A THIRD TREASURY OF
THE FAMILIAR

RALPH L. WOODS, the popular anthol-
ogist, is the author of scores of magazine
articles and is editor of *Behold the Man,* a
collection of writings about Christ.

A Third Treasury of the Familiar

EDITED BY *Ralph L. Woods*

THE MACMILLAN COMPANY

The Macmillan Company
866 Third Avenue, New York, N.Y. 10022
Collier-Macmillan Canada Ltd., Toronto, Ontario

Library of Congress Catalog Card Number: 79-109455

FIRST PRINTING

Printed in the United States of America

ACKNOWLEDGMENTS

Grateful acknowledgment is made to the following for their cooperation in granting permission to reprint herein the copyrighted material listed below:

ANDERSON HOUSE, PUBLISHERS, for lines from *Winterset* by Maxwell Anderson, copyright 1935 by Anderson House, copyright renewed 1963 by Gilda Oakleaf Anderson, all rights reserved, reprinted by permission of Anderson House.

EDWARD ARNOLD (PUBLISHERS) LTD., for two verses from Harry Graham's *Ruthless Rhymes for Heartless Homes*.

A. S. BARNES AND CO., INC., for "Two Sides of War" from Grantland Rice's *The Final Answer and Other Poems*, copyright 1955.

THE BELL-MCCLURE SYNDICATE, for H. I. Phillip's column "Guests at a Ground-Breaking," September 20, 1948.

GEOFFREY BLES LTD., London, from *The Screwtape Letters* by C. S. Lewis.

BOBBS-MERRILL CO., INC., for "A Parting Guest" from *The Biographical Edition of the Complete Works of James Whitcomb Riley*, reprinted by permission of the publishers, Bobbs-Merrill Co., Inc.

THE BODLEY HEAD, London, for Anatole France's "The Procurator of Judea," from *Mother of Pearl*, translated by John Chapman.

THE BOOK-OF-THE-MONTH CLUB, INC., for Roger William Riis's "I Admire the Human Race," copyright 1951 by The Book-of-the-Month Club, Inc.

(iv)

CONSTANCE M. BROUN AND HEYWOOD HALE BROUN, for Heywood Broun's "The Unknown Soldier," copyright 1919, 1945, by Heywood Hale Broun.

MR. SIMON CAMPBELL, for Joseph Campbell's "The Old Woman."

CHATTO AND WINDUS, LTD., for "Strange Meeting" and "Anthem for Doomed Youth," both by Wilfred Owen.

J. CURWEN AND SONS LTD., for the lyrics of the hymn "Now the Day Is Over" by Sabine Baring-Gould.

THE LITERARY TRUSTEES OF WALTER DE LA MARE and THE SOCIETY OF AUTHORS, as their representatives, for Walter de la Mare's "All That's Past."

J. M. DENT AND SONS LTD., for "Do Not Go Gentle Into That Good Night," from *Collected Poems of Dylan Thomas*; "The Donkey" from G. K. Chesterton's *The Wild Knight and Other Poems*.

DODD, MEAD AND CO., INC., for "Peace" by Rupert Brooke from *The Collected Poems of Rupert Brooke*, copyright 1915 by Dodd, Mead and Co., Inc., copyright renewed 1943 by Edward Marsh; passages from *Scott's Last Expedition* by Robert F. Scott, copyright 1913, 1941, by Dodd, Mead and Co., Inc.; "Elegy in a Country Churchyard" from *The Collected Poems of G. K. Chesterton*, copyright 1932 by Dodd, Mead and Co., Inc., copyright renewed 1959 by Oliver Chesterton; "The Procurator of Judea" from Anatole France's *Mother of Pearl*, translated by John Chapman, reprinted by permission of Dodd, Mead and Co., Inc.

DOUBLEDAY AND CO., INC., from the R. L. Devonshire translation of R. Vallery-Radot's *Life of Pasteur*; from Don Marquis's *archy and mehitabel*.

GERALD DUCKWORTH AND CO. LTD., for Reginald Arkell's poem "Rumour" from *All the Rumours*.

FABER AND FABER LTD., for "Musée des Beaux Arts" and "The Unknown Citizen" from W. H. Auden's *Collected Shorter Poems, 1927–1957*; "I Think Continually of Those Who Were Truly Great" from Stephen Spender's *Collected Poems 1928–1953*; "The Love Song of J. Alfred Prufrock" from *Collected Poems 1909–1962*, by T. S. Eliot.

JOHN FARQUHARSON, LTD., for passage from James Hilton's *Lost Horizon*.

HARCOURT, BRACE AND WORLD, INC., for "The Love Song of J. Alfred Prufrock" from *Collected Poems 1909–1962* by T. S. Eliot, copyright 1936, by Harcourt Brace and World, Inc., copyright © 1963, 1964, by T. S. Eliot, reprinted by permission of the publisher; lines from T. S. Eliot's *Murder in the Cathedral* and from his *The Cocktail Party*, reprinted by permission of the publisher, Harcourt, Brace and World, Inc.

HARPER AND ROW, PUBLISHERS, for passage from pp. 505–506 *You Can't Go Home Again* by Thomas Wolfe, copyright 1940 by Maxwell Perkins as Executor; renewed 1968 by Paul Gitlin, reprinted by permission of Harper and Row, Publishers; "The Treasurer's Report" from *Benchley Beside Himself* by Robert Benchley, copyright 1930 by Robert C. Benchley, renewed 1958 by Gertrude Benchley; "The Commuter" from *The Lady is Cold* by E. B. White, copyright 1925, 1953, by E. B. White, originally appeared in *The New Yorker*, and reprinted by permission of Harper and Row, Publishers.

HARVARD UNIVERSITY PRESS and THE LOEB CLASSICAL LIBRARY, for a passage from the H. Rushton Fairclough translation of Horace's *Epistles*, Book I.

by Georgie Yeats; "The Darkling Thrush," "Afterwards," and "Great Things" by Thomas Hardy, copyright 1925 by The Macmillan Co.; "The Bells of Heaven," copyright 1917 by The Macmillan Co., renewed 1945 by Ralph Hodgson; from *The Screwtape Letters* by C. S. Lewis, © C. S. Lewis 1961; "Laugh and Be Merry," "Tewkesbury Road" by John Masefield; copyright 1912 by The Macmillan Co., renewed 1940 by John Masefield; "Poetry" by Marianne Moore, copyright 1935 by Marianne Moore, renewed 1963 by Marianne Moore and T. S. Eliot; "In Distrust of Merit" by Marianne Moore, copyright 1944 by Marianne Moore; "Mr. Flood's Party" by Edwin Arlington Robinson, copyright 1921 by Edwin Arlington Robinson, renewed 1949 by Ruth Nivison; "A Glass of Beer" by James Stephens, copyright 1918 by The Macmillan Co., renewed 1946 by James Stephens.

THE MACMILLAN COMPANY OF CANADA, LTD., for passages from Thomas Hardy's *Far From The Madding Crowd* and from *The Return of the Native*; and "The Darkling Thrush," "Great Things," and "Afterwards," all from *The Collected Poems of Thomas Hardy,* by permission of the Estate of Thomas Hardy; "The Bells of Heaven" from *Collected Poems of Ralph Hodgson,* permission of Mrs. Hodgson; and all by permission of Macmillan and Co. Ltd. of London, and The Macmillan Co. of Canada, Ltd.

VIRGIL MARKHAM, for Edwin Markham's "The Place of Peace," "Rules for the Road," "Victory in Defeat," and "Outwitted."

MILLS MUSIC INC., for lyrics of "School Days," copyright 1906 by Gus Edwards Music Co., copyright © renewed 1934 by Mills Music Inc. and Shapiro Bernstein and Co. Inc.

WILLIAM MORROW AND COMPANY, INC., from *Lost Horizon* by James Hilton, copyright 1933, 1936, by James Hilton, copyright © renewed 1960 by Alice Hilton.

MRS. ELIZABETH K. MORTON, for "Who Walks With Beauty" from David Morton's *Ships in Harbor.*

JOHN MURRAY, PUBLISHER, for passages from Lionel Giles's translation of *The Sayings of Lao Tzu,* in the series *The Wisdom of the East,* published by John Murray.

OTTO NATHAN, TRUSTEE, ESTATE OF ALBERT EINSTEIN, for passages from Albert Einstein in *Living Philosophies,* published by Simon and Schuster, Inc., copyright, 1931, and from *Einstein on Peace,* ed. by Nathan and Norden, Simon and Schuster, Inc., copyright, 1960.

NEW DIRECTIONS PUBLISHING CORP., for "Strange Meeting" and "Anthem for Doomed Youth" from Wilfred Owen's *Collected Poems,* copyright Chatto and Windus, Ltd. 1946, © 1963, reprinted by permission of New Directions Publishing Corp.; "Do Not Go Gentle Into That Good Night," from Dylan Thomas's *Collected Poems,* copyright 1952 by Dylan Thomas, permission of New Directions Publishing Corp.

MAYER U. NEWFIELD, for Samuel Ulman's "Youth."

HAROLD OBER ASSOCIATES, INC., for Corey Ford's "How to Guess Your Age," copyright 1949, 1959 by Corey Ford; and for "The Black Man Speaks," copyright 1943 by Langston Hughes, and from his *Simple Takes A Wife,* copyright 1953 by Langston Hughes.

(vii)

THE OPEN CHURCH FOUNDATION, for Orin L. Crane's "Slow Me Down, Lord."

THE OPEN COURT PUBLISHING CO., for passages from *The Gospel of Buddha*, translated by Paul Carus.

OXFORD UNIVERSITY PRESS, INC., New York, "Music I Heard" from *Collected Poems* by Conrad Aiken, copyright 1953 by Conrad Aiken; "God's Grandeur" and "The Windhover" by Gerard Manley Hopkins.

OXFORD UNIVERSITY PRESS, London, for G. K. Chesterton's "O God of Earth and Altar."

A. D. PETERS AND COMPANY, for "Fatigue," "On His Books," "On Lady Poltagrue, a Public Peril," and "Epitaph on a Politician," all by Hilaire Belloc, published by Gerald Duckworth and Co., Ltd., reprinted by permission of A. D. Peters and Co.

RANDOM HOUSE, INC., for "The Musée des Beaux Arts" and "The Unknown Citizen" from *Collected Shorter Poems 1927–1957* by W. H. Auden, copyright 1940, renewed 1968 by W. H. Auden; "I Think Continually of Those Who Were Truly Great" reprinted from *Collected Poems 1928–1953*, copyright 1934, renewed 1962 by Stephen Spender.

DON RUSSELL, for Nixon Waterman's "To Know All Is to Forgive All" from Nixon Waterman's *A Rose to the Living and Other Poems*, copyright 1929, 1957.

ST. MARTIN'S PRESS, for "Back" from Wilfred Gibson's *Collected Poems,* also with the permission of Macmillan and Co. Ltd., Michael Gibson, executor of Estate of Wilfred Gibson.

SCHOCKEN BOOKS, INC., for a passage from *Ten Rungs* by Martin Buber, translated by Olga Marx, copyright © 1947 by Schocken Books, Inc.

CHARLES SCRIBNER'S SONS, for "For a Dead Lady" from Edwin Arlington Robinson's *The Town Down the River*, copyright 1910 by Charles Scribner's Sons; renewal copyright 1948 by Ruth Nivison; "The House of the Hill," "Credo," and "Luke Havergal" from Edwin Arlington Robinson's *The Children of the Night* (1897); an excerpt from Thomas Wolfe's *Of Time and the River*, copyright 1935 by Charles Scribner's Sons, renewal copyright © 1963 by Paul Gitlin, Administrator C.T.A.; from the R. G. Smith translation of Martin Buber's *I and Thou*.

THE SOCIETY OF AUTHORS, as the literary representative of The Estate of A. E. Housman and Jonathan Cape Ltd., publishers of A. E. Housman's *Collected Poems,* for "With Rue My Heart Is Laden" and "Loveliest of Trees."

MRS. JAMES THURBER, for "The Secret Life of Walter Mitty" from *My World and Welcome to It*, copyright © 1942 James Thurber, published by Harcourt, Brace and World, Inc., originally printed in *The New Yorker.*

UNIVERSITY OF NORTH CAROLINA PRESS, for the lyrics of "John Henry" from Guy B. Johnson's *John Henry: Tracking Down a Legend.*

THE VIKING PRESS, INC., for a passage from Arthur Miller's *The Death of A Salesman,* copyright 1949 by Arthur Miller; "The Velvet Hand" from *Times Three* by Phyllis McGinley, copyright 1945 by Phyllis McGinley, both used by permission of The Viking Press, Inc.

A. P. WATT AND SON, for "Elegy in a Country Churchyard" from *Collected Poems of G. K. Chesterton,* by permission of Miss D. E. Collins, the copyright

To DAVID CHRISTOPHER HUOT
My Eight-Year-Old Grandson
A Ready Reader, Artful Persuader,
And Accomplished Charmer

Preface

When *A Treasury of the Familiar* was published in 1942, I dared to conjecture that if the book proved a commercial success it would be followed some years later by *A Second Treasury of the Familiar* containing riches that did not get into the first volume. That is what happened in 1950.

When *A Second Treasury of the Familiar* was published, I firmly concluded that this category of literature was reasonably well taken care of for a long time to come.

However, during the intervening twenty years I have been repeatedly reminded by reading, by friends, and by an awareness of what was happening in the nation and the world that there is ample warrant—perhaps even need—for *A Third Treasury of the Familiar*.

So it was that ten years ago I began to gather material and make notes, in case I should decide to venture for the third time into the field of the familiar.

My decision to go ahead with this book was due in substantial measure to acute comments made in late 1968 by William A. Caldwell, daily columnist and associate editor of *The Record*, of Hackensack, New Jersey. While writing about *A Treasury of the Familiar* with amiable exasperation, Mr. Caldwell said the book reveals to contemporary youth the values and the "platitudes" the world lives by. He suggested that the volume is a "child's code book" to the thinking and conversation of older generations.

Though the Caldwell column did not recommend involuntary retirement for the earlier volumes, and though the book-buying public continues its generous patronage of them, nevertheless it became clear that a third volume could make at least a modest contribution toward narrowing the generation gap. The older generation could be exposed to literature that has become familiar in recent years, and the younger generation could be reminded that literature of earlier decades has a surprising relevance to the present. George MacDonald's nineteenth-century poem "Obedience" is a particularly striking illustration of the latter.

A Third Treasury of the Familiar repeats nothing found in the two earlier books. Nor has an attempt been made to have it fit any formula other than faithfulness to the principle of familiarity, popularity, and wide general appeal to the American people.

Before I began work on the present volume, I thought that almost all the literary standbys were already in the two earlier books. But this proved not to be the case. Witness herein the vast amount of famous prose and poetry from such venerable authors as Emily Dickinson, Robert and Elizabeth Browning, John Donne, Cicero, Walt Whitman, Longfellow, Demosthenes, Shakespeare, Lincoln, Jefferson, Mark Twain, Emerson, Wordsworth, Keats, Thoreau, Byron, both Oliver Wendell Holmeses, Shelley, Dr. Johnson, Gibbon, Stevenson, from the Bible, and from other familiar and much-loved men and women who have richly endowed our literature and deeply influenced our tastes and thinking.

It is particularly interesting to note some older selections that were not widely popular two decades ago and have now become generally familiar. Either they have a special relevance to us now, or the test of time has allowed them increased recognition and acceptance. For example: Orin L. Crane's "Slow Me Down, Lord"; T. S. Eliot's "The Love Song of J. Alfred Prufrock"; "A Prayer by a Confederate Soldier," (Author Unknown); a 1692 prose-poem usually titled "Go Placidly" that, for reasons not difficult to appreciate, has been frequently quoted in recent years; Horace Mann's early nineteenth-century plea for public education; passages from Oriental sages and philosophers that have interested young people; many hymns that are now far more widely known because of the ecumenical movement; passages from the ancient wisdom of Judaism which have gained an admiring audience well beyond the Jewish community; excerpts from U.S. Supreme Court decisions that have a special relevance today.

And, of course, the present volume contains many selections that originated or became quite famous in the past decade or so: notable passages from John F. Kennedy; Lyndon B. Johnson addressing Congress on civil rights; President Eisenhower's warning about the military-industrial complex; General MacArthur's farewell to West Point; President Nixon's inaugural plea for restraint; Irving Berlin's "God Bless America," which threatens the primacy of "The Star

Spangled Banner"; Martin Buber's "I–Thou" philosophy; the words of the first men to walk on the moon; "Parkinson's Law"; key material on nuclear explosions; the poetry of Auden, Spender, MacLeish, Ransom, Benét, and others.

Incidentally, the tremendous expansion of high school and college education, and the concurrent rise in the general level of education, have given wider familiarity to much prose and poetry that previously had been known and enjoyed by a smaller number of people.

Although I would hope to do other books in the uncertain years ahead, I am positive that *A Third Treasury of the Familiar* is the last of this series as far as I am concerned. Perhaps two or more decades from now someone else will undertake still another volume. In that event, I wish the project well.

Meanwhile, I will be content if this latest volume is given a place alongside its continuingly popular predecessors.

R. L. W.

Let Fate do her worst; there are relics of joy,
Bright dreams of the past, which she cannot destroy;
Which come in the night-time of sorrow and care,
And bring back the features that joy used to wear.
Long; long be my heart with such memories fill'd!
Like the vase, in which roses have been distill'd—
You may break, you may shatter the vase, if you will,
But the scent of the roses will hang 'round it still.

—THOMAS MOORE

A THIRD TREASURY OF
THE FAMILIAR

FOR EVERYTHING GIVE THANKS

Helena Isabella Tupper

For all that God in mercy sends,
For health and children, home and friends,
For comfort in the time of need,
For every kindly word and deed,
For happy thoughts and holy talk,
For guidance in our daily walk,
    For everything give thanks!

For beauty in this world of ours,
For verdant grass and lovely flowers,
For song of birds, for hum of bees,
For refreshing summer breeze,
For hill and plain, for streams and wood,
For the great ocean's mighty flood,
    For everything give thanks!

For sweet sleep which comes with night,
For the returning morning light,
For the bright sun that shines on high,
For the stars glittering in the sky,
For these and everything we see,
O Lord, our hearts we lift to thee.
    For everything give thanks!

A LESSON

Sa'di

(TRANSLATOR: Sir Edwin Arnold)

Never did I complain of the chances of fortune, nor make a wry face at the resolution of fate, but once, when I was brought to the pass of going barefooted, and had nothing with which to buy shoes. Just then I entered the mosque at Kusa with a heavy heart, and there I observed a person who had no feet at all. At this I offered up praise and thanks to the Almighty God, and gladly submitted to this accident of being shoeless.

OH, THE WILD JOY OF LIVING

Robert Browning

Oh, the wild joy of living! the leaping from rock up to rock,
The strong rending of boughs from the fir-tree, the cool silver shock
Of the plunge in the pool's living water, the hunt of the bear,
And the sultriness showing the lion couched in his lair.
And the meal, the rich dates yellowed over the gold dust divine,
And the locust-flesh steeped in the pitcher, the full draft of wine,
And the sleep in the dried river-channel where bulrushes tell
That the water was wont to go marbling so softly and well.
How good is man's life, the mere living! how fit to employ
All the heart and the soul and the senses forever in joy!

THE THINKING REED

Blaise Pascal

Man is but a reed—the weakest thing in nature—but he is a reed that thinks. It is not necessary that the whole universe should arm itself to crush him. A vapor, a drop of water, is enough to kill him. But if the universe should crush him, man would still be nobler than that which slays him, for he knows that he dies; but of the advantage which it has over him the universe knows nothing. Our dignity consists, then, wholly in thought. Our elevation must come from this, not from space and time, which we cannot fill. Let us, then, labor to think well: that is the fundamental principle of morals.

THE ROAD NOT TAKEN

Robert Frost

Two roads diverged in a yellow wood,
And sorry I could not travel both
And be one traveler, long I stood
And looked down one as far as I could
To where it bent in the undergrowth;

Then took the other, as just as fair,
And having perhaps the better claim,
Because it was grassy and wanted wear;
Though as for that the passing there
Had worn them really about the same.

And both that morning equally lay
In leaves no step had trodden black.
Oh, I kept the first for another day!
Yet knowing how way leads on to way,
I doubted if I should ever come back.

I shall be telling this with a sigh
Somewhere ages and ages hence:
Two roads diverged in a wood, and I—
I took the one less traveled by,
And that has made all the difference.

ON CROSSING A STREAM BEFORE YOU REACH IT

Abraham Lincoln

Many years ago, when I was a young lawyer, and Illinois was little settled, except on her southern border, I, and other lawyers, used to ride the circuit; journeying with the judge from county-seat to county-seat in quest of business. Once, after a long spell of pouring rain, which had flooded the whole country, transforming small creeks into rivers, we were often stopped by these swollen streams, which we with difficulty crossed. Still ahead of us was the Fox River, larger than all the rest; and we could not help saying to each other, "If these streams give us so much trouble, how shall we get over Fox River?" Darkness fell before we had reached that stream; and we all stopped at a log tavern, had our horses put out, and resolved to pass the night. Here we were right glad to fall in with the Methodist Presiding Elder of the circuit*, who rode it in all weather, knew all its ways, and could tell us about Fox River. So we all gathered around him, and asked him if he knew about the crossing of Fox River. "Oh, yes," he replied, "I know all about Fox River. I have crossed it often and understand it well; but I have one fixed rule with regard to Fox River: I never cross it till I reach it."

AWAY WITH FUNERAL MUSIC

Robert Louis Stevenson

Away with funeral music—set
  The pipe to powerful lips—
The cup of life's for him that drinks
  And not for him that sips.

---

* Peter Cartwright, whom Lincoln had once defeated for Congress.

SCHOOL DAYS*

Will D. Cobb

Nothing to do, Nellie Darling;
Nothing to do, you say.
Let's take a trip on memory's ship,
Back to the by-gone days.
Sail to the old village school house,
Anchor outside the school door,
Look in and see, there's you and there's me,
A couple of kids once more.

Chorus
School days, school days, dear old golden rule days;
Readin' and 'ritin' and 'rithmetic,
Taught to the tune of a hick'ry stick,
You were my queen in calico,
I was your bashful, barefoot beau,
And you wrote on my slate,
"I love you, Joe,"
When we were a couple of kids.

'Member the hill, Nellie Darling,
And the oak tree that grew on its brow?
They've built forty stories upon that old hill
And the oak's an old chestnut now.
'Member the meadows so green, dear,
So fragrant with clover and maize?
Into new city lots and preferred business plots,
They've cut them up since those days.

THIS IS MY LETTER TO THE WORLD

Emily Dickinson

This is my letter to the world,
That never wrote to me,—
The simple news that Nature told,
With tender majesty.

Her message is committed
　　To hands I cannot see;
For love of her, sweet countrymen,
　　Judge tenderly of me.

ADAM AND EVE

Holy Bible, Genesis 2:7–9, 15–19, 21–25; 3:1–13, 16–23

And the Lord God formed man of the dust of the ground, and breathed into his nostrils the breath of life; and man became a living soul.

And the Lord God planted a garden eastward in Eden: and there he put the man whom he had formed.

And out of the ground made the Lord God to grow every tree that is pleasant to the sight, and good for food; the tree of life also in the midst of the garden, and the tree of knowledge of good and evil. . . .

And the Lord God took the man, and put him into the garden of Eden, to dress it and to keep it.

And the Lord God, commanded the man, saying, Of every tree of the garden thou mayest freely eat:

But of the tree of the knowledge of good and evil, thou shalt not eat of it: for in the day that thou eatest thereof thou shalt surely die.

And the Lord God said, It is not good that the man should be alone, I will make him an help meet for him.

And out of the ground the Lord God formed every beast of the field, and every fowl of the air; and brought them unto Adam to see what he would call them: and whatsoever Adam called every living creature, that was the name thereof. . . .

And the Lord God caused a deep sleep to fall upon Adam, and he slept: and he took one of his ribs, and closed up the flesh instead thereof;

And the rib, which the Lord God had taken from man, made he a woman, and brought her unto the man.

And Adam said, This is now bone of my bones, and flesh of my flesh: she shall be called woman, because she was taken out of man.

Therefore shall a man leave his father and his mother, and shall cleave unto his wife: and they shall be one flesh.

And they were both naked, the man and his wife, and were not ashamed.

Now the serpent was more subtle than any beast of the field which the Lord God had made. And he said unto the woman, Yea, hath God said, Ye shall not eat of every tree of the garden?

And the woman said unto the serpent, We may eat of the fruit of the trees of the garden:

But of the fruit of the tree which is in the midst of the garden, God hath said, Ye shall not eat of it, neither shall ye touch it, lest ye die.

And the serpent said unto the woman, Ye shall not surely die:

For God doth know that in the day ye eat thereof, then your eyes shall be opened; and ye shall be as gods, knowing good and evil.

And when the woman saw that the tree was good for food, and that it was pleasant to the eyes, and a tree to be desired to make one wise she took of the fruit thereof, and did eat; and gave also unto her husband with her, and he did eat.

And the eyes of them both were opened, and they knew that they were naked: and they sewed fig leaves together, and made themselves aprons.

And they heard the voice of the Lord God walking in the garden in the cool of the day: and Adam and his wife hid themselves from the presence of the Lord God, amongst the trees of the garden.

And the Lord God called unto Adam, and said unto him, Where art thou?

And he said, I heard thy voice in the garden, and I was afraid, because I was naked: and I hid myself.

And he said, Who told thee that thou wast naked? Hast thou eaten of the tree, whereof I commanded thee that thou shouldest not eat?

And the man said, The woman whom thou gavest to be with me, she gave me of the tree and I did eat.

And the Lord God said unto the woman, What is this that thou hast done? And the woman said, The serpent beguiled me and I did eat. . . .

Unto the woman he said, I will greatly multiply thy sorrow, and thy conception: in sorrow thou shalt bring forth children; and thy desire shall be to thy husband, and he shall rule over thee.

And unto Adam he said, Because thou hast harkened unto the voice of thy wife, and hast eaten of the tree of which I commanded thee, saying, Thou shalt not eat of it: cursed is the ground for thy sake: in sorrow shalt thou eat of it all the days of thy life:

Thorns also and thistles shall it bring forth to thee: and thou shalt eat the herb of the field:

In the sweat of thy face shalt thou eat bread, till thou return unto the ground; for out of it wast thou taken: for dust thou art, and unto dust shalt thou return.

And Adam called his wife's name Eve; because she was the mother of all living.

Unto Adam also, and to his wife, did the Lord God make coats of skins, and clothed them.

And the Lord God said, Behold, the man is become as one of us, to know good and evil: and now, lest he put forth his hand, and take also of the tree of life, and eat, and live for ever;

Therefore the Lord God sent him forth from the garden of Eden to till the ground from whence he was taken.

FLATTERY

Jonathan Swift

'Tis an old maxim in the schools,
That flattery's the food of fools;
Yet now and then your men of wit
Will condescend to take a bit.

I–THOU

Martin Buber

The primary word *I–Thou* can be spoken only with the whole being. Concentration and fusion into the whole being can never take place through my agency, nor can it ever take place without me. I become through my relation to the *Thou*; as I become *I*, I say *Thou*.

All real living is meeting.

THE POWER OF LITTLES

Anonymous

Great events, we often find,
  On little things depend,
And very small beginnings
  Have oft a mighty end.

Letters joined make words,
  And words to books may grow,
As flake on flake descending
  Form an avalanche of snow.

A single utterance may good
  Or evil thought inspire;
One little spark enkindled
  May set a town on fire.

What volumes may be written
  With little drops of ink!
How small a leak, unnoticed,
  A mighty ship will sink!

A tiny insect's labor
  Makes the coral strand,
And mighty seas are girdled
  With grains of golden sand.

A daily penny, saved,
  A fortune may begin;
A daily penny, squandered,
  May lead to vice and sin.

Our life is made entirely
  Of moments multiplied,
As little streamlets, joining,
  Form the ocean's tide.

Our hours and days, our months and years,
  Are in small moments given:
They constitute our time below—
  Eternity in heaven.

MR. DOOLEY'S TRIUMPHAL ARCH

Finley Peter Dunne

When ye build yer triumphal arch to yer conquerin' hero, Hinnissey, build it out of bricks so the people will have somethin' convanient to throw at him as he passes through.

IN DEFENSE OF YOUTH'S EXCESSES

Robert Louis Stevenson

When the old man waggles his head and says, "Ah, so I thought when I was your age," he has proved the youth's case. Doubtless, whether from growth of experience or decline of animal heat, he thinks so no longer; but he thought so while he was young; and all men have thought so while they were young, since there was dew in the morning or hawthorn in May; and here is another young man adding his vote to those of previous generations and riveting another link to the chain of testimony. It is as natural and as right for a young man to be imprudent and exaggerated, to live in swoops and circles, and beat about his cage like any other wild thing newly captured, as it is for old men to turn grey, or mothers to love their offspring, or heroes to die for something worthier than their lives. . . .

You need repent none of your youthful vagaries. They may have been over the score on one side, just as those of age are probably over the score on the other. But they had a point; they not only befitted your age and expressed its attitude and passions, but they had a relation to what was outside of you, and implied criticisms on the existing state of things, which you need not allow to have been undeserved, because you now see that they were partial. All error, not merely verbal, is a strong way of stating that the current truth is incomplete. The follies of youth have a basis in sound reason, just as much as the embarrassing questions put by babes and sucklings. Their most antisocial acts indicate the defects of our society. When the torrent sweeps the man against a boulder, you must expect him to scream, and you need not be surprised if the scream is sometimes a theory. Shelley, chafing at the Church of England, discovered the cure of all evils in universal atheism. Generous lads irritated at the injustices of society, see nothing for it but the abolishment of everything and Kingdom Come of anarchy. Shelley was a young fool; so are these cock-sparrow revolutionaries. But it is better to be a fool than to be dead. It is better to emit a scream in the shape of a theory than to be entirely insensible to the jars and incongruities of life and take everything as it comes in a forlorn stupidity. Some people swallow the universe like a pill; they travel on through the world, like smiling images pushed from behind. For God's sake give me the young man who has brains enough to make a fool of himself!

A HYMNE TO GOD THE FATHER

John Donne

I

Wilt thou forgive that sinne where I begunne,
    Which is my sin, though it were done before?
Wilt thou forgive those sinnes, through which I runne,
    And do run still: though still I do deplore?
        When thou hast done, thou hast not done,
            For, I have more.

II

Wilt thou forgive that sinne by which I have wonne
    Others to sinne? and, made my sinne their doore?
Wilt thou forgive that sinne which I did shunne
    A yeare, or two: but wallowed in, a score?
        When thou hast done, thou hast not done,
            For, I have more.

III

I have a sinne of feare, that when I have spunne
    My last thred, I shall perish on the shore;
Sweare by thy selfe, that at my death thy sonne
    Shall shine as he shines now, and heretofore;
        And, having done that, Thou haste done,
            I feare no more.

THE HORRORS OF SPRING

Ambrose Bierce

Spring is with us with its oldtime stock of horrors—birds blaspheming in the trees; flowers loading the lukewarm air with odious exhalations; grass with snakes in it; matronly cows to gore the unwary. The blue of the sky and the green of the earth renew their immemorial feud, murdering one another in cold blood all along the line of the horizon. Hideous ferns erect themselves in the gulches where the poison oak unsheathes his leaves to work his ghastly joke upon the culler of simples. Fleas call the roll and perfect their organization; spiders hang their poddy carcasses face-high above the trail. 'Come, gentle spring, ethereal mildness, come.' Come with lute, come with clamor of geese, yelling of dogs, deep diapason of the strolling bull, and frequent thud of country lasses falling over their own feet.

THE BLACK MAN SPEAKS

Langston Hughes

I swear to the Lord
I still can't see
Why Democracy means
Everybody but me.

PRESIDENT JOHN F. KENNEDY'S INAUGURAL ADDRESS

We observe today not a victory of party but a celebration of freedom—symbolizing an end as well as a beginning—signifying renewal as well as change. For I have sworn before you and Almighty God the same solemn oath our forebears prescribed nearly a century and three-quarters ago.

The world is very different now. For man holds in his mortal hands the power to abolish all forms of human poverty and all forms of human life. And yet the same revolutionary beliefs for which our forebears fought are still at issue around the globe—the belief that the rights of man come not from the generosity of the state but from the hand of God.

We dare not forget today that we are the heirs of that first revolution. Let the word go forth from this time and place, to friend and foe alike, that the torch has been passed to a new generation of Americans—born in this century, tempered by war, disciplined by a hard and bitter peace, proud of our ancient heritage—and unwilling to witness or permit the slow undoing of those human rights to which this nation has always been committed, and to which we are committed today at home and around the world.

Let every nation know, whether it wishes us well or ill, that we shall pay any price, bear any burden, meet any hardship, support any friend, oppose any foe to assure the survival and the success of liberty.

This much we pledge—and more.

To those old allies whose cultural and spiritual origins we share, we pledge the loyalty of faithful friends. United, there is little we cannot do in a host of new cooperative ventures. Divided, there is little we can do—for we dare not meet a powerful challenge at odds and split asunder.

To those new states whom we welcome to the ranks of the free, we pledge our word that one form of colonial control shall not have passed away merely to be replaced by a far more iron tyranny. We shall not always expect to find them supporting our view. But we shall always hope to find them strongly supporting their own freedom—and to remember that, in the past, those who foolishly sought power by riding the back of the tiger ended up inside.

To those peoples in the huts and villages of half the globe struggling to break the bonds of mass misery, we pledge our best efforts to help them help themselves, for whatever period is required—not because the Communists may be doing it, not because we seek their votes, but because it is right. If a free society cannot help the many who are poor, it cannot save the few who are rich.

To our sister republics south of our border, we offer a special pledge—to convert our good words into good deeds—in a new alliance for progress—to assist free men and free governments in casting off the chains of poverty. But this peaceful revolution of hope cannot become the prey of hostile powers. Let all our neighbors know that we shall join with them to oppose aggression or subversion anywhere in the Americas. And let every other power know that this hemisphere intends to remain the master of its own house.

To that world assembly of sovereign states, the United Nations, our last best hope in an age where the instruments of war have far outpaced the instruments of peace, we renew our pledge of support—to prevent it from becoming merely a forum for invective—to strengthen its shield of the new and the weak—and to enlarge the area in which its writ may run.

Finally, to those nations who would make themselves our adversary, we offer not a pledge but a request: that both sides begin anew the quest for peace, before the dark powers of destruction unleashed by science engulf all humanity in planned or accidental self-destruction.

We dare not tempt them with weakness. For only when our arms are sufficient beyond doubt can we be certain beyond doubt that they will never be employed.

But neither can two great and powerful groups of nations take comfort from our present course—both sides overburdened by the cost of modern weapons, both rightly alarmed by the steady spread of the deadly atom, yet both racing to alter that uncertain balance of terror that stays the hand of mankind's final war.

So let us begin anew—remembering on both sides that civility is not a sign of weakness, and sincerity is always subject to proof. Let us never negotiate out of fear. But let us never fear to negotiate.

Let both sides explore what problems unite us instead of belaboring those problems which divide us.

Let both sides, for the first time, formulate serious and precise proposals for the inspection and control of arms—and bring the absolute power to destroy other nations under the absolute control of all nations.

Let both sides seek to invoke the wonders of science instead of its terrors. Together let us explore the stars, conquer the deserts, eradicate disease, tap the ocean depths and encourage the arts and commerce.

Let both sides unite to heed in all corners of the earth the command of Isaiah—to "undo the heavy burdens . . . [and] let the oppressed go free."

And if a beachhead of cooperation may push back the jungles of suspicion, let both sides join in creating a new endeavor—not a new balance of power, but a new world of law, where the strong are just and the weak secure and the peace preserved.

All this will not be finished in the first 100 days. Nor will it be finished in the first 1,000 days, nor in the life of this Administration, nor even perhaps in our lifetime on this planet. But let us begin.

In your hands, my fellow citizens, more than mine, will rest the final success or failure of our course. Since this country was founded, each generation of Americans has been summoned to give testimony to its national loyalty. The graves of young Americans who answered the call to service surround the globe.

Now the trumpet summons us again—not as a call to bear arms, though arms we need—not as a call to battle, though embattled we are—but a call to bear the burden of a long twilight struggle year in and year out, "rejoicing in hope, patient in tribulation"— a struggle against the common enemies of man: tyranny, poverty, disease and war itself.

Can we forge against these enemies a grand and global alliance, north and south, east and west, that can assure a more fruitful life for all mankind? Will you join in that historic effort?

In the long history of the world, only a few generations have been granted the role of defending freedom in its hour of maximum danger. I do not shrink from this responsibility—I welcome it. I do not believe that any of us would exchange places with any other people or any other generation. The energy, the faith, the devotion which we bring to this endeavor will light our country and all who serve it—and the glow from that fire can truly light the world.

And so, my fellow Americans: ask not what your country can do for you—ask what you can do for your country.

My fellow citizens of the world: ask not what America will do for you, but what together we can do for the freedom of man.

Finally, whether you are citizens of America or citizens of the world, ask of us here the same high standards of strength and sacrifice which we ask of you. With a good conscience our only sure reward, with history the final judge of our deeds, let us go forth to lead the land we love, asking His blessing and His help, but knowing that here on earth God's work must truly be our own.

(January 20, 1961)

THE FROG

Anonymous

What a wonderful bird the frog are—
When he stand he sit almost;
When he hop, he fly almost.

He ain't got no sense hardly;
He ain't got no tail hardly either,
When he sit, he sit on what he ain't got almost.

A CROAKER

Benjamin Franklin

There are croakers in every country, always boding its ruin. Such a one then lived in Philadelphia; a person of note, an elderly man, with a wise look and a very grave manner of speaking; his name was Samuel Mickle. This gentleman, a stranger to me, stopt one day at my door, and asked me if I was the young man who had lately opened a new printing-house. Being answered in the affirmative, he said he was sorry for me, because it was an expensive undertaking, and the expense would be lost; for Philadelphia was a sinking place, the people already half-bankrupts, or near being so; all appearances to the contrary, such as new buildings and the rise of rents, being to his certain knowledge fallacious; for they were, in fact, among the things that would soon ruin us. And he gave me such a detail of misfortunes now existing, or that were soon to exist, that he left me half melancholy. Had I known him before I engaged in this business, probably I never should have done it. This man continued to live in this decaying place, and to declaim in the same strain, refusing for many years to buy a house there, because all was going to destruction; and at last I had the pleasure of seeing him give five times as much for one as he might have bought it for when he first began his croaking.

(From *The Autobiography of Benjamin Franklin*)

CHERRY–RIPE

Thomas Campion

There is a garden in her face
  Where roses and white lilies grow;
A heavenly paradise is that place,
  Wherein all pleasant fruits do flow;

There cherries grow which none may buy,
Till 'Cherry-Ripe' themselves do cry.

Those cherries fairly do enclose
    Of orient pearl a double row,
Which when her lovely laughter shows,
    They look like rose-buds fill'd with snow:
Yet them nor peer nor prince can buy,
Till 'Cherry-Ripe' themselves do cry.

Her eyes like angels watch them still;
    Her brows like bended bows do stand,
Threat'ning with piercing frowns to kill
    All that attempt with eye or hand
Those sacred cherries to come nigh,
—Till 'Cherry-Ripe' themselves do cry!

PARKINSON'S LAW, OR THIS RISING PYRAMID

C. Northcote Parkinson

Work expands so as to fill the time available for its completion. General recognition of this fact is shown in the proverbial phrase "It is the busiest man who has time to spare." Thus, an elderly lady of leisure can spend the entire day in writing and dispatching a postcard to her niece at Bognor Regis. An hour will be spent in finding the postcard, another in hunting for spectacles, half an hour in a search for the address, an hour and a quarter in composition, and twenty minutes in deciding whether or not to take an umbrella when going to the mailbox in the next street. The total effort that would occupy a busy man for three minutes all told may in this fashion leave another person prostrate after a day of doubt, anxiety, and toil.

Granted that work (and especially paperwork) is thus elastic in its demands on time, it is manifest that there need be little or no relationship between the work to be done and the size of the staff to which it may be assigned. A lack of real activity does not, of necessity, result in leisure. A lack of occupation is not necessarily revealed by a manifest idleness. The thing to be done swells in importance and complexity in direct ratio with the time to be spent. This fact is widely recognized, but less attention has been paid to its wider implications, more especially in the field of public administration. Politicians and taxpayers have assumed (with occasional phases of doubt) that a rising total in the number of civil servants must reflect a growing volume of work to be done. Cynics, in questioning this belief, have imagined that the multiplication of officials must have left some of them idle or all of them able to work for shorter hours. But this is a matter in which faith and doubt seem equally misplaced. The fact is that the number of officials and the quantity of the work are not related to each other at all. The rise in the total of those employed is governed by Parkinson's Law and would be much the same whether the volume of the work were to increase, diminish, or even disappear.

ONE WEPT WHOSE ONLY CHILD WAS DEAD

Alice Meynell

One wept whose only child was dead,
New-born, ten years ago.
"Weep not; he is in bliss," they said.
She answered, "Even so,

"Ten years ago was born in pain
A child, not now forlorn.
But oh, ten years ago, in vain,
A mother, a mother was born."

SWEET ADELINE

Richard H. Gerard

In the evening when I sit alone a-dreaming
Of days gone by love—to me so dear,
There's a picture that in fancy 'oft appearing
Brings back the time love—when you were near;
It is then I wonder where you are my darling,
And if your heart to me is still the same,
For the sighing wind and the nightingale a-singing
Are breathing only your sweet name.

Chorus
Sweet Adeline, My Adeline,
At night, dear heart, for you I pine,
In all my dreams your fair face beams;
You're the flower of my heart,
Sweet Adeline.

THE BEGINNING OF THE NUCLEAR AGE

Albert Einstein
Old Grove Road
Nassau Point
Peconic, Long Island
August 2, 1939

F. D. Roosevelt
President of the United States
White House
Washington, D. C.

SIR:

Some recent work by E. Fermi and L. Szilard, which has been communicated to me in manuscript, leads me to expect that the element uranium may be turned into a new and important source of energy in the immediate future. Certain aspects of the situation seem to call for watchfulness and, if necessary, quick action on the part of the Administration. I believe, therefore, that it is my duty to bring to your attention the following facts and recommendations.

In the course of the last four months, it has been made probable—through the work of Joliot in France as well as Fermi and Szilard in America—that it may become possible to set up nuclear chain reactions in a large mass of uranium, by which vast amounts of power and large quantities of new radium-like elements would be generated. Now it appears almost certain that this could be achieved in the immediate future.

This new phenomenon would also lead to the construction of bombs and it is conceivable—though much less certain—that extremely powerful bombs of a new type may thus be constructed. A single bomb of this type, carried by boat or exploded in a port, might very well destroy the whole port together with some of the surrounding territory. However, such bombs might very well prove to be too heavy for transportation by air.

(The letter from which the above is a quotation was delivered to President Roosevelt on October 11, 1939, by Alexander Sachs.)

GOD

John Banister Tabb

I see Thee in the distant blue;
But in the violet's dell of dew,
Behold, I *breathe and touch* Thee too.

GO PLACIDLY

Anonymous

Go placidly amid the noise and the haste, and remember what peace there may be in silence. As far as possible without surrender be on good terms with all persons. Speak your truth quietly and clearly; and listen to others, even the dull and ignorant; they too have their story. Enjoy your achievements as well as your plans. Keep interested in your own career, however humble; it is a real possession in the changing fortunes of time. Be yourself.

Take kindly the counsels of years, gracefully surrendering the things of youth. Nurture strength of spirit to shield you in sudden misfortune. But do not distress yourself with imaginings. Many fears are born of fatigue and loneliness. You are a child of the universe no less than the trees and the stars; you have a right to be here. And whether or not it is clear to you, no doubt the universe is unfolding as it should. Therefore be at peace with God, whatever you conceive Him to be; and whatever your labors and aspirations, in the noisy confusion of life, keep peace with your soul. With all its sham, drudgery and broken dreams, it is still a beautiful world.

(1692)

NOW SLEEPS THE CRIMSON PETAL

Alfred, Lord Tennyson

Now sleeps the crimson petal, now the white;
Nor waves the cypress in the palace walk;
Nor winks the gold fin in the porphyry font:
The fire-fly wakens: waken thou with me.

Now droops the milkwhite peacock like a ghost,
And like a ghost she glimmers on to me.

Now lies the Earth all Danae to the stars,
And all thy heart lies open unto me.

Now slides the silent meteor on, and leaves
A shining furrow, as thy thoughts in me.

Now folds the lily all her sweetness up,
And slips into the bosom of the lake:
So fold thyself, my dearest, thou, and slip
Into my bosom and be lost in me.

UPON THE DEATH OF SIR ALBERT MORTON'S WIFE

Sir Henry Wotton

He first deceased; she for a little tried
To live without him, liked it not, and died.

JOAN OF ARC

Thomas De Quincey

What is to be thought of *her?* What is to be thought of the poor
shepherd girl from the hills and forests of Lorraine, that—like the
Hebrew shepherd boy from the hills and forests of Judea—rose
suddenly out of the quiet, out of the safety, out of the religious

inspiration, rooted in deep pastoral solitudes, to a station in the van of armies, and to the more perilous station at the right hand of kings? The Hebrew boy inaugurated his patriotic mission by an *act*, by a victorious *act*, such as no man could deny. But so did the girl of Lorraine, if we read her story as it was read by those who saw her nearest. Adverse armies bore witness to the boy as no pretender; but so they did to the gentle girl. Judged by the voice of all who saw them *from a station of good–will*, both were found true and loyal to any promises involved in their first acts. Enemies it was that made the difference between their subsequent fortunes. The boy rose to a splendor and a noon day prosperity, both personal and public, that rang through the records of his people, and became a by-word amongst his posterity for a thousand years, until the sceptre was departing from Judah. The poor, forsaken girl, on the contrary, drank not herself from that cup of rest which she had secured for France. She never sang together with the songs that rose in her native Domrémy, as echoes to the departing steps of the invaders. She mingled not in the festal dances of Vaucouleurs which celebrated in rapture the redemption of France. No! for her voice was then silent; no! for her feet were dust. Pure, innocent, noble-hearted girl! whom, from earliest youth, ever I believed in as full of truth and self-sacrifice, this was amongst the strongest pledges of *thy* truth, that never once—no, not for a moment of weakness— didst thou revel in the vision of coronets and honors from man. Coronets for thee! Oh no! Honors, if they come when all is over, are for those that share thy blood. Daughter of Domrémy, when the gratitude of thy kind shall awaken, thou wilt be sleeping the sleep of the dead. Call her, King of France, but she will not hear thee. Cite her by the apparitors to come and receive a robe of honor, but she will be found *en contumace*. When the thunders of universal France, as even yet may happen, shall proclaim the grandeur of the poor shepherd girl that gave up all for her country, thy ear, young shepherd girl, will have been deaf for five centuries. To suffer and to do, that was thy portion in this life; that was thy destiny; and not for a moment was it hidden from thyself. Life, thou saidst, is short; and the sleep which is in the grave is long; let me use that life, so transitory, for the glory of those heavenly dreams destined to comfort the sleep which is so long! This pure creature—pure from every suspicion of even a visionary self-interest, even as she was pure in senses more obvious—never once did this holy child, as regarded herself, relax from her belief in the darkness that was traveling to meet her. She might not prefigure the very manner of her death; she saw not in vision, the aerial altitude of the fiery scaffold, the spectators without end on every road pouring into Rouen as to a coronation, the surging smoke, the volleying flames, the hostile faces all around, the pitying eye that lurked but there, until nature and imperishable truth broke loose from artificial restraints;—these might not be apparent through the mists of the hurrying future. But the voice that called her to death, *that* she heard forever.

Great was the throne of France even in those days, and great was he that sat upon it; but well Joanna knew that not the throne, nor he that sat upon it, was for *her*; but on the contrary, that she was for *them*; not she by them, but they by her, should rise from the dust. Gorgeous were the lilies of France, and for centuries had the privilege to spread their beauty over land and sea, until in another century the wrath of God and man combined to wither them; but well Joanna knew, early at Domrémy she had read that bitter truth, that the lilies of France would decorate no garland for *her*. Flower nor bud, bell nor blossom, would ever bloom for *her*.

THE LAST INVOCATION

Walt Whitman

At the last, tenderly,
From the walls of the powerful, fortress'd house,
From the clasp of the knitted locks—from the keep of the
    well-closed doors,
Let me be wafted.

Let me glide noiselessly forth;
With the key of softness unlock the locks—with a whisper,
Set ope the doors, O Soul!

Tenderly! be not impatient!
(Strong is your hold, O mortal flesh!
Strong is your hold, O love.)

JESUS CHRIST

Ralph Waldo Emerson

Jesus Christ belonged to the true race of prophets. He saw with open eyes the mystery of the soul. Drawn by its severe harmony, ravished with its beauty, he lived in it, and had his being there. Alone in all history he estimated the greatness of man. One man was true to what is in you and me. He saw that God incarnates himself in man, and evermore goes forth anew to take possession of his World.

O TO BE UP AND DOING

Robert Louis Stevenson

O to be up and doing,
Unfearing and unashamed to go
In all the uproar and the press
About my human business!
My undissuaded heart I hear
Whisper courage in my ear.
With voiceless calls, the ancient earth
Summons me to a daily birth,
Thou, O my love, ye, O my friends—
The gist of life, the end of ends—
To laugh, to love, to live, to die
Ye call me by the ear and eye!

In general, the art of government consists in taking as much money as possible from one class of citizens to give to the other.

—Voltaire

(24)

WHO HAS SEEN THE WIND

Christina Rossetti

Who has seen the wind?
  Neither I nor you:
But when the leaves hang trembling,
  The wind is passing through.

Who has seen the wind?
  Neither you nor I:
But when the trees bow down their heads,
  The wind is passing by.

CONSTITUTION AND COURT

Charles Evans Hughes

We are under a Constitution, but the Constitution is what the judges say it is, and the judiciary is the safeguard of our liberty and of our property under the Constitution.

(1907)

THE WITCHES' BREW

William Shakespeare

First Witch: Round about the cauldron go:
In the poison'd entrails throw.
Toad, that under cold stone
Days and nights has thirty one
Swelter'd venom sleeping got,
Boil thou first i' the charmed pot.
All: Double, double toil and trouble;
Fire burn and cauldron bubble.
Second Witch: Fillet of a fenny snake,
In the cauldron boil and bake;
Eye of newt and toe of frog,
Wool of bat and tongue of dog,

Adder's fork and blind-worm's sting,
Lizard's leg and howlet's wing,
For a charm of powerful trouble,
Like a hell-broth boil and bubble.
All: Double, double toil and trouble;
Fire burn and cauldron bubble.
Third Witch: Scale of dragon, tooth of wolf,
Witches' mummy, maw and gulf
Of the ravin'd salt-sea shark,
Root of hemlock digg'd i' the dark,
Liver of blaspheming Jew,
Gall of goat and slips of yew
Sliver'd in the moon's eclipse,
Nose of Turk and Tartar's lips,
Finger of birth-strangled babe
Ditch-deliver'd by a drab,
Make the gruel thick and slab:
Add thereto a tiger's chaudron,
For the ingredient of our cauldron.
All: Double, double toil and trouble;
Fire burn and cauldron bubble.
Second Witch: Cool it with a baboon's blood,
Then the charm is firm and good.

(From *Macbeth*)

WILLY LOMAN, SALESMAN

Arthur Miller

(*Linda Loman is defending her husband, to her two grown sons:*)

I don't say he's a great man. Willy Loman never made a lot of
money. His name was never in the paper. He's not the finest character that ever lived. But he's a human being, and a terrible thing is
happening to him. So attention must be paid. He's not to be allowed
to fall into his grave like an old dog. Attention, attention must be
finally paid to such a person. You called him crazy . . . A lot of
people think he's lost his—balance. But you don't have to be very
smart to know what his trouble is. The man is exhausted. . . . A small
man can be just as exhausted as a great man. He works for a company
thirty-six years this March, opens up unheard-of-territories to their

trademark, and now in his old age they take his salary away. . . . For five weeks he's been on straight commission, like a beginner, an unknown! . . . When he brought them business, when he was young, they were glad to see him. But now his old friends, the old buyers that loved him so and always found some order to hand him in a pinch—they're all dead, retired. He used to be able to make six, seven calls a day in Boston. Now he takes his valises out of the car and puts them back and takes them out again and he's exhausted. Instead of walking he talks now. He drives seven hundred miles, and when he gets there no one knows him any more, no one welcomes him. . . . How long can that go on? How long? You see what I'm sitting here and waiting for? And you tell me he has no character? The man who never worked a day but for your benefit. When does he get a medal for that? . . .

(After Willy Loman's suicide, an old business friend speaks to the dead man's sons:)

Nobody dast blame this man. You don't understand: Willy was a salesman. And for a salesman, there is no rock bottom to the life. He don't put a bolt to a nut, he don't tell you the law or give you medicine. He's a man way out there in the blue riding on a smile and a shoeshine. And when they start not smiling back—that's an earthquake. And then you get yourself a couple of spots on your hat, and you're finished. Nobody dast blame this man. A salesman is got to dream, boy. It comes with the territory.

(From The Death of a Salesman)

THE RAINY DAY

Henry Wadsworth Longfellow

The day is cold, and dark, and dreary;
It rains, and the wind is never weary;
The vine still clings to the mouldering wall,
But at every gust the dead leaves fall,
    And the day is dark and dreary.

My life is cold, and dark, and dreary;
It rains, and the wind is never weary;
My thoughts still cling to the mouldering Past,
But the hopes of youth fall thick in the blast,
    And the days are dark and dreary.

Be still, sad heart; and cease repining;
Behind the clouds is the sun still shining;
Thy fate is the common fate of all,
Into each life some rain must fall,
  Some days must be dark and dreary.

THE GOLDEN RULE

Mahabharata, c. 800 B.C.: Deal with others as thou wouldst thyself be dealt by. Do nothing to thy neighbor which thou wouldst not have him to thee hereafter.

Dadistan-I dinik, Zend-Avesta, c. 700 B.C.: That nature only is good when it shall not do unto another whatever is not good for its own self.

Undana Varga, c. 500 B.C.: Hurt not others with that which pains yourself.

Confucius, 5th century B.C.: Tuan-mu Tzv said, "What I do not wish others to do unto me I also wish not to do unto others." Do not unto others what you would not they should do unto you.

Panchatantra, c. 200 B.C.: Ponder well the maxim: Never do to other persons what would pain thyself.

Hillel Ha-Babli, c. 30 B.C.: Whatsoever thou wouldst that men should not do to thee, do not do that to them. This is the whole law. The rest is only explanation.

St. Luke, c. A.D. 75: As ye would that men should do to you, do ye also to them likewise.

St. Matthew, c. A.D. 75: All things whatsoever ye would that men should do to you, do ye even so to them; for this is the law and the prophets.

Mohammed, 7th century A.D.: Say not, if people are good to us, we will do good to them, and if people oppress us we will oppress them: but resolve that if people do good to you, you will do good to them, and if they oppress you, oppress them not again.

(28)

THE MORAL WARFARE

John Greenleaf Whittier

Our fathers to their graves have gone,
   Their strife is past,—their triumph won;
But sterner trials await the race
   Which rises in their honored place,—
A moral warfare with the crime
   And folly of an evil time.

So let it be. In God's own might
   We gird us for the coming fight,
And, strong in Him whose cause is ours
   In conflict with unholy powers,
We grasp the weapons He has given,—
   The Light, the Truth, and Love of Heaven.

When the Rev. Edward Everett Hale was chaplain of the United States Senate, he was asked if he prayed for the Senators.

"No," he said, "I look at the Senators and pray for the country."

THE CHILD'S WORLD

William Brighty Rands

Great, wide, beautiful, wonderful World,
With the wonderful water round you curled,
And the wonderful grass upon your breast,
World, you are beautifully dressed.

The wonderful air is over me,
And the wonderful wind is shaking the tree—
It walks on the water, and whirls the mills,
And talks to itself on the top of the hills.

You friendly Earth, how far do you go,
With the wheat-fields that nod and the rivers that flow,
With cities and gardens and cliffs and isles,
And the people upon you for thousands of miles?

Ah! you are so great, and I am so small,
I hardly can think of you, World, at all;
And yet, when I said my prayers to-day,
My mother kissed me, and said, quite gay,

"If the wonderful World is great to you,
And great to father and mother too,
You are more than the Earth, though you are such a dot!
You can love and think, and the Earth cannot!"

EPIGRAM

Alexander Pope

You beat your pate, and fancy wit will come:
Knock as you please, there's nobody at home.

THE DROP OF HONEY

Thousand and One Nights

(TRANSLATOR: Richard Burton)

A certain hunter used to chase wild beast in wold, and one day he came upon a grotto in the mountains, where he found a hollow full of bees' honey. So he took somewhat thereof in a waterskin he had with him and, throwing it over his shoulder, carried it to the city, followed by a hunting dog which was dear to him. He stopped at the shop of an oilman and offered him the honey for sale and he bought it. Then he emptied out the skin, that he might see it, and in the act a drop fell to the ground, whereupon the flies flocked to it and a bird swooped down upon the flies. Now the oilman had a cat, which sprang upon the bird, and the huntsman's dog, seeing the cat, sprang upon it and slew it; whereupon the oilman sprang upon the dog and slew it, and the huntsman in turn sprang upon the oilman and slew him. Now the oilman was of one village and the huntsman of another; and when the people of the two places heard what had passed, they took up arms and weapons and rose one on the other in wrath and the two lines met; nor did the sword leave its play amongst them, till there died of them much people, none knoweth their number saye Almighty Allah.

VICTORY IN DEFEAT

Edwin Markham

Defeat may serve as well as victory
To shake the soul and let the glory out.
When the great oak is straining in the wind,
The boughs drink in new beauty and the trunk
Sends down a deeper root on the windward side.
Only the soul that knows the mighty grief
Can know the mighty rapture. Sorrows come
To stretch out spaces in the heart for joy.

UNSPOKEN WAR PRAYER

Mark Twain

Oh, Lord Our Father, our young patriots, idols of our hearts, go forth to battle. Be Thou near them! With them—in spirit—we also go from the sweet peace of our beloved firesides to smite the foe.

Oh, Lord our God, help us to tear their soldiers to bloody shreds with our shells; help us to cover their smiling fields with the pale forms of their patriot dead; help us to drown the thunder of the guns with the wounded, writhing in pain; help us to lay waste their humble homes with the hurricane of fire; help us to wring the hearts of their unoffending widows with unavailing grief; help us to turn them out roofless with their little children to wander unfriended over wastes of their desolated land in rags and hunger and thirst, sport of the sun-flames of summer and the icy winds of winter, broken in spirit, worn with travail, imploring Thee for the refuge of the grave and denied it—for our sakes, who adore Thee, Lord, blast their hopes, blight their lives, protract their bitter pilgrimage, make heavy their steps, water their way with their tears, stain the white snow with the blood of their wounded feet! We ask of One who is the spirit of Love and Who is the ever-faithful refuge and friend of all that are sore beset, and seek His aid with humble and contrite hearts. Grant our prayer, Oh Lord, and thine shall be the praise and honor and glory, now and forever, Amen.

A LAMENT

Percy Bysshe Shelley

O world! O life! O time!
On whose last steps I climb,
    Trembling at that where I had stood before;
When will return the glory of your prime?
        No more—Oh, never more!

Out of the day and night
A joy has taken flight;
    Fresh spring, and summer, and winter hoar,
Move my faint heart with grief, but with delight
        No more—Oh, never more!

"When I use a word," Humpty Dumpty said, "it means just what I choose it to mean—neither more nor less."
                        —Lewis Carroll

RAIN SONG

Robert Loveman

It isn't raining for me,
  It's raining daffodils;
In every dimpled drop I see
  Wild flowers on the hills.
The clouds of gray engulf the day
  And overwhelm the town;
It isn't raining rain to me,
  It's raining roses down.

It isn't raining rain to me,
  But fields of clover bloom,
Where any buccaneering bee
  Can find a bed and room.
A health unto the happy,
  A fig for him who frets!
It isn't raining rain to me,
  It's raining violets.

THE VOW

Antipater

Once, when she fell sick, Bacchylis, the sponge of the cups of Bacchus, addressed Demeter on her knees. She implored her somewhat in this fashion:

"If I escape from the wave of this evil fever, for the space of a hundred suns in my sight I shall not drink but fresh spring water and avoid Bacchus and wine."

But when she was cured of her illness, on the very first day she invented a remarkable way to get out of her pledge.

Taking a sieve and looking upward through its close meshes, she saw even more than a hundred suns.

ALEXANDER POPE'S EPITAPH FOR SIR ISAAC NEWTON

Nature and Nature's Laws lay hid in Night:
GOD said, *Let Newton be*! and all was light.

THE SECRET LIFE OF WALTER MITTY

James Thurber

"We're going through!" The Commander's voice was like thin ice breaking. He wore his full-dress uniform, with the heavily braided white cap pulled down rakishly over one cold gray eye. "We can't make it, sir. It's spoiling for a hurricane, if you ask me." "I'm not asking you, Lieutenant Berg," said the Commander. "Throw on the power lights! Rev her up to 8,500! We're going through!" The pounding of the cylinders increased: ta-pocketa-pocketa-pocketa-*pocketa-pocketa*. The Commander stared at the ice forming on the pilot window. He walked over and twisted a row of complicated dials. "Switch on No. 8 auxiliary!" he shouted. "Switch on No. 8 auxiliary!" repeated Lieutenant Berg. "Full strength in No. 3 turret!" shouted the Commander. "Full strength in No. 3 turret!" The crew, bending to their various tasks in the huge, hurtling eight-engined Navy hydroplane, looked at each other and grinned. "The Old Man ain't afraid of Hell!" . . .

"Not so fast! You're driving too fast!" said Mrs. Mitty. "What are you driving so fast for?"

"Hmm?" said Walter Mitty. He looked at his wife, in the seat beside him, with shocked astonishment. She seemed grossly unfamiliar, like a strange woman who had yelled at him in a crowd. "You were up to fifty-five," she said. "You know I don't like to go more than forty. You were up to fifty-five." Walter Mitty drove on toward Waterbury in silence, the roaring of the SN 202 through the worst storm in twenty years of Navy flying faded in the remote, intimate airways of his mind. "You're tensed up again," said Mrs. Mitty. "It's one of your days. I wish you'd let Dr. Renshaw look you over." Walter Mitty stopped the car in front of the building where his wife went to have her hair done. "Remember to get those overshoes while I'm having my hair done," she said. "I don't need overshoes," said Mitty. She put her mirror back into her bag. "We've

(34)

been all through that," she said, getting out of the car. "You're not a young man any longer." He raced the engine a little. "Why don't you wear your gloves? Have you lost your gloves?" Walter Mitty reached in a pocket and brought out the gloves. He put them on, but after she had turned and gone into the building and he had driven on to a red light, he took them off again. "Pick it up, brother!" snapped a cop as the light changed, and Mitty hastily pulled on his gloves and lurched ahead. He drove around the streets aimlessly for a time and then he drove past the hospital on his way to the parking lot.

"It's the millionaire banker, Wellington McMillan," said the pretty nurse. "Yes?" said Walter Mitty, removing his gloves slowly. "Who has the case?" "Dr. Renshaw and Dr. Benbow, but there are two specialists here, Dr. Remington from New York and Mr. Pritchard–Mitford from London. He flew over." A door opened down a long, cool corridor and Dr. Renshaw came out. He looked distraught and haggard. "Hello, Mitty," he said. "We're having the devil's own time with McMillan, the millionaire banker and close personal friend of Roosevelt. Obstreosis of the ductal tract. Tertiary. Wish you'd take a look at him." "Glad to," said Mitty.

In the operating room there were whispered introductions: "Dr. Remington, Dr. Mitty. Mr. Pritchard–Mitford, Dr. Mitty." "I've read your book on streptothricosis," said Pritchard–Mitford, shaking hands. "A brilliant performance, sir." "Thank you," said Walter Mitty. "Didn't know you were in the States, Mitty," grumbled Remington. "Coals to Newcastle, bringing Mitford and me up here for a tertiary." "You are very kind," said Mitty. A huge, complicated machine, connected to the operating table, with many tubes and wires, began at this moment to go pocketa-pocketa-pocketa. "The new anesthetizer is giving way!" shouted an interne. "There is no one in the east who knows how to fix it!" "Quiet, man!" said Mitty, in a low, cool voice. He sprang to the machine, which was going pocketa-pocketa-queep-pocketa-queep. He began fingering delicately a row of glistening dials. "Give me a fountain pen!" he snapped. Someone handed him a fountain pen. He pulled a faulty piston out of the machine and inserted the pen in its place. "That will hold for ten minutes," he said. "Get on with the operation." A nurse hurried over and whispered to Renshaw, and Mitty saw the man turn pale. "Coreopsis has set in," said Renshaw nervously. "If you would take over, Mitty?" Mitty looked at him and at the craven figure of Benbow, who drank, and at the grave, uncertain faces of the two great specialists. "If you wish," he said. They slipped a white gown on

(35)

him; he adjusted a mask and drew on thin gloves; nurses handed him shining . . .

"Back it up, Mac! Look out for that Buick!" Walter Mitty jammed on the brakes. "Wrong lane, Mac," said the parking-lot attendant, looking at Mitty closely. "Gee. Yeh," muttered Mitty. He began cautiously to back out of the lane marked "Exit Only." "Leave her sit there," said the attendant. "I'll put her away." Mitty got out of the car. "Hey, better leave the key." "Oh," said Mitty, handing the man the ignition key. The attendant vaulted into the car, backed it up with insolent skill, and put it where it belonged.

They're so damn cocky, thought Walter Mitty, walking along Main Street; they think they know everything. Once he had tried to take his chains off, outside New Milford, and he had got them wound around the axles. A man had had to come out in a wrecking car and unwind them, a young, grinning garageman. Since then Mrs. Mitty always made him drive to a garage to have the chains taken off. The next time, he thought, I'll wear my right arm in a sling; they won't grin at me then. I'll have my right arm in a sling and they'll see I couldn't possibly take the chains off myself. He kicked at the slush on the sidewalk. "Overshoes," he said to himself, and he began looking for a shoe store.

When he came out into the street again, with the overshoes in a box under his arm, Walter Mitty began to wonder what the other thing was his wife had told him to get. She had told him, twice, before they set out from their house for Waterbury. In a way he hated these weekly trips to town—he was always getting something wrong. Kleenex, he thought, Squibb's, razor blades? No. Toothpaste, toothbrush, bicarbonate, cardorundumn, initiative and referendum? He gave it up. But she would remember it. "Where's the what-its-name." A newsboy went by shouting something about the Waterbury trial.

"Perhaps this will refresh your memory." The District Attorney suddenly thrust a heavy automatic at the quiet figure on the witness stand. "Have you ever seen this before?" Walter Mitty took the gun and examined it expertly. "This is my Webley–Vickers 50.80," he said calmly. An excited buzz ran around the courtroom. The Judge rapped for order. "You are a crack shot with any sort of firearms, I believe?" said the District Attorney, insinuatingly. "Objection!" shouted Mitty's attorney. "We have shown that the defendant could not have fired the shot. We have shown that he wore his right arm in a sling on the night of the fourteenth of July." Walter Mitty raised his hand briefly and the bickering attorneys were stilled. "With any known make of gun," he said evenly, "I could have killed Gregory Fitzhurst at three hundred feet *with my left hand.*"

Pandemonium broke loose in the courtroom. A woman's scream rose above the bedlam and suddenly a lovely, dark-skinned girl was in Walter Mitty's arms. The District Attorney struck at her savagely. Without rising from his chair, Mitty let the man have it on the point of the chin. "You miserable cur!" . . .

"Puppy biscuit," said Walter Mitty. He stopped walking and the buildings of Waterbury rose up out of the misty courtroom and sur- rounded him again. A woman who was passing laughed. "He said 'Puppy Biscuit'," she said to her companion. "That man said 'Puppy Biscuit' to himself." Walter Mitty hurried on. He went into an A.&P., not the first one he came to but a smaller one farther up the street. "I want some biscuit for small, young dogs," he said to the clerk. "Any special brand, sir?" The greatest pistol shot in the world thought a moment. "It says 'Puppies Bark for It' on the box," said Walter Mitty.

His wife would be through at the hairdresser's in fifteen minutes, Mitty saw in looking at his watch, unless they had trouble drying it; sometimes they had trouble drying it. She didn't like to get to the hotel first; she would want him to be there waiting for her as usual. He found a big leather chair in the lobby, facing a window, and he put the overshoes and the puppy biscuit on the floor beside it. He picked up an old copy of *Liberty* and sank down into the chair. "Can Germany Conquer the World Through the Air?" Walter Mitty looked at the pictures of bombing planes and of ruined streets.

. . . "The cannonading has got the wind up in young Raleigh, sir," said the sergeant. Captain Mitty looked up at him through tousled hair. "Get him to bed," he said wearily. "With the others. I'll fly alone." "But you can't, sir," said the sergeant anxiously. "It takes two men to handle that bomber and the Archies are pounding hell out of the air. Von Richtman's circus is between here and Saulier." "Some- body's got to get that ammunition dump," said Mitty. "I'm going over. Spot of brandy?" He poured a drink for the sergeant and one for himself. War thundered and whined around the dugout and battered at the door. There was a rending of wood and splinters flew through the room. "A bit of a near thing," said Captain Mitty carelessly. "The box barrage is closing in," said the sergeant. "We only live once, sergeant," said Mitty with his faint, fleeting smile. "Or do we?" He poured another brandy and tossed it off. "I never see a man could hold his brandy like you, sir," said the sergeant. "Begging your pardon, sir." Captain Mitty stood up and strapped on his huge Webley–Vickers automatic. "It's forty kilometers through hell, sir," said the sergeant. Mitty finished one last brandy. "After all," he said softly, "what isn't?" The pounding of the cannon increased; there was the rat-tat-tatting of machine guns, and from somewhere came the menacing pocketa-pocketa-pocketa of the new flame-throwers. Walter Mitty walked to the door of the dugout humming "Auprès de Ma Blonde." He turned and waved to the sergeant. "Cheerio!" he said.

Something struck his shoulder. "I've been looking all over this hotel for you," said Mrs. Mitty. "Why do you have to hide in this old chair? How did you expect me to find you?" "Things close in," said Walter Mitty vaguely. "What?" Mrs. Mitty said. "Did you get the what's-its-name? The puppy biscuit? What's in that box?" "Over-shoes," said Mitty. "Couldn't you have put them on in the store?" "I was thinking," said Walter Mitty. "Does it ever occur to you that I am sometimes thinking?" She looked at him. "I'm going to take your temperature when I get you home," she said.

They went out through the revolving doors that made a faintly derisive whistling sound when you pushed them. It was two blocks to the parking lot. At the drugstore on the corner she said, "Wait here for me. I forgot something. I won't be a minute." Walter Mitty lighted a cigarette. It began to rain, rain with sleet in it. He stood up against the wall of the drugstore, smoking . . . He put his shoulders back and his heels together. "To hell with the handker-chief," said Walter Mitty scornfully. He took one last drag on his cigarette and snapped it away. Then with that faint, fleeting smile playing about his lips, he faced the firing squad; erect and motion-less, proud and disdainful, Walter Mitty the Undefeated, inscrutable to the last.

THE VALUE OF SILENCE

When someone twitted Calvin Coolidge for his habitual silence, he replied, "Well, I found out early in life that you didn't have to explain something you hadn't said."

DAYBREAK

Henry Wadsworth Longfellow

A Wind came up out of the sea,
And said, "O mists, make room for me."

It hailed the ships, and cried, "Sail on,
Ye mariners, the night is gone."

And hurried landward far away,
Crying, "Awake! it is the day."

It said unto the forest, "Shout!
Hang all your leafy banners out!"

It touched the wood-bird's folded wing,
And said, "O bird, awake and sing."

And o'er the farms, "O chanticleer,
Your clarion blow; the day is near."

It whispered to the fields of corn,
"Bow down, and hail the coming morn."

It shouted through the belfry-tower,
"Awake, O bell! proclaim the hours."

It crossed the churchyard with a sigh,
And said, "Not yet! in quiet lie."

FAITH

Anonymous

Fear knocked at the door.
Faith answered.
There was no one there.

(From a sign over an
old inn at Bray, England)

THE DOER OF GOOD

Oscar Wilde

It was night-time, and He was alone.

And He saw afar off the walls of a round city, and went toward the city.

And when He came near He heard within the city the tread of the feet of joy, and the laughter of the mouth of gladness, and the loud noise of many lutes. And he knocked at the gate and certain of the gate-keepers opened to Him.

And He beheld a house that was of marble, and had fair pillars of marble before it. The pillars were hung with garlands, and within and without there were torches of cedar. And He entered the house.

And when He had passed through the hall of chalcedony and the hall of jasper, and reached the long hall of feasting, He saw lying on a couch of sea-purple one whose hair was crowned with red roses and whose lips were red with wine.

And He went behind him and touched him on the shoulder, and said to him: "Why do you live like this?"

And the young man turned round and recognized Him, and made answer, and said: "But I was a leper once, and you healed me. How else should I live?"

And He passed out of the house and went again into the street.

And after a little while He saw one whose face and raiment were painted and whose feet were shod with pearls. And behind her came slowly, as a hunter, a young man who wore a cloak of two colors. Now the face of the woman was as the fair face of an idol, and the eyes of the young man were bright with lust.

And He followed swiftly, and touched the hand of the young man, and said to him: "Why do you look at this woman in such wise?"

And the young man turned round and recognized Him, and said: "But I was blind once, and you gave me sight. At what else should I look?"

And He ran forward and touched the painted raiment of the woman, and said to her: "Is there no other way in which to walk save the way of sin?"

And the woman turned round and recognized Him, and laughed, and said: "But you forgave me my sins, and the way is a pleasant way."

And He passed out of the city.

And when He had passed out of the city, He saw, seated by the roadside, a young man who was weeping.

And He went toward him and touched the long locks of his hair, and said to him: "Why are you weeping?"

And the young man looked up and recognized Him, and made answer: "But I was dead, and you raised me from the dead. What else should I do but weep?"

ON HEARING A LADY PRAISE A CERTAIN REVEREND DOCTOR'S EYES

George Outram

I cannot praise the Doctor's eyes;
I never saw his glance divine;
He always shuts them when he prays,
And when he preaches he shuts mine.

From TO A HIGHLAND GIRL

William Wordsworth

Sweet Highland Girl, a very shower
Of beauty is thy earthly dower!
Twice seven consenting years have shed
Their utmost bounty on thy head:
And these grey rocks; that household lawn;
Those trees, a veil just half withdrawn;
This fall of water that doth make
A murmur near the silent lake;
This little bay; a quiet road
That holds in shelter thy Abode—
In truth together do ye seem
Like something fashioned in a dream. . . .
   With earnest feeling I shall pray
For thee when I am far away:
For never saw I mien, or face,
In which more plainly I could trace

Benignity and home-bred sense
Ripening in perfect innocence. . . .
　　Now thanks to Heaven! that of its grace
Hath led me to this lonely place.
Joy have I had; and going hence
I bear away my recompense.
In spots like these it is we prize
Our Memory, feel that she hath eyes:
Then, why should I be loth to stir?
I feel this place was made for her;
To give new pleasure like the past,
Continued long as life shall last.
Nor am I loth, though pleased at heart,
Sweet Highland Girl! from thee to part:
For I, methinks, till I grow old,
As fair before me shall behold,
As I do now, the cabin small,
The lake, the bay, the waterfall;
And Thee, the Spirit of them all!

From ON FRIENDSHIP

William Cowper

The man that hails you Tom or Jack,
And proves, by thumping on your back,
His sense of your great merit,
Is such a friend that one had need
Be very much his friend indeed
To pardon or to bear it.

THERE IS A REALM WHERE THE RAINBOW NEVER FADES

George D. Prentice

It cannot be that the earth is man's only abiding place. It cannot
be that our life is a mere bubble cast up by eternity to float a moment
on its waves and then sink into nothingness. Else why is it that

glorious aspirations which leap like angels from the temple of our hearts are forever wandering unsatisfied? Why is it that all the stars that hold festival around the midnight throne are set above the grasp of our limited faculties, forever mocking us with their unapproachable glory? And, finally, why is it that bright forms of human beauty presented to our view are taken from us, leaving the thousand streams of our affections to flow back in Alpine torrents upon our hearts? There is a realm where the rainbow never fades; where the stars will be spread out before us like islands that slumber in the ocean, and where the beautiful beings which now pass before us like shadows will stay in our presence forever.

THE SATISFIED TIGER

Cosmo Monkhouse

There was a young lady of Niger
Who smiled as she rode on a tiger;
They returned from the ride
With the lady inside,
And the smile on the face of the tiger.

THIS ONLY GRANT ME

Abraham Cowley

This only grant me, that my means may lie
Too low for envy, for contempt too high.
   Some honor I would have,
Not from great deeds, but good alone;
Th' unknown are better than the ill-known.
   Rumor can ope the grave;
Acquaintance I would have; but when 't depends
Not on the number, but the choice of friends.

Books should, not business, entertain the light,
And sleep, as undisturbed as death, the night.

(43)

My house a cottage, more
Than palace, and fitting be
For all my use, no luxury.
  My garden painted o'er
With Nature's hand, not Art's; and pleasures yield,
Horace might envy in his Sabine field.

Thus would I double my life's fading space,
For he that runs it well, twice runs his race.
  And in this true delight,
These unbought sports, that happy state,
I would not fear nor wish my fate,
  But boldly say each night,
Tomorrow let my sun his beams display,
Or in clouds hide them; I have lived today.

CENSORSHIP

Dwight D. Eisenhower

Don't join the book burner. Don't think you are going to conceal thoughts by concealing evidence that they ever existed. Don't be afraid to go to the library and read every book, so long as that document doesn't offend our own ideas of decency; that should be the only censorship.

(At Dartmouth College, June 14, 1953)

THE HOUSE AND THE ROAD

Josephine Preston Peabody

The little Road says, Go,
The little House says, Stay;
And O, it's bonny here at home,
But I must go away.

The little Road, like me,
Would seek and turn and know;
And forth I must, to learn the things
The little Road would show!

And go I must, my dears,
And journey while I may,
Though heart be sore for the little House
That had no word but Stay.

Maybe, no other way
Your child could ever know
Why a little House would have you stay,
When a little Road says, Go.

I DIED FOR BEAUTY

Emily Dickinson

I died for beauty, but was scarce
Adjusted in the tomb,
When one who died for truth was lain
In an adjoining room.

He questioned softly why I failed?
"For beauty," I replied.
And I for truth—the two are one;
We brethren are," he said.

And so, as kinsmen met a-night,
We talked between the rooms,
Until the moss had reached our lips,
And covered up our names.

GREATER LOVE HATH NO MAN

Holy Bible, John 15:13–16

Greater love hath no man than this, that a man lay down his life for his friends.

Ye are my friends, if ye do whatsoever I command you.

Henceforth I call you not servants; for the servant knoweth not what his lord doeth: but I have called you friends . . .

Ye have not chosen me, but I have chosen you.

TEWKESBURY ROAD

John Masefield

It is good to be out on the road, and going one knows not where,
   Going through meadow and village, one knows not whither nor why;
Through the grey light drift of the dust, in the keen, cool rush of the air,
   Under the flying white clouds, and the broad blue lift of the sky.

And to halt at the chattering brook, in the tall green fern at the brink
   Where the harebell grows, and the gorse, and the fox-gloves purple and white;
Where the shy-eyed delicate deer troop down to the brook to drink
   When the stars are mellow and large at the coming on of night.

O, to feel the beat of the rain, and the homely smell of the earth,
   Is a tune for the blood to jig to, a joy past power of words;
And the blessed green comely meadows are all a-ripple with mirth
   At the noise of the lambs at play and the dear wild cry of the birds.

LINCOLN REPARTEE

A foreign diplomat unexpectedly walked in on Abraham Lincoln when he was shining his shoes.

"I am astonished, Mr. President," he said, "to find you blacking your own shoes."

"Whose shoes do you shine?" asked Lincoln.

JOHN KEATS' FAREWELL LETTER TO FANNY BRAWNE

MY DEAREST GIRL,

I have been a walk this morning with a book in my hand, but as usual I have been occupied with nothing but you: I wish I could say in an agreeable manner. I am tormented day and night. They talk of my going to Italy. 'Tis certain I shall never recover if I am to be so long separate from you: yet with all this devotion to you I cannot persuade myself into any confidence of you.

Past experience connected with the fact of my long separation from you gives me agonies which are scarcely to be talked of. When your mother comes I shall be very sudden and expert in asking her whether you have been to Mrs. Dilke's, for she might say no to make me easy. I am literally worn to death, which seems my only recourse. I cannot forget what has pass'd. What? nothing with a man of the world, but to me dreadful.

I will get rid of this as much as possible. When you were in the habit of flirting with Brown you would have left off, could your own heart have felt one half of one pang mine did. Brown is a good sort of Man—he did not know he was doing me to death by inches. I feel the effect of every one of those hours in my side now; and for that cause, though he had done me many services, though I know his love and friendship for me, though at this moment I should be without pence were it not for his assistance, I will never see or speak to him until we are both old men, if we are to be. I will resent my heart having been made a football. You will call this madness. I have heard you say that it was not unpleasant to wait a few years—you have amusements—your mind is away—you have not brooded over one idea as I have, and how should you?

You are to be an object intensely desirable—the air I breathe in a room empty of you is unhealthy. I am not the same to you—no—you can wait—you have a thousand activities—you can be happy without me. Any party, any thing to fill up the day has been enough.

How have you pass'd this month? Who have you smil'd with? All this may seem savage in me. You do not feel as I do—you do not know what it is to love—one day you may—your time is not come.

Ask yourself how many unhappy hours Keats has caused you in Loneliness. For myself I have been a Martyr the whole time, and for this reason I speak, the confession is forc'd from me by the torture.

I appeal to you by the blood of that Christ you believe in; Do not write to me if you have done anything this month which it would have pained me to have seen. You may have altered—if you have not—if you still behave in dancing rooms and other societies as I have seen you—I do not want to live—if you have done so I wish this coming night may be my last.

I cannot live without you, and not only you but chaste you; virtuous you. The Sun rises and sets, the day passes, and you follow the bent of your inclination to a certain extent—you have no conception of the quantity of miserable feeling that passes through me in a day.—Be serious! Love is not a plaything—and again do not write unless you can do it with a crystal conscience. I would sooner die for want of you than—

Yours for ever
J. Keats

(A few months after this letter was written, Keats died of tuberculosis.)

SHENANDOAH

Anonymous

Oh, Shenandoah, I long to hear you,
    Away, you rolling river,
Oh, Shenandoah, I long to hear you,
    Away, we're bound away,
    'Cross the wide Missouri.

The white man loved the Indian maiden,
    Away, you rolling river,
With notions his canoe was laden,
    Away, we're bound away,
    'Cross the wide Missouri.

Oh, Shenandoah, I love your daughter,
    Away, you rolling river,
I'll take her 'cross the rolling water,
    Away, we're bound away,
    'Cross the wide Missouri.

Oh, Shenandoah, I'm bound to leave you,
    Away, you rolling river,
Oh, Shenandoah, I'll not deceive you,
    Away, we're bound away,
    'Cross the wide Missouri.

A WELCOME

Thomas O. Davis

Come in the evening, or come in the morning,
Come when you're looked for, or come without warning,
Kisses and welcomes you'll find here before you,
And the oftener you come here the more I'll adore you.

TAOISM

Lao Tzu

(TRANSLATOR: Lionel Giles)

When your work is done and fame has been achieved, then retire into the background; for this is the Way of Heaven.

Those who follow the Way desire not excess; and thus without excess they are for ever exempt from change.

All things alike do their work, and then we see them subside. When they have reached their bloom, each returns to its origin. Returning to their origin means rest or fulfilment of destiny. This reversion is an eternal law. To know that law is to be enlightened. Not to know it, is misery and calamity. He who knows the eternal law is liberal-minded. Being liberal-minded, he is just. Being just, he is kingly. Being kingly, he is akin to Heaven. Being akin to Heaven, he possesses Tao. Possessed of Tao he endures for ever. Though his body perish, yet he suffers no harm.

LIVES OF GREAT MEN

Anonymous

Lives of great men all remind us
As their pages o'er we turn,
That we're apt to leave behind us
Letters that we ought to burn.

FORBEARANCE

Ralph Waldo Emerson

Hast thou named all the birds without a gun?
Loved the wood rose, and left it on its stalk?
At rich men's tables eaten bread and pulse?
Unarmed, faced danger with a heart of trust?
And loved so well a high behavior,
In man or maid, that thou from speech refrained,
Nobility more nobly to repay?
O, be my friend, and teach me to be thine!

THE PARTING OF SIR THOMAS MORE FROM HIS DAUGHTER MARGARET

William Roper

When Sir Thomas More came from Westminster to the Tower-ward again, his daughter, my wife, desirous to see her father, whom she thought she should never see in this world after, and also to have his final blessing, gave attendance about the Tower Wharf, where she knew he should pass by before he could enter into the Tower. There tarrying for his coming home, as soon as she saw him, after his blessing upon her knees reverently received, she hastening towards him, and without consideration of care of herself pressing in among the midst of the throng and company of the guard that with halberds and bills went round about him, hastily ran to him, and there openly in the sight of them all embraced him, took him about the neck, and kissed him. Who well liking her most natural and dear daughterly affection towards him, gave her his fatherly blessing, and many godly words of comfort besides. For whom after she was departed, she, not satisfied with her former sight of him, and like one that had forgotten herself, being all ravished with the entire love of her dear father, having respect neither to herself nor to the press of the people and multitude that were about him, suddenly turned back again, ran to him as before, took him about the neck, and divers times together most lovingly kissed him; and at last, with a full heavy heart, was feign to depart from him, the beholding whereof was to many of them that were present thereat so lamentable, that it made them for very sorrow thereof to mourn and weep.

THE TONGUE

Phillips Burrows Strong

"The boneless tongue, so small and weak,
Can crush and kill," declared the Greek.

"The tongue destroys a greater horde,"
The Turk asserts, "than does the sword."

A Persian proverb wisely saith,
"A lengthy tongue—an early death."

Or sometimes takes this form instead,
"Don't let your tongue cut off your head."

"The tongue can speak a word whose speed,"
Says the Chinese, "outstrips the steed";

While Arab sages this impart,
"The tongue's great storehouse is the heart."

From Hebrew with the maxim sprung,
"Though feet should slip, ne'er let the tongue."

The sacred writer crown the whole:
"Who keeps the tongue doth keep his soul."

WHEN IN THE CHRONICLE OF WASTED TIME

William Shakespeare

When in the chronicle of wasted time
I see descriptions of the fairest wights,
And beauty making beautiful old rhyme
In praise of ladies dead and lovely knights,
Then, in the blazon of sweet beauty's best,
Of hand, of foot, of lip, of eye, of brow,
I see their antique pen would have express'd
Even such a beauty as you master now.

So all their praises are but prophecies
Of this our time, all you prefiguring;
And, for they look'd but with divining eyes,
They had not skill enough your worth to sing:
   For we, which now behold these present days,
   Have eyes to wonder, but lack tongues to praise.
(From his Sonnets)

FRANCIS BACON TO SIR EDWARD COKE

Mr. Attorney, I respect you, I fear you not; and the less you speak of your own greatness, the more I will think of it.

QUO VADIS, DOMINE?

Henry K. Sienkiewicz

(TRANSLATOR: J. Curtin)

At dawn . . . two dark figures were stealing along the Appian Way towards the valley of the Campania. One of them was Nazarius, the other the Apostle, Peter, who was leaving Rome and his distracted brethren. In the East the sky was already assuming a slight tinge of green, which changed gradually into a saffron color. From out the shadows appeared trees with silvery foliage, white marble villas and the arches of aqueducts stretching along the plain toward the city. The green tinge of the sky was becoming shot with gold. Soon the rays began to redden and illuminate the Alban Hills, which appeared as if wrapped in a violet frame. The dawn was mirrored in drops of dew trembling on the leaves of trees. The haze grew thinner and un-veiled a wider view of the plain, the houses that dotted it, the cemeteries, towns and groups of trees, among which gleamed the white columns of temples.

The road was deserted. The peasants who brought vegetables to the city had evidently not yet harnessed their horses. The blocks of stone with which the road was paved as far as the mountains echoed from the wooden-soled shoes of the wayfarers.

The sun rose over the hills, and then a wonderful vision burst upon the Apostle. It seemed to him that the golden disc, instead of rising higher in the sky, came gliding down from the heights and moved along the road. Then Peter stopped and said: "Didst thou see the brightness approaching us?"

"I see nothing," replied Nazarius.

Peter, shading his eyes with his hands, continued:

"Some figure is approaching us in the gleam of the sun."

But no sound of footsteps reached their ears. Nazarius saw only that the trees in the distance were trembling as if shaken, and that the light was spreading more widely over the valley. With amazement in his eyes he looked at the Apostle.

"Rabbi, what troubles thee?" he cried in alarm.

Peter dropped his staff; his eyes looked straight ahead, his mouth was open, his face expressed wonder, delight, ecstasy.

Suddenly he fell upon his knees, with his hands stretched out, and cried:

"O Christ! O Christ!" and he pressed his face towards the earth, as though kissing someone's feet. Then the voice of the old man was heard, choked with tears.

"Quo Vadis, Domine?" ("Whither goest Thou, O Lord?")

Nazarius did not catch the answer, but to Peter's ears came the sad, sweet voice, which said: "As thou art deserting my people, I go to Rome to be crucified a second time."

The Apostle lay on the ground, his face in the dust, motionless and silent. It seemed to Nazarius that he had fainted, or perhaps even that he was dead. But suddenly he arose, and without a word, turned back toward the City of the Seven Hills.

The lad, seeing this, repeated like an echo:

"Quo Vadis, Domine?"

"To Rome," replied the Apostle.

And he returned.

ASLEEP IN THE DEEP

Arthur J. Lamb

Stormy the night and the waves roll high,
Bravely the ship doth ride;
Hark! while the light-house bell's solemn cry
Rings o'er the sullen tide.

(53)

There on the deck see two lovers stand,
Heart to heart beating and hand in hand,
Though death be near, she knows no fear,
While at her side is the one ever dear.

Chorus
Loudly the bell in the old tower rings,
Bidding us list to the warning it brings;
Sailor, take care! Sailor, take care!
Danger is near thee, Beware! Beware!
Many brave hearts are asleep in the deep,
So beware! beware!

THE WIDOW'S MITE

Holy Bible, Luke 21:1–4

And he looked up, and he saw the rich men casting their gifts into the treasury.

And he saw also a certain poor widow casting in thither two mites.

And he said, Of a truth I say unto you, that this poor widow hath cast in more than they all.

For all these have of their abundance cast in unto the offerings of God: but she of her penury hath cast in all the living that she had.

GLOUCESTER MOORS

William Vaughan Moody

A mile behind is Gloucester town
Where the fishing fleets put in,
A mile ahead the land dips down
And the woods and farms begin.
Here, where the moors stretch free
In the high blue afternoon,
Are the marching sun and talking sea,
And the racing winds that wheel and flee
On the flying heels of June.

Jill-o'er-the-ground is purple blue,
Blue is the quaker-maid,
The wild geranium holds its dew
Long in the boulder's shade.
Wax-red hangs the cup
From the huckleberry boughs,
In barberry bells the grey moths sup
Or where the choke-berry lifts high-up
Sweet bowls for their carouse.

Over the shelf of the sandy cove
Beach-peas blossom late.
By copse and cliff the swallows rove
Each calling to its mate.
Seaward the sea-gulls go,
And the land-birds all are here;
The green-gold flash was a vireo,
And yonder flame where the march-flags grow
Was a scarlet tanager.

This earth is not the steadfast place
We landsmen build upon;
From deep to deep she varies face,
And while she comes is gone.
Beneath my feet I feel
Her smooth bulk heave and dip;
With velvet plunge and soft upreel
She swings and steadies to her keel
Like a gallant, gallant ship.

These summer clouds she sets for sail,
The sun is her masthead light,
She tows the moon like a pinnace frail
Where her phosphor wake churns bright.
Now hid, now looming clear,
On the face of the dangerous blue
The star fleets tack and wheel and veer,
But on, but on does the old earth steer
As if her port she knew.

God, dear God! Does she know her port,
Though she goes so far about?
Or blind astray, does she make her sport
To brazen and chance it out?

I watched her when captains passed:
She were better captainless.
Men in the cabin, before the mast,
But some were reckless and some aghast,
And some sat gorged at mess.

By her battened hatch I leaned and caught
Sounds from the noisome hold,—
Cursing and sighing of souls distraught
And cries too sad to be told.
Then I strove to go down and see;
But they said, "Thou art not of us!"
I turned to those on the deck with me
And cried, "Give help!" But they said, "Let be:
Our ship sails faster thus."

Jill-o'er-the-ground is purple blue,
Blue is the quaker-maid,
The alder-clump where the brook comes through
Breeds cresses in its shade.
To be out of the moiling street
With its swelter and its sin!
Who has given to me this sweet,
And given my brother dust to eat?
And when will his wage come in?

Scattering wide or blown in ranks,
Yellow and white and brown,
Boats and boats from the fishing banks
Come home to Gloucester town.
There is cash to pursue and spend,
There are wives to be embraced,
Hearts to borrow and hearts to lend,
And hearts to take and keep to the end,—
O little sails, make haste!

But thou, vast outbound ship of souls,
What harbor town for thee?
What shapes, when thy arriving tolls,
Shall crowd the banks to see?

Shall all the happy shipmates then
Stand singing brotherly?
Or shall a haggard ruthless few
Warp her over and bring her to,
While the many broken souls of men
Fester down in the slaver's pen,
And nothing to say or do?

THE GEORGIA FUNERAL

Henry W. Grady

I attended a funeral once in Pickens County in my State [Georgia]. A funeral is not usually a cheerful object to me unless I could select the subject. I think I could, perhaps, without going a hundred miles from here, find the material for one or two cheerful funerals. Still, this funeral was peculiarly sad. It was a poor "one gallus" fellow, whose breeches struck him under the armpits and hit him at the other end about the knee. . . . They buried him in the midst of a marble quarry: they cut through solid marble to make his grave: and yet a little tombstone they put above him was from Vermont. They buried him in the heart of a pine forest, and yet the pine coffin was imported from Cincinnati. They buried him within touch of an iron mine, and yet the nails in his coffin and the iron in the shovel that dug his grave was imported from Pittsburgh. They buried him by the side of the best sheep-grazing country on earth, and yet the wool in the coffin bands and the coffin bands themselves were brought from the North. The South didn't furnish a thing on earth for that funeral but the corpse and the hole in the ground. There they put him away and the clods rattled down on his coffin, and they buried him in a New York coat and a Boston pair of shoes and a pair of breeches from Chicago and a shirt from Cincinnati, leaving him nothing to carry into the next world with him to remind him of the country in which he lived, and for which he fought for four years, but the chill of blood in his veins and the marrow in his bones.

(1889)

TIME

Anonymous

Time is
Too slow for those who wait,
Too swift for those who Fear,
Too long for those who Grieve,
Too short for those who Rejoice;
But for those who Love
Time is
Eternity.

OCTOBER'S BRIGHT BLUE WEATHER

Helen Hunt Jackson

O suns and skies and clouds of June,
  And flowers of June together,
Ye cannot rival for one hour
  October's bright blue weather.

When loud the humblebee makes haste,
  Belated, thriftless vagrant,
And Golden Rod is dying fast,
  And lanes with grapes are fragrant;

When Gentians roll their fringes tight,
  To save them for the morning,
And chestnuts fall from satin burrs
  Without a sound of warning;

When on the ground red apples lie
  In piles like jewels shining,
And redder still on old stone walls
  Are leaves of woodbine twining;

When all the lovely wayside things
  Their white-winged seeds are sowing,
And in the fields, still green and fair,
  Late aftermaths are growing;

When springs run low, and on the brooks,
    In idle golden freighting,
Bright leaves sink noiseless in the hush
    Of woods, for winter waiting;

When comrades seek sweet country haunts,
    By twos and twos together,
And count like misers, hour by hour,
    October's bright blue weather.

O suns and skies and flowers of June,
    Count all your boasts together,
Love loveth best of all the year
    October's bright blue weather.

A CHILD

John Earle

Is a Man in a small Letter, yet the best copy of *Adam* before he tasted of *Eve* or the apple; and he is happy whose small practice in the world can only write this Character. He is nature's fresh picture newly drawn in oil, which time, and much handling, dims and defaces. His Soul is yet a white paper unscribbled with observations of the world, wherewith, at length, it becomes a blurred notebook. He is purely happy, because he knows no evil, nor hath made means by sin to be acquainted with misery. He arrives not at the mischief of being wise, nor endures evils to come, by foreseeing them. He kisses and loves all, and, when the smart of the rod is past, smiles on his beater. Nature and his Parents alike dandle him, and 'tice him on with a bait of sugar to a draught of wormwood. He plays yet, like a young Prentice the first day, and is not come to his task of melancholy. All the language he speaks yet is tears, and they serve him well enough to express his necessity. His hardest labor is his tongue, as if he were loath to use so deceitful an Organ; and he is best company with it when he can but prattle. We laugh at his foolish sports, but his game is our earnest; and his drums, rattles, and hobby-horses, but the Emblems and mocking of man's business. His father hath writ him as his own little story, wherein he reads those days of his life that he cannot remember, and sighs to see what innocence he has out-lived. The elder he grows, he is a stair lower from God; and like his first father, much worse in his breeches. He is the Christian's example, and the old man's relapse; the one imitates his pureness, and the other falls into his simplicity. Could he put off his body with his little coat, he had not eternity without a burden, and exchanged but one Heaven for another.

THERE WAS A ROARING IN THE WIND ALL NIGHT

William Wordsworth

There was a roaring in the wind all night;
The rain came heavily and fell in floods;
But now the sun is rising calm and bright;
The birds are singing in the distant woods;
Over his own sweet voice the Stock-dove broods;
The Jay makes answer as the Magpie chatters;
And all the air is filled with pleasant noise of waters.

All things that love the sun are out of doors;
The sky rejoices in the morning's birth;
The grass is bright with rain-drops;—on the moors
The hare is running races in her mirth;
And with her feet she from the plashy earth
Raises a mist, that, glittering in the sun,
Runs with her all the way, wherever she doth run.

EPITAPH ON SIR JOHN VANBRUGH, ARCHITECT

Abel Evans

Under this stone, Reader, survey
Dead Sir John Vanbrugh's house of clay.
Lie heavy on him, Earth! for he
Laid many heavy loads on thee!

TAXES

Benjamin Franklin

Taxes are indeed very heavy; but if those laid on by the government were the only ones we had to pay, we might more easily discharge them; but we have many others, and much more grievous ones to some of us. We are taxed quite as heavily by idleness, three times as much by our pride, and four times as much by our folly; and from these taxes the commissioners cannot easily deliver us by allowing an abatement.

SHALL I COMPARE THEE TO A SUMMER'S DAY?

William Shakespeare

Shall I compare thee to a summer's day?
Thou art more lovely and more temperate:
Rough winds do shake the darling buds of May,
And summer's lease hath all too short a date:
Sometimes too hot the eye of heaven shines,
And every fair form from fair sometimes declines,
By chance or nature's changing course untrimm'd;
But thy eternal summer shall not fade,
Nor lose possession of that fair thou owest;
Nor shall Death brag thou wander'st in his shade,
When in eternal lines to time thou grow'st:
   So long as men can breathe, or eyes can see,
   So long lives this, and this gives life to thee.

                         (From his *Sonnets*)

SOMETIMES

Thomas S. Jones, Jr.

Across the fields of yesterday
   He sometimes comes to me,
A little lad just back from play—
   The lad I used to be.

And yet he smiles so wistfully
Once he has crept within,
I wonder if he hopes to see
The man I might have been.

SAMUEL JOHNSON'S VIEW ON HAPPY MARRIAGES

Boswell: Pray, Sir, do you suppose that there are fifty women in the world, with any one of whom a man may be as happy, as with any one woman in particular?

Johnson: Ay, Sir, fifty thousand.

Boswell: Then, Sir, you are not of opinion with some who imagine that certain men and certain women are made for each other; and that they cannot be happy if they miss their counterpart?

Johnson: To be sure, not, Sir. I believe marriages in general would be as happy, and often more so, if they were all made by the Lord Chancellor, upon a due consideration of characters and circumstances, without the parties having any choice in the matter.

MARY'S A GRAND OLD NAME

George M. Cohan

My mother's name was Mary, she was so good and true;
Because her name was Mary, she called me Mary, too.
She wasn't gay or airy, but plain as she could be;
I'd hate to be contrary, and call myself Marie.

Chorus
For it is Mary, Mary, plain as any name can be;
But with propriety, society will say Marie.
But it was Mary, Mary, long before the fashions came;
And there is something there that sounds so fair,
It's a grand old name!

Now, when her name is Mary, there is no falseness there;
When to Marie she'll vary, she'll surely bleach her hair.
Though Mary's ordinary, Marie is fair to see;
Don't ever fear sweet Mary, beware of sweet Marie!

(62)

LINCOLN ON SWAPPING HORSES

I have not permitted myself, gentlemen, to conclude that I am the best man in the country, but I am reminded in this connection of an old Dutch farmer who remarked it was not best to swap horses while crossing a stream.

(June 9, 1864)

HE HEARS WITH GLADDENED HEART THE THUNDER

Robert Louis Stevenson

He hears with gladdened heart the thunder
  Peal, and loves the falling dew;
He knows the earth above and under—
  Sits and is content to view.

He sits beside the dying ember,
  God for hope and man for friend,
Content to see, glad to remember,
  Expectant of the certain end.

HOW TO GUESS YOUR AGE

Corey Ford

It seems to me that they are building staircases steeper than they used to. The risers are higher, or there are more of them, or something. Maybe this is because it is so much farther today from the first to the second floor, but I've noticed it is getting harder to make two steps at a time any more. Nowadays it is all I can do to make one step at a time.

Another thing I've noticed is the small print they're using lately. Newspapers are getting farther and farther away when I hold them, and I have to squint to make them out. The other day I had to back halfway out of a telephone booth in order to read the number on the coin box. It is obviously ridiculous to suggest that a person my age needs glasses, but the only other way I can find out what's going on is to have somebody read aloud to me, and that's not too satisfactory because people speak in such low voices these days that I can't hear them very well.

Everything is farther than it used to be. It's twice the distance from my house to the station now, and they've added a fair-sized hill that I never noticed before. The trains leave sooner too. I've given up running for them, because they start faster these days when I try to catch them. You can't depend on timetables any more, and it's no use asking the conductor. I ask him a dozen times a trip if the next station is where I get off, and he always says it isn't. How can you trust a conductor like that? Usually I gather up my bundles and put on my hat and coat and stand in the aisle a couple of stops away, just to make sure I don't go past my destination. Sometimes I make doubly sure by getting off at the station ahead.

A lot of other things are different lately. Barbers no longer hold up a mirror behind me when they've finished, so I can see the back of my head, and my wife has been taking care of the tickets lately when we go to the theater. They don't use the same material in clothes any more, either. I've noticed that all my suits have a tendency to shrink, especially in certain places such as around the waist or in the seat of pants, and the laces they put in shoes nowadays are harder to reach.

Revolving doors revolve much faster than they used to. I have to let a couple of openings go past me before I jump in, and by the time I get up nerve enough to jump out again I'm right back in the street where I started. It's the same with golf. I'm giving it up because these modern golf balls they sell are so hard to pick up when I stoop over. I've had to quit driving, too; the restrooms in filling stations are getting farther and farther apart. Usually I just stay home at night and read the papers, particularly the obituary columns. It's funny how much more interesting the obituary columns have been getting lately.

Even the weather is changing. It's colder in winter and the summers are hotter than they used to be. I'd go away, if it wasn't so far. Snow is heavier when I try to shovel it, and I have to put on rubbers whenever I go out, because rain today is wetter than the rain we used to get. Draughts are more severe too. It must be the way they build windows now.

People are changing too. For one thing, they're younger than they used to be when I was their age. I went back recently to an alumni reunion at the college I graduated from in 1943—that is,

1933—I mean, 1923—and I was shocked to see the mere tots they're admitting as students these days. The average age of the freshman class couldn't have been more than seven. They seem to be more polite than in my time, though; several undergraduates called me "Sir," and one of them asked if he could help me across the street.

On the other hand, people my own age are so much older than I am. I realize that my generation is approaching middle age (I define middle age roughly as the period between 21 and 110) but there is no excuse for my classmates tottering into a state of advanced senility. I ran into my old roommate at the bar, and he'd changed so much that he didn't recognize me. "You've put on a little weight, George," I said.

"It's this modern food," George said. "It seems to be more fattening."

"How about another martini?" I said. "Have you noticed how much weaker the martinis are these days?"

"Everything is different," said George. "Even the food you get. It's more fattening."

"How long since I've seen you, George?" I said. "It must be several years."

"I think the last time was right after the election," said George.

"What election was that?"

George thought for a moment. "Harding."

I ordered a couple more martinis. "Have you noticed these martinis are weaker than they used to be?" I said.

"It isn't like the old days," George said. "Remember when we'd go down to the speak, and order some Orange Blossoms, and maybe pick up a couple of flappers? Boy, could they neck! Hot diggety!"

"You used to be quite a cake-eater, George," I said. "Do you still do the Black Bottom?"

"I put on too much weight," said George. "This food nowadays seems to be more fattening."

"I know," I said, "you mentioned that just a minute ago."

"Did I?" said George.

"How about another martini?" I said. "Have you noticed the martinis aren't as strong as they used to be?"

"Yes," said George, "you said that twice before."

"Oh," I said. . . .

I got to thinking about poor old George while I was shaving this morning, and I stopped for a moment and looked at my own reflection in the mirror. They don't seem to use the same kind of glass in mirrors any more.

(65)

NEEDLESS WORRY

Ralph Waldo Emerson

Some of your hurts you have cured,
   And the sharpest you still have survived,
But what torments of grief you endured
   From evils which never arrived!

ADVERTISE!

Mark Twain

(*When Mark Twain edited a paper in Missouri, one of his subscribers wrote him that he had found a spider in the paper and wanted to know whether it meant good luck or bad. Mark Twain replied:*) "Old Subscriber: Finding a spider in your paper was neither good luck nor bad luck for you. The spider was merely looking over our paper to see which merchant is not advertising so that he can go to that store, spin his web across the door and lead a life of undisturbed peace ever afterward."

OLD AGE

Edmund Waller

The seas are quiet when the winds give o'er;
So calm are we when passions are no more.
For then we know how vain it was to boast
Of fleeting things, so certain to be lost.
Clouds of affection from our younger eyes
Conceal that emptiness which age descries.

The soul's dark cottage, batter'd and decay'd,
Lets in new light through chinks that Time hath made
Stronger by weakness, wiser men become
As they draw near to their eternal home.
Leaving the old, both worlds at once they view
That stand upon the threshold of the new.

DAYS OF THE WEEK

Anonymous

Monday for wealth,
Tuesday for health,
Wednesday the best day of all:
Thursday for crosses,
Friday for losses,
Saturday no luck at all.

LA BELLE DAME SANS MERCI

John Keats

O what can ail thee, knight-at-arms,
  Alone and palely loitering?
The sedge has wither'd from the lake,
  And no birds sing.

O what can ail thee, knight-at-arms,
  So haggard and so woe-begone?
The squirrel's granary is full,
  And the harvest's done.

I see a lily on thy brow
  With anguish moist and fever dew;
And on thy cheeks a fading rose
  Fast withereth too.

I met a lady in the meads,
  Full beautiful—a faëry's child,
Her hair was long, her foot was light,
  And her eyes were wild.

I made a garland for her head,
  And bracelets too, and fragrant zone;
She look'd at me as she did love,
  And made sweet moan.

(67)

I set her on my pacing steed,
　　And nothing else saw all day long,
For sidelong would she bend, and sing
　　A faëry's song.

She found me roots of relish sweet,
　　And honey wild, and manna dew,
And sure in language strange she said,
　　"I love thee true!"

She took me to her elfin grot,
　　And there she wept and sigh'd full sore,
And there I shut her wild, wild eyes
　　With kisses four.

And there she lulled me asleep,
　　And there I dream'd,—ah! woe betide!
The latest dream I ever dream'd
　　On the cold hill's side.

I saw pale kings and princes too,
　　Pale warriors, death-pale were they all;
They cried—"La Belle Dame sans Merci
　　Hath thee in thrall!"

I saw their starved lips in the gloam,
　　With horrid warning gaped wide,
And I awoke and found me here,
　　On the cold hill's side.

And this is why I sojourn here,
　　Alone and palely loitering,
Though the sedge is wither'd from the lake,
　　And no birds sing.

Those who make peaceful revolution impossible will
make violent revolution inevitable.
　　　　　　　　　　(John F. Kennedy, March 12, 1962)

THE FABLE OF THE SLIM GIRL WHO
TRIED TO KEEP A DATE THAT WAS NEVER MADE

George Ade

Once upon a Time there was a slim Girl with a Forehead which was Shiny and Protuberant, like a Bartlett Pear. When asked to put Something in an Autograph Album she invariably wrote the Following, in a tall, dislocated Back–Hand:

> Life is Real; Life is Earnest,
> And the Grave is not its Goal.

That's the kind of Girl she was.

In her own Town she had the Name of being a Cold Proposition, but that was because the Primitive Yokels of a One-Night Stand could not Attune Themselves to the Views of one who was troubled with Ideals. Her Soul Panted for the Higher Life.

Alas, the Rube Town in which she Hung Forth was given over to Croquet, Mush and Milk Sociables, a lodge of Elks and two married Preachers who doctored for the Tonsilitis. So what could the Poor Girl do?

In All the Country around there was not a Man who came up to her Plans and Specifications for a Husband. Neither was there any Man who had any time for Her. So she led a lonely Life, dreaming of the One—the Ideal. He was a big and pensive Literary Man, wearing a Prince Albert coat, a neat Derby Hat and godlike Whiskers. When He came he would enfold Her in his Arms and whisper Emerson's *Essays* to her.

But the Party failed to show up.

Often enough she put on her Chip Hat and her Black Lisle Gloves and Sauntered in front of the Occidental Hotel, hoping that the Real Thing would be there. But she always saw the same old line of Four-Flush Drummers from Chicago and St. Louis, smoking Horrid Cigars and talking about the Percentages of the League Teams.

She knew that these Gross Creatures were not prone to chase mere Intellectual Splendor, so she made no effort to Flag them.

When she was Thirty-four years of age and was able to recite "Lucile" without looking at the Book she was Married to a Janitor of the name of Ernest. He had been kicked in the Head by a Mule when young and believed everything he read in the Sunday Papers. His pay was Twenty-three a month, which was high, if you knew Ernest.

His wife wore a red Mother Hubbard all during the Remainder of her Life.

This is invariably a Sign of Blasted Hopes.

Moral: *Never live in a Jay Town.*

ILL FARES THE LAND

Oliver Goldsmith

Ill fares the land, to hastening ills a prey,
Where wealth accumulates, and men decay;
Princes and lords may flourish or may fade;
A breath can make them, as a breath has made;
But a bold peasantry, their country's pride,
When once destroy'd, can never be supplied.

THE GARDEN OF PROSERPINE

Algernon Charles Swinburne

Here, where the world is quiet;
    Here, where all trouble seems
Dead winds' and spent waves' riot
    In doubtful dreams of dreams;
I watch the green field growing
For reaping folk and sowing,
For harvest-time and mowing,
    A sleepy world of streams.

I am tired of tears and laughter,
    And men that laugh and weep;
Of what may come hereafter
    For men that sow to reap:
I am weary of days and hours,
Blown buds of barren flowers,
Desires and dreams and powers
    And everything but sleep.

Here life has death for neighbour,
   And far from eye or ear
Wan waves and wet winds labour,
   Weak ships and spirits steer;
They drive adrift, and whither
They wot not who make thither;
But no such winds blow hither,
   And no such things grow here.

No growth of moor or coppice,
   No heather-flower or vine,
But bloomless buds of poppies,
   Green grapes of Proserpine,
Pale beds of blowing rushes
Where no leaf blooms or blushes
Save this whereout she crushes
   For dead men deadly wine.

Pale, without name or number,
   In fruitless fields of corn,
They blow themselves and slumber
   All night till light is born;
And like a soul belated,
In hell and heaven unmated,
By cloud and mist abated
   Comes out of darkness morn.

Though one were strong as seven,
   He too with death shall dwell,
Nor wake wth wings in heaven,
   Nor weep for pains in hell;
Though one were fair as roses,
His beauty clouds and closes;
And well though love reposes
   In the end it is not well.

Pale, beyond porch and portal,
   Crowned with calm leaves, she stands
Who gathers all things mortal
   With cold immortal hands;

Her languid lips are sweeter
Than Love's, who fears to greet her
To men that mix and meet her
　　From many times and lands.

She waits for each and other,
　　She waits for all men born;
Forgets the earth her mother,
　　The life of fruits and corn;
And spring and seed and swallow
Take wing for her and follow
Where summer song rings hollow
　　And flowers are put to scorn.

There go the loves that wither,
　　The old loves with wearier wings;
And all dead years draw thither,
　　And all disastrous things;
Dead dreams of days forsaken,
Blind buds that snows have shaken,
Wild leaves that winds have taken,
　　Red strays of ruined springs.

We are not sure of sorrow,
　　And joy was never sure;
Today will die tomorrow;
　　Time stoops to no man's lure;
And love, grown faint and fretful,
With lips but half regretful
Sighs, and with eyes forgetful
　　Weeps that no loves endure.

From too much love of living,
　　From hope and fear set free,
We thank with brief thanksgiving
　　Whatever gods may be
That no life lives for ever;
That dead men rise up never;
That even the weariest river
　　Winds somewhere safe to sea.

Then star nor sun shall waken,
   Nor any change of light:
Nor sound of waters shaken,
   Nor any sound or sight:
Nor wintry leaves nor vernal,
Nor days nor things diurnal:
Only the sleep eternal
In an eternal night.

THE PUBLIC SCHOOL EXTOLLED BY HORACE MANN, ITS EARLY AMERICAN ADVOCATE

Without undervaluing any other human agency it may be safely affirmed that the common school, improved and energized as it can easily be, may become the most effective and benignant of all the forces of civilization. Two reasons sustain this position. In the first place, there is a universality in its operation, which can be affirmed of no other institution whatever. If administered in the spirit of justice and conciliation, all the rising generation may be brought within the circle of its reformatory and elevating influences. And, in the second place, the materials upon which it operates are so pliant and ductile as to be susceptible of assuming a greater variety of forms than any other earthly work of the Creator. The inflexibility and ruggedness of the oak, when compared with the lithe sapling or the tender germ, are but feeble emblems to typify the docility of childhood when contrasted with the obduracy and intractableness of man. It is these inherent advantages of the common school, which, in our own State [Massachusetts], have produced results so striking, from a system so imperfect, and an administration so feeble. . . .

The true business of the schoolroom connects itself, and becomes identical, with the great interests of society. The former is the infant, immature state of those interests; the latter their developed, adult state. As "the child is father to the man," so may the training of the schoolroom expand into the institutions and fortunes of the State. . . .

Now, surely nothing but universal education can counterwork this tendency to the domination of capital and the servility of labor. If one class possesses all the wealth and education, while the residue of society is ignorant and poor, it matters not by what name the relation between them may be called: the latter, in fact and in truth, will be the servile dependents and subjects of the former. But if education be equally diffused, it will draw property after it by the strongest of all attractions; for such a thing never did happen, and never can happen, as that an intelligent and practical body of men should be permanently poor. . . .

The very terms "public school" and "common school" bear upon their face that they are schools which the children of the entire community may attend. Every man not on the pauper-list is taxed for their support. . . . He is taxed to support them as a *preventive* means against dishonesty, against fraud, and against violence, on the same principle that he is taxed to support criminal courts as a *punitive* means against the same offenses. He is taxed to support schools, on the same principle that he is taxed to support paupers,—because a child without education is poorer and more wretched than a man without bread. He is taxed to support schools, on the same principle that he would be taxed to defend the nation against foreign invasion, or against rapine committed by a foreign foe,—because the general prevalence of ignorance, superstition, and vice, will breed Goth and Vandal at home more fatal to the public well-being than any Goth or Vandal from abroad. And, finally, he is taxed to support schools, because they are the most effective means of developing and training those powers and faculties in a child, by which, when he becomes a man, he may understand what his highest interests and his highest duties are, and may be in fact, and not in name only, a free agent.

(1848)

EXPLANATION

Josh Billings

I hate to be a kicker,
   I always long for peace,
But the wheel that does the squeaking,
   Is the one that gets the grease.

TO THE FRINGED GENTIAN

William Cullen Bryant

Thou blossom, bright with autumn dew,
And colored with the heaven's own blue,
That openest when the quiet light
Succeeds the keen and frosty night;

Thou comest not when violets lean
O'er wandering brooks and springs unseen,
Or columbines, in purple dressed,
Nod o'er the ground bird's hidden nest.

Thou waitest late, and com'st alone,
When woods are bare and birds are flown,
And frosts and shortening days portend
The aged year is near his end.

Then doth thy sweet and quiet eye
Look through its fringes to the sky,
Blue—blue—as if that sky let fall
A flower from its cerulean wall.

I would that thus, when I shall see
The hour of death draw near to me,
Hope, blossoming within my heart,
May look to heaven as I depart.

THE WIT OF WINSTON CHURCHILL

On Stanley Baldwin, when the latter was Prime Minister: Baldwin occasionally stumbles over the truth, but he always hastily picks himself up and hurries on as if nothing happened.

On Sir Stafford Cripps: There but for the grace of God goes God.

On Charles Beresford: When my Right Honorable friend rose to his feet a few minutes ago, he had not the least idea of what he was going to say. Moreover, he did not know what he was saying when

(75)

speaking. And when he sat down, he was doubtless unable to remember what he had said.

On Clement Atlee: A modest man, and I know of no one with more to be modest about.

When the Nazis invaded Russia, Churchill pledged aid to Russia: If Hitler invaded Hell, I would make at least a favorable reference to the devil in the House of Commons.

Referring to Stanley Baldwin, known for his honesty: It is a fine thing to be honest, but it is also very important to be right.

Referring to Ramsay Macdonald, in the House of Commons, January, 1931: I remember, when I was a child, being taken to the celebrated Barnum's Circus, which contained an exhibition of freaks and monstrosities, but the exhibit on the program which I most desired to see was . . . "The Boneless Wonder." My parents judged that that spectacle would be too revolting and demoralizing for youthful eyes, and I have waited fifty years to see The Boneless Wonder sitting on the Treasury Bench.

On R. H. S. Crossman: The Honorable Member is never lucky in the coincidence of his facts with the truth.

Broadcast, October 21, 1940: We are waiting for the long-promised invasion. So are the fishes.

On his 75th Birthday (1949): I am ready to meet my Maker. Whether my Maker is prepared for the great ordeal of meeting me is another matter.

From an address at the Convocation of the Massachusetts Institute of Technology, March 20, 1949: The Dean of the humanities spoke with awe "of an approaching scientific ability to control men's thoughts with precision."—I shall be very content to be dead before that happens.

THEY ARE NOT LONG

Ernest Dowson

They are not long, the weeping and the laughter,
  Love and desire and hate:
I think they have no portion in us after
    We pass the gate.

They are not long, the days of wine and roses:
  Out of a misty dream
Our path emerges for awhile, then closes
    Within a dream.

MUSIC, WHEN SOFT VOICES DIE

Percy Bysshe Shelley

Music when soft voices die,
Vibrates in the memory—
Odours, when sweet violets sicken,
Live within the sense they quicken.

Rose leaves, when the rose is dead,
Are heaped for the beloved's bed;
And so thy thoughts, when thou art gone,
Love itself shall slumber on.

SYDNEY SMITH'S STORY OF MRS. PARTINGTON

    I do not mean to be disrespectful, but the attempt of the Lords to stop the progress of reform reminds me very forcibly of the great storm of Sidmouth, and of the conduct of the excellent Mrs. Partington on that occasion. In the winter of 1824 there set in a great flood upon that town—the tide rose to an incredible height—the waves rushed in upon the houses—and everything was threatened with destruction. In the midst of this sublime storm, Dame Partington, who lived upon the beach, was seen at the door of her house with mop and pattens, trundling her mop, and squeezing out the seawater, and vigorously pushing away the Atlantic Ocean. The Atlantic was roused. Mrs. Partington's spirit was up; but I need not tell you that the contest was unequal. The Atlantic Ocean beat Mrs. Partington. She was excellent at slop or a puddle, but she should not have meddled with a tempest.

(1831)

DO NOT GO GENTLE INTO THAT GOOD NIGHT

Dylan Thomas

Do not go gentle into that good night,
Old age should burn and rave at close of day;
Rage, rage against the dying of the light.

Though wise men at their end know dark is right,
Because their words had forked no lightning they
Do not go gentle into that good night.

Good men, the last wave by, crying how bright
Their frail deeds might have danced in a green bay,
Rage, rage against the dying of the light.

Wild men who caught and sang the sun in flight,
And learn, too late, they grieved it on its way,
Do not go gentle into that good night.

Grave men, near death, who see with blinding sight
Blind eyes could blaze like meteors and be gay,
Rage, rage against the dying of the light.

And you, my father, there on the sad height,
Curse, bless, me now with your fierce tears, I pray.
Do not go gentle into that good night.
Rage, rage against the dying of the light.

DANIEL WEBSTER IN REPLY TO HAYNE

When my eyes shall be turned to behold for the last time the sun in heaven, may I not see him shining on the broken and dishonored fragments of a once glorious Union; on States dissevered, discordant, belligerent; on a land rent with civil feuds, or drenched, it may be, in fraternal blood! Let their last feeble and lingering glance rather behold the gorgeous ensign of the Republic, now known and honored throughout the earth, still full high advanced, its arms and trophies streaming in their original lustre, not a stripe erased or polluted, not a single star obscured. Bearing for its motto, no such miserable interrogatory as "What is all this worth?" nor those other words of delusion and folly, "Liberty first and Union afterward"; but everywhere, spread all over in characters of living light, blazing on all its ample folds, as they float over the sea and over the land, and in every wind under the whole heavens, that other sentiment, dear to every true American heart,—Liberty and Union, now and forever, one and inseparable!

(United States Senate, January 26, 1830)

GOD'S WORK

Charlotte Cushman

God conceived the world, that was poetry;
He formed it, that was sculpture;
He colored it, that was painting;
He peopled it with living beings, that was the
    grand, divine, eternal drama.

THE BIBLE

John Greenleaf Whittier

We search the world for truth. We cull
The good, the true, the beautiful,
From graven stone and written scroll,
And all old flower-fields of the soul;

(79)

And, weary seekers of the best,
We come back laden from our quest,
To find that all the sages said
Is in the Book our mothers read.

MAJOR GENERAL ISRAEL PUTNAM AND THE WOLF

David Humphreys

The first years on a new farm are not exempt from disasters and disappointments which can only be remedied by stubborn and patient industry. Our farmer, sufficiently occupied in building a house and barn, felling woods, making fences, sowing grain, planting orchards and taking care of his stock, had to encounter in turn the calamities occasioned by drought in summer, blast in harvest, loss of cattle in winter, and the desolation of his sheepfold by wolves. On one night he had seventy fine sheep and goats killed besides many lambs and kids wounded. This havoc was committed by a she-wolf which, with her annual whelps, had for several years infested the vicinity. The young were commonly destroyed by the vigilance of the hunters, but the old one was too sagacious to come within reach of gunshot. Upon being closely pursued, she would generally fly to the western woods and return the next winter with another litter of whelps.

This wolf at length became such an intolerable nuisance that Mr. Putnam entered into a combination with five of his neighbors to hunt alternately until they could destroy her. Two, by rotation, were to be constantly in pursuit. It was known that having lost the toes from one foot by a steel trap, she made one track shorter than the other. By this vestige, the pursuers recognized in a light snow the route of this pernicious animal. Having followed her to the Connecticut River and found she had turned back in a direct course towards Pomfret, they immediately returned, and by ten o'clock the next morning the bloodhounds had driven her into a den about three miles distant from the house of Mr. Putnam. The people soon collected with dogs, guns, straw, fire, and sulphur to attack the common enemy. With this apparatus several unsuccessful efforts were made to force her from the den. The hounds came back badly wounded and refused to return. The smoke of blazing straw had no effect; nor did the fumes of burnt limestone with which the cavern was filled compel her to quit the retirement. Wearied with such fruitless attempts, which had brought the time to ten o'clock at night, Mr. Putnam tried once more to make his dog enter—but in vain. He proposed to his Negro man to go down into the cavern and shoot the wolf; the Negro declined the hazardous service. Then it was that their master, angry at the disappointment and declaring that he was ashamed to have a coward in his family, resolved himself to destroy the ferocious beast, lest she should escape through some unknown fissure of the rock. His neighbors strongly remonstrated against the perilous enterprise; but he, knowing that wild animals were intimidated by fire, and having provided several strips of birch bark, the only combustible material which he could obtain that would afford light in this deep and darksome cave, prepared for his descent. Having accordingly divested himself of his coat and waistcoat, and having a long rope fastened round his legs, by which he might be pulled back at a concerted signal, he entered head foremost, with the blazing torch in his hand.

The aperture of the den on the east side of a very high ledge of rocks is about two feet square. From thence it descends obliquely fifteen feet; then running horizontally about ten more, it ascends gradually sixteen feet towards its termination. The sides of this subterraneous cavity are composed of smooth and solid rocks which seem to have been divided from each other by some former earthquake. The top and bottom are also of stone, and the entrance in winter, being covered with ice, is exceedingly slippery. It is in no place high enough for a man to raise himself upright nor in any part more than three feet in width.

Having groped his passage to the horizontal part of the den, the most terrifying darkness appeared in front of the dim circle of light afforded by his torch. It was as silent as the house of death. None but monsters of the desert had ever before explored this solitary mansion of horror. He, cautiously proceeding onward, came to the ascent, which he slowly mounted on his hands and knees until he discovered the glaring eyeballs of the wolf, who was sitting at the extremity of the cavern. Startled at the sight of the fire, she gnashed her teeth and gave a sullen growl. As soon as he had the necessary discovery, he kicked the rope as a signal for pulling him out. The people at the mouth of the den, who had listened with painful anxiety—hearing the growling of the wolf and supposing their friend to be in the most imminent danger—drew him forth with such celerity that his shirt was stripped over his head and his skin severely lacerated. After he had adjusted his clothes and loaded his gun with nine buckshot, holding a torch in one hand and the musket in the other, he descended a second time. When he drew nearer than before, the wolf, assuming a still more fierce and terrible appearance—howling, rolling her eyes, snapping her teeth, and dropping her head between her legs—was evidently in the attitude and on the point of springing at him. At the critical instant he leveled and fired at her head. Stunned with the shock and suffocated with the smoke, he immediately found himself drawn out of the cave; but having refreshed himself and permitted the smoke to dissipate, he went down the third time. Once more he came within sight of the wolf, who appearing very passive, he applied the torch to her nose; and perceiving her dead, he took hold of her ears, then kicking the rope still tied round his legs, the people above, with no small exultation, dragged them both out together.

I have offered these facts in greater detail because they contain a display of character and because they have been erroneously related in several European publications and very much mutilated in the history of Connecticut, a work as replete with falsehood as destitute of genius, lately printed in London.

(1788)

BEER

George Arnold

     Here
     With my beer
I sit,
While golden moments flit.
     Alas!
     They pass
Unheeded by;
And, as they fly,
     I,
     Being dry,
     Sit idly sipping here
     My beer.

Oh, finer far
Than fame or riches are
The graceful smoke-wreaths of this cigar!

Why
Should I
Weep, wail, or sigh?
What if luck has passed me by?
What if my hopes are dead,
My pleasures fled?
Have I not still
My fill
Of right good cheer,—
Cigars and beer?

Go, whining youth,
Forsooth!
Go, weep and wail,
Sigh and grow pale,
Weave melancholy rhymes
On the old times,
Whose joys like shadowy ghosts appear,—
But leave me to my beer!
Gold is dross,
Love is loss;
So, if I gulp my sorrows down,
Or see them drown
In foamy draughts of old nut-brown,
Then do I wear the crown
Without a cross!

TO THE CUCKOO

William Wordsworth

O blithe new-comer! I have heard,
I hear thee and rejoice:
O Cuckoo! shall I call thee Bird,
Or but a wandering Voice?

While I am lying on the grass
Thy twofold shout I hear;
From hill to hill it seems to pass,
At once far off and near.

Though babbling only to the vale
  Of sunshine and of flowers,
Thou bringest unto me a tale
  Of visionary hours.

Thrice welcome, darling of the Spring!
  Even yet thou art to me
No bird, but an invisible thing,
  A voice, a mystery;

The same whom in my school-boy days
  I listen'd to; that Cry
Which made me look a thousand ways
  In bush, and tree, and sky.

To seek thee did I often rove
  Through woods and on the green;
And thou wert still a hope, a love;
  Still longed for, never seen.

And I can listen to thee yet;
  Can lie upon the plain
And listen, till I do beget
  That golden time again.

O blessed Bird! the earth we pace
  Again appears to be
An unsubstantial, fairy place,
  That is fit home for Thee!

THE MAN WHO HAD MORE SENSE THAN EDUCATION

Panchatantra

In a certain town were four Brahman who lived in friendship. Three of them had reached the far shore of all scholarship, but lacked sense. The other found scholarship distasteful; he had nothing but sense.

One day they met for consultation. "What is the use of attainments," said they, "if one does not travel, win the favor of kings, and acquire money? Whatever we do, let us all travel."

But when they had gone a little way, the eldest of them said: "One of us, the fourth, is a dullard, having nothing but sense. Now nobody gains the favorable attention of kings by simple sense without scholarship. Therefore we will not share our earnings with him. Let him turn back and go home."

Then the second said: "My intelligent friend, you lack scholarship. Please go home." But the third said: "No, no. This is no way to behave. For we have played together since we were little boys. Come along, my noble friend. You shall have a share of all the money we earn."

With this argument they continued their journey, and in a forest they found the bones of a dead lion. Thereupon one of them said: "A good opportunity to test the ripeness of our scholarship. Here lies some kind of creature, dead. Let us bring it to life by means of the scholarship we have honestly won."

Then the first said: "I know how to assemble the skeleton." The second said: "I can supply skin, flesh, and blood." The third said: "I can give it life."

So the first assembled the skeleton, the second provided skin, flesh, and blood. But while the third was intent on giving the breath of life, the man of sense advised against it, remarking: "This is a lion. If you bring him to life, he will kill every one of us."

"You simpleton!" said the other, "it is not I who will reduce scholarship to a nullity."

"In that case," came the reply, "wait a moment, while I climb this convenient tree."

When this had been done, the lion was brought to life, rose up, and killed all three. But the man of sense, after the lion had gone elsewhere, climbed down and went home.

MY LIFE IS LIKE THE SUMMER ROSE

Richard Henry Wilde

My life is like the summer rose
That opens to the morning sky,
But ere the shades of evening close,
Is scattered on the ground—to die!

(85)

Yet on the rose's humble bed
The sweetest dews of night are shed,
As if she wept the waste to see,—
But none shall weep a tear for me!

My life is like the autumn leaf
That trembles in the moon's pale ray;
Its hold is frail,—its date is brief,
Restless,—and soon to pass away!
Yet, ere that leaf shall fall and fade,
The parent tree will mourn its shade,
The winds bewail the leafless tree,—
But none shall breathe a sigh for me!

My life is like the prints which feet
Have left on Tampa's desert strand;
Soon as the rising tide shall beat,
All trace will vanish from the sand;
Yet, as if grieving to efface
All vestige of the human race,
On that lone shore loud moans the sea,—
But none, alas! shall mourn for me!

THE BOYS AND THE FROG

Aesop

A troop of boys were playing at the edge of a pond, when, perceiving a number of Frogs in the water, they began to pelt them with stones. They had already killed many of the poor creatures, when one Frog more hardy than the rest put his head above the water and cried: "Stop your cruel sport, my lads; consider, what is Play to you, is Death to us."

ELIZABETH L. H.

Ben Jonson

Wouldst thou hear what man can say
In a little? Reader, stay,
Underneath this stone doth lie
As much Beauty as could die;
Which in life did harbour give
To more virtue than doth live.
If at all she had a fault,
Be sure it's buried in this vault.
One name was Elizabeth,
The other, let it sleep with death:
Fitter, where it died, to tell
Than that it lived at all. Farewell!

THE FATEFUL CHOICE

Bernard M. Baruch

We are here to make a choice between the quick and the dead. That is our business. Behind the black portent of the new atomic age lies a hope which, seized upon with faith, can work out salvation. If we fail, then we have damned every man to be the slave of fear. Let us not deceive ourselves; we must elect world peace or world destruction.

(From an address to the United Nations, June 14, 1946)

ISOLATION

Matthew Arnold

We were apart; yet day by day,
I bade my heart more constant be.
I bade it keep the world away,
And grow a home for only thee;
Nor fear'd but thy love likewise grew,
Like mine, each day, more tried, more true.

(87)

The fault was grave! I might have known,
What far too soon, alas! I learn'd—
The heart can bind itself alone,
And faith may oft be unreturn'd.
Self-sway'd our feelings ebb and swell—
Thou lov'st no more;—Farewell! Farewell!

(From *To Marguerite*)

A UNIVERSITY

Robert M. Hutchins

Now, a university is a place that is established and will function for the benefit of society, provided it is a center of independent thought. It is a center of independent thought and criticism that is created in the interest of the progress of society, and the one reason that we know that every totalitarian government must fail is that no totalitarian government is prepared to face the consequences of creating free universities.

It is important for this purpose to attract into the institution men of the greatest capacity, and to encourage them to exercise their independent judgment.

Education is a kind of continuing dialogue, and a dialogue assumes, in the nature of the case, different points of views.

The civilization, which I work and which I am sure every American is working toward, could be called a civilization of the dialogue, where instead of shooting one another when you differ, you reason things out together.

In this dialogue, then, you cannot assume that you are going to have everybody thinking the same way or feeling the same way. It would be unprogressive if that happened. The hope of eventual development would be gone. More than that, of course, it would be very boring.

A university, then, is a kind of continuing Socratic conversation on the highest level for the very best people you can think of, you can bring together, about the most important questions, and the thing that you must do to the uttermost possible limits is to guarantee those men the freedom to think and to express themselves.

Now, the limits on this freedom cannot be merely prejudice, because although our prejudices might be perfectly satisfactory, the prejudices of our successors, or of those who are in a position to bring pressure to bear on the institution, might be subversive in the real sense, subverting the American doctrine of free thought and free speech.

KISS ME AGAIN

Henry Blossom

Sweet summer breeze,
Whispering trees,
Stars shining above;
Roses in bloom, wafted perfume,
Sleepy birds dreaming of love.
Safe in your arms, far from alarms,
Daylight shall come but in vain.
Tenderly pressed close to your breast,
Kiss me, kiss me again.
Kiss me again! Kiss me!
Kiss me again!

BENJAMIN DISRAELI'S ESTIMATE OF WILLIAM E. GLADSTONE

A sophisticated rhetorician inebriated with the exuberance of his own verbosity, and gifted with an egotistical imagination that can at all times command an interminable and inconsistent series of arguments to malign an opponent and to glorify himself.

He's the kind of politician who follows you through a revolving door and then comes out ahead of you.
—Anonymous

NATURE

Henry Wadsworth Longfellow

As a fond mother, when the day is o'er,
   Leads by the hand her little child to bed,
   Half willing, half reluctant to be led,
   And leaves his broken playthings on the floor,
Still gazing at them through the open door,
   Nor wholly reassured and comforted
   By promises of others in their stead,
   Which, though more splendid, may not please him more;
So Nature deals with us, and takes away
   Our playthings one by one, and by the hand
   Leads us to rest so gently, that we go
Scarce knowing if we wish to go or stay,
   Being too full of sleep to understand
   How far the unknown transcends the what we know.

THE MOUNTAINS ARE A LONELY FOLK

Hamlin Garland

   The mountains they are silent folk,
     They stand afar—alone;
   And the clouds that kiss their brows at night
     Hear neither sign nor groan.
     Each bears him in his ordered place
     As soldiers do, and bold and high
   They fold their forests round their feet
     And bolster up the sky.

   Perched on the loftiest throne in the world, man is still
sitting on his own behind.
                —Michel de Montaigne

PETER'S TEARS

Thomas Hood

After much dissension and strife,
Some wonder that Peter should weep for his wife;
But his tears on her grave are nothing surprising,
He's laying her dust, for fear of it rising.

A PEACEFUL LIFE, A LONG LIFE

Balthasar Gracian

To live, let live. Peacemakers not only live; they rule life. Hear,
see, and be silent. A day without dispute brings sleep without dreams.
Long life and a pleasant one is life enough for two: that is the fruit
of peace. He has all that makes nothing of what is nothing to him.
There is no greater perversity than to take everything to heart.
There is equal folly in troubling our heart about what does not
concern us and in not taking to heart what does.

MUSIC I HEARD

Conrad Aiken

Music I heard with you was more than music,
And bread I broke with you was more than bread;
Now that I am without you, all is desolate;
All that was once so beautiful is dead.

Your hands once touched this table and this silver
And I have seen your fingers hold this glass,
These things do not remember you, beloved,—
And yet your touch upon them will not pass.

For it was in my heart you moved among them,
And blessed them with your hands and with your eyes;
And in my heart they will remember always,—
They knew you once, O beautiful and wise.

THE THREE RINGS

Giovanni Boccaccio

Saladin, Sultan of Babylon, . . . called to mind a rich Jew of Alexandria, named Melchizedeck, . . . sent for the Jew, received him in a most gracious manner, and making him sit down, thus addressed him:

"Worthy man, I hear from divers persons that thou are very wise and knowing in religious matters; wherefore I would gladly know from thee which religion thou judgest to be the true one, viz., the Jewish, the Mohammedan, or the Christian?"

The Jew (truly a wise man) found that Saladin had a mind to trap him, and must gain his point should he exalt any one of the three religions above the others; after considering, therefore, for a little how best to avoid the snare, his ingenuity at last supplied him with the following answer:

"The question which your Highness has proposed is very curious; and that I may give you my sentiments, I must beg leave to tell you a short story. I remember often to have heard of a great and rich man, who among his rare and precious jewels had a ring of exceeding beauty and value. Being proud of possessing a thing of such worth, and desirous that it should continue forever in his family, he declared, by will, that to whichsover of his sons he should give this ring, him he designed for his heir, and that he should be respected as the head of the family. That son to whom the ring was given, made the same law with respect to his descendants, and the ring passed one to another in long succession, till it came to a person who had three sons, all virtuous and dutiful to their father, and all equally beloved by him. Now the young men, knowing what depended upon the ring, and ambitious of superiority, began to entreat their father, who was now grown old, everyone for himself, that he would give the ring to him. The good man, equally fond of all, was at a loss which to prefer; and, as he had promised all, and wished to satisfy all, he privately got an artist to make two other rings, which were so alike the first, that he himself scarcely knew the true one. When he found his end approaching, he secretly gave one ring to each of his sons; and they, after his death, all claimed the honor and estate, each disputing with his brothers, and producing the ring; and the rings were found so much alike, that the true one could not be distinguished. To law then they went, as to which should succeed, nor is that question yet decided. And thus it has happened, my Lord, with regard to the three laws given by God the Father, concerning which you proposed your question: everyone believes he is the true heir of God, has his laws, and obeys his commandments; but which is the right is uncertain, in like manner as with the rings.

EVENING SONG

Sidney Lanier

Look off, dear Love, across the sallow sands,
  And mark yon meeting of the sun and sea,
How long they kiss in sight of all the lands,
  Ah, longer, longer, we!

Now in the sea's red vintage melts the sun,
  As Egypt's pearl dissolved in rosy wine,
And Cleopatra night drinks all. 'Tis done.
  Love, lay thine hand in mine.

Come forth, sweet stars, and comfort heaven's heart;
  Glimmer, ye waves, round else unlighted sands.
O night! divorce our sun and sky apart,
  Never our lips, our hands.

ON A CLERGYMAN'S HORSE BITING HIM

Anonymous

The steed bit his master;
How came this to pass?
He heard the good pastor
Cry "All flesh is grass."

THUS PITEOUSLY LOVE CLOSED

George Meredith

Thus piteously Love closed what he begat:
The union of this ever-diverse pair!
These two were rapid falcons in a snare,
Condemned to do the flitting of the bat.
Lovers beneath the singing sky of May
They wandered once; clear as the dew on flowers:
But they fed not on the advancing hours:
Their hearts held cravings for the buried day.
Then each applied to each that fatal knife,
Deep questioning, which probes to endless dole.
Ah, what a dusty answer gets the soul
When hot for certainties in this our life!—
In tragic hints here see what evermore
Moves dark as yonder midnight ocean's force,
Thundering like ramping hosts of warrior horse,
To throw that faint thin line upon the shore!

As he [Samuel Johnson] opened a note which his servant brought
to him, he said, "An odd thought strikes me: we shall receive no
letters in the grave."

—James Boswell

POP! GOES THE WEASEL

Anonymous

A penny for a spool of thread,
A penny for a needle,
That's the way the money goes,
Pop! goes the weasel.
All around the cobbler's bench
The monkey chased the weasel,
The monkey thought 'twas all in fun,
Pop! goes the weasel.

Potatoes for an Irishman's taste,
A doctor for the measles,
A fiddler always for a dance,
Pop! goes the weasel.
Blood-pudding for a Dutchman's meal,
A workman for a chisel,
The tune that everybody sings
Pop! goes the weasel.

Major Wood has put the rum sellers through,
The Maine law's sad and evil,
We cannot get our toddy now,
Pop! goes the weasel.
The butcher, when he charges for meat,
Sticks in the bone and gristle,
But that's the way the money goes,
Pop! goes the weasel.

From round about the countrymen's barn
The mice begin to mizzle;
For when they poke their noses out,
Pop! goes the weasel!
The painter works with ladder and brush,
The artist with the easel,
The fiddler always snaps the strings at
Pop! goes the weasel!

NEW OCCASIONS TEACH NEW DUTIES

James Russell Lowell

New occasions teach new duties; Time makes ancient good uncouth;
They must upward still, and onward, who would keep abreast of
    Truth;
Lo, before us gleam her camp-fires! we ourselves must Pilgrims be,
Launch our Mayflower, and steer boldly through the desperate
    winter sea,
Nor attempt the Future's portal with the Past's blood-rusted key.

(From *The Present Crisis*)

ONE WORLD

Johann Amos Comenius

We are all citizens of one world, we are all of one blood. To hate a man because he was born in another country, because he speaks a different language, or because he take a different view on this subject or that, is a great folly. Desist, I implore you, for we are all equally human. . . . Let us have but one end in view, the welfare of humanity.

WHO WALKS WITH BEAUTY

David Morton

Who walks with Beauty has no need of fear;
The sun and moon and stars keep pace with him,
Invisible hands restore the ruined year,
And time, itself, grows beautifully dim.
One hill will keep the footprints of the moon,
That came and went a hushed and secret hour;
One star at dusk will yield the lasting boon;
Remembered Beauty's white, immortal flower.
Who takes of Beauty wine and daily bread,
Will know no lack when bitter years are lean;
The brimming cup is by, the feast is spread,—
The sun and moon and stars his eyes have seen,
Are for his hunger and the thirst he slakes:
The wine of Beauty and the bread he breaks.

A FAREWELL TO A FELLOW–EDITOR

William Allen White

Editor Phillips, late editor, owner and publisher of the Emporia *Daily and Weekly Democrat*, has left for parts unknown, probably to the horror and consternation of the parts, and certainly for the general betterment of this community. Far be it from this paper to say aught that would cast an unwarranted aspersion upon an earnest though unfortunate gentleman. It is not the purpose of the *Gazette* to be sensational nor to exaggerate interesting facts. But as a matter of news and stated in the precise terms of scientific description, without coloring the statement by loose vernacular, the simple, homely truth demands that it be said of Phillips that he was, is and will be while he lives on this easy old earth, the most picturesque, unique, original, shameless, deliberate, conscienceless, malicious and indefatigable dead-beat that ever pressed the sidewalk of Commercial Street with his velvety feline feet. It is but just to him to add that he was not a harsh or irascible man. He did not exact tribute with either club or buzz saw. He had the soft, self-deprecatory, insinuating voice of a cooing dove; and he glided into his machinations with the gentle, noiseless, hypnotic sinuosity of a rubber-tired rattlesnake. He was as bland as a sunrise and as deadly as a pestilence.

Not only did he have the face to charge for a total circulation of 150 copies, advertising rates that would make reputable editors blush whose papers circulated by the thousand; but Editor Phillips actually got those rates. Earth was a wilderness of suckers for him. He put the marks of his easy touch all over the town and when advertisers were coy he cut their advertisements from other papers, charged up the account, waited till the store keeper was out and traded out the amount of his account and twice as much besides. Rebuffs and insults rebounded from him without denting his pachyderm complacency, nor rubbing the creamed and mantled waters of stagnant moral sense.

Poor old Phillips, he has left us. We may never look upon his like again—thank Heaven—until the sulphurous blazes of perdition illuminate the job lot in the deepest part of the seventh pit.

(*Emporia Gazette*, 1889)

CARELESS SEEMS THE GREAT AVENGER

James Russell Lowell

Careless seems the great Avenger; history's pages but record
One death-grapple in the darkness 'twixt old systems and the Word;
Truth forever on the scaffold, Wrong forever on the throne,—
Yet that scaffold sways the Future, and, behind the dim unknown,
Standeth God within the shadow, keeping watch above his own.

(From *The Present Crisis*)

(97)

WE HAVE LIVED AND LOVED TOGETHER

Charles Jefferys

We have lived and loved together
  Through many changing years;
We have shared each other's gladness
  And wept each other's tears;
I have known ne'er a sorrow
  That was long unsoothed by thee;
For thy smiles can make a summer
  Where darkness else would be.

Like the leaves that fall around us
  In autumn's fading hours,
Are the traitor's smiles, that darken
  When the cloud of sorrow lowers;
And though many such we've known, love,
  Too prone, alas, to range,
We both can speak of one love
  Which time can never change.

We have lived and loved together
  Through many changing years;
We have shared each other's gladness
  And wept each other's tears.
And let us hope the future
  As the past has been will be:
  I will share with thee my sorrows,
  And thou thy joys with me.

THE SOUL SELECTS

Emily Dickinson

The soul selects her own society,
Then shuts the door;
On her divine majority
Obtrude no more.

Unmoved, she notes the chariot's pausing
At her low gate;
Unmoved, an emperor is kneeling
Upon her mat.
I've known her from an ample nation
Choose one;
Then close the valves of her attention
Like stone.

POWER FROM GOD

Holy Bible, Isaiah 40:28–31

Hast thou not known? hast thou not heard, that the everlasting God, the Lord, the Creator of the ends of the earth, fainteth not, neither is weary? there is no searching of his understanding.

He giveth power to the faint; and to them that have no might he increaseth strength.

Even the youths shall faint and be weary, and the young men shall utterly fall; But they that wait upon the Lord shall renew their strength; they shall mount up with wings as eagles; they shall run, and not be weary; and they shall walk, and not faint.

LOVE AT FIRST SIGHT

Christopher Marlowe

It lies not in our power to love or hate,
For will in us is overruled by fate.
When two are stripped, long ere the course begins,
We wish that one should lose, the other win;
And one especially do we affect
Of two gold ingots, like in each respect:
The reason no man knows; let it suffice
What we behold is censured by our eyes.
Where both deliberate, the love is slight:
Who ever loved, that loved not at first sight?
(From Hero and Leander)

MAN WILL PREVAIL

William Faulkner

Our tragedy today is a general and universal physical fear so long sustained by now that we can even bear it. There are no longer problems of the spirit. There is only the question: when will I be blown up? Because of this, the young man or woman writing today has forgotten the problems of the human heart in conflict with itself which alone can make good writing because only that is worth writing about, worth the agony and the sweat.

He must learn them again. He must teach himself that the basest of all things is to be afraid; and teaching himself that, forget it forever, leaving no room in his workshop for anything but the old verities and truths of the heart, the old universal truths lacking which any story is ephemeral and doomed—love and honor and pity and pride and compassion and sacrifice. Until he does so he labors under a curse. He writes not of love but of lust, of defeats in which nobody loses anything of value, of victories without hope and worst of all without pity or compassion. His griefs grieve on universal bones, leaving no scars. He writes not of the heart, but of the glands.

Until he relearns these things he will write as though he stood among and watched the end of man. It is easy to say that man is immortal simply because he will endure; but when the last ding-dong of doom has clanged and faded from the last worthless rock hanging tideless in the last red and dying evening, that even then there will still be one more sound: that of his puny inexhaustible voice, still talking. I refuse to accept this. I believe that man will not merely endure: he will prevail. He is immortal, not because he alone among creatures has an inexhaustible voice, but because he has a soul, a spirit capable of compassion and sacrifice and endurance. The poet's, the writer's, duty is to write about these things. It is his privilege to help man endure by lifting his heart, by reminding him of the courage and honor and hope and pride and compassion and pity and sacrifice which have been the glory of his past. The poet's voice need not merely be the record of man, it can be one of the props, the pillars to help him endure and prevail.

(From Nobel Prize Speech, January, 1951)

THE UNKNOWN CITIZEN

(To Js/o7/M 378 This Marble Monument is Erected by the State)

W. H. Auden

He was found by the Bureau of Statistics to be
One against whom there was no official complaint,
And all the reports on his conduct agree
That, in the modern sense of an old-fashioned word, he was a saint,
For in everything he did he served the Greater Community.
Except for the War till the day he retired
He worked in a factory and never got fired,
But satisfied his employers, Fudge Motors Inc.
Yet he wasn't a scab or odd in his views,
For his Union reports that he paid his dues,
(Our report on his Union shows it was sound)
And our Social Psychology workers found
That he was popular with his mates and liked a drink.
The Press are convinced that he bought a paper every day
And that his reactions to advertisements were normal in every way.
Policies taken out in his name prove that he was fully insured,
And his Health-card shows he was once in hospital but left it cured.
Both Producers Research and High-Grade Living declare
He was fully sensible to the advantages of the Installment Plan
And had everything necessary to the Modern Man,
A phonograph, a radio, a car and a frigidaire.
Our researchers into Public Opinion are content
That he held the proper opinions for the time of year;
When there was peace, he was for peace; when there was war,
	he went.
He was married and added five children to the population,
Which our Eugenist says was the right number for a parent of his
	generation,
And our teachers report that he never interfered with their education.
Was he free? Was he happy? The question is absurd:
Had anything been wrong, we should certainly have heard.

THE BATTLE OF LEXINGTON

Joseph Warren

Watertown, April 26th, 1775

In provincial congress of Massachusetts,
to the inhabitants of Great Britain.

FRIENDS; and fellow subjects—Hostilities are at length commenced in this colony by the troops under the command of general Gage, and it being of the greatest importance, that an early, true, and authentic account of this inhuman proceeding should be known to you, the congress of this colony have transmitted the same, and from want of a session of the hon. continental congress, think it proper to address you on the alarming occasion.

By the clearest depositions relative to this transaction, it will appear that on the night preceding the nineteenth of April instant, a body of the king's troops, under the command of colonel Smith, were secretly landed at Cambridge, with an apparent design to take or destroy the military and other stores, provided for the defense of this colony, and deposited at Concord—that some inhabitants of the colony, on the night aforesaid, whilst traveling peaceably on the road, between Boston and Concord, were seized and greatly abused by armed men, who appeared to be officers of general Gage's army; that the town of Lexington, by these means, was alarmed, and a company of the inhabitants mustered on the occasion—that the regular troops on their way to Concord, marched into the said town of Lexington, and the said company, on their approach, began to disperse—that, notwithstanding this, the regulars rushed on with great violence and first began hostilities, by firing on said Lexington company, whereby they killed eight, and wounded several others— that the regulars continued their fire, until those of said company, who were neither killed nor wounded, had made their escape—that colonel Smith, with the detachment then marched to Concord, where a number of provincials were again fired on by the troops, two of them killed and several wounded, before the provincials fired on them, and provincials were again fired on by the troops, produced an engagement that lasted through the day, in which many of the provincials and more of the regular troops were killed and wounded.

To give a particular account of the ravages of the troops, as they retreated from Concord to Charlestown, would be very difficult, if not impracticable; let it suffice to say, that a great number of the houses on the road were plundered and rendered unfit for use, several were burnt, women in child-bed were driven by the soldiery naked into the streets, old men peaceably in their houses were shot dead, and such scenes exhibited as would disgrace the annals of the most uncivilized nation.

These, brethren, are marks of the ministerial vengeance against this colony, for refusing with her sister colonies, a submission to slavery; but they have not yet detached us from our royal sovereign. We profess to be his loyal and dutiful subjects, and so hardly dealt with as we have been, are still ready with our lives and fortunes, to defend his person, family, crown and dignity. Nevertheless, to the persecution and tyranny of his cruel ministry we will not tamely submit—appealing to Heaven for the justice of our cause, we determine to die or be free. . . .

By order,
Joseph Warren, President

SIT DOWN, SAD SOUL

Bryan Waller Procter

Sit down, sad soul, and count
  The moments flying:
Come,—tell the sweet amount
  That's lost by sighing!
How many smiles?—a score?
Then laugh, and count no more;
  For day is dying.

Lie down, sad soul, and sleep,
  And no more measure
The flight of Time, nor weep
  The loss of leisure;
But here, by this lone stream,
Lie down with us and dream
  Of starry treasure.

We dream; do thou the same:
  We love—forever;
We laugh; yet few we shame,
  The gentle, never.

(103)

Stay, then, till Sorrow dies;
Then—hope and happy skies
Are thine forever!

HANUKKAH HYMN

Anonymous

Rock of Ages, let our song
Praise Thy saving power;
Thou, amidst the raging foes,
Wast our sheltering tower.
Furious, they assailed us,
But Thine arm availed us,
And Thy word
Broke their sword
When our own strength failed us.

Kindling new the holy lamps,
Priest approved in suffering,
Purified the nation's shrine,
Brought to God their offering.
And His courts surrounding,
Hear, in joy abounding,
Happy throngs
Singing songs
With a mighty sounding.

Children of the martyr race,
Whether free or fettered,
Wake the echoes of the songs
Where ye may be scattered.
Yours the message cheering
That the time is nearing
Which will see
All men free,
Tyrants disappearing.

MY SYMPHONY

William Ellery Channing

To live with small means—to seek elegance rather than luxury, and refinement rather than fashion, to be worthy, not respectable, and wealthy, not rich—to study hard, think quietly, talk gently, act frankly, to listen to stars and birds, babes and sages, with open heart —to bear all cheerfully—do all bravely, await occasions,—hurry never—in a word to let the spiritual, unbidden and unconscious, grow up through the common. This is to be my symphony.

SAILING TO BYZANTIUM

William Butler Yeats

That is no country for old men. The young
In one another's arms, birds in the trees,
—Those dying generations—at their song,
The salmon-falls, the mackerel-crowded seas,
Fish, flesh, or fowl, commend all summer long
Whatever is begotten, born, and dies.
Caught in that sensual music all neglect
Monuments of unageing intellect.

An aged man is but a paltry thing,
A tattered coat upon a stick, unless
Soul clap its hands and sing, and louder sing
For every tatter in its mortal dress,
Nor is there singing school but studying
Monuments of its own magnificence;
And therefore I have sailed the seas and come
To the holy city of Byzantium.

O sages standing on God's holy fire
As in the gold mosaic of a wall,
Come from the holy fire, perne in a gyre,
And be the singing-masters of my soul.

Consume my heart away; sick with desire
And fastened to a dying animal
It knows not what it is; and gather me
Into the artifice of eternity.

Once out of nature I shall never take
My bodily form from any natural thing,
But such a form as Grecian goldsmiths make
Of hammered gold and gold enamelling
To keep a drowsy Emperor awake;
Or set upon a golden bough to sing
To lords and ladies of Byzantium
Of what is past, or passing, or to come.

REPARTEE

Anonymous

Loud brayed an ass. Quoth Kate, "My dear,"
(To spouse with scornful carriage)
"One of your relations I hear."
"Yes, love," said he, "by marriage."

WE WILL SPEAK OUT

James Russell Lowell

We will speak out, we will be heard,
   Though all earth's systems crack;
We will not bate a single word,
   Nor take a letter back.
Let liars fear, let cowards shrink,
   Let traitors turn away;
Whatever we have dared to think
   That dare we also say.
We speak the truth, and what care we
   For hissing and for scorn,
While some faint gleamings we can see
   Of Freedom's coming morn?

THE NOBLEST OCCUPATION

Montaigne

(TRANSLATOR: William Hazlitt)

What egregious fools are we! He hath passed his life in idleness, say we: "Alas, I have done nothing this day." What? have you not lived? It is not only the fundamental but the noblest of your occupation. "Had I been placed or thought fit for the managing of great affairs, I would have showed what I could have performed." Have you known how to meditate and manage your life? you have accomplished the greatest work of all. . . . Have you known how to compose your manners? you have done more than he who hath composed books. Have you known how to take rest? you have done more than he who hath taken Empires and Cities. The glorious masterpiece of man is to live to the purpose. All other things, as to reign, to govern, to hoard up treasure, to thrive and to build, are for the most part but appendixes and supports thereunto.

THE RETREAT

Henry Vaughan

Happy those early days, when I
Shined in my Angel-infancy!
Before I understood this place
Appointed for my second race,
Or taught my soul to fancy aught
But a white, celestial thought;
When yet I had not walk'd above
A mile or two from my first Love,
And looking back, at that short space
Could see a glimpse of His bright face;
When on some gilded cloud or flower
My gazing soul would dwell an hour,
And in those weaker glories spy
Some shadows of eternity;
Before I taught my tongue to wound
My conscience with a sinful sound,

Or had the black art to dispense
A several sin to every sense,
But felt through all this fleshly dress
Bright shoots of everlastingness.
O how I long to travel back,
And tread again that ancient track!
That I might once more reach that plain,
Where first I left my glorious train;
From whence th' enlighten'd spirit sees
That shady City of Palm trees!
But ah! my soul with too much stay
Is drunk, and staggers in the way:—
Some men a forward motion love,
But I by backward steps would move;
And when this dust falls to the urn,
In that state I came, return.

OUR FLAG

Mark Twain

And our flag—another pride of ours, our chiefest! When we have
seen it in far lands—glimpsing it unexpectedly in that strange sky,
waving its welcome and benediction to us—we have caught our
breaths, and uncovered our heads, and couldn't speak, for a moment,
for the thought of what it was to us and the great ideals it stood for.

FROM E TENEBRIS

Oscar Wilde

Come down, O Christ, and help me! reach thy hand,
  For I am drowning in a stormier sea
  Than Simon on thy lake of Galilee:
The wine of life is spilt upon the sand,
My heart is as some famine-murdered land
  Whence all good things have perished utterly,
  And well I know my soul in Hell must lie
If I this night before God's throne should stand.

The house of everyone is to him as his castle and fortress, as well
for his defense against injury and violence as for his repose.
—Sir Edward Coke (1552–1634)

NOT BY BREAD ALONE

James Terry White

If thou of fortune be bereft,
And thou dost find but two loaves left
To thee—sell one, and with the dole
Buy hyacinths to feed thy soul.

But not alone does beauty bide
Where bloom and tint and fragrance hide;
The minstrel's melody may feed
Perhaps a more insistent need.

But even beauty, howe'er blent
To ear and eye, fails to content;
Only the heart, with love afire,
Can satisfy the soul's desire.

(From *The Greek Anthology*)

BUILDING OF THE GREAT PYRAMID

Herodotus

(TRANSLATOR: George Rawlinson)

Till the death of Rhampsinitus, the priests said, Egypt was excel-
lently governed, and flourished greatly; but after him Cheops succeeded to the throne, and plunged into all manner of wickedness.
He closed the temples, and forbade the Egyptians to offer sacrifice,
compelling them instead to labor, and one and all, in his service. Some
were required to drag blocks of stone down to the Nile from the

quarries in the Arabian range of hills; others received the blocks after they had been conveyed acros the river, and drew them to the range of hills called the Libyan. A hundred thousand men labored constantly, and were relieved every three months by a fresh lot. It took ten years' oppression of the people to make the causeway for the conveyance of the stones, a work not much inferior, in my judgment, to the pyramid itself. This causeway is five furlongs in length; ten fathoms wide, and in height, at the highest part, eight fathoms. It is built of polished stone, and is covered with carvings of animals. To make it took ten years, as I said—or rather to make the causeway, the works on the mound where the pyramid stands, and the underground chambers, which Cheops intended as vaults for his own use; these last were built on a sort of island, surrounded by water introduced from the Nile by a canal. The pyramid itself was twenty years in building. It is a square, eight hundred feet each way, and the height the same, built entirely of polished stone, fitted together with the utmost care. The stones of which it is composed are none of them less than thirty feet in length.

The pyramid was built in steps, battlement-wise, as it it called, or, according to others, altar-wise. After laying the stones for the base, they raised the remaining stones to their places by means of machines formed of short wooden planks. The first machine raised them from the ground to the top of the first step. On this there was another machine, which received the stone upon its arrival, and conveyed it to the second step, whence a third machine advanced it still higher. Either they had as many machines as there were steps in the pyramid, or possibly they had but a single machine, which, being easily moved, was transferred from tier to tier as the stone rose—both accounts are given, and therefore I mention both. The upper portion of the pyramid was finished first, then the middle, and finally the part which was lowest and nearest the ground. There is an inscription in Egyptian characters on the pyramid which records the quantity of radishes, onions, and garlick consumed by the laborers who constructed it; and I perfectly well remember that the interpreter who read the writing to me said that the money expended in this way was 1600 talents of silver. If this then is a true record, what a vast sum must have been spent on the iron tools used in the work, and on the feeding and clothing of the laborers, considering the length of time the work lasted, which has already been stated, and the additional time—no small space, I imagine—which must have been occupied by the quarrying of the stones, their conveyance, and the formation of the underground apartments.

(From *The History*)

O AMIABLE LOVELY DEATH

William Shakespeare

Death, death; O amiable lovely death!
Thou odoriferous stench! sound rottenness!
Arise forth from the couch of lasting night,
Thou hate and terror to prosperity,
And I will kiss thy detestable bones
And put my eyeballs in thy vaulty brows
And ring these fingers with thy household worms
And stop this gap of breath with fulsome dust
And be a carrion monster like thyself:
Come, grin on me, and I will think thou smilest,
And buss thee as thy wife. Misery's love,
O, come to me!

(From King John)

TRUTH

Francis Bacon

Truth, which only doth judge itself, teacheth that the inquiry of truth, which is the love-making or wooing of it, the knowledge of truth, which is the presence of it, and the belief of truth, which is the enjoying of it, is the sovereign good of human nature.

A DIRGE

James Shirley

The glories of our blood and state,
  Are shadows, not substantial things.
There is no armour against fate,
  Death lays his icy hand on Kings,
        Sceptre and Crown
        Must tumble down,
And in the dust be equal made
With the poor crooked scythe and spade.

(111)

Some men with swords may reap the field,
  And plant fresh laurels where they kill,
But their strong nerves at last must yield,
  They tame but one another still;
      Early or late
      They stoop to fate,
And must give up their murmuring breath,
When they, pale Captives, creep to death.

The garlands wither on your brow,
  Then boast no more your mighty deeds,
Upon death's purple Altar now,
  See, where the Victor–victim bleeds.
      Your heads must come
      To the cold Tomb;
Only the actions of the just
Smell sweet, and blossom in their dust.

AN UNHAPPY ARTIST

Thomas Fuller

   Zeuxis the curious picturer painted a boy holding a dish full of
grapes in his hand, done so lively that the birds being deceived
flew to peck the grapes.
   However, Zeuxis was unhappy in his workmanship, explaining
that had he made the boy as lively as the grapes the birds would
have been afraid to touch them.

                                                          (1642)

   A man is in general better pleased when he has a good
dinner upon his table than when his wife talks Greek.
                                            —Samuel Johnson

PEACE

Rupert Brooke

Now, God be thanked Who has matched us with His hour,
  And caught our youth, and wakened us from sleeping,
With hand made sure, clear eye, and sharpened power,
  To turn, as swimmers into cleanness leaping,
Glad from a world grown old and cold and weary,
  Leave the sick hearts that honour could not move,
And half-men, and their dirty songs and dreary,
  And all the little emptiness of love!

Oh! we, who have known shame, we have found release there,
  Where there's no ill, no grief, but sleep has mending,
    Naught broken save this body, lost but breath;
Nothing to shake the laughing heart's long peace there
  But only agony, and that has ending;
    And the worst friend and enemy is but Death.

FRANKENSTEIN COMPLETES HIS MONSTER

Mary Wollstonecraft Shelley

It was on a dreary night of November that I beheld the accomplishment of my toils. With an anxiety that almost amounted to agony, I collected the instruments of life around me, that I might infuse a spark of being into the lifeless thing that lay at my feet. It was already one in the morning; the rain pattered dismally against the panes, and my candle was nearly burnt out, when, by the glimmer of the half-extinguished light, I saw the dull yellow eye of the creature open; it breathed hard, and a convulsive motion agitated its limbs.

How can I describe my emotions at this catastrophe, or how delineate the wretch whom with such infinite pains and care I had endeavored to form? His limbs were in proportion, and I had selected his features as beautiful. Beautiful!—Great God! His yellow skin scarcely covered the work of muscles and arteries beneath; his hair was of a lustrous black, and flowing; his teeth of a pearly whiteness; but these luxuriances only formed a more horrid contrast with his watery eyes, that seemed almost of the same color as the dun white sockets in which they were set, his shrivelled complexion and straight black lips.

The different accidents of life are not so changeable as the feelings of human nature. I had worked hard for nearly two years, for the sole purpose of infusing life into an inanimate body. For this I had deprived myself of rest and health. I had desired it with an ardor that far exceeded moderation; but now that I had finished, the beauty of the dream vanished, and breathless horror and disgust filled my heart. Unable to endure the aspect of the being I had created, I rushed out of the room, and continued a long time traversing my bedchamber, unable to compose my mind to sleep. At length lassitude succeeded to the tumult I had before endured; and I threw myself on the bed in my clothes, endeavoring to seek a few moments of forgetfulness. But it was in vain; I slept, indeed, but I was disturbed by the wildest dreams. I thought I saw Elizabeth, in the bloom of health, walking in the streets of Ingolstadt. Delighted and surprised, I embraced her; but as I imprinted the first kiss on her lips, they became livid with the hue of death; her features appeared to change, and I thought that I held the corpse of my dead mother in my arms; a shroud enveloped her form, and I saw the grave worms crawling in the folds of the flannel. I started from my sleep with horror; a cold dew covered my forehead, my teeth chattered, and every limb became convulsed: when, by the dim and yellow light of the moon, as it forced its way through the window shutters, I beheld the wretch—the miserable monster whom I had created. He held up the curtain of my bed; and his eyes, if eyes they may be called, were fixed on me. His jaws opened, and he muttered some inarticulate sounds, while a grin wrinkled his cheeks. He might have spoken, but I did not hear; one hand was stretched out, seemingly to detain me, but I escaped, and rushed downstairs. I took refuge in the courtyard belonging to the house which I inhabited; where I remained during the rest of the night, walking up and down in the greatest agitation, listening attentively, catching and fearing each sound as if it were to announce the approach of the demoniacal corpse to which I had so miserably given life.

Oh! no mortal could support the horror of that countenance. A mummy again endued with animation could not be so hideous as that wretch. I had gazed on him while unfinished; he was ugly then; but when those muscles and joints were rendered capable of motion, it became a thing such as even Dante could not have conceived.

(From *Frankenstein*, 1818)

WITH EVERY RISING OF THE SUN

Ella Wheeler Wilcox

With every rising of the sun
Think of your life as just begun.

The past has shrived and buried deep
All yesterdays—there let them sleep. . . .

Concern yourself with but today,
Woo it and teach it to obey,

Your wish and will. Since time began
Today has been the friend of man. . . .

You and today! a soul sublime
And the great pregnant hour of time.

With God between to bind the twain—
Go forth I say—attain—attain.

THE INVISIBLE BRIDGE

Gelett Burgess

I'd never Dare to Walk across
A Bridge I could Not See;
For Quite Afraid of Falling off,
I fear that I should be!

THE TERROR OF THE INFINITE

Blaise Pascal

When I consider the shortness of my life, lost in an eternity before and behind, "passing away as the remembrance of a guest who tarrieth but a day," the little space I fill or behold in the infinite immensity of spaces, of which I know nothing and which know nothing of me—when I reflect on this, I am filled with terror, and wonder why I am *here* and not *there*, for there was no reason why it should be the one rather than the other; why *now* rather than *then*. Who set me here? By whose command and rule were this time and place appointed me? How many kingdoms know nothing of us! The eternal silence of those infinite spaces terrifies me.

FIVE REASONS FOR DRINKING

Dean Henry Aldrich

If all be true that I do think,
There are five reasons we should drink:
Good wine—a friend—or being dry—
Or lest we should be by and by—
Or any other reason why.

LOVE IN THE VALLEY

George Meredith

Under yonder beech-tree single on the green-sward,
  Couch'd with her arms behind her golden head,
Knees and tresses folded to slip and ripple idly,
  Lies my young love sleeping in the shade.
Had I the heart to slide an arm beneath her,
  Press her parting lips as her waist I gather slow,
Waking in amazement she could not but embrace me:
  Then would she hold me and never let me go?

Shy as the squirrel and wayward as the swallow,
  Swift as the swallow along the river's light
Circleting the surface to meet his mirror'd winglets,
  Fleeter she seems in her stay than in her flight.
Shy as the squirrel that leaps among the pine-tops,
  Wayward as the swallow overhead at set of sun,
She whom I love is hard to catch and conquer,
  Hard, but O the glory of the winning were she won!

THE END OF A FAMOUS HISTORICAL WORK

Edward Gibbon

I have presumed to mark the moment of conception; I shall now commemorate the hour of my final deliverance. It was on the day, or rather night, of the 27th of June, 1787, between the hours of eleven and twelve, that I wrote the last lines of the last page [of *The Decline and Fall of the Roman Empire*] in a summer-house in my garden. After laying down my pen, I took several turns in a *berceau*, or covered walk of acacias, which commands a prospect of the country, the lake, and the mountains. The air was temperate, the sky was serene, the silver orb of the moon was reflected from the waters, and all nature was silent. I will not dissemble the first emotions of joy on recovery of my freedom, and, perhaps, the establishment of my fame. But my pride was soon humbled, and a sober melancholy was spread over my mind, by the idea that I had taken an everlasting leave of an old and agreeable companion, and that whatsoever might be the future date of my *History*, the life of the historian must be short and precarious.

A WORTHY FOOL

William Shakespeare

A fool, a fool! I met a fool i' the forest,
A motley fool; a miserable world!
As I do live by food, I met a fool;
Who laid him down and bask'd in the sun,
And rail'd on Lady Fortune in good terms,
In good set terms, and yet a motley fool.
"Good morrow, fool," quoth I. "No sir," quoth he,
"Call me not fool till heaven hath sent me fortune:"
And then he drew a dial from his poke,
And looking on it with lack-lustre eye,
Says very wisely, "It is ten o'clock:
Thus we may see," qouth he, "how the world wags:
'Tis but an hour ago since it was nine;
And after one hour more 'twill be eleven;
And so, from hour to hour, we ripe and ripe,

(117)

And then, from hour to hour, we rot and rot;
And thereby hangs a tale." When I did hear
The motley fool thus moral on the time,
My lungs began to crow like chanticleer,
That fools should be so deep-contemplative;
And I did laugh sans intermission
An hour by his dial. O noble fool!
A worthy fool! Motley's the only wear.

(From *As You Like It*)

O SONS OF EARTH

Alexander Pope

O sons of earth! attempt ye still to rise
By mountains piled on mountains to the skies?
Heaven still with laughter the vain toil surveys,
And buries madmen in the heaps they raise.

Know all the good that individuals find,
Or God and Nature meant to mere mankind,
Reason's whole pleasure, all the joys of sense,
Lie in three words—Health, Peace, and Competence.

THE LAST MESSAGES OF ROBERT FALCON SCOTT

(Scott reached the South Pole in 1912, but he and his
fellow-explorers perished on the return journey.)

March 17th. I can only write at lunch and then only occasionally.
The cold is intense, *minus* 40° at midday. My companions are
unendingly cheerful, but we are all on the verge of serious frost-
bites, and though we constantly talk of fetching through I don't
think any of us believes it in his heart.

We are cold on the march now, and at all times except meals.
Yesterday we had to lay up for a blizzard, and today we move

(118)

dreadfully slow. We are now at No. 14 pony camp, only two pony marches from One Ton Depot. We leave here our theodolite, a camera, and Oates's sleeping-bag. Diaries, etc. and geological specimens carried at Wilson's special request, will be found with us or on our sledge.

Sunday, March 18th.— . . . My right foot has gone, nearly all the toes—two days ago I was proud possessor of best feet. These are the steps of my downfall. . . . Bowers takes first place in condition, but there is not much to choose after all. The others are still confident of getting through—or pretend to be—I don't know! We have the last *half* full of oil in our primus and a very small quantity of spirit—this alone between us and thirst. The wind is fair for the moment, and that is perhaps a fact to help. . . .

Thursday, March 22 and 23.—Blizzard bad as ever—Wilson unable to start—tomorrow last chance—no fuel and only one or two of food left—must be near the end. Have decided it shall be natural—we shall march for the depot with or without our effects and die in our tracks.

Thursday, March 29th.—Since the 21st we have had a continuous gale with W.S.W. and S.W. We had fuel to make two cups of tea apiece and bare food for two days on the 20th. Every day we have been ready to start for our depot 13 *miles* away, but outside the door of the tent it remains a scene of whirling drift. I do not think we can hope for any better things now. We shall stick it out to the end, but we are getting weaker, of course, and the end cannot be far. It seems a pity but I do not think I can write more. R. Scott.

CAPTAIN SCOTT'S "MESSAGE TO THE PUBLIC"

Had we lived, I should have had a tale to tell of the hardihood, endurance, and courage of my companions which would have stirred the heart of every Englishman. These rough notes and our dead bodies must tell the tale, but surely, surely, a great rich country like ours will see that those who are dependent on us are properly provided for.

R. Scott

SCOTT'S LETTER TO MRS. E. A. WILSON

My Dear Mrs. Wilson:—If this letter reaches you Bill and I will have gone out together. We are very near it now and I should like you to know how splendid he was at the end—everlastingly cheerful and ready to sacrifice himself for others, never a word of blame to me for leading him into this mess. He is not suffering, luckily, at least only minor discomforts.

His eyes have a comfortable blue look of hope and his mind is peaceful with the satisfaction of his faith in regarding himself as part of a great scheme of the Almighty. I can do no more to comfort you than to tell you that he died as he lived, a brave, true man—the best of comrades and staunchest of friends.

My whole heart goes out to you in pity.—Yours,

R. Scott

SCOTT'S LETTER TO MRS. BOWERS

My Dear Mrs. Bowers:—I am afraid this will reach you after one of the heaviest blows of your life.

I write when we are very near the end of our journey, and I am finishing it in company with two gallant, noble gentlemen. One of these is your son. He had come to be one of my closest and soundest friends, and I appreciate his wonderful upright nature, his ability and energy. As the troubles have thickened his dauntless spirit ever shone brighter and he has remained cheerful, hopeful, and indomitable to the end.

The ways of Providence are inscrutable, but there must be some reason why such a young, vigorous and promising life is taken.

My whole heart goes out to you in pity for you.—Yours,

R. Scott

To the end he has talked of you and his sisters. One sees what a happy home he must have had and perhaps it is well to look back on nothing but happiness.

He remains unselfish, self-reliant and splendidly hopeful to the end, believing in God's mercy to you.

LEAVE ME, O LOVE WHICH REACHEST BUT TO DUST

Sir Philip Sidney

Leave me, O love which reachest but to dust,
And thou, my mind, aspire to higher things!
Grow rich in that which never taketh rust:
Whatever fades, but fading pleasure brings.
Draw in thy beams, and humble all thy might
To that sweet yoke where lasting freedoms be;
Which breaks the clouds and opens forth the light
That doth both shine and give us sight to see.
O, take fast hold! let that light be thy guide
In this small course which birth draws out to death,
And think how evil becometh him to slide
Who seeketh heaven, and comes of heavenly breath.
    Then farewell, world; thy uttermost I see:
    Eternal Love, maintain thy life in me.

DR. SAMUEL JOHNSON ON COURT–MARTIALS

James Boswell

Talking of a court-martial that was sitting upon a very momentous public occasion, he expressed much doubt of an enlightened decision; and said that perhaps there was not a member of it who in the whole course of his life had ever spent an hour by himself in balancing probabilities.

I would rather sit on a pumpkin, and have it all to myself, than to be crowded on a velvet cushion.

                    —Henry Thoreau

QUA CURSUM VENTUS

Arthur Hugh Clough

As ships, becalmed at eve, that lay
  With canvas drooping, side by side,
Two towers of sail at dawn of day
  Are scarce long leagues apart described;

When fell the night, unsprung the breeze,
  And all the darkling hours they plied,
Nor dreamt but each the self-same seas
  By each was cleaving, side by side;

E'en so—but why the tale reveal
  Of those, whom year by year unchanged,
Brief absence joined anew to feel,
  Astounded, soul from soul estranged?

At dead of night their sails were filled,
  And onward each rejoicing steered—
Ah, neither blame, for neither willed,
  Or wist, what first with dawn appeared!

To veer, how vain! On, onward strain,
  Brave barks! In light, in darkness too,
Through winds and tides one compass guides—
  To that, and your own selves, be true.

But O blithe breeze, and O great seas,
  Though ne'er, that earliest parting past,
On your wide plain they join again,
  Together lead them home at last.

One port, methought, alike they sought,
  One purpose hold where'er they fare,—
O bounding breeze, O rushing seas!
  At last, at last, unite them there!

JOHN HAY, PRESIDENT LINCOLN'S SECRETARY, RECORDS IN HIS DIARY THE OCCASION OF THE GETTYSBURG ADDRESS

In the morning of the 19th, I got a beast and rode out with the President and suite to the Cemetery in procession. The procession formed itself in an orphanly sort of way, and moved out with very little help from anybody; and after a little delay Mr. Everett took his place on the stand—and Mr. Stockton made a prayer which thought it was an oration—and Mr. Everett spoke as he always does, perfectly, and the President, in a firm free way, with more grace than is his wont, said a half-dozen lines of consecration—and the music wailed, and we went home through crowded and cheering streets.

(November, 1863)

MY DAYS AMONG THE DEAD

Robert Southey

My days among the dead are past;
　Around me I behold,
Wher'er these casual eyes are cast,
　The mighty minds of old:
My never-failing friends are they,
With whom I converse day by day.

With them I take delight in weal
　And seek relief in woe;
And while I understand and feel
　How much to them I owe,
My cheeks have often been bedewed
With tears of thoughtful gratitude.

My thoughts are with the Dead; with them
　I live in long-past years,
Their virtues love, their faults condemn,
　Partake their hopes and fears;
And from their lessons seek and find
Instruction with an humble mind.

My hopes are with the Dead; anon
  My place with them will be,
And I with them shall travel on
  Through all Futurity;
Yet leaving here a name, I trust,
That will not perish in the dust.

INNUENDO

Learned Hand

I had rather take my chance that some traitors will escape detection
than spread abroad a spirit of general suspicion and distrust, which
accepts rumor and gossip in place of undismayed and unintimidated
inquiry.

(1952)

COME ALL YE FAIR AND TENDER MAIDENS

Anonymous

Come all ye fair and tender maidens,
Take warning how you court young men,
They're like a star of a summer's morning,
First they'll appear, and then they're gone.

They'll tell you some lovin' story,
They'll swear to you their love is true,
Straight-way they'll go and court another,
And that's the love they had for you.

Oh, do you remember our days of courtin'
When your head lay upon my breast?
You could make me believe
  With the fallin' of your arm
That the sun rose in the West.

If I'd a known before I courted
That love it was such a killin' thing,
I'd a locked my heart in a box of golden
And fastened it up with a silver pin.

I wish I was a little sparrow,
And I had wings and I could fly,
I'd fly away to my own true lover,
And when he'd speak I would deny.

But I am no little sparrow,
I have no wings, neither can I fly,
I'll sit right down in my grief and sorrow,
And let my troubles pass me by.

WINSTON CHURCHILL'S LAST MESSAGE AS PRIME MINISTER

It only remains for me to express to the British people, for whom
I have acted in these perilous years, my profound gratitude for the
unflinching, unswerving support which they have given me during
my task, and for the many expressions of kindness which they have
shown towards their servant.

(July, 1945)

MIMNERMUS IN CHURCH

William (Johnson) Cory

You promise heavens free from strife,
    Pure truth, and perfect change of will;
But sweet, sweet is this human life,
    So sweet, I fain would breathe it still;
Your chilly stars I can forego,
This warm kind world is all I know.

You say there is no substance here,
    One great reality above:
Back from that void I shrink in fear,
    And child-like hide myself in love:

(125)

Show me what angels feel. Till then
I cling, a mere weak man, to men.

You bid me lift my mean desires
    From faltering lips and fitful veins
To sexless souls, ideal quires,
    Unwearied voices, wordless strains:
My mind with fonder welcome owns
One dear dead friend's remember'd tones.

Forsooth the present we must give
    To that which cannot pass away;
All beauteous things for which we live
    By laws of time and space decay.
But O, the very reason why
I clasp them, is because they die.

MR. DOOLEY ON OLD AGE

Finley Peter Dunne

"Manny a man that cudden't direct ye to th' dhrug store on th' corner whin he was thirty will get a respectful hearin' whin age has further impaired his mind. . . ."

"Why," said Mr. Hennessy, "ye'd give annythin' to be twinty-five agin."

"I wuddn't," said Mr. Dooley. "Why shud I want to grow old agin?"

ONE WORD IS TOO OFTEN PROFANED

Percy Bysshe Shelley

One word is too often profaned
    For me to profane it,
One feeling too falsely disdain'd
    For thee to disdain it;

One hope is too like despair
For prudence to smother,
And Pity from thee more dear
Than that from another.

I can give not what men call love;
But wilt thou accept not
The worship the heart lifts above
And the Heavens reject not,—
The desire of the moth for the star,
Of the night for the morrow,
The devotion to something afar
From the sphere of our sorrow?

AN EXCHANGE OF LETTERS BETWEEN KING DARIUS III OF PERSIA AND ALEXANDER THE GREAT, KING OF MACEDONIA, 334 B.C.

Darius to Alexander

From the capital of the kings of the world: As long as the sun shines on the head of Iskander [Alexander] the robber, etc. etc., let him know that the King of Heaven has bestowed on me the dominion of the earth, and that the Almighty has granted to me the surface of the four quarters. Providence has also eminently distinguished me with glory, exaltation, majesty, and with multitudes of devoted champions and confederates.

A report has reached us that you have gathered to yourself numbers of thieves and reprobates, the multitude of whom has so elated your imagination that you propose through their co-operation to procure the crown and throne, lay waste our kingdom, and destroy our land and people.

Such crude resolves are perfectly consistent with the infatuation of the men of Room. It now behooves you, on reading the contents of this epistle, to return instantly from the place to which you have advanced. As to this criminal movement which has proceeded from you, be under no alarm from our majesty and correction, as you are not yet ranked among the number of those who merit our vengeance and punishment. Behold! I send you a coffer full of gold, and an assload of sesame, to give you by these two objects an idea of the extent of my wealth and powers. I also send you a scourge and a ball: the latter, that you may amuse yourself with a diversion suitable to your age; the former, to serve for your chastisement.

Alexander to Darius

From Zu-ul-kurnain [Alexander] to him who pretends to be king of kings; that the very hosts of Heaven stand in awe of him; and that the inhabitants of the world are by him enlightened! How then can it be worthy of such a person to be afraid of a contemptible foe like Iskander?

Does not Dárá [Darius] know that the High and Mighty Lord gives power and dominion to whomsoever He wills? And also, whenever a feeble mortal regards himself as a God, and conqueror over the hosts of Heaven, beyond doubt the indignation of the Almighty brings down ruin on his kingdom?

How can the person doomed to death and corruption be a God, he from whom his kingdom is taken away and who leaves the enjoyment of the world to others?

Lo! I have resolved to meet you in battle, and therefore march towards your realms. I profess myself the weak and humble servant of God, to whom I address my prayers and look for victory and triumph, and whom I adore.

Along with the letter in which you make a display of your great power you have sent me a scourge, a ball, a coffer filled with gold, and an assload of sesame; all of which I refer to good fortune and regard as auspicious signs. The scourge portends that I shall be the instrument of your castigation and become your ruler, preceptor, and director. The ball indicates that the surface of the earth and the circumference of the globe shall be my lieutenants. The coffer of gold, which is part of your treasure, denotes that your riches shall soon be transferred to me. And as to the sesame, although the grains are many in number, it is however soft to the touch and of all kinds of food the least noxious and disagreeable.

In return I send you a kaffis of mustard seed, that you may taste and acknowledge the bitterness of my victory. And whereas through presumption you have exalted yourself, and have become proud through the grandeur of your kingdom, and pretend to be a Divinity on earth, and have even raised to the heavens this standard *I truly am your supreme lord*; and although by the enumeration of your numbers, preparations, and might you have endeavored to alarm me; yet I confidently trust in the interposition of Divine Providence, that it will please the Almighty to make thy boasting attended by the reproach of mankind; and that in the same proportion as you have magnified yourself He may bring on you humiliation and grant me victory over you. My trust and reliance are in the Lord. And so farewell.

(Alexander won victory in the two battles that followed.)

LUCIFER IN STARLIGHT

George Meredith

On a starred night Prince Lucifer uprose.
Tired of his dark dominion swung the fiend
Above the rolling ball in cloud part screened,
Where sinners hugged their specter of repose.
Poor prey to his hot fit of pride were those.
And now upon his western wing he leaned,
Now his huge bulk o'er Afric's sands careened,
Now the black planet showed Arctic snows.
Soaring through wider zones that pricked his scars
With memory of the old revolt from Awe,
He reached a middle height, and at the stars,
Which are the brain of heaven, he looked, and sank.
Around the ancient track marched, rank on rank,
The arm of unalterable law.

POLITICAL PROMISES

Said Representative Charles S. Hartman of Montana, in 1896:
"It is true that the Populist party has a number of different remedies for the situation. And I am advised that they are about to add three additional planks to their platform. One of them is to make a cross between the lightning bug and the honeybee for the purpose of enabling the bee to work at night. Another, that of breeding the centipede with the hog, for the purpose of having a hundred hams to each animal. And I am told they have a further visionary scheme of budding strawberries into milkweeds, so that everybody can have strawberries and cream from the same plant."

(129)

DEPARTURE

Coventry Patmore

It was not like your great and gracious ways!
Do you, that have naught other to lament,
Never, my Love, repent
Of how, that July afternoon,
You went,
With sudden, unintelligible phrase,
And frightened eye,
Upon your journey of so many days
Without a single kiss, or a good-bye?
I knew, indeed, that you were parting soon;
And so we sate, within the low sun's rays,
You whispering to me, for your voice was weak,
Your harrowing praise.
Well, it was well
To hear such things speak,
And I could tell
What made your eyes a growing gloom of love,
As a warm South wind sombres a March grove.
And it was like your great and gracious ways
To turn your talk on daily things, my Dear,
Lifting the luminous, pathetic lash
To let the laughter flash,
Whilst I drew near,
Because you spoke so low that I could scarcely hear.
But all at once to leave me at the last,
More at the wonder than the loss aghast,
With huddled, unintelligible phrase,
And frightened eye,
And go your journey of all days
With not one kiss, or a good-bye,
And the only loveless look the look with which
    you passed:
'Twas all unlike your great and gracious ways.

PRESIDENT KENNEDY TO THE UNITED NATIONS, SEPTEMBER 25, 1961

Unconditional war can no longer lead to unconditional victory. It can no longer concern the great powers alone. For a nuclear disaster, spread by wind and water and fear, could well engulf the great and the small, the rich and the poor, the committed and the uncommitted alike. Mankind must put an end to war or war will put an end to mankind.

The mere existence of modern weapons—ten million times more powerful than any that the world has ever seen, and only minutes away from any target on earth—is a source of horror and discord and distrust.

Men no longer maintain that disarmament must await the settlement of all disputes, for disarmament must be a part of any permanent settlement. And man may no longer pretend that the quest for disarmament is a sign of weakness, for in a spiraling arms race a nation's security may be shrinking even as its arms increase.

For peace is not solely a matter of military or technical problems, it is primarily a problem of politics and people. And unless man can match his strides in weaponry and technology with equal strides in social and political development, our great strength, like that of the dinosaur, will become incapable of proper control and, like the dinosaur, vanish from the earth.

And as we extend the rule of law on earth, so must we also extend it to man's new domain: Outer space.

Terror is not a new weapon. Throughout history it has been used by those who could not prevail either by persuasion or example. But inevitably they fail, either because men are not afraid to die for a life worth living, or because the terrorists themselves came to realize that free men cannot be frightened by threats and that aggression would meet its own response.

But I come here today to look across this world of threats to a world of peace. In that search we cannot expect any final triumph, for new problems will always arise. We cannot expect that all nations will adopt like systems, for conformity is the jailer of freedom and the enemy of growth. Nor can we expect to reach our goal by contrivance, by fiat or even by the wishes of all.

But however close we sometimes seem to that dark and final abyss, let no man of peace and freedom despair. For he does not stand alone. If we all can persevere, if we can in every land and office look beyond our own shores and ambitions, then surely the

(131)

age will dawn in which the strong are just and the weak secure and the peace preserved.

Ladies and gentlemen of this Assembly, the decision is ours. Never have the nations of the world had so much to lose or so much to gain. Together we shall save our planet or together we shall perish in its flames. Save it we can and save it we must, and then shall we earn the eternal thanks of mankind and, as peace-makers, the eternal blessing of God.

WHAT IS TO COME

William Ernest Henley

What is to come we know not. But we know
That what has been was good—was good to show,
Better to hide, and best of all to bear.
We are the masters of the days that were;
We have lived, we have loved, we have suffered . . . even so.

Shall we not take the ebb who had the flow?
Life was our friend. Now, if it be our foe—
Dear, though it spoil, and break us!—need we care
        What is to come?
Let the great winds their worst and wildest blow,
Or the gold weather round us mellow slow;
We have fulfilled ourselves, and we can dare
And we can conquer, though we may not share
In the rich quiet of the afterglow
        What is to come.

BE NOT AFRAID OF LIFE

William James

These, then, are my last words to you: Be not afraid of life. Believe that life *is* worth living and your belief will help create the fact. The "scientific" proof that you are right may not be clear before the day of judgment (or some stage of being which that expression may serve to symbolize) is reached. But the faithful fighters of this hour, or the beings that then and there will represent them, may turn to the faint-hearted, who here decline to go on, with words like those with which Henry IV greeted the tardy Crillon after a great battle had been gained: "Hang yourself, brave Crillon! We fought at Arques, and you were not there!"

THE MORON

Anonymous

See the happy moron,
He doesn't give a damn!
I wish I were a moron—
My God! Perhaps I am!

ALL THAT'S PAST

Walter de la Mare

Very old are the woods;
    And the buds that break
Out of the brier's boughs,
    When March winds wake,
So old with their beauty are—
    Oh, no man knows
Through what wild centuries
    Roves back the rose.
Very old are the brooks;
    And the rills that rise
Where snow sleeps cold beneath
    The azure skies
Sing such a history
    Of come and gone,
Their every drop is as wise
    As Solomon.

(133)

Very old are we men;
  Our dreams are tales
Told in dim Eden
  By Eve's nightingales;
We wake and whisper awhile,
  But, the day gone by,
Silence and sleep like fields
  Of amaranth lie.

WHERE LOVE IS, THERE GOD IS ALSO

Leo N. Tolstoy

(TRANSLATOR: Nathan Haskell Dole)

In the city lived the shoemaker, Martuin Avdyeitch. He lived in a
basement, in a little room with one window. The window looked out
on the street. Through the window he used to watch the people
passing by; although only their feet could be seen, yet by the boots,
Martuin Avdyeitch recognized the people. Martuin Avdyeitch had
lived long in one place, and had many acquaintances. Few pairs of
boots in his district had not been in his hands once and again. Some
he would halfsole, some he would patch, some he would stitch
around, and occasionally he would also put on new uppers. And
through the window he often recognized his work.

Avdyeitch had always been a good man; but as he grew old, he
began to think more about his soul, and get nearer to God. Martuin's
wife had died when he was still living with his master. His wife left
him a boy three years old. None of their other children had lived.
All the eldest had died in childhood. Martuin at first intended to
send his little son to his sister in the village, but afterward he felt
sorry for him; he thought to himself:—

"It will be hard for my little Kapitoshka to live in a strange family.
I shall keep him with me."

And Avdyeitch left his master, and went into lodgings with his
little son. But God gave Avdyeitch no luck with his children. As
Kapitoshka grew older, he began to help his father, and would have
been a delight to him, but a sickness fell on him, he went to bed,
suffered a week, and died. Martuin buried his son, and fell into
despair. So deep was this despair that he began to complain of God.

Martuin fell into such a melancholy state, that more than once he prayed to God for death, and reproached God because He had not taken him who was an old man, instead of his beloved only son. Avdyeitch also ceased to go to church.

And once a little old man from the same district came from Troitsa [a famous monastery] to see Avdyeitch; for seven years he had been wandering about. Avdyeitch talked with him, and began to complain about his sorrows.

"I have no desire to live any longer," he said, "I only wish I was dead. That is all I pray God for. I am a man without anything to hope for now."

And the little old man said to him:—

"You don't talk right, Martuin, we must not judge God's doings. The world moves, but not by our skill, but by God's will. God decreed for your son to die,—for you—to live. So it is for the best. And you are in despair, because you wish to live for your own happiness."

"But what should one live for?" asked Martuin.

And the little old man said:—

"We must live for God, Martuin. He gives you life, and for His sake you must live. When you begin to live for Him, you will not grieve over anything, and all will seem easy to you."

Martuin kept silent for a moment, and then said, "But how can one live for God?"

And the little old man said:—

"Christ has taught us how to live for God. You know how to read? Buy a Testament and read it; there you will learn how to live for God. Everything is explained there."

And these words kindled a fire in Avdyeitch's heart. And he went that very same day, bought a New Testament in large print, and began to read.

At first Avdyeitch intended to read only on holidays; but as he began to read, it so cheered his soul that he used to read every day. At times he would become so absorbed in reading, that all the kerosene in the lamp would burn out, and still he could not tear himself away. And so Avdyeitch used to read every evening.

And the more he read, the clearer he understood what God wanted of him, and how one should live for God; and his heart kept growing easier and easier. . . .

Once it happened that Martuin read till late into the night. He was reading the Gospel of Luke. He was reading over the sixth chapter and he was reading the verses:

(135)

And unto him that smiteth thee on the one cheek offer also the other; and him that taketh away thy cloak forbid not to take thy coat also. Give to every man that asketh of thee; and of him that taketh away thy goods, ask them not again. And as ye would that men should do to you, do ye also to them likewise. . . .

Avdyeitch read these words, and joy filled his soul. He took off his spectacles, put them down on the book, leaned his elbows on the table, and became lost in thought. . . . He wanted to go to bed, but he felt loath to tear himself away from the book. And he began to read farther in the seventh chapter. . . . He reached the forty-fourth verse, and began to read:—

And he turned to the woman, and said unto Simon, Seest thou this woman? I entered into thine house, thou gavest me no water for my feet; but she hath washed my feet with tears, and wiped them with the hair of her head. Thou gavest me no kiss; but this woman since the time I came in hath not ceased to kiss my feet. My head with oil thou didst not anoint; but this woman hath anointed my feet with ointment.

He finished reading these verses, and thought to himself:—

Thou gavest me no water for my feet, thou gavest me no kisses. My head with oil thou didst not anoint.

And again Avdyeitch took off his spectacles, put them down on the book, and again he became lost in thought.

"It seems that Pharisee must have been such a man as I am. I, too, apparently have thought only of myself,—how I might have my tea, be warm and comfortable, but never to think about my guest. He thought about himself, but there was not the least care taken of the guest. And who was his guest? The Lord Himself. If He had come to me, should I have done the same way?"

Avdyeitch rested his head upon both his arms, and did not notice that he fell asleep.

"Martuin!" suddenly seemed to sound in his ears.

Martuin started from his sleep:—

"Who is here?"

He turned around, glanced toward the door—no one.

Again he fell into a doze. Suddenly, he plainly heard:—

"Martuin! Ah, Martuin! look tomorrow on the street. I am coming."

Martuin awoke, rose from the chair, began to rub his eyes. He himself could not tell whether he heard those words in his dream, or in reality. He turned down his lamp, and went to bed.

At daybreak next morning, Avdyeitch rose, made his prayer to God, lighted the stove, put on the shchi[1] and the kasha,[2] put the water in the samovar, and put on his apron, and sat down by the window to work . . . looking out more than he was working. When anyone passed by in boots which he did not know, he would bend down, look out of the window, in order to see, not only the feet, but also the face.

The dvornik[3] passed by in new felt boots, the water-carrier passed by; then there came up to the window an old soldier of Nicholas's time in an old pair of laced felt boots, with a shovel in his hands. Avdyeitch recognized him by his felt boots. The old man's name was Stepanuitch; and a neighboring merchant out of charity, gave him a home with him. He was required to assist the dvornik. Stepanuitch began to shovel away the snow from in front of Avdyeitch's window. Avdyeitch glanced at him, and took up his work again.

"Pshaw! I must be getting crazy in my old age," said Avdyeitch, and laughed at himself. "Stepanuitch is clearing away the snow, and I imagine that Christ is coming to see me. I was entirely out of my mind, old dotard that I am!"

Avdyeitch sewed about a dozen stitches, and then felt impelled to look through the window again. He looked out again through the window, and saw Stepanuitch had leaned his shovel against the wall, and was warming himself, and resting. He was an old, broken-down man; evidently he had not strength enough even to shovel the snow. Avdyeitch said to himself:—

"I will give him some tea; by the way, the samovar has only just gone out." Avdyeitch laid down his awl, rose from his seat, put the samovar on the table, poured out the tea, and tapped with his finger at the glass. Stepanuitch turned around, and came to the window. Avdyeitch beckoned to him, and went to open the door.

"Come in, warm yourself a little," he said. "You must be cold."

"May Christ reward you for this! my bones ache," said Stepanuitch.

Stepanuitch came in, and shook off the snow, tried to wipe his feet, so as not to soil the floor, but staggered.

"Don't trouble to wipe your feet. I will clean it up myself; we are used to such things. Come in and sit down," said Avdyeitch. "Here, drink a cup of tea."

And Avdyeitch filled two glasses, and handed one to his guest: while he himself poured his tea into a saucer, and began to blow it.

Stepanuitch finished drinking his glass of tea, turned the glass

[1] cabbage-soup
[2] gruel
[3] house-porter

(137)

upside down, put the half-eaten lump of sugar on it, and began to express his thanks. But it was evident he wanted some more.

"Have some more," said Avdyeitch, filling both his own glass and his guest's. Avedyeitch drank his tea, but from time to time glanced out into the street.

"Are you expecting anyone?" asked his guest.

"Am I expecting anyone? I am ashamed even to tell whom I expect. I am, and I am not, expecting someone; but one word has kindled a fire in my heart. Whether it is a dream, or something else, I do not know. Don't you see, brother, I was reading yesterday the Gospel about Christ, the Batyushka; how He suffered, how He walked on the earth. I suppose you have heard about it?"

"Indeed I have," replied Stepanuitch, "but we are people in darkness, we can't read."

"Well, now, I was reading about that very thing,—how He walked on the earth; I read, you know, how He came to the Pharisee, and the Pharisee did not treat Him hospitably. Well, and so, my brother, I was reading yesterday, about this very thing, and was thinking to myself how he did not receive Christ, the Batyushka, with honor. Suppose, for example, He should come to me, or anyone else, I said to myself, I should not even know how to receive Him. And he gave Him no reception at all. Well! while I was thus thinking, I fell asleep, brother, and I heard someone call me by name. I got up; the voice, just as if someone whispered, said, 'Be on the watch; I shall come to-morrow.' And this happened twice. Well! would you believe it, it got into my head? I scolded myself—and yet I am expecting Him, the Batyushka."

Stepanuitch shook his head, and said nothing; he finished drinking his glass of tea, and put it on the side; but Avdyeitch picked up the glass again, and filled it once more.

"Drink some more for your good health. You see, I have an idea that, when the Batyushka went about this earth, He disdained no one, and had more to do with the simple people. He always went to see the simple people. He picked out His disciples more from among folk like such sinners as we are, from the working class. Said He, whoever exalts himself, shall be humbled and he who is humbled shall become exalted. Said He, you call me Lord, and, said He, I wash your feet. Whoever wishes, said He, to be the first, the same shall be a servant to all. Because, said He, blessed are the poor, the humble, the kind, the generous."

And Stepanuitch forgot about his tea; he was an old man, and easily moved to tears. He was listening, and the tears rolled down his face.

"Come, now, and have more tea," said Avdyeitch; but Stepanuitch made the sign of the cross, thanked him, turned down his glass, and arose.

"Thanks to you," he said, "Martuin Avdyeitch, for treating me kindly, and satisfying me, soul and body."

"You are welcome; come in again; always glad to see a friend," said Avdyeitch.

Stepanuitch departed; and Martuin poured out the rest of the tea, drank it up, put away the dishes, and sat down again by the window to work, to stitch on a patch. He kept stitching away, and at the same time looking through the window. He was expecting Christ, and was all the while thinking of Him and His deeds, and his head was filled with all the different speeches of Christ.

Two soldiers passed by; one wore boots furnished by the crown, and the other one, boots that he had made; then the master of the next house passed by in shining galoshes; then a baker with a basket passed by. All passed by; and now there came also by the window a woman in woolen stockings and rustic bashmaks on her feet. She passed by the window, and stood still near the window-case.

Avdyeitch looked at her from the window, and saw it was a stranger, a woman poorly clad, and with a child; she was standing by the wall with her back to the wind trying to wrap up the child, and she had nothing to wrap it up in. The woman was dressed in shabby summer clothes; and from behind the frame Avdyeitch could hear the child crying, and the woman trying to pacify it; but she was not able to pacify it.

Avdyeitch got up, went to the door, ascended the steps, and cried:—

"My good woman! Hey! my good woman!"

The woman heard him and turned around.

"Why are you standing in the cold with the child? Come into my room, where it is warm; you can manage it better. Here, this way!"

The woman was astonished. She saw an old, old man in his apron, with spectacles on his nose, calling her to him. She followed him. They descended the steps and entered the room; the old man led the woman to his bed.

"There," said he, "sit down, my good woman, nearer to the stove; you can get warm and nurse the little one."

"I have no milk for him. I myself have not eaten anything since morning," said the woman; but, nevertheless, she took the baby to her breast.

Avdyeitch shook his head, went to the table, brought out the bread and a dish, opened the oven door, poured into the dish some cabbage soup, took out the pot with the gruel, but it was not cooked as yet; so he filled the dish with shchi only, and put it on the table. He got the bread, took the towel down from the hook, and spread it upon the table.

"Sit down," he said, "and eat, my good woman; and I will mind the little one. You see, I once had children of my own; I know how to handle them."

The woman crossed herself, sat down at the table, and began to eat; while Avdyeitch took a seat on the bed near the infant. Avdyeitch kept smacking and smacking to it with his lips; but it was a poor kind of smacking, for he had no teeth. The little one kept on crying. And it occurred to Avdyeitch to threaten the little one with his finger; he waved his finger before the child's mouth, because his finger was black, and soiled with wax. And the little one looked at the finger, and became quiet; then it began to smile, and Avdyeitch also was glad. While the woman was eating, she told him who she was, and whither she was going.

Said she:—

"I am a soldier's wife. It is now seven months since they sent my husband away off, and no tidings. I lived out as a cook; the baby was born; no one cared to keep me with a child. This is the third month that I have been struggling along without a place. I ate up all I had. I wanted to engage as a wet-nurse—no one would take me—I am too thin, they say. I have just been to the merchant's wife, where lives a young woman I know, and so they promised to take us in. I thought that was the end of it. But she told me to come next week. And she lives a long way off. I got tired out; and it tired him, too, my heart's darling. Fortunately, our landlady takes pity on us for the sake of Christ, and gives us a room, else I don't know how I should manage to get along."

Avdyeitch sighed, and said:—

"Haven't you any warm clothes?"

"Now is the time, friend, to wear warm clothes; but yesterday I pawned my last shawl for a twenty-kopek piece."

The woman came to the bed, and took the child; and Avdyeitch rose, went to the partition, rummaged round, and succeeded in finding an old coat.

"Na!" said he; "It is a poor thing, yet you may turn it to some use."

The woman looked at the coat and looked at the old man; she took the coat, and burst into tears; and Avdyeitch turned away his head; crawling under the bed, he pushed out a little trunk, rummaged in it, and sat down again opposite the woman.

And the woman said:—

"May Christ bless you, little grandfather. He must have sent me to your window. My little baby would have frozen to death. When I started out it was warm, but now it has grown cold. And He, the Batyushka, led you to look through the window and take pity on me, an unfortunate."

Avdyeitch smiled, and said:—

"Indeed, He did that! I have been looking through the window, my good woman, for some wise reason."

And Martuin told the soldier's wife his dream, and how he had heard the voice,—how the Lord promised to come and see him that day.

"All things are possible," said the woman. She rose, put on the coat, wrapped up her little child in it; and as she started to take leave, she thanked Avdyeitch again.

"Take this, for Christ's sake," said Avdyeitch, giving her a twenty-kopek piece; "redeem your shawl."

The woman went away. Avdyeitch ate some shchi, washed the dishes, and sat down again to work. While he was working he still remembered the window; when the window grew darker he immediately looked out to see who was passing by. Acquaintances passed by and strangers passed by, and there was nothing out of the ordinary.

But here Avdyeitch saw an old apple woman had stopped in front of his window. She carried a basket of apples. Only a few were left, as she had evidently sold them nearly all out; and over her shoulder she carried a bag full of chips. She must have gathered them up in some new building, and was on her way home. One could see that the bag was heavy on her shoulder; she tried to shift it to the other shoulder. So she lowered the bag on the sidewalk, stood the basket with the apples on a little post, and began to shake down the splinters in the bag. And while she was shaking the bag, a little boy in a torn cap came along, picked up an apple from the basket, and was about to make his escape; but the old woman noticed it, turned around, and caught the youngster by his sleeve. The little boy began to struggle, tried to tear himself away; but the old woman grasped him with both hands, knocked off his cap, and caught him by the hair.

The little boy was screaming, the old woman was scolding. Avdyeitch lost no time in putting away his awl; he threw it upon the floor, sprang to the door,—he even stumbled on the stairs, and dropped his spectacles,—and rushed out into the street.

The old woman was pulling the youngster by his hair, and was scolding and threatening to take him to the policeman; the youngster was defending himself, and denying the charge.

"I did not take it," he said; "What are you licking me for? Let me go!"

Avdyeitch tried to separate them. He took the boy by his arm, and said:—

"Let him go, babushka; forgive him, for Christ's sake."

"I will forgive him so that he won't forget it till the new broom grows. I am going to take the little villain to the police."

Avdyeitch began to entreat the old woman:—

"Let him go, babushka," he said, "he will never do it again. Let him go, for Christ's sake."

The old woman let him loose; the boy started to run, but Avdyeitch kept him back.

"Ask the babushka's forgiveness," he said, "and don't you ever do it again; I saw you take the apple."

The boy burst into tears, and began to ask for forgiveness.

"There now! that's right; and here's an apple for you."

And Avdyeitch took an apple from the basket, and gave it to the boy.

"I will pay you for it, babushka," he said to the old woman.

"You ruin them that way, the good-for-nothings," said the old woman. "He ought to be treated so that he would remember it for a whole week."

"Eh, babushka, babushka," said Avdyeitch, "that is right according to our judgment, but not according to God's. If he is to be whipped for an apple, then what ought to be done to us for our sins?"

The old woman was silent.

And Avdyeitch told her of the parable of the master who forgave a debtor all that he owed him, and how the debtor went and began to choke one who owed him.

The old woman listened, and the boy stood listening.

"God has commanded us to forgive," said Avdyeitch, "else we, too, may not be forgiven. All should be forgiven, and the thoughtless especially."

The old woman shook her head, and sighed.

"That's so," said she; "but the trouble is that they are very much spoiled."

"Then we who are older must teach them," said Avdyeitch.

"That's just what I say," remarked the old woman. "I myself have had seven of them,—only one daughter is left."

And the old woman began to relate where and how she lived with her daughter, and how many grandchildren she had. "Here," she said, "my strength is only so-so, and yet I have to work. I pity the youngsters—my grandchildren—but what nice children they are!

No one gives me such a welcome as they do. Aksintka won't go to anyone but me. 'Babushka, dear babushka, loveliest'."

And the old woman grew quite sentimental.

"Of course, it is a childish trick. God be with him," said she, pointing to the boy.

The woman was just about to lift the bag on her shoulder, when the boy ran up and said:—

"Let me carry it, babushka; it is on my way."

The old woman nodded her head, and put the bag on the boy's back.

And side by side they passed along the street.

And the old woman even forgot to ask Avdyeitch to pay for the apple. Avdyeitch stood motionless, and kept gazing after them; and he heard them talking all the time as they walked away. After Avdyeitch saw them disappear, he returned to his room; he found his eye-glasses on the stairs,—they were not broken; he picked up his awl, and sat down to work again.

After working a little while, it grew darker, so that he could not see to sew; he saw the lamplighter passing by to light the street-lamps.

"It must be time to make a light," he said to himself; so he got his little lamp ready, hung it up, and betook himself again to his work. He had one boot already finished; he turned it around, looked at it; "Well done." He put away his tools, swept off the cuttings, cleared off the bristles and ends, took the lamp, set it on the table, and took down the Gospels from the shelf. He intended to open the book at the very place where he had yesterday put a piece of leather as a mark, but it happened to open at another place; and the moment Avdyeitch opened the Testament, he recollected his last night's dream. And as soon as he remembered, it seemed as if he heard someone stepping about behind him. Avdyeitch looked around and saw—there, in the dark corner, it seemed as if people were standing; he was at a loss to know who they were. And a voice whispered in his ear:—

"Martuin—ah, Martuin; did you not recognize me?"

"Who?" exclaimed Avdyeitch.

"Me," repeated the voice. "It was I; and Stepanuitch stepped forth from the dark corner; he smiled, and like a little cloud faded away, and soon vanished.

"And it was I," said the voice.

From the dark corner stepped the woman with her child; the woman smiled, the child laughed, and they also vanished.

"And it was I," continued the voice; both the old woman and the boy with the apple, stepped forward; both smiled and vanished.

(143)

Avdyeitch's soul rejoiced; he crossed himself, put on his spactacles, and began to read the Evangelists where it happened to open. On the upper part of the page he read:—

For I was an hungered, and ye gave me meat; I was thirsty, and ye gave me drink; I was a stranger, and ye took me in.

And on the lower part of the page he read this:—

Inasmuch as ye have done it unto one of the least of these my brethren, ye have done it unto me.—St. Matthew, Chapter xxv.

And Avdyeitch understood that his dream had not deceived him; that the Saviour really called on him that day, and that he really received Him.

TODAY

Mary F. Butts

Build a little fence of trust
Around Today,
Fill the space with loving work
And therein stay.
Look not through the sheltering bars
Upon Tomorrow;
God will help thee bear what comes
Of joy or sorrow.

STILL TO BE NEAT

Ben Jonson

Still to be neat, still to be drest
As you were going to a feast;
Still to be powder'd, still perfum'd:
Lady, it is to be presum'd,
Though art's hid causes are not found,
All is not sweet, all is not sound.

Give me a look, give me a face
That makes simplicity a grace;

Robes loosely flowing, hair as free:
Such sweet neglect more taketh me
Than all th' adulteries of art;
They strike mine eyes, but not my heart.

SHAKESPEARE

Ben Jonson

I remember the players have often mentioned it as an honor to
Shakespeare, that in his writing (whatsoever he penned) he never
blotted out a line. My answer hath been, "Would he had blotted a
thousand," which they thought a malevolent speech. I had not told
posterity this but for their ignorance who chose that circumstance to
commend their friend by wherein he most faulted; and to justify
mine own candor, for I loved the man, and do honor his memory on
this side of idolatry as much as any. He was, indeed, honest, and of
an open and free nature; had an excellent phantasy, brave notions,
and gentle expressions, wherein he flowed with that facility that
sometimes it was necessary he should be stopped. *"Sufflaminandus
enat,"* as Augustus said of Haterius. His wit was in his own power;
would the rule of it had been so, too! Many times he fell into those
things, could not escape laughter, as when he said in the person of
Caesar, one speaking to him, "Caesar, thou dost me wrong." He
replied, "Caesar never did wrong but with just cause"; and such like,
which were ridiculous. But he redeemed his vices with his virtues.
There was ever more in him to be praised than to be pardoned.

I HAVE SEEN A CURIOUS CHILD

William Wordsworth

I have seen
A curious child, who dwelt upon a tract
Of inland ground, applying to his ear
The convolutions of a smooth-lipped shell;
To which, in silence hushed, his very soul
Listened intensely; and his countenance soon

(145)

Brightened with joy; for from within were heard
Murmurings, whereby the monitor expressed
Mysterious union with its native sea.
Even such a shell the universe itself
Is to the ear of Faith; and there are times,
I doubt not, when to you it doth impart
Authentic tidings of invisible things;
Of ebb and flow, and ever-during power;
And central peace, subsisting at the heart
Of endless agitation.

(From The Excursion, Book Four)

MR. DOOLEY ON THE SUPREME COURT

Finley Peter Dunne

No matter whether th' constitution follows th' flag or not, th' supreme coort follows th' iliction returns.

THE PESSIMIST

Ben King

Nothing to do but work,
Nothing to eat but food,
Nothing to wear but clothes
To keep one from going nude.

Nothing to breathe but air,
Quick as a flash 'tis gone;
Nowhere to fall but off,
Nowhere to stand but on.

Nothing to comb but hair
Nowhere to sleep but in bed,
Nothing to weep but tears,
Nothing to bury but dead.

Nothing to sing but songs,
Ah, well, alas! alack!
Nowhere to go but out,
Nowhere to come but back.

Nothing to see but sights,
Nothing to quench but thirst,
Nothing to have but what we've got;
Thus thro' life we are cursed.

Nothing to strike but a gait;
Everything moves that goes.
Nothing at all but common sense
Can ever withstand these woes.

JESUS AND THE CHILDREN

Holy Bible, Mark 10:13–16

And they brought young children to him, that he should touch them: and his disciples rebuked those that brought them.

But when Jesus saw it, he was much displeased, and said unto them, Suffer the little children to come unto me, and forbid them not; for such is the kingdom of God.

Verily I say unto you, Whosoever shall not receive the kingdom of God as a little child, he shall not enter therein.

And he took them up in his arms, put his hands upon them, and blessed them.

THE PULLEY

George Herbert

When God at first made Man,
Having a glass of blessings standing by—
Let us (said He) pour on him all we can;
Let the world's riches, which dispersèd lie,
            Contract into a span.

So strength first made a way,
Then beauty flow'd, then wisdom, honour, pleasure:
When almost all was out, God made a stay,
Perceiving that, alone of all His treasure,
Rest in the bottom lay.

For if I should (said He)
Bestow this jewel also on My creature,
He would adore My gifts instead of Me,
And rest in Nature, not the God of Nature:
So both should losers be.

Yet let him keep the rest,
But keep them with repining restlessness;
Let him be rich and weary, that at least,
If goodness lead him not, yet weariness
May toss him to My breast.

ZEST FOR LIFE

William Allen White

I have never been bored an hour in my life. I get up every morning wondering what new strange glamorous thing is going to happen and it happens at fairly regular intervals. Lady Luck has been good to me and I fancy she has been good to every one. Only some people are dour, and when she gives them the come hither with her eyes, they look down or turn away and lift an eyebrow. But me, I give her the wink and away we go.

MAGNA EST VERITAS

Coventry Patmore

Here, in this little Bay,
Full of tumultuous life and great repose,
Where, twice a day,
The purposeless, glad ocean comes and goes,

Under high cliffs, and far from the huge town,
I sit me down.
For want of me the world's course will not fail:
When all its work is done, the lie shall rot;
The truth is great, and shall prevail,
When none cares whether it prevail or not.

I SOUGHT MY SOUL

Anonymous

I sought my soul,
   But my soul I could not see.
I sought my God,
   But my God eluded me.
I sought my brother,
   And I found all three.

BOY DEFINED

Anonymous

Nature's answer to that false belief that there is no such thing as
perpetual motion. A boy can swim like a fish, run like a deer, climb
like a squirrel, balk like a mule, bellow like a bull, eat like a pig, or
act like a jackass, according to climatic conditions. He is a piece of
skin stretched over an appetite; a noise covered with smudges. . . .
He is a growing animal of superlative promise, to be fed, watered,
and kept warm, a joy forever, a periodic nuisance, the problem of
our times, the hope of a nation. Every boy born is evidence that
God is not yet discouraged of man.

IN THE GARDEN*

C. Austin Miles

I come to the garden alone,
While the dew is still on the roses;
  And the voice I hear,
  Falling on my ear;
The Son of God discloses.

Chorus:
And He walks with me, and He talks with me
And He tells me I am His own,
  And the joy we share
  As we tarry there,
None other has ever known.

He speaks, and the sound of His voice
Is so sweet the birds hush their singing
  And the melody,
  That He gave to me;
Within my heart is ringing.

I'd stay in the garden with Him
Though the night around me be falling,
  But He bids me go;
  Through the voice of woe,
His voice to me is calling.

POLITICS DEFINED

Oscar Ameringer

    The art of obtaining money from the rich and votes from the poor, on the pretext of protecting each from the other.

ENJOYMENT OF THE WORLD

Thomas Traherne

You never enjoy the world aright, till the Sea itself floweth in your veins, till you are clothed with the heavens, and crowned with the stars; and perceive yourself to be the sole heir of the whole world, and more than so, because men are in it who are every one sole heirs as well as you. Till you can sing and rejoice and delight in God, as misers do in gold, and Kings in sceptres, you never enjoy the world.

Till your spirit filleth the whole world, and the stars are your jewels; till you are as familiar with the ways of God in all Ages as with your walk and table; till you are intimately acquainted with that shady nothing out of which the world was made: till you love men so as to desire their happiness, with a thirst equal to the zeal of your own; till you delight in God for being good to all: you never enjoy the world.

Till you remember how lately you were made, and how wonderful it was when you came into it; and more rejoice in the palace of your glory, than if it had been made but to-day morning.

THE NIGHT PIECE, TO JULIA

Robert Herrick

Her eyes the glow-worm lend thee;
The shooting stars attend thee;
   And the elves also,
   Whose little eyes glow
Like the sparks of fire, befriend thee.

No Will-o'-the-Wisp mislight thee,
Nor snake or slow-worm bite thee;
   But on, on thy way,
   Not making a stay,
Since ghosts there's none to affright thee.

Let not the dark thee cumber;
What though the moon does slumber?

The stars of the night
Will lend thee their light
Like tapers clear without number.

Then, Julia, let me woo thee,
Thus, thus to come unto me;
    And when I shall meet
    Thy silv'ry feet,
My soul I'll pour into thee.

A MAN TO THE UNIVERSE

Stephen Crane

A man said to the universe:
"Sir, I exist!"
"However," replied the universe,
"The fact has not created in me
A sense of obligation."

CAPTAIN AHAB'S MONOMANIA

Herman Melville

His three boats stove around him, and oars and men both whirling in the eddies; one captain, seizing the line-knife from his broken prow, had dashed at the whale, as an Arkansas duelist at his foe, blindly seeking with a six-inch blade to reach the fathom-deep life of the whale. That captain was Ahab. And then it was, that suddenly sweeping his sickle-shaped lower jaw beneath him, Moby Dick had reaped away at Ahab's leg, as a mower a blade of grass in the field. No turbaned Turk, no hired Venetian or Malay, could have smote him with more seeming malice. Small reason was there to doubt, then, that ever since that almost fatal encounter, Ahab had cherished a wild vindictiveness against the whale, all the more fell for that in his frantic morbidness he at last came to identify with him, not only all his bodily woes, but all his intellectual and spiritual exasperations. The White Whale swam before him as the monomaniac incarnation of all those malicious agencies which some deep men feel eating in them, till they are left living on with half a heart and half a lung. That intangible malignity which has been from the beginning; to whose dominion even the modern Christians ascribe one-half of the worlds; which the ancient Ophites of the east reverenced in their statue devils;—Ahab did not fall down and worship it like them; but deliriously transferring its idea to the abhorred White Whale, he pitted himself, all mutilated, against it. All that most maddens and torments; all that stirs up the lees of things; all truth with malice in it; all that cracks the sinews and cakes the brain; all the subtle demonisms of life and thought; all evil, to crazy Ahab, were visibly personified, and made practically assailable in Moby Dick. He piled upon the whale's white hump the sum of all the general rage and hate felt by his whole race from Adam down; and then, as if his chest had been a mortar, he burst his hot heart's shell upon it. . . .

When by this collision forced to turn towards home, and for long months of days and weeks, Ahab and anguish lay stretched together in one hammock, rounding in mid winter that dreary, howling Patagonian Cape; then it was, that his torn body and gashed soul bled into one another; and so interfusing, made him mad. That it was only then, on the homeward voyage, after the encounter, that the final monomania seized him, seems all but certain from the fact that, at intervals during the passage, he was a raving lunatic; and, though unlimbed of a leg, yet such vital strength yet lurked in his Egyptian chest, and was moreover intensified by his delirium, that his mates were forced to lace him fast, even there, as he sailed, raving in his hammock. In a strait-jacket, he swung to the mad rockings of the gales. And, when running into the more sufferable latitudes, the ship, with mild stun'sails spread, floated across the tranquil tropics, and, to all appearances, the old man's delirium seemed left behind with the Cape Horn swells, and he came forth from his dark den into the blessed light and air even then, when he bore that firm collected front, however pale, and issued his calm orders once again; and his mates thanked God the direful madness was now gone; even then, Ahab, in his hidden self, raved on. . . . Not one jot of Ahab's broad madness had been left behind; so in that broad madness, not one jot of his great natural intellect had perished. That before living agent, now became the living instrument. If such a furious trope may stand, his special lunacy stormed his general sanity, and carried it, and turned all its concentrated cannon upon its own mad mark; so that far from having lost his strength, Ahab, to that one end, did now possess a thousand fold more potency than ever he had sanely brought to bear upon any one reasonable object. . . .

Now, in his heart, Ahab had some glimpses of this, namely: all my means are sane, my motive and object mad. . . . Nevertheless, so well did he succeed in that dissembling, that when with his ivory leg he stepped ashore at last, no Nantucketer thought him otherwise than but naturally grieved, and that to the quick, with the terrible casualty which had overtaken him.

The report of his undeniable delirium at sea was likewise popularly ascribed to a kindred cause. And so too, all the added moodiness which always afterwards, to the very day of sailing in the Pequod on the present voyage, sat brooding on his brow. Nor is it so very unlikely, that far from distrusting his fitness for another whaling voyage, on account of such dark symptoms, the calculating people of that prudent isle were inclined to harbor the conceit, that for those very reasons he was all the better qualified and set on edge, for a pursuit so full of rage and wildness as the bloody hunt of whales. Gnawed within and scorched without, with the infixed, unrelenting fangs of some incurable idea; such an one, could he be found, would seem the very man to dart his iron and lift his lance against the most appalling of all brutes. . . . Be all this as it may, certain it is, that with the mad secret of his unabated rage bolted up and keyed in him, Ahab had purposely sailed upon the present voyage with the one only and all-engrossing purpose of hunting the White Whale. Had any one of his old acquaintances on shore but half dreamed of what was lurking in him then, how soon would their aghast and righteous souls have wrenched the ship from such a fiendish man! They were bent on profitable cruises, the profit to be counted down in dollars from the mint. He was intent on an audacious, immitigable, and supernatural revenge.

Here, then, was this grey-headed, ungodly old man, chasing with curses a Job's whale round the world, at the head of a crew, too, chiefly made up of mongrel renegades, and castaways, and cannibals —morally enfeebled also, by the incompetence of mere unaided virtue or right-mindedness in Starbuck, the invulnerable jollity of indifference and recklessness in Stubb, and the pervading mediocrity in Flask. Such a crew, so officered, seemed specially picked and packed by some infernal fatality to help him to his monomaniac revenge. How it was that they so aboundingly responded to the old man's ire—by what evil magic their souls were possessed, that at times his hate seemed almost theirs; the White Whale as much their insufferable foe as his; how all this came to me—what the White Whale was to them, or how to their unconscious understandings,

also, in some dim, unsuspected way, he might have seemed the gliding great demon of the seas of life,—all this to explain, would be to
dive deeper than Ishmael can go.

(From *Moby Dick*, 1851)

THE VELVET HAND

Phyllis McGinley

I call that parent rash and wild
Who'd reason with a six-year child,
Believing little twigs are bent
By calm, considered argument.

In bandying words with progeny,
There's no percentage I can see,
And people who, imprudent, do so,
Will wonder how their troubles grew so.

Now underneath this tranquil roof
Where sounder theories have their proof,
Our life is sweet, our infants happy.
In quietude dwell Mammy and Pappy.

We've sworn a stern, parental vow
That argument we won't allow.
Brooking no juvenile excess here,
We say a simple No or Yes, here,
And then, when childish wails begin

We don't debate.
We just give in.

THE VICAR OF BRAY

Thomas Fuller, in his *Worthies of England* (1662), tells the story
of the legendary Vicar of Bray, in Berkshire county, during the reigns
of Henry VIII, Edward VI, Queen Mary, and Queen Elizabeth.

This particular Vicar adroitly adjusted his religious loyalties to those of the reigning monarch, as a consequence of which he was first a Catholic, then a Protestant, again a Catholic, and finally a Protestant.

When charged with being a chronic turncoat, an unconstant changeling, and a man without principle, the Vicar replied: "Not so. I have always kept my principle, which is to live and die the Vicar of Bray."

ISABELLA CONDEMNS TYRANNY

William Shakespeare

O, it is excellent
To have a giant's strength; but it is tyrannous
To use it like a giant. . . .
Could great men thunder
As Jove himself does, Jove would ne'er be quiet,
For every pelting, petty officer
Would use his heaven for thunder.
Nothing but thunder! Merciful Heaven,
Thou rather with thy sharp and sulphurous bolt
Split'st the unwedgeable and gnarled oak
Than the soft myrtle; but man, proud man,
Drest in a little brief authority,
Most ignorant of what he's most assured,
His glassy essence, like an angry ape,
Plays such fantastic tricks before high heaven
As make the angels weep; who, with our spleens,
Would all themselves laugh mortal.

(From *Measure for Measure*)

PRIDE, THE NEVER-FAILING VICE OF FOOLS

Alexander Pope

Of all the Causes which conspire to blind
Man's erring judgment, and misguide the mind,
What the weak head with strongest bias rules,
Is *Pride*, the never-failing vice of fools.

Whatever nature has in worth denied,
She gives in large recruits of needful pride;
For as in bodies, thus in souls, we find
What wants in blood and spirits, swell'd with wind:
Pride, where wit fails, steps into our defense,
And fill up all the mighty Void of sense.
If once right reason drives that cloud away,
Truth breaks upon us with resistless day.
Trust not yourself; but your defects to know,
Make use of ev'ry friend—and ev'ry foe.

(From *Essay on Criticism*)

RESOLUTION

Abraham Lincoln

I am not bound to win, but I am bound to be true. I am not bound to succeed but I am bound to live up to what light I have. I must stand with anybody that stands right: stand with him while he is right and part with him when he goes wrong.

ALADDIN

James Russell Lowell

When I was a beggarly boy,
  And lived in a cellar damp,
I had not a friend nor a toy,
  But I had Aladdin's lamp;
When I could not sleep for the cold,
  I had fire enough in my brain,
And builded, with roofs of gold,
  My beautiful castles in Spain!

Since then I have toiled day and night,
  I have money and power good store,
But I'd give all my lamps of silver bright
  For the one that is mine no more.

(157)

Take, Fortune, whatever you choose;
You gave, and may snatch again;
I have nothing 'twould pain me to lose,
For I own no more castles in Spain!

DUTY

Robert Louis Stevenson

There is an idea abroad among moral people that they should make their neighbors good. One person I have to make good: myself. But my duty to my neighbor is much more nearly expressed by saying that I have to make him happy—if I may.

A BAG OF TOOLS

R. L. Sharpe

Isn't it strange
That princes and kings,
And clowns that caper
In sawdust rings,
And common people
Like you and me
Are builders for eternity?

Each is given a bag of tools,
A shapeless mass,
A book of rules;
And each must make—
Ere life has flown—
A stumbling block
Or a steppingstone.

OBEDIENCE

George Macdonald

I said, "Let me walk in the fields."
  He said, "No, walk in the town."
I said, "There are no flowers there."
  He said, "No flowers, but a crown."

I said, "But the skies are black;
  There is nothing but noise and din."
And He wept as he sent me back;
  "There is more," He said; "there is sin."

I said, "But the air is thick,
  And fogs are veiling the sun."
He answered, "Yet souls are sick,
  And souls in the dark undone."

I said, "I shall miss the light,
  And friends will miss me, they say."
He answered, "Choose to-night,
  If *I* am to miss you, or they."

I pleaded for time to be given.
  He said, "Is it hard to decide?
It will not seem hard in heaven
  To have followed the steps of your Guide."

I cast one look at the fields,
  Then set my face to the town;
He said, "My child, do you yield?
  Will you leave the flowers for the crown?"

Then into His hand went mine,
  And into my heart came He;
And I walk in a light divine
  The path I had feared to see.

DAY DEFINED

Lewis Carroll

The day is the same length of time
as anything that is the same length
as *it*.

THE GREAT COMMANDMENT

Holy Bible, Matthew 22:34–40

But when the Pharisees had heard that he had put the Sadducees
to silence, they were gathered together.

Then one of them, which was a lawyer, asked him a question,
tempting him, and saying,

Master, which is the great commandment in the law?

Jesus said unto him, Thou shalt love the Lord thy God with all
thy heart, and with all thy soul, and with all thy mind.

This is the first and great commandment.

And the second is like unto it. Thou shalt love thy neighbor
as thyself.

On these two commandments hang all the law and the prophets.

MY LIFE CLOSED TWICE

Emily Dickinson

My life closed twice before its close;
It yet remains to see
If Immortality unveil
A third event to me,

So huge, so hopeless to conceive,
   As these that twice befell:
Parting is all we know of heaven,
   And all we need of hell.

WORDS FROM THE FIRST MEN ON THE MOON, NEIL A. ARMSTRONG AND EDWIN A. ALDRIN, JR., AND MICHAEL COLLINS, WHO REMAINED IN THE COMMAND SPACESHIP COLUMBIA

HOUSTON [The Mission Control center] (4 P.M.): *Eagle* [the lunar landing craft, undocked from the command ship *Columbia*], you are go for powered descent. Over. . . .

HOUSTON: Coming up one minute to ignition.

EAGLE (4:05 P.M.): Altitude about 46,000 feet, continuing to descend. Ignition about ten per cent.

HOUSTON: *Eagle*, everything's looking good here. Over. . . .

HOUSTON: We're still go. Altitude 27,000 feet.

EAGLE: Bravo on time. Throttle down better than the simulator.

HOUSTON: Roger. Altitude now 21,000 feet still looking very good. Velocity down now to 1,200 feet per second. You look great to us, *Eagle*. . . .

HOUSTON (4:12 P.M.): Seven minutes 30 seconds into the burn. Altitude 16,300 feet.

HOUSTON: We're go. Altitude 9,200 feet. You're looking great. Descent rate 129 feet per second. *Eagle*, you're looking great, coming up on nine minutes.

HOUSTON: We're now in the approach phase. Everything looking good. Altitude 5,200 feet.

EAGLE: Manual control is good.

HOUSTON: Altitude 4,200 feet. You are go for landing. Over.

EAGLE: Roger go for landing, 3,000 feet. We're go. We're go. Two thousand feet. Into the AGS 47 degrees.

HOUSTON: Roger.

HOUSTON: *Eagle*, looking great. You're go. Altitude 1,600 feet . . . 1,400 feet, still looking very good.

EAGLE: 35 degrees. 35 degrees. 750 coming down to 23; 700 feet 21 down, 33 degrees; 600 feet down to 19; 540 down to 15; 400 feet down at 9 three forward; 350 feet down at 4; 300 feet down 3½; 47 forward; on one a minute 1½ down; 270 . . . 50 down at 2½; 19 forward. Altitude velocity lights down 15 forward, 11 forward; 200 feet 4½ down 5½ down 6½ down, 5½ down, nine forward; 120 feet 100 feet 3½ down, nine forward, 5 per cent 75 feet looking good down ½, six forward.

HOUSTON: Sixty seconds.

EAGLE: Lights on; down 2½. Forward, forward 40 feet down 2½ picking up some dust; 30 feet 2½ down shadow, four forward, four forward, drifting to the right a little.

HOUSTON: Thirty seconds.

EAGLE: Contact light. Okay, engines stop. Engine arm off.

HOUSTON: We copy. You're down, Eagle.

EAGLE: Houston. Tranquillity Base here. The *Eagle* has landed. . . .

HOUSTON: Roger, Tranquillity, we copy you on the ground. You've got a bunch of guys about to turn blue. We're breathing again. Thanks a lot.

TRANQUILLITY BASE: Thank you.

HOUSTON: You're looking good here.

TRANQUILLITY BASE: A very smooth touchdown.

HOUSTON: You are stay for TL [the first step in the lunar operation]. Over.

TRANQUILLITY BASE: Roger. Stay for TL. . . .

COLUMBIA [The command spacecraft]: How do you read me?

HOUSTON: *Columbia*, he has landed Tranquillity Base. *Eagle* is at Tranquillity. I read you five by. Over.

COLUMBIA: Yes, I heard the whole thing.

HOUSTON: Well, it's a good show.

COLUMBIA: Fantastic.

TRANQUILLITY BASE: I'll second that. . . .

HOUSTON: We have an unofficial time for that touchdown of 102 hours, 45 minutes, 42 seconds and we will update that. . . .

TRANQUILLITY BASE: Houston, that may have seemed like a very long final phase but the auto targeting was taking us right into a football field-sized crater with a large number of big boulders and rocks for about one or two craters diameter around it and it required us to fly manually over the rock field to find a reasonably good area.

HOUSTON: We copy. It was beautiful from here, Tranquillity. Over.

TRANQUILLITY BASE: We'll get to the details of what's around here, but it looks like a collection of just about every shape, angularity, granularity, about every variety of rock you could find. The colors are pretty much depending on how you are looking relative to the zero phase length. There doesn't appear to be too much of a general color at all. However, it looks as though some of the rocks and boulders, of which there are quite a few in the near area—it looks as though they're going to have some interesting colors to them. Over. . . .

HOUSTON: Roger. Tranquillity. Be advised there are lots of smiling faces in this room and all over the world. Over. . . .

TRANQUILLITY BASE: Thank you, Houston, the guys that bet that we wouldn't be able to tell precisely where we are are the winners today. We were a little busy worrying about program alarms and things like that in the part of the descent where we would normally be picking out our landing spot; and aside from a good look at several of the craters we came over in the final descent, I haven't been able to pick out the things on the horizon as a reference yet.

HOUSTON: Rog, Tranquillity. No sweat. We'll figure out—we'll figure out. Over.

TRANQUILLITY BASE: You might be interested to know that I don't think we noticed any difficulty at all in adapting to one-sixth G. It seems immediately natural to live in this environment. ... [Unintelligible] ... window, with relatively level plain cratered with a large number of craters of the 5-to-50-foot variety. And some ridges small, 20 to 30 feet high, I would guess. And literally thousands of little ones—and two-foot craters around the area. We see some angular blocks out several hundred feet in front of us that are probably two feet in size and have angular edges. There is a hill in view just about on the ground track ahead of us. Difficult to estimate, but might be a half a mile or a mile . . . I'd say the color of the local surface is very comparable to that we observed from orbit at this sun angle—about 10 degrees sun angle or that nature. It's pretty much without color. It's gray and it's very white as you look into the zero phase line. And it's considerably darker grey, more like an ashen grey, as you look out 90 degrees to the sun. Some of the surface rocks in close here that have been fractured or disturbed by the rocket engine plume are coated with this light gray on the outside. But where they have been broken, they display a dark, very dark, gray interior and it looks like it could be country basalt. . . . From the surface we could not see any stars out the window, but on my overhead patch I'm looking at the earth. It's big and bright, beautiful. Buzz [Aldrin] is going to give a try at seeing some stars through the optics. . . .

HOUSTON: We have some heart rates for Neil Armstrong [in command of the craft that landed on the moon] during that powered descent to lunar surface. At the time the burn was initiated, Armstrong's heart rate was 110. At touchdown on the lunar surface, he had a heart rate of 156 beats per minute, and the flight surgeon reports that his heart rate is now in the 90's. We do not have biomedical data on Buzz Aldrin. We have an up date on that touchdown time . . . 102 hours, 45 minutes, 40 seconds, which would have been 12 minutes, 36 seconds after initiating the powered descent. . . . . . It appears that the spacecraft *Eagle* touched down at 799 degrees north, or just about on the lunar equator, and 23.46 degrees east longitude, which would have put it about four miles from the targeted landing point downrange. . . .

TRANQUILLITY BASE: This is the LM pilot [Buzz Aldrin]. I'd like to take this opportunity to ask every person listening in, whoever, wherever they may be, to pause for a moment and contemplate the events of the past few hours and to give thanks in his or her own way. Over. . . .

HOUSTON: We have an interesting phenomena here in the Mission Control Center, Houston, something we've never seen before. Our visual of the lunar module—our visual display of the lunar module—our visual display standing still, our velocity digitals for our Tranquillity Base now reading zero. Reverting, if we could, to the terminology of an earlier form of transportation—the railroad —what we're witnessing now is man's very first trip into space with a station-stop along the route. . . .

TRANQUILLITY BASE: I think we'll be ready to start EVA [Extra Vehicular Activity—walking on the moon] in about a half hour or so. We are beginning our EVA prep. . . .

TRANQUILLITY BASE (9:45 P.M.): Houston, Tranquillity. You'll find that the area around the ladder is in a complete dark shadow, so we're going to have some problem with TV. But I'm sure you'll see the—you'll get a picture from the lighted horizon. . . . Neil's got his antenna up now. Let's see if he comes through any better now. Okay, Houston, this is Neil [Armstrong]. How do you read?

HOUSTON: Neil, this is Houston, reading you beautifully. . . .

TRANQUILLITY BASE: Houston, this is Tranquillity. We're standing by for a cabin depress.

HOUSTON: You are go for cabin depressureization. . . .

TRANQUILLITY BASE: Okay, the vent window is clear. I remove lever from the engine cover. . . . Lock system, decks, exit check, blue locks are checked, lock locks, red locks, perch locks, and on this side the perch locks and lock locks—both sides, body locks, and the calm. . . .

HOUSTON: In the control center a clock has been set up to record the operating time on Neil's life support system. EVA will be counted from that time.

TRANQUILLITY BASE: Cabin repress closed. Now come the gymnastics. Air pressure going toward zero. Standby LM suit circuit 36 to 43. That's verified. FIT GA pressure about 4.5, 4.75 and coming down. We'll open the hatch when we get to zero. Do you want to bring down one of your visors now or leave them up? We can put them down if we need them. We have visor down.

HOUSTON (10:33 P.M.): Coming up on five minutes of operation of Neil Armstrong's portable life support system now. (10:37 P.M. Neil, this is Houston, what's your status on hatch opening?
TRANQUILLITY BASE: Everything is go here. We're just waiting for the cabin pressure to bleed to a low enough pressure to open the hatch. It's about .1 on our gauge now. I'd hate to tug on that thing. Alternative would be to open that one too.
HOUSTON: We're seeing a relatively static pressure on your cabin. Do you think you can open the hatch at this pressure?
TRANQUILLITY BASE: We're going to try it. The hatch is coming open. [Aldrin] Hold it from going closed and I'll get the valve turner. I'd better get up first.
ALDRIN: Your window cleared yet?
ARMSTRONG: It was, yeah.
ALDRIN: Mine hasn't cleared yet.
[The following is a conversation between Armstrong and Aldrin:] Bical pump secondary circuit breaker open. Back to lean—this way. Radar circuit breakers open. Well, I'm looking head-on at it. I'll get it. Okay. My antenna's out. Right. Okay, now we're ready to hook up the LEC. Okay. Now we need to hook this. Your visor. Yep. Your back is up against the perch. Now you're clear. Over toward me. Straight down, to your left a little bit. Plenty of room. You're lined up nicely.
     Toward me a little bit. Down. Okay. Now you're clear. You're catching the first hinge. The what hinge? All right, move. Roll to your left. Okay, now you're clear. You're lined up on the platform. Put your left foot to the right a little bit. Okay that's good. More left. Good.
ARMSTRONG: Okay, Houston, I'm on the porch. . . .
ALDRIN: Halt where you are a minute, Neil.
ARMSTRONG AND ALDRIN: Okay. Everything's nice and straight in here. Okay. can you pull the door open a little more? Right.
HOUSTON: We're getting a picture on TV.
ALDRIN: You've got a good picture, huh?
HOUSTON: There's a great deal of contrast in it and currently it's upside down on monitor. But we can make out a fair amount of detail.
ARMSTRONG: Okay, will you verify the position, the opening I ought to have on the camera.
HOUSTON: The what? We can see you coming down the ladder now.
ARMSTRONG: Okay. I just checked getting back up to that first

(165)

step. It didn't collapse too far. But it's adequate to get back up. It's a pretty good little jump. I'm at the foot of the ladder. The LM foot beds are only depressed in the surface about one or two inches, although the surface appears to be very, very fine-grained as you get close to it. It's almost like a powder. It's very fine. I'm going to step off the LM now.

That's one small step for a man, one giant leap for mankind.

The surface is fine and powdery. I can pick it up loosely with my toe. It does adhere in fine layers like powdered charcoal to the sole and sides of my boots. I only go in a small fraction of an inch, maybe an eighth of an inch but I can see the footprints of my boots and the treads in the fine sandy particles.

There seems to be no difficulty in moving around this and we suspect that it's even perhaps easier than the simulations of 1/6 G that we performed in various simulations on the ground. Actually no trouble to walk around.

The descent engine did not leave a crater of any size. It has about one foot clearance on the ground. We're essentially on a very level place here. I can see some evidence of rays emanating from the descent engine, but a very insignificant amount.

Okay, Buzz, are we ready to bring down the camera?

ALDRIN: I'm all ready. I think it's squared away and in good shape. But you'll have to play out all the LEC. Looks like it's coming out nice and evenly.

It's quite dark here in the shadow and a little hard for me to see if I have a good footing. I'll work my way over into the sunlight here without looking directly into the sun.

ARMSTRONG: Looking up at the LM, I'm standing directly in the shadow now looking up at . . . in the windows I can see everything quite clearly. The light is sufficiently bright backlighted into the front of the LM that everything is clearly visible.

I'll step out and take some of my first pictures here.

ALDRIN: Are you going to get the contingency sample [from moon's surface]? Okay. That's good.

ARMSTRONG: The contingency sample is down and it's up. Like it's a little difficult to dig through the crust. It's very interesting. It's a very soft surface but here and there where I plug with the contingency sample collector I run into very hard surface but it appears to be very cohesive material of the same sort. I'll try to get a rock in here.

HOUSTON: Oh, that looks beautiful from here, Neil.

ARMSTRONG: It has a stark beauty all its own. It's like much of the high desert of the United States. It's different but it's very pretty out here. Be advised that a lot of the rock samples out here, the hard rock samples have what appears to be vesicles on the surface. This has been about six or eight inches into the surface. It's easy to push on it. I'm sure I could push it in farther, but it's hard for me to bend down farther than that.

ALDRIN: Ready for me to come out?

ARMSTRONG: Yeah. Just stand by for a second, I'll move this over the handrail.

ALDRIN: Okay?

ARMSTRONG: All right, that's got it. Are you ready?

ALDRIN: All set. . . .

ALDRIN: How far are my feet from the . . .

ARMSTRONG: You're right at the edge of the porch.

ALDRIN: Small little foot movement. Porch. Arching of the back . . . without any trouble at all. Now I want to back up and partially close the hatch—making sure not to lock it on my way out.

ARMSTRONG: Good thought.

ALDRIN: That's our home for the next couple of hours; we want to take care of it. I'm on the top step. It's a very simple matter to hop down from one step to the next.

ARMSTRONG: Yes, I found that to be very comfortable, and walking is also very comfortable, Houston. You've got three more steps and then a long one.

ALDRIN: I'm going to leave that one foot up there and both hands down to about the fourth rung up.

ARMSTRONG: A little more. About one inch. There you got it. That's a good step.

ALDRIN: About a three footer. Beautiful view.

ARMSTRONG: Ain't that somethin'? . . .

HOUSTON (1:37 P.M.): You're cleared for take-off.

TRANQUILLITY BASE: Roger. Understand. We're No. 1 on the runway.

HOUSTON (1:38 P.M.): We have confirmation on the ground that the ascent propulsion system propellant has been pressurized. . . .

TRANQUILLITY BASE: Okay. I assume we're go for lift-off and will proceed with the ascent feeds.

HOUSTON (1:44 P.M.): A little less than ten minutes here. Everything looks good. (1:50 P.M.) *Eagle*, you're looking good to us. We'll continue to monitor now at 3 minutes 12 seconds away from ignition as crew of Eagle goes through their pre-launch checklist. Guidance reports both navigation systems on *Eagle* are looking good.

TRANQUILLITY BASE: Nine, eight, seven, six, five, first stage engine on ascent. Proceed. Beautiful. 26, 36 feet per second up.

(167)

Little pitch over, very smooth, very quiet ride. There's that one crater down there.

HOUSTON (1:54 P.M.): A thousand feet high, 80 feet per second vertical rise. Twenty-six hundred feet altitude. *Eagle*, Houston. One minute and you're looking good. A hundred thirty feet vertical rise rate.

EAGLE: A little bit of slow wallowing back and forth. Not very much thruster activity.

HOUSTON: Mighty fine. *Eagle*, you're go at three minutes. Everything's looking good.

EAGLE: Right. This is . . . This is H dot max now. Right down U.S. 1.

HOUSTON: Height's now approaching 32,000 feet. *Eagle*, four minutes. You're going right down the track. Everything is great.

EAGLE: Horizontal velocity approaching 2,500 feet per second. We've got Sabine now to our right now.

HOUSTON: Some 120 miles to go until insertion [with command ship *Columbia*]. . . .

EAGLE: *Eagle* is back in orbit, having left Tranquillity Base, and leaving behind a replica from our Apollo patch with an olive branch.

HOUSTON: Roger. We copy. The whole world is proud of you. (3:26 P.M.) Less than a minute away from acquisition of the spacecraft *Columbia* coming around on the near side of the moon, on the 26th revolution. Some three minutes, 11 seconds away from *Eagle*'s appearance on the lunar frontside. We have AOS [Acquisition of Signal] of the spacecraft *Columbia*. Range between *Eagle* and *Columbia* now showing 67.5 nautical miles, Range rate—closure rate—121 feet per second. . . .

EAGLE (4:31 P.M.): Mike [Collins in *Columbia*], if you want our target delta V, I'll give it to you.

COLUMBIA: Ready to copy.

EAGLE: 127 03 3082 plus 22.7 plus 1.1, minus 10.6.

HOUSTON (5:23 P.M.): Less than a minute away from acquisition of the spacecraft *Columbia*. Hopefully flying within a few feet of it will be *Eagle*. Docking should take place about ten minutes from now according to the flight plan. However, this is a crew-option matter. . . .

EAGLE (5:27 P.M.): Okay, Mike. I'll try to get positioned here. Then you got it.

COLUMBIA: How did the roll attitude look? I'll stop. As a matter of fact, I could stop right here, if you like that.

EAGLE (5:30 P.M.): I'm not going to do a thing, Mike. I'm just letting her hold in attitude.
EAGLE (5:36 P.M.): We're all yours, *Columbia*.
COLUMBIA: Okay. . . .
HOUSTON (7:20 P.M.): Hello *Eagle*, Houston. Do you read?
COLUMBIA: Read you loud and clear. We're all three back inside. The hatch is installed. We're ready to . . . Everything's going well.

> (July 21 and 22, 1969)
> (*The historic voyage to the moon terminated with a successful splashdown in the Pacific Ocean on July 24 at 12:50 P.M., Eastern daylight time, 950 miles southwest of Hawaii, and 11 miles from the prime recovery ship, the U.S. aircraft carrier Hornet.*)

YOUR FRIEND

Anonymous

If your friend has got a heart,
There is something fine in him;
Cast away his darkest part,—
Cling to what's divine in him.

EPILOGUE TO *ASOLANDO*

Robert Browning

At the midnight in the silence at sleep-time,
    When you set your fancies free,
Will they pass to where—by death, fools think, imprisoned—
Low he lies who once so loved you, whom you loved so,
        —Pity me?

(169)

O to love so, be so loved, yet so mistaken!
    What had I on earth to do
With the slothful, with the mawkish, the unmanly?
        —Being—who?

One who never turned his back but marched breast forward,
    Never doubted clouds would break,
Never dreamed, though right were worsted, wrong would
        triumph,
Held we fall to rise, are baffled to fight better,
        Sleep to wake.
No, at noonday in the bustle of man's work-time
    Greet the unseen with a cheer!
Bid him forward, breast and back as either should be,
"Strive and thrive!" cry "Speed,—fight on, fare ever
        There as here!"

FRIENDS

George W. Childs

Do not keep the alabaster box of your love and tenderness sealed up until your friends are dead. Fill their lives with sweetness. Speak approving, cheering words while their ears can hear them, and while their hearts can be thrilled and made happier. The kind things you mean to say when they are gone, say before they go. The flowers you mean to send for their coffin, send to brighten and sweeten their homes before they leave them. If my friends have alabaster boxes laid away, full of fragrant perfumes of sympathy and affection, which they intend to break over my body, I would rather they would bring them out in my weary and troubled hours and open them, that I may be refreshed and cheered while I need them. I would rather have a plain coffin without flowers, a funeral without a eulogy, than a life without the sweetness and love emanating from sympathy. Let us learn to anoint our friends while they are yet among the living. Post-mortem kindness does not cheer the burdened heart; flowers on the coffin cast no fragrance backward over the weary way.

YOUTH

Samuel Ullman

Youth is not a time of life; it is a state of mind, it is not a matter of rosy cheeks, red lips and supple knees; it is a matter of the will, a quality of the imagination, a vigor of the emotions; it is the freshness of the deep springs of life.

Youth means the temperamental predominance of courage over timidity of the appetite, for adventure over the love of ease. This often exists in a man of sixty more than a boy of twenty. Nobody grows old merely by a number of years. We grow old by deserting our ideals.

Years may wrinkle the skin, but to give up enthusiasm wrinkles the soul. Worry, fear, self-distrust bows the heart and turns the spirit back to dust.

Whether sixty or sixteen, there is in every human being's heart the lure of wonder, the unfailing child-like appetite of what's next, and the joy of the game of living. In the center of your heart and my heart there is a wireless station; so long as it receives messages of beauty, hope, cheer, courage and power from men and from the Infinite, so long are you young.

When the aerials are down, and your spirit is covered with snows of cynicism and the ice of pessimism, then you are grown old, even at twenty, but as long as your aerials are up, to catch waves of optimism, there is hope you may die young at eighty.

THE PLACE OF PEACE

Edwin Markham

At the heart of the cyclone tearing the sky
And flinging the clouds and towers by,
　　Is a place of central calm;
So here in the roar of mortal things,
I have a place where my spirit sings,
　　In the hollow of God's Palm.

(171)

THE TREASURER'S REPORT

Robert Benchley

*The report is delivered by an Assistant Treasurer who has been
called in to pinch-hit for the regular Treasurer, who is ill. He is not
a very good public-speaker, but after a few minutes of confusion is
caught up by the spell of his own oratory and is hard to stop.*

I shall take but a very few moments of your time this evening,
for I realize that you would much rather be listening to this interesting entertainment than to a dry financial statement . . . but I am
reminded of a story—which you have probably all of you heard.

It seems that there were two Irishmen walking down the street
when they came to a—oh, I should have said in the first place that
the parrot which was hanging out in front of the store—or rather
belonging to one of these two fellows—the first Irishman, that is—
we—well, anyway, this parrot.—

*(After a slight cogitation, he realizes that, for all practical purpose,
the story is as good as lost; so he abandons it entirely and, stepping
forward, drops his facile, story-telling manner and assumes a quite
spurious businesslike air.)*

Now, in connection with reading this report, there are one or
two points which Dr. Murnie wanted brought up in connection
with it, and he asked me to bring them up in connec—to bring
them up.

In the first place, there is the question of the work which we are
trying to do up there at our little place at Silver Lake, a work which
we feel not only fills a very definite need in the community but also
fills a very definite need—er—in the community. I don't think that
many members of the Society realize just how big the work is that
we are trying to do up there. For instance, I don't think that it is
generally known that most of our boys are between the age of
fourteen. We feel that, by taking the boy at this age, we can get
closer to his real nature—for a boy has a very real nature, you may
be sure—and bring him into closer touch not only with the school,
the parents, and with each other, but also the town in which they
live, the country to whose flag they pay allegiance, and to the—
ah— (trailing off) town in which they live.

Now the fourth point which Dr. Murnie wanted brought up was
that in connection with the installation of the new furnace last Fall.
There seems to have been considerable talk going around about this

not having been done quite as economically as it might—have—been
—done, when, as a matter of fact, the whole thing was done just as
economically as possible—in fact, even more so. I have here a report
of the Furnace Committee, showing just how the whole thing was
handled from start to finish.

(*Reads from report, with considerable initial difficulty with the
stiff cover.*)

Bids were submitted by the following firms of furnace contractors,
with a clause stating that if we did not engage a firm to do the work
for us we should pay them nothing for submitting the bids. This
clause alone saved us a great deal of money.

The following firms, then, submitted bids:

Merkle, Wybigant Co., the Eureka Dust Bin and Shaker Co.,
the Elite Furnace Shop, and Harris, Birnbauer and Harris. The bid
of Merkle, Wybignant being the lowest, Harris, Birnbauer were
selected to do the job.

(*Here a page is evidently missing from the report, and a hurried
search is carried on through all the pages, without result.*)

Well, that pretty well clears up that end of the work.

Those of you who contributed so generously last year to the
floating hospital have probably wondered what became of the money.

I was speaking on this subject only last week at our up-town
branch, and, after the meeting, a dear little old lady, dressed all in
lavender, came up on the platform, and laying her hand on my arm,
said: "Mr. So-and-so (calling me by name), Mr. So-and-so, what the
hell did you do with all the money we gave you last year?" Well,
I just laughed and pushed her off the platform, but it has occurred
to the committee that perhaps some of you, like that little old lady,
would be interested in knowing the disposition of the funds.

Now, Mr. Rossiter, unfortunately our treasurer—or rather Mr.
Rossiter our *treasurer, unfortunately* is confined at his home tonight
with a bad head-cold and I have been asked (*he hears someone
whispering at him from the wings, but decides to ignore it*) and I
have been asked if I would (*the whisperer will not be denied, so he
goes over to the entrance and receives a brief message, returning
beaming and laughing to himself*).

Well the joke seems to be on *me*! Mr. Rossiter has *pneumonia!*

Following, then, is a summary of the Treasurer's report:

(*Reads in a very business-like manner*).

During the year 1929—and by that is meant 1928—the Choral
Society received the following in donations:

B.L.G. $500
G.K.M. 500
Lottie and Nellie W. 500
In memory of a happy summer at Rye Beach .. 10
Proceeds of a sale of coats and hats left in the
    boat house 1.55
And then the Junior League gave a perform-
    ance of "Pinafore" for the benefit of the
    Fund which, unfortunately, resulted in a
    deficit of $300
Then, from dues and charges 2,354.75

And, following the installation of the new furnace, a saving in coal amounting to $374.75—which made Dr. Murnie very happy, you may be sure. Making a total of receipts amounting to $3,645.75. This is all, of course, reckoned as of June.

In the matter of expenditures, the Club has not been so fortunate. There was the unsettled condition of business, and the late Spring, to contend with, resulting in the following—er—rather discouraging figures, I am afraid.

Expenditures $23,574.85
Then there was a loss, owing to—
    several things—of 3,326.70
Car-fare 4,452.25
And then, Mrs. Rawlin's expense account,
    when she went down to see the work
    they are doing in Baltimore, came to
    $256.50, but I am sure that you will all
    agree that it was worth it to find out—er
    —what they are doing in Baltimore.
And then, Mrs. Rawlin's expense account
    and Ends 2,537.50
Making a total disbursement of (hurriedly)
                             $416,546.75
or a net deficit of—ah—several thousand
    dollars.

Now these figures bring us down only to October. In October my sister was married, and the house was all torn up, and in the general confusion we lost track of the figures for May and August. All those wishing to approximate figures for May and August, how-ever, may obtain them from me in the vestry after the dinner, where I will be with pledge cards for those of you who wish to subscribe over and above your annual dues, and I hope that each and every one of you here tonight will look deep into his heart and (archly) into his pocketbook, and see if he cannot find it there to help us put this thing over with a bang (accompanied by a wholly ineffectual gesture representing a bang) and to help and make this just the biggest and best year the Armenians have ever had—I thank you.

(Exits, bumping into proscenium.)

EPITAPH OF SARAH SEXTON

Here lies the body of Sarah Sexton,
Who never did aught to vex one.
Not like the woman under the next stone.
      (Thomas Sexton's first wife was buried under the
        next stone. Church-yard, Newmarket, England)

YOU NEVER CAN TELL

Ella Wheeler Wilcox

You never can tell when you send a word
    Like an arrow shot from a bow
By an archer blind, be it cruel or kind,
    Just where it may chance to go.
It may pierce the breast of your dearest friend,
    Tipped with its poison or balm,
To a stranger's heart in life's great mart
    It may carry its pain or its calm.

HALLUCINATION

Lewis Carroll

"I see nobody on the road," said Alice.
"I only wish I had such eyes," the White King remarked in a fretful tone. "To be able to see Nobody! And at that distance, too! Why it's as much as I can do to see real people by this light!"

(175)

A SONG FOR ST. CECILIA'S DAY

November 22, 1687

John Dryden

1

From Harmony, from heav'nly Harmony
  This universal Frame began;
   When Nature underneath a heap
    Of jarring Atomes lay,
  And cou'd not heave her Head,
The tuneful Voice was heard from high,
   Arise, ye more than dead.
Then cold and hot and moist and dry
  In order to their Stations leap,
   And MUSICK'S pow'r obey.
From Harmony, from heavenly Harmony
  This universal Frame began:
   From Harmony to Harmony
Through all the Compass of the Notes it ran,
The Diapason closing full in Man

2

What Passion cannot MUSICK raise and quell?
   When *Jubal* struck the corded Shell,
  His listening Brethren stood around,
   And, wond'ring, on their Faces fell
  To worship that Celestial Sound:
Less than a God they thought there could not dwell
   Within the hollow of that Shell,
   That spoke so sweetly, and so well.
What Passion cannot MUSICK raise and quell?

3

  The TRUMPETS loud Clangor
   Excites us to Arms
  With shrill Notes of Anger
   And mortal Alarms.
  The double double double beat
   Of the thund'ring DRUM
   Cryes, heark the Foes come;
Charge, Charge, 'tis too late to retreat.

4

The soft complaining FLUTE
In dying Notes discovers
The Woes of hopeless Lovers,
Whose Dirge is whisper'd by the warbling LUTE.

5

Sharp VIOLINS proclaim
Their jealous Pangs and Desperation,
Fury, frantick Indignation,
Depth of Pains and Height of Passion,
For the fair, disdainful Dame.

6

But oh! what Art can teach
What human Voice can reach
The sacred ORGANS Praise?
Notes inspiring holy Love,
Notes that wing their heavenly Ways
To mend the Choires above.

7

Orpheus cou'd lead the savage race,
And Trees uprooted left their Place,
Sequacious of the Lyre;
But bright CECILIA rais'd the Wonder high'r:
When to her Organ vocal Breath was given,
An angel heard, and straight appear'd
Mistaking Earth for Heav'n.

Grand Chorus.
As from the Pow'r of Sacred Lays
The Spheres began to move,
And sung the great Creator's Praise
To all the bless'd above;
So, when the last and dreadful Hour
This crumbling Pageant shall devour,
The TRUMPET shall be heard on high,
The dead shall live, the living die,
And MUSICK shall untune the Sky.

NAPOLEON BONAPARTE BLAMES HIS FAILURES ON NATURE

I frightened them pretty well with my invasion of England, didn't I? What was the public talk about it at the time? Well, you may have joked about it in Paris, but Pitt wasn't laughing in London. Never was the English oligarchy in greater peril!

I had made a landing possible; I had the finest army that ever existed, that of Austerlitz; what more can be said? In four days I could have reached London; I would not have entered as a conqueror but as a liberator; I would have acted the part of William III again, but with greater generosity. The discipline of my army would have been perfect; and it would have behaved in London as it might in Paris. From there I would have operated from south and north, under the colors of the Republic, the European regeneration which later I was on the point of effecting from north to south, under monarchical forms. The obstacles before which I failed did not proceed from men but from the elements: in the south it was the sea destroyed me; and in the north it was the fire of Moscow and the ice of winter; so there it is, water, air, fire, all nature and nothing but nature; these were the opponents of a universal regeneration commanded by Nature herself! The problems of Nature are insoluble.

CHEERFULNESS

Anonymous

I'm glad the sky is painted blue;
　And the earth is painted green;
And such a lot of nice fresh air
　All sandwiched in between.

PRAYER

John Greenleaf Whittier

Dear Lord and Father of mankind,
  Forgive our foolish ways!
Reclothe us in our rightful mind,
In purer lives Thy service find,
  In deeper reverence, praise.

Drop Thy still dews of quietness,
Till all our strivings cease;
Take from our souls the strain and stress,
And let our ordered lives confess
  The beauty of Thy peace.

TWO VIEWS OF THE SAME SHIP

Midrash

I am standing upon the seashore; a ship at my side spreads her
white sails to the morning breeze and starts for the blue ocean. She
is an object of beauty and strength, and I stand and watch her until
—at length—she hangs like a speck of white cloud just where the
sea and sky come down to mingle with each other. Then someone
at my side says, "There! She's gone!" Gone where? Gone from my
sight—that is all. She is just as large in mast and hull and spar as
she was when she left my side and is just as able to bear her load of
living freight to the place of destination. Her diminished size is in
me, not in her; and just at the moment when someone at my side
says, "There! She's gone!", there are other eyes watching her coming
and other voices ready to take up the glad shout, "There she comes!"
And that is dying.

MEET ME IN ST. LOUIS

Andrew B. Sterling

When Louis came home to the flat,
He hung up his coat and his hat,
He gazed all around, but no wifey he found,
So he said "Where can Flossie be at?"
A note on the table he spied,
He read it just once, then he cried.
It ran, "Louis dear, it's too slow for me here,
So I think I will go for a ride."

Chorus
"Meet me in St. Louis, Louis,
Meet me at the fair,
Don't tell me the lights are shining any place but there;
We will dance the Hoochee Koochee,
I will be your tootsie wootsie,
If you will meet me in St. Louis, Louis,
Meet me at the fair."

The dresses that hung in the hall,
Were gone, she had taken them all;
She took all his rings
And the rest of his things;
A picture he missed from the wall.

"What! Moving?" the janitor said,
Your rent is paid three months ahead."
"What good is the flat?" said poor Louis,
"Read that." And the janitor smiled as he read.
                                        (Chorus)

THE GOVERNMENT OF ALL

Chief Justice John Marshall

If any one proposition could command the universal assent of mankind, we might expect it would be this: that the government of the Union, though limited in its powers, is supreme within its sphere of

(180)

action. This would seem to result necessarily from its nature. It is the government of all; its powers are delegated by all; it represents all, and acts for all. Though any one State may be willing to control its operations, no State is willing to allow others to control them. The nation, on those subjects on which it can act, must necessarily bind its component parts. But this question is not left to mere reason: the people have, in express terms, decided it, by saying, "this Constitution, and the laws of the United States, which shall be made in pursuance thereof," "shall be the supreme law of the land," and by requiring that the members of the State legislatures, and the officers of the executive and judicial departments of the States, shall take the oath of fidelity to it.

The government of the United States, then, though limited in its powers, is supreme; and its laws, when made in pursuance of the Constitution, form the supreme law of the land, "anything in the constitution or laws of any State to the contrary notwithstanding."

(M'Culloch v. Maryland, 1819)

EVENSONG

Robert Louis Stevenson

The embers of the day are red
Beyond the murky hill.
The kitchen smokes; the bed
In the darkling house is spread:
The great sky darkens overhead,
And the great woods are shrill.
So far have I been led,
Lord, by Thy will:
So far have I followed, Lord, and wondered still.
The breeze from the embalmed land
Blows sudden towards the shore,
And claps my cottage door.
I hear the signal, Lord—I understand.
The night at Thy command
Comes. I will eat and sleep and will not question more.

OUR LADY'S TUMBLER*

(TRANSLATOR: Isabel Butler)

A certain minstrel came and went for so long in diverse places, and so wasted his strength, that at last, weary of the world, he withdrew into a holy order. His horses, his garments, his money, and all that he had he put therein, and left the world, for he would follow its ways no more. Thus, then, he came into a monastery which, men say, was that of Clairvaux. Now, though the youth was of much worship, and fair and well made and goodly, he yet knew no craft of which the folk there stood in any need. For he had lived only by tumbling and leaping and dancing; and though he knew right well how to leap and spring, he knew naught besides.

Now when he was come into the monastery and saw the tonsured brethren who let no word fall from their lips, but spoke among themselves by signs, the minstrel was much abashed and ill at ease, for he knew not how to share by word or deed in that which was the practice of the place; so was he dejected and heavy at heart. He saw the monks and the lay brothers each serving God in his place and after the manner appointed to him. Then he said, "Holy Mary, alas, and woe is me! what do I do here? There is no one so base in all the convent but strives to serve God in his own manner; but I have no trade that is of service to me here. Truly a poor creature am I in a goodly place." Then he wept to relieve his grief, and wished he were dead.

When he had bemoaned himself thus, he went away through the cloister, looking this way and that, until he came into a crypt; there he crouched down by an altar, drawing himself as close to it as he might. Above the altar was a statue of Our Lady, the Holy Mary, and he did not go astray when he came into that place. "I will do what I have been taught to do, and I will serve the Mother of God here in her monastery by my own trade! the others serve by singing, and I will serve by tumbling." He took off his cloak and disrobed himself, and laid his garments beside the altar.

Then he turned to the image, and looking up at it very humbly: "Lady," said he, "into your care I commit me, body and soul. Gentle Lady, Sweet Queen, do not despise me that which I know, for I would serve you in all good faith, and so God may help me, without offense. I know not how to read or to sing, but right gladly will I show you my most chosen tricks of tumbling."

* Abridged

Then he began to leap and to spring, now up and now down, beginning first with small capers, and then leaping higher and higher. Then he did the French trick and the trick of Champagne, and the tricks they do in Britanny, and then the trick of Lorraine; and he did them all with great travail. "Lady," he said, "this is good disport and I do it for no other save for you and your Son before all, so God may help me, I do not. I know not how to worship you in any other way. Henceforth will I be your minstrel. In God's name despise me not." Then he turned away and made a spring, "Lady," he said, "so God may save me, this thing did I never before. This trick is wholly new, and is not for common folk." So long did he leap and skip and dance, and never ceased till he was so spent that he could no longer hold himself upright, but sank down for very weariness and fell to the ground exhausted. "Lady," said he, "I can do no more now, but in sooth I will come again."

The good man continued long in this way of life, but at length he was thrown into much trouble. For a monk took note of him, and blamed him, that he came not to matins; and he marvelled what became of him, and what was the service that he did, and how he earned his bread. Now the monk so followed him, and so watched and spied upon him, that he saw him perform all his tricks.

He went to the abbot and told the whole story, and the abbot arose and said to the monk: "Now do not spread this abroad, but be silent, for by your vows I command you." And the abbot and monk watched all the convert's devotions, and all his leaping and dancing; and they saw how he bowed before the image, and how he skipped and sprang till his strength failed him.

And the abbot watched and straightway saw a Lady come down to him from the vault, and with her came angels and archangels from heaven, who came about the minstrel and gave him comfort and consolation. Then they hastened to serve him, for they longed to reward him for the service that he had paid to their Lady, that most Sweet Wonder.

The holy fathers tell us that thus it befell the minstrel. And now let us pray to God, who is above all, that He grant us to serve Him so well that we may deserve His love. Here ends the story of Our Lady's Tumbler.

(From an old French legend)

THE OPTIMIST

Anonymous

The optimist fell ten stories;
At each window bar
He shouted to his friend
"All right so far."

PRAYER FOR A LITTLE HOUSE

Florence Bone

God send us a little home
To come back to when we roam—
Low walls and fluted tiles,
Wide windows, a view for miles;
Red firelight and deep chairs;
Small white bed upstairs;
Great talk in little nooks;
Dim color, rows of books;
One picture on each wall;
Not many things at all.
God send us a little ground—
Tall trees standing round,
Homely flowers in brown sod,
Overhead thy stars, O God!
God bless when winds blow
Our home and all we know.

DESTINY

John Oliver Hobbes

Men heap together mistakes of their lives, and create a monster which they call Destiny. Some take a mournful pleasure in contemplating the ugliness of the idol: these are called Stoics. Others build it a temple like Solomon's, and worship the temple. These are called Epicureans.

(184)

THE DIVINE OFFICE OF THE KITCHEN

God walks among the pots and pipkins—St. Teresa

Cecily Hallack

Lord of the pots and pipkins, I have no time to be
A saint by doing lovely things and vigiling with Thee,
By watching in the twilight dawn, and storming Heaven's gates,
Make me a saint by getting meals, and washing up the plates!

Lord of the pots and pipkins, please, I offer Thee my souls,
The tiresomeness of tea leaves, and the sticky porridge bowls!
Remind me of the things I need, not just to save the stairs,
But so that I may perfectly lay tables into prayers.

Accept my roughened hands because I made them so for Thee!
Pretend my dishmop is a bowl, which heavenly harmony
Makes on a fiddle frying pan; it is so hard to clean,
And, ah, so horrid! dear Lord, the music that I mean!

Although I must have Martha hands, I have a Mary mind,
And when I black the boots, I try Thy sandals, Lord, to find.
I think of how they trod our earth, what time I scrub the floor.
Accept this meditation when I haven't time for more!

Vespers and Compline come to pass by washing supper things.
And, mostly I am very tired; and all the heart that sings
About the morning's work, is gone, before me into bed.
Lend me, dear Lord, Thy Tireless Heart to work in me instead!

My matins are said overnight to praise and bless Thy Name
Beforehand for tomorrow's work, which will be just the same;
So that it seems I go to bed still in my working dress,
Lord make Thy Cinderella soon a heavenly Princess.

Warm all the kitchen with Thy Love and light it with Thy Peace!
Forgive the worrying, and make the grumbling words to cease.
Lord, who laid Breakfast on the shore, forgive the world which saith
"Can any good thing come to God out of poor Nazareth?"

(185)

THE GOLDEN MEAN

Confucius

(TRANSLATOR: James Legge)

While there are no stirring of pleasure, anger, sorrow or joy, the mind may be said to be in the state of EQUILIBRIUM. When these feelings have been stirred, and they act in their due degree, there ensues what may be called the state of HARMONY. This EQUILIBRIUM is the great root *from which grow all the human actings* in the world, and this HARMONY is the Unique path *which they all should pursue.*

Let the states of equilibrium and harmony exist in perfection, and a happy order will prevail throughout heaven and earth, and all things will be nourished and flourish.

I CAN STAND ANY SOCIETY

Mark Twain

I'm quite sure that . . . I have no race prejudices, and I think I have no color prejudices nor creed prejudices. Indeed, I know it. I can stand any society. All I care to know is that a man is a human being— that is enough for me; he can't be any worse.

From CORINNA'S GOING A-MAYING

Robert Herrick

Get up, get up for shame! The blooming morn
  Upon her wings presents the god unshorn.
  See how Aurora throws her fair
  Fresh-quilted colors through the air:
  Get up, sweet slug-a-bed, and see
  The dew bespangling herb and tree!
Each flower has wept, and bowed toward the east

Above an hour since, yet you not dressed;
   Nay! not so much as out of bed?
   When all the birds have matins said
   And sung their thankful hymns, 'tis sin.
   Nay, profanation to keep in,
Whenas a thousand virgins on this day
Spring sooner than the lark, to fetch in May.

         *   *   *   *

Come, let us go, while we are in our prime,
And take the harmless folly of the time!
   We shall grow old apace, and die
   Before we know our liberty.
   Our life is short, and our days run
   As fast away as does the sun.
And as a vapor, or a drop of rain
Once lost, can ne'er be found again,
   So when or you or I are made
   A fable, song, or fleeting shade,
   All look, all liking, all delight
   Lies drowned with us in endless night.
Then while time serves, and we are but decaying,
Come, my Corinna, come, let's go a-Maying.

THE DEFINITION OF LOVE

Andrew Marvell

My love is of a birth as rare
As 'tis for object strange and high;
It was begotten by Despair
Upon Impossibility.

Magnanimous Despair alone
Could show me so divine a thing,
Where feeble Hope could ne'er have flown
But vainly flapt its tinsel wing.

And yet I quickly might arrive
Where my extended soul is fixt,
But Fate does iron wedges drive,
And always crowds itself betwixt.

(187)

For Fate with jealous eye does see
Two perfect loves, nor lets them close:
Their union would her ruin be,
And her tyrannic pow'r depose.

And therefore her decrees of steel
Us as the distant poles have plac'd,
(Though Love's whole world on us does wheel)
Not by themselves to be embrac'd,

Unless the giddy heaven fall
And earth some new convulsion tear,
And, us to join, the world should all
Be cramp'd into a planisphere.

As lines, so loves oblique may well
Themselves in every angle greet;
But ours, so truly parallel,
Though infinite, can never meet.

Therefore the love which doth us bind,
But Fate so enviously debars,
Is the conjunction of the mind,
And opposition of the stars.

PLINY THE YOUNGER DESCRIBES THE ERUPTION OF VESUVIUS IN 79 A.D.

(TRANSLATOR: William Melmoth)

Your request that I would send you an account of my uncle's death, in order to transmit a more exact relation of it to posterity, deserves my acknowledgments. He was at that time with the fleet under his command at Misenum. On the 24th of August, about one in the afternoon, my mother desired him to observe a cloud which appeared of a very unusual size and shape. He had just taken a turn in the sun, and, after bathing himself in cold water, and making a light luncheon, gone back to his books: he immediately arose and went out upon a rising ground from whence he might get a better sight of this very uncommon appearance. A cloud, from which mountain was uncertain, at this distance [but it was found afterwards to come from Mount Vesuvius], was ascending, the appearance of which I cannot give you a more exact description of than by likening it to that of a pine tree, for it shot up to a great height in the form of a very tall trunk, which spread itself out at the top into a sort of branches; occasioned, I imagine, either by a sudden gust of air that impelled it, the force of which decreased as it advanced upwards, or the cloud itself being pressed back again by its own weight, expanded in the manner I have mentioned; it appeared sometimes bright and sometimes dark and spotted, according as it was either more or less impregnated with earth and cinders. This phenomenon seemed to a man of such learning and research as my uncle extraordinary and worth further looking into. He ordered a light vessel to be got ready, and gave me leave, if I liked, to accompany him. I said I had rather go on with my work; and it so happened he had himself given me something to write out. As he was coming out of the house, he received a note from Rectina, the wife of Bassus, who was in the utmost alarm at the imminent danger which threatened her; for her villa lying at the foot of Mount Vesuvius, there was no way of escape but by sea; she earnestly entreated him therefore to come to her assistance. He accordingly changed his first intention, and what he had begun from a philosophical, he now carried out in a noble and generous spirit. He ordered the galleys to put to sea, and went himself on board with an intention of assisting not only Rectina, but several other towns which lay thickly strewn along that beautiful coast. Hastening then to the place from whence others fled with the utmost terror, he steered his course direct to the point of danger, and with so much calmness and presence of mind as to be able to make and dictate his observations upon the motion and all the phenomena of that dreadful scene. He was now so close to the mountain that the cinders, which grew thicker and hotter the nearer he approached, fell into the ships, together with pumice-stones, and black pieces of burning rock: they were in danger too not only of being a-ground by the sudden retreat of the sea, but also from the vast fragments which rolled down from the mountain, and obstructed all the shore. Here he stopped to consider whether he should turn back again; to which the pilot advising him, "Fortune," said he, "favours the brave; steer to where Pomponianus is." Pomponianus was then at Stabiae, separated by a bay, which the sea, after several insensible windings, forms with the shore. He had already sent his baggage on board; for though he was not at that time in actual danger, yet being within sight of it, and indeed extremely near, if it should in the least increase, he was determined to put to sea as soon as the wind, which was blowing dead in-shore, should go down. It was favourable, however, for carrying my uncle to Pomponianus, whom he found in the greatest consternation: he embraced him tenderly, encouraging and urging him to keep up his spirits, and the more effectually to soothe his fears by seeming unconcerned himself, ordered a bath to be got ready, and then, after having bathed, sat down to supper with great cheerfulness, or at least (what is just as heroic) with every appearance of it. Meanwhile broad flames shone out in several places from Mount Vesuvius, which the darkness of the night contributed to render still brighter and clearer. But my uncle, in order to soothe the apprehensions of his friend, assured him it was only the burning of the villages, which the country people had abandoned to the flames: after this he retired to rest, and it is most certain he was so little disquieted as to fall into a sound sleep: for his breathing which on account of his corpulence, was rather heavy and sonorous, was heard by the attendants outside. The court which led to his apartment being now almost filled with stones and ashes, if he had continued there any time longer, it would have been impossible for him to have made his way out. So he was awoke and got up, and went to Pomponianus and the rest of his company, who were feeling too anxious to think of going to bed. They consulted together whether it would be most prudent to trust to the houses, which now rocked from side to side with frequent and violent concussions as though shaken from their very foundations; or fly to the open fields, where the calcined stones and cinders, though light indeed, yet fell in large showers, and threatened destruction. In this choice of dangers they resolved for the fields: a resolution which, while the rest of the company were hurried into by their fears, my uncle embraced upon cool and deliberate consideration. They went out then, having pillows tied upon their heads with napkins; and this was their whole defence against the storm of stones that fell round them. It was now day everywhere else, but *there* a deeper darkness prevailed than in the thickest night; which however was in some degree alleviated by torches and other lights of various kinds. They thought proper to go farther down upon the shore to see if they might safely put out to sea, but found the waves still running extremely high, and boisterous. There my uncle, laying himself down upon a sail-cloth, which was spread for him, called twice for some cold water, which he drank, when immediately the flames, preceded by a strong whiff of sulphur, dispersed the rest of the party, and obliged him to rise. He raised himself up with the assistance of two of his servants, and instantly fell down dead; suffocated, as I conjecture, by some gross and noxious vapour, having always had a weak throat, which was often inflamed. As soon as it was light again, which was not till the third day after this melancholy accident, his body was found entire, and without any marks of violence upon it, in the dress in which he fell, and looking more like a man asleep than dead.

THE HEIGHT OF THE RIDICULOUS

Oliver Wendell Holmes

I wrote some lines once on a time
   In wondrous merry mood,
And thought, as usual, men would say
   They were exceeding good.

They were so queer, so very queer,
   I laughed as I would die;
Albeit, in the general way,
   A sober man am I.

I called my servant, and he came;
   How kind it was of him
To mind a slender man like me,
   He of the mighty limb.

"These to the printer," I exclaimed,
   And, in my humorous way,
I added, (as a trifling jest),
   "There'll be the devil to pay."

He took the paper, and I watched,
   And saw him peep within;
At the first line he read, his face
   Was all upon the grin.

He read the next; the grin grew broad,
   And shot from ear to ear;
He read the third, a chuckling noise
   I now began to hear.

The fourth, he broke into a roar;
  The fifth; his waistband split;
The sixth; he burst five buttons off,
  And tumbled in a fit.

Ten days and nights with sleepless eye,
  I watched that wretched man,
And since, I never dare to write
  As funny as I can.

LAST ENTRY IN GEORGE WASHINGTON'S DIARY BEFORE HE BECAME PRESIDENT

April 16, 1789. About ten o'clock I bade adieu to Mount Vernon, to private life, and to domestic felicity, and with a mind oppressed with more anxious and painful sensations than I have words to express, set out for New York. . . . With the best disposition to render service to my country in obedience to its calls, but with less hope of answering its expectations.

BED IN SUMMER

Robert Louis Stevenson

In winter I get up at night
And dress by yellow candle-light.
In summer, quite the other way,
I have to go to bed by day.

I have to go to bed and see
The birds still hopping on the tree,
Or hear the grown-up people's feet
Still going past me in the street.

And does it not seem hard to you,
When all the sky is clear and blue,
And I should like so much to play,
To have to go to bed by day?

REALISM AND DUTY

Ralph Waldo Emerson

There is a time in every man's education when he arrives at the conviction that envy is ignorance; that imitation is suicide; that he must take himself, for better or for worse, as his portion; that, though the wide universe is full of good, no kernel of nourishing corn can come to him but through his toil bestowed on that plot of ground which is given him to till.

ALL THAT GLITTERS IS NOT GOLD

Anonymous

Just an ivy-covered cottage with a brooklet running near,
Just an aged couple seated in the door;
Sadly thinking of their Mary, to their fond hearts ever dear.
In wounded pride she left them years before;
And as they stood there at parting, the couple old and gray,
They begged her not to leave them all alone.
"If you leave us," said the father,
"You may feel regret some day.
Remember child, the motto in your home:

Chorus
"All is not gold that glitters;
All is not pure that shines.
Follow your mother's teachings,
And happiness will be thine;
Lovers may seek your favor,
Boast of their wealth untold,
But all through your life, remember child
All that glitters is not gold."

It is many years ago now, since the people old and gray,
Crossed the stream of death and landed on life's shore;
Now the neighbors are in wonder, for 'twas only yesterday,
That a stranger knocked upon the cottage door;

(193)

She asked a few short questions, then in sadness turned away,
And wandered to the churchyard down the lane;
As she placed a bunch of daisies where her kind old parents lay,
She seemed to hear their parting words again.

COMMITMENT

James Russell Lowell

They are slaves who fear to speak
For the fallen and the weak;
They are slaves who will not choose
Hatred, scoffing, and abuse.
Rather than in silence shrink,
From the truth they needs must think;
They are slaves who dare not be
In the right with two or three.

PHINEAS T. BARNUM REVEALS HIS PROMOTION METHODS

Some men have a peculiar genius for writing a striking advertisement, one that will arrest the attention of the reader at first sight. Sometimes a man makes himself popular by a unique sign or a curious display in his window. Recently I observed a swing sign extending over the sidewalk in front of a store, on which was the inscription in plain letters,
DON'T READ THE OTHER SIDE.
Of course, I did, and so did everybody else, and I learned that the man had made an independence by first attracting the public to his business in that way and then using his customers well afterwards. . . .
I thoroughly understand the art of advertising, not merely by means of printer's ink, which I have always used freely, and to which I confess myself so much indebted for my success, but by turning every possible circumstance to my account. It was my monomania to make my American Museum [New York] the town wonder and town talk. As an illustration, one morning a stout, hearty-looking man,

came into my ticket-office, and begged some money. I asked him why he did not work and earn his living? He replied that he could get nothing to do and that he would be glad of any job at a dollar a day. I handed him a quarter of a dollar, told him to go out and get his breakfast and return, and I would employ him at light labor at a dollar and a half a day. When he returned I gave him five common bricks.

"Now," said I, "go and lay a brick on the sidewalk at the corner of Broadway and Anne Street; another close by the Museum; a third diagonally across the way at the corner of Broadway and Vesey Street, by the Astor House; put down the fourth on the sidewalk in front of St. Paul's Church, opposite; then, with a fifth brick in hand, take up a rapid march from one point to the other, making the circuit, exchanging your brick at every point, and say nothing to anyone."

"What is the object of this?" inquired the man.

"No matter," I replied; "all you need to know is that it brings you fifteen cents wages per hour. It is a bit of my fun, and to assist me properly you must seem to be as deaf as a post; wear a serious countenance; answer no questions; pay no attention to any one; but attend faithfully to the work and at the end of every hour by St. Paul's Church show this ticket at the Museum door; enter, walking solemnly through every hall in the building, pass out, and resume your work."

With the remark that it was "all one to him, so long as he could earn his living," the man placed his bricks and began his round. Half an hour afterwards, at least five hundred people were watching his mysterious movements. He had assumed a military step and bearing, and looking as sober as a judge, he made no response whatever to the constant inquiries as to the object of his singular conduct. At the end of the first hour, the sidewalks in the vicinity were packed with people all anxious to solve the mystery. The man, as directed, then went into the Museum, devoting fifteen minutes to a solemn survey of the halls, and afterwards returning to his round. This was repeated every hour till sundown and whenever the man went into the Museum a dozen or more persons would buy tickets and follow him, hoping to gratify their curiosity in regard to the purpose of his movements. This was continued for several days—the curious people who followed the man into the Museum considerably more than paying his wages—till finally the policeman to whom I had imparted my object, complained that the obstruction of the sidewalk by crowds had become so serious that I must call in my "brick man." This trivial incident excited considerable talk and amusement; it advertised me; and it materially advanced my purpose of making a lively corner near the Museum. . . .

I kept a band of music on the balcony of the Museum and announced "Free Music for the Millions." People said, "Well, that Barnum is a liberal fellow to give us music for nothing," and they flocked down to hear my outdoor free concerts. But I took pains to select and maintain the poorest band I could find—one whose discordant notes would drive the crowd into the Museum, out of earshot of my outside orchestra. Of course, the music was poor. When people expect to get "something for nothing" they are sure to be cheated, and generally deserve to be, and so, no doubt, some of my out-door patrons were sorely disappointed; but when they came inside and paid to be amused and instructed, I took care to see that they not only received the full worth of their money, but were more than satisfied.

(1855)

PARTING AT MORNING

Robert Browning

Round the cape of a sudden came the sea,
And the sun looked over the mountain's rim:
And straight was a path of gold for him,
And the need of a world of men for me.

BENJAMIN FRANKLIN, AT THE CONSTITUTIONAL CONVENTION, SUPPORTS THE CONSTITUTION

I confess that there are several parts of this Constitution which I do not at present approve, but I am not sure I shall never approve them. For, having lived long, I have experienced many instances of being obliged, by better information or fuller consideration, to change opinions, even on important subjects, which I once thought right, to be found otherwise. It is therefore that, the older I grow, the more apt I am to doubt my own judgment, and to pay more respect to the judgment of others. Most men, indeed, as well as most sects in religion, think themselves in possession of all truth, and that wherever others differ from them, it is so far error. Steele, a Protestant, in a dedication, tells the Pope, that the only difference between our churches, in their opinions of the certainty of their doctrines, is "the Church of Rome is infallible, and the Church of England is never in the wrong." But though many private persons think almost as highly of their own infallibility as of that of their sect, few express it so naturally as a certain French lady, who, in a dispute with her sister, said, "I don't know how it happens, sister, but I meet with nobody but myself that is always in the right."

In these sentiments, Sir, I agree to this Constitution, with all its faults, if they are such; . . . I doubt, too, whether any other Convention we can obtain may be able to make a better Constitution. For, when you assemble a number of men to have the advantage of their joint wisdom, you inevitably assemble with those men all their prejudices, their passions, their errors of opinion, their local interests, and their selfish views. From such an assembly can a perfect production ever be expected? It therefore astonishes, me, sir, to find this system approaching so near to perfection as it does. . . . Thus I consent, sir, to this Constitution because I expect no better, and because I am not sure that it is not the best. The opinions I have had of its errors I sacrifice to the public good. I have never whispered a syllable of them abroad. Within these walls they were born, and here they shall die.

(September 17, 1787)

THE GIRL SCOUT LAWS

1. A Girl Scout's honor is to be trusted.
2. A Girl Scout is loyal.
3. A Girl Scout's duty is to be useful and to help others.
4. A Girl Scout is a friend to all and a sister to every other Girl Scout.
5. A Girl Scout is courteous.
6. A Girl Scout is a friend to animals.
7. A Girl Scout obeys orders.
8. A Girl Scout is cheerful.
9. A Girl Scout is thrifty.
10. A Girl Scout is clean in thought, word and deed.

FUNICULI, FUNICULA

Luigi Denza

Some think the world is made for fun and frolic,
And so do I! And so do I!
Some think it well to be all melancholic,
To pine and sigh, to pine and sigh.
But I, I love to spend my time in singing
Some joyous song, some joyous song;
To set the air with music bravely ringing
Is far from wrong! Is far from wrong!

Chorus
Hearken! Hearken! Music sounds afar!
Hearken! Hearken! Music sounds afar!
Funiculi, funicula, funiculi, funicula!
Joy is everywhere, funiculi, funicula!

Ah me! 'Tis strange that some should take to sighing,
And like it well! And like it well!
For me, I have not thought it worth the trying,
So cannot tell! So cannot tell!
With laugh, and dance, and song, the day soon passes,
Full soon is gone, full soon is gone;
For mirth was made for joyous lad and lasses
To call their own! To call their own!

WHEN LOVE RULES ON EARTH

Martin Buber

When senseless hatred reigns on earth, and men hide their faces
from one another, then heaven is forced to hide its face. But when
love comes to rule on earth, and men reveal their faces to one
another, then the splendor of God will be revealed.

From THE LOTOS-EATERS

Alfred, Lord Tennyson

"Courage!" he said, and pointed toward the land,
"This mounting wave will roll us shoreward soon."
In the afternoon they came unto a land
In which it seemed always afternoon.
All round the coast the languid air did swoon,
Breathing like one that hath a weary dream.
Full-faced above the valley stood the moon;
And like a downward smoke, the slender stream
Along the cliff to fall and pause and fall did seem.

A land of streams! some, like a downward smoke,
Slow-dropping veil of thinnest lawn, did go;
And some through wavering lights and shadows broke,
Rolling a slumbrous sheet of foam below.
They saw the gleaming river seaward flow
From the inner land; far off, three mountain-tops,
Three silent pinnacles of aged snow,
Stood sunset-flushed; and, dewed with showery drops,
Up-clomb the shadowy pine above the woven copse.

The charmed sunset lingered low and on
In the red West; through mountain clefts the dale
Was seen far inland, and the yellow down
Bordered with palm, and many a winding vale
And meadow, set with slender galingale;
A land where all things always seemed the same!
And round about the keel with faces pale,
Dark faces pale against that rosy flame,
The mild-eyed melancholy Lotos-eaters came.

Branches they bore of that enchanted stem,
Laden with flower and fruit, whereof they gave
To each, but whoso did receive of them
And taste, to him the gushing of the wave
Far far away did seem to mourn and rave
On alien shores; and if his fellow spake,
His voice was thin, as voices from the grave;
And deep-asleep he seemed, yet all awake,
And music in his ears his beating heart did make.

(199)

They sat them down upon the yellow sand
Between the sun and moon upon the shore;
And sweet it was to dream of Fatherland,
Of child, and wife, and slave; but evermore
Most weary seemed the sea, weary the oar,
Weary the wandering fields of barren foam.
Then someone said, "We will return no more";
And all at once they sang, "Our island home
Is far beyond the wave; we will no longer roam."

THE SPHYNX

Alexander W. Kinglake

And near the Pyramids, more wondrous, and more awful than all else in the land of Egypt, there sits the lonely Sphynx. Comely the creature is, but the comeliness is not of this world; the once worshipped beast is a deformity and a monster to this generation, and yet you can see that those lips, so thick and heavy, were fashioned according to some ancient mould of beauty—some mould of beauty now forgotten—forgotten because that Greece drew forth Cytherea, from the flashing foam of the Aegean, and in her image created new forms of beauty, and made it a law among men that the short and proudly wreathed lips should stand for a sign and the main condition of loveliness through all generations to come. Yet still there lives on the race of those who were beautiful in the fashion of the elder world, and Christian girls of Coptic blood will look on you with the sad, serious gaze, and kiss your charitable hand with the big pouting lips of the very Sphynx.

Laugh and mock if you will at the worship of stone idols, but mark ye this, ye breakers of images, that in one regard, the stone idol bears awful semblance of Deity—unchangefulness in the midst of change—the same seeming will, and intent for ever and ever inexorable! Upon ancient dynasties of Ethiopians and Egyptian kings—upon Greek and Roman, upon Arab and Ottoman conquerors—upon Napoleon dreaming of an Eastern Empire—upon battle and pestilence—upon the ceaseless misery of the Egyptian race—upon keen-eyed travellers—Herodotus yesterday, and Warburton today—upon all and more this unworldly Sphynx has watched, and watched like a Providence with the same earnest eyes, the same sad, tranquil mien. And we, we shall die, and Islam will wither away, and the Englishman straining far over to hold his loved India, will plant a firm foot on the banks of the Nile, and sit in the seats of the Faithful, and still that sleepless rock will lie watching and watching the works of the new busy race, with those same sad, earnest eyes, and the same tranquil mien everlasting. You dare not mock at the Sphynx.

MARY MORISON

Robert Burns

O Mary, at thy window be,
   It is the wish'd, the trysted hour!
Those smiles and glances let me see,
   That make the miser's treasure poor:
How blythely wad I bide the stoure,
   A weary slave frae sun to sun,
Could I the rich reward secure,
   The lovely Mary Morison.

Yestreen, when to the trembling string
   The dance gaed thro' the lighted ha',
To thee my fancy took its wing,
   I sat, but neither heard nor saw:
Tho' this was fair, and that was braw,
   And yon the toast of a' the town,
I sigh'd, and said amang them a',
   "Ye are na Mary Morison."

O Mary, canst thou wreck his peace,
   Wha for thy sake wad gladly die?
Or canst thou break that heart of his,
   Whase only faut is loving thee?
If love for love thou wilt na gie,
   At least be pity to me shown!
A thought ungentle canna be
   The thought o' Mary Morison.

JESUS EATS WITH SINNERS

Holy Bible, Mark 2:15–17

And it came to pass, that, as Jesus sat at meat in his house, many publicans and sinners sat also together with Jesus and his disciples: for there were many, and they followed him.

And when the scribes and Pharisees saw him eat with publicans and sinners, they said unto his disciples, How is it that he eateth and drinketh with publicans and sinners?

When Jesus heard it, he saith unto them, They that are whole have no need of the physician, but they that are sick: I came not to call the righteous, but sinners to repentance.

ODE TO THE CONFEDERATE DEAD

(Magnolia Cemetery, Charleston, S.C.)

Henry Timrod

Sleep sweetly in your humble graves,
   Sleep, martyrs of a fallen cause;
Though yet no marble column craves
   The pilgrim here to pause.

In seeds of laurel in the earth
   The blossom of your fame is blown,
And somewhere, waiting for its birth,
   The shaft is in the stone!

Meanwhile, behalf the tardy years
   Which keep in trust your storied tombs,
Behold! your sisters bring their tears,
   And these memorial blooms.

Small tributes! but your shades will smile
   More proudly on these wreaths today,
Than when some cannon-moulded pile
   Shall overlook this bay.

Stop, angels, hither from the skies!
    There is no holier spot of ground
Than where defeated valor lies,
    By mourning beauty crowned!

(1866)

OFFICE SEEKERS

Harried night and day by office seekers, President Lincoln once said, "This human struggle and scramble for office, for a way to live without work, will finally test the strength of our institutions."

NATURE AND ART

Alexander Pope

First follow Nature, and your judgment frame
By her just standard, which is still the same:
Unerring NATURE, still divinely bright,
One clear, unchang'd, and universal light,
Life, force, and beauty, must to all impart,
At once the source, and end, and test of Art.
Art from that fund each just supply provides,
Works without show, and without pomp presides;
In some fair body thus th' informing soul
With spirits feeds, with vigor fills the whole,
Each motion guides, and ev'ry nerve sustains;
Itself unseen, but in th' effects, remains.
Some, to whom Heav'n in wit has been profuse,
Want as much more, to turn it to its use;
For wit and judgment often are at strife,
Tho' meant each other's aid, like man and wife.
'T is more to guide, than spur the Muse's steed;
Restrain his fury, than provoke his speed;
The winged courser, like a gen'rous horse,
Shows most true mettle when you check his course.
Those RULES of old discovered, not devis'd,
Are Nature still, but Nature methodiz'd.
Nature, like liberty, is but restrain'd
By the same laws which first herself ordain'd.

(From *Essay on Criticism*)

From PRESIDENT NIXON'S INAUGURAL ADDRESS

Greatness comes in simple trappings.

The simple things are the ones most needed today if we are to surmount what divides us and cement what unites us. To lower our voices would be a simple thing.

In these difficult years, America has suffered from a fever of words; from inflated rhetoric that promises more than it can deliver; from angry rhetoric that fans discontents into hatreds; from bombastic rhetoric that postures instead of persuading.

We cannot learn from one another until we stop shouting at one another—until we speak quietly enough so that our words can be heard as well as our voices.

We shall plan now for the day when our wealth can be transferred from the destruction of war abroad to the urgent needs of our people at home.

The American dream does not come to those who fall asleep.

But we are approaching the limits of what government alone can do.

Our greatest need now is to reach beyond government, to enlist the legions of the concerned and the committed. What has to be done has to be done by government and people together or it will not be done at all. The lesson of past agony is that without the people we can do nothing; with the people we can do everything.

The essence of freedom is that each of us shares in the shaping of his own destiny. Until he has been part of a cause larger than himself, no man is truly whole.

The way to fulfillment is in the use of our talents; we achieve nobility in the spirit that inspires that use.

As we measure what can be done, we shall promise only what we know we can produce; but as we chart our goals we shall be lifted by our dreams.

No man can be fully free while his neighbor is not. To go forward at all is to go forward together.

Let us take as our goal: where peace is unknown, make it welcome; where peace is fragile, make it strong; where peace is temporary, make it permanent.

I know America. I know the heart of America is good.

I speak from my own heart, and the heart of my country, the deep concern we have for those who suffer and those who sorrow.

I have taken an oath today in the presence of God and my countrymen: To uphold and defend the Constitution of the United States. And to that oath, I now add this sacred commitment: I shall consecrate my office, my energies and all the wisdom I can summon, to the cause of peace among nations.

Let this message be heard by strong and weak alike.

The peace we seek—the peace we seek to win—is not victory over any other people, but the peace that comes with healing in its wings; with compassion for those who have suffered; with understanding for those who have opposed us; with the opportunity for all the peoples of this earth to choose their own destiny.

Our destiny offers not the cup of despair, but the chalice of opportunity. So let us seize it, not in fear, but in gladness—and "riders on the earth together," let us go forward, firm in our faith, steadfast in our purpose, cautious of the dangers; but sustained by our confidence in the will of God and the promise of man.

(January 20, 1969)

THEN LAUGH

Bertha Adams Backus

Build for yourself a strongbox,
   Fashion each part with care;
When it's strong as your hand can make it,
   Put all your troubles there;
Hide there all thoughts of your failures,
   And each bitter cup that you quaff;
Lock all your heartaches within it,
   Then sit on the lid and laugh.

Tell no one its contents,
   Never its secrets share;
When you've dropped in your care and worry
   Keep them forever there;
Hide them from sight so completely
   That the world will never dream half;
Fasten the strongbox securely—
   Then sit on the lid and laugh.

MOHAMMED AND THE MOUNTAIN

Francis Bacon

Mohammed indicated to the people that he would call a mountain to him, and from the top of it offer up his prayers for the observers of his law. The people assembled. Mohammed called the mountain to come to him, again and again; and when the mountain stood still he was never a whit abashed, but said, "If the mountain will not come to Mohammed, Mohammed will go to the mountain."

ENCOUNTERING GOD

Walt Whitman

Why should I wish to see God better than this day?
I see something of God each hour of the twenty-four,
    and each moment then,
In the faces of men and women I see God, and in my
    own face in the glass,
I find letters from God dropt in the street, and
    every one is sign'd by God's name,
And I leave them where they are, for I know that
    wheresoe'er I go,
Others will punctually come for ever and ever.

ABRIDGMENT OF FREEDOM

James Madison

I believe there are more instances of the abridgment of the freedom of the people by gradual and silent encroachments of those in power than by violent and sudden usurpations.

SIX-YEAR-OLD HENRY ADAMS IS TAKEN IN HAND BY
A FORMER PRESIDENT OF THE UNITED STATES

Henry Adams

He knew his grandfather John Quincy Adams only as an old man of seventy-five or eighty who was friendly and gentle with him, but except that he heard his grandfather always called "the President," and his grandmother "the Madam," he had no reason to suppose that his Adams grandfather differed in character from his Brooks grandfather who was equally kind and benevolent. . . . Henry Adams never knew a boy of his generation to like a master, and the tasks of remaining on friendly terms with one's own family, in such a relation, was never easy.

All the more singular it seemed afterwards to him that his first serious contact with the President should have been a struggle of will, in which the old man almost necessarily defeated the boy, but instead of leaving, as usual in such defeats, a lifelong sting, left rather an impression of as fair treatment as could be expected from a natural enemy. The boy met seldom with such restraint. He could not have been much more than six years old at the time—seven at the utmost—and his mother had taken him to Quincy for a long stay with the President during the Summer. What became of the rest of the family he quite forgot; but he distinctly remembered standing at the house door one summer morning in a passionate outburst of rebellion against going to school. Naturally his mother was the immediate victim of his rage; that is what mothers are for, and boys also; but in this case the boy had his mother at an unfair disadvantage, for she was a guest, and had no means of enforcing obedience. Henry showed a certain tactical ability by refusing to start, and he met all efforts at compulsion by successful, though too vehement protest. He was in fair way to win, and was holding his own, with sufficient energy, at the bottom of the long staircase which led up to the President's library, when the door opened, and the old man slowly came down. Putting on his hat, he took the boy's hand without a word, and walked with him, paralyzed by awe, up the road to town. After the first moments of consternation at this interference in a domestic dispute, the boy reflected that an old gentleman close on to eighty would never trouble himself to walk near a mile on a hot summer morning over a shadeless road to take a boy to school, and that it would be strange if a lad imbued with the passion of freedom could not find a corner to dodge around, somewhere before reaching the school door. Then and always, the boy insisted that this reasoning justified his apparent submission; but the old man did not stop, and the boy saw all his strategical points turned, one after another, until he found himself seated inside the school, and obviously the center of curious if not malevolent criticism. Not till then did the President release his hand and depart.

The point was that this act, contrary to the inalienable rights of boys, and nullifying the social compact, ought to have made him dislike his grandfather for life. He could not recall that it had this effect even for a moment. With a certain maturity of mind, the child must have recognized that the President, though a tool of tyranny, had done his disreputable work with a certain intelligence. He had shown no temper, no irritation, no personal feelings, and had made no display of force. Above all, he had held his tongue. During their long walk he had said nothing; he had uttered no syllable of revolting cant about the duty of obedience and the sickedness of resistance to law; he had shown no concern in the matter; hardly even a consciousness of the boy's existence. Probably his mind at that moment was actually troubling itself little about his grandson's iniquities, and much about the iniquities of President Polk, but the boy . . . gave his grandfather credit for intelligent silence. For this forbearance he felt instinctive respect.

(From *The Education of Henry Adams*)

FAITH

Robert Browning

If I stoop
Into a dark tremendous sea of
    cloud,
It is but for a time; I press God's
    lamp
Close to my breast; its splendor
    soon or late
Will pierce the gloom: I shall
    emerge one day.
You understand me? I have said
    enough?

THE TWELVE MONTHS

Gregory Gander

Snowy, Flowy, Blowy,
Showery, Flowery, Bowery,
Hoppy, Choppy, Droppy,
Breezy, Sneezy, Freezy.

FREE SPEECH

Justice Oliver Wendell Holmes

The most stringent protection of free speech would not protect a man in falsely shouting fire in a theatre and causing a panic. . . The question in every case is whether the words used are used in such circumstances and are of such a nature as to create a clear and present danger that they will bring about the substantive evils that Congress has a right to prevent.

(Schenck v. *U.S.,* 1919)

TRUST IN GOD

Norman Macleod

Courage, brother! do not stumble,
Though thy path be dark as night;
There's a star to guide the humble,
Trust in God and do the Right.

One of the things we have to be thankful for is that we don't get as much government as we pay for.
—C. H. Kettering

RIDICULOUS EXCESS

William Shakespeare

Therefore, to be possess'd with double pomp,
To guard a title that was rich before,
To gild refined gold, to paint the lily,
To throw a perfume on the violet,
To smooth the ice, or add another hue
Unto the rainbow, or with taper-light
To seek the beauteous eye of heaven to garnish,
Is wasteful and ridiculous excess.

(From *King John*)

STRANGE MEETING

Wilfred Owen

It seemed that out of battle I escaped
Down some profound dull tunnel, long since scooped
Through granites which titanic wars had groined.
Yet also there encumbered sleepers groaned,
Too fast in thought or death to be bestirred.
Then, as I probed them, one sprang up, and stared
With piteous recognition in fixed eyes,
Lifting distressful hands as if to bless.
And by his smile, I knew that sullen hall,
By his dead smile I knew we stood in Hell.
With a thousand pains that vision's face was grained;
Yet no blood reached there from the upper ground,
And no guns thumped, or down the flues made moan.
"Strange friend," I said, "here is no cause to mourn."
"None," said the other, "save the undone years,
The hopelessness. Whatever hope is yours,
Was my life also; I went hunting wild
After the wildest beauty in the world,
Which lies not calm in eyes, or braided hair,
But mocks the steady running of the hour.
And if it grieves, grieves richlier than here.
For by my glee might many men have laughed,

And of my weeping something had been left,
Which must die now. I mean the truth untold,
The pity of war, the pity war distilled.
Now men will go content, with what we spoiled.
Or, discontent, boil bloody, and be spilled.
They will be swift with swiftness of the tigress,
None will break ranks, though nations trek from progress.
Courage was mine, and I had mystery,
Wisdom was mine, and I had mastery;
To miss the march of this retreating world
Into vain citadels that are not walled.
Then, when much blood had clogged their chariot-wheels,
I would go up and wash them from sweet wells,
Even with truths that lie too deep for taint.
I would have poured my spirit without stint
But not through wounds; not on the cess of war.
Foreheads of men have bled where no wounds were.
I am the enemy you killed, my friend.
I knew you in this dark; for so you frowned
Yesterday through me as you jabbed and killed.
I parried; but my hands were loath and cold.
Let us sleep now . . ."

JAMES BOSWELL CALLS ON SAMUEL JOHNSON

He received me very courteously; but, it must be confessed that
his apartment, and furniture, and morning dress, were sufficiently
uncouth. His brown suit of clothes looked very rusty; he had on a
little old shrivelled unpowdered wig, which was too small for his
head; his shirt-neck and knees of his breeches were loose; his black
worsted stockings ill drawn up; and he had a pair of unbuckled
shoes by way of slippers. But all these slovenly particularities were
forgotten the moment he began to talk. Some gentlemen, whom I
do not recollect, were sitting with him; and when they went away,
I also rose; but he said to me, "Nay, don't go."—"Sir," said I, "I am
afraid that I intrude upon you. It is benevolent to allow me to sit
and hear you." He seemed pleased with this compliment, which I
sincerely paid him, and answered, "Sir, I am obliged to any man
who visits me."—I have preserved the following short minute of
what passed this day.
"Madness frequently discovers itself merely by unnecessary devia-

tion from the usual modes of the world. My poor friend Smart showed the disturbance of his mind, by falling upon his knees, and saying his prayers in the street, or in any other unusual place. Now although, rationally speaking, it is greater madness not to pray at all, than to pray as Smart did, I am afraid there are so many who do not pray, that their understanding is not called in question."

Concerning the unfortunate poet, Christopher Smart, who was confined in a mad-house, he had, at another time, the following conversation with Dr. Burney.—BURNEY. "How does poor Smart do, Sir; is he likely to recover?" JOHNSON. "It seems as if his mind had ceased to struggle with the disease; for he grows fat upon it." BURNEY. "Perhaps, Sir, that may be from want of exercise." JOHNSON. "No, Sir; he has partly as much exercise as he used to have, for he digs in the garden. Indeed, before his confinement, he used for exercise to walk to the alehouse; but he was *carried* back again. I did not think he ought to be shut up. His infirmities were not noxious to society. He insisted on people praying with him; and I'd as lief pray with Kit Smart as anyone else. Another charge was, that he did not love clean linen; and I have no passion for it."

Johnson continued. "Mankind have a great aversion to intellectual labor; but even supposing knowledge to be easily attainable, more people would be content to be ignorant than would take even a little trouble to acquire it.

"The morality of an action depends on the motive from which we act. If I fling half a crown to a beggar with intention to break his head, and he picks it up and buys victuals with it, the physical effect is good; but, with respect to me, the action is very wrong. So, religious exercises, if not performed with an intention to please God, avail us nothing. As our Savior says of those who perform them from other motives, 'Verily they have their reward.'"

Talking of Garrick, he said, "He is the first man in the world for sprightly conversation."

When I rose a second time, he again pressed me to stay, which I did.

He told me that he generally went abroad at four in the afternoon, and seldom came home till two in the morning. I took the liberty to ask if he did not think it wrong to live thus, and not make more use of his great talents. He owned it was a bad habit. On reviewing, at the distance of many years, my journal of this period, I wonder how, at my first visit, I ventured to talk to him so freely, and that he bore it with so much indulgence.

Before we parted, he was so good as to promise to favor me with his company one evening at my lodgings; and, as I took my leave, shook me cordially by the hand. It is almost needless to add, that I felt no little elation at having now so happily established an acquaintance of which I had been so long ambitious.

TO HIS COY MISTRESS

Andrew Marvell

Had we but World enough, and Time,
This coyness, Lady, were no crime.
We would sit down, and think this way
To walk, and pass our love's long day.
Thou by the Indian Ganges' side
Should'st rubies find: I by the tide
of Humber should complain. I Would
Love you ten years before the Flood:
And you should if you please refuse
Till the conversion of the Jews.
My vegetable love should grow
Vaster than empires, and more slow.
An hundred years should go to praise
Thine eyes, and on thy forehead gaze.
Two hundred to adore each breast:
But thirty thousand to the rest.
An age at least to every part,
And the last stage should show your heart.
For, Lady, you deserve this state;
Nor would I love at lower rate.
  But at my back I always hear
Time's winged chariot drawing near:
And yonder before us lie
Deserts of vast Eternity.
Thy beauty shall no more be found
Nor, in thy marble vault, shall sound
My echoing song: then worms shall try
That long preserved virginity;
And your quaint honour turn to dust;
And into ashes all my lust.
The grave's a fine and private place,
But none I think do there embrace.

(213)

Now therefore, while the youthful hue
Sits on thy skin by morning dew,
And while thy willing soul transpires
At every pore with instant fires,
Now let us sport us while we may;
And now, like amorous birds of prey,
Rather at once our time devour,
Than languish in his slow-chapt power.
Let us roll all our strength, and all
Our sweetness, up into one ball:
And tear our pleasures with rough strife,
Through the iron gates of life.
Thus, though we cannot make our sun
Stand still, yet we will make him run.

WHAT YOU ARE SEEKING IS HERE

Horace

Whatever hour God has given for your weal, take it with grateful hand nor put off joys from year to year; so that in whatever place you have been you may say that you have lived happily. For if 'tis reason and wisdom that takes away cares and not a site commanding a wide expanse of sea, they change their clime, not their mind, who rush across the sea. 'Tis a busy idleness that is our bane; with yachts and cars we seek to make life happy. What you are seeking is here.

TO THOMAS MOORE

Lord Byron

My boat is on the shore,
    And my bark is on the sea;
But, before I go, Tom Moore,
    Here's a double health to thee!

Here's a sigh to those who love me,
    And a smile to those who hate;
And, whatever sky's above me,
    Here's a heart for every fate.

(214)

Though the ocean roar around me,
    Yet it still shall bear me on;
Though a desert should surround me,
    It hath springs that may be won.

Were the last drop in the well,
    As I gasp'd upon the brink,
Ere my fainting spirit fell,
    'Tis to thee that I would drink.

With what water, as this wine,
    The libation I would pour
Should be—Peace with thine and mine
    And a health to thee, Tom Moore.

BOOKS

Richard de Bury

Books delight us when prosperity smiles upon us; they comfort us inseparably when stormy fortune frowns on us. They lend validity to human compacts, and no serious judgments are propounded without their help. Arts and sciences, all the advantages of which no mind can enumerate, consist in books. How highly must we estimate the wondrous power of books, since through them we survey the utmost bounds of the world and time, and contemplate the things that are as well as those that are not, as it were in the mirror of eternity. In books we climb mountains and scan the deepest gulfs of the abyss; in books we behold the finny tribes that may not exist outside of their native waters, distinguish the properties of streams and springs and of various lands; from books we dig out gems and metals and the materials of every kind of mineral, and learn the virtues of herbs and trees and plants, and survey at will the wholy progeny of Neptune, Ceres, and Pluto.

Books are masters who instruct us without words of anger, without bread or money. If you approach them they are not asleep. If you seek them, they do not hide, if you blunder they do not scold, if you are ignorant, they do not laugh at you.

FAUSTUS FACES HIS DOOM

Christopher Marlowe

O Faustus,
Now hast thou but one bare hour to live,
And then thou must be damned perpetually!
Stand still, you ever-moving spheres of heaven,
That time may cease, and midnight never come;
Fair Nature's eye, rise, rise again, and make
Perpetual day; or let this hour be but
A year, a month, a week, a natural day,
That Faustus may repent and save his soul!
O lente, lente currite, noctis equi!
The stars move still, time runs, the clock will strike,
The devil will come, and Faustus must be dam'd.
O, I'll leap up to heaven!—Who pulls me down?—
See, where Christ's blood streams in the firmament!
One drop of blood will save me: O my Christ!—
Rend not my heart for naming of my Christ;
Yet will I call on him; O, spare me, Lucifer!—
Where is it now? 'tis gone:
And, see, a threatening arm, an angry brow!
Mountains and hills, come, come, and fall on me,
And hide me from the heavy wrath of heaven!
No!
Then will I headlong run into the earth:
Gape, earth! O, no, it will not harbour me!
You stars that reigned at my nativity,
Whose influence hath allotted death and hell,
Now draw up Faustus, like a foggy mist,
Into the entrails of yon labouring cloud,
That, when you vomit forth into the air,
My limbs may issue from your smoky mouths;
But let my soul mount and ascend to heaven!
O, half the hour is past! 'twill all be past anon.
O, if my soul must suffer for my sin,
Impose some end to my incessant pain;
Let Faustus live in hell a thousand years,
A hundred thousand, and at last be sav'd!
No end is limited to damned souls.
Why were thou not a creature wanting soul?
Or why is this immortal that thou hast?

O, Pythagoras' metempsychosis, were that true,
This soul should fly from me, and I be chang'd
Into some brutish beast! all beasts are happy,
For, when they die,
Their souls are soon dissolv'd in elements;
But mine must live still to be plagu'd in hell.
Curst be the parents that engender'd me!
No, Faustus, curse thyself, curse Lucifer
That hath depriv'd thee of the joys of heaven.
It strikes, it strikes! Now, body turn to air,
Or Lucifer will bear thee quick to hell!
O soul, be chang'd into small water-drops,
And fall into the ocean, ne'er be found!

THAT ENERGY EQUALS MASS TIMES THE SPEED OF LIGHT SQUARED

Albert Einstein

$E = mc^2$, where E is the energy in ergs, m the mass in grams and c the velocity of light (that is 3×10^{10} cm. per second).

THE POWER OF SPIRIT

When Svetaketu, at his father's bidding, had brought a ripe fruit from the banyan tree, the father said to him,
   "Split the fruit in two, dear son."
   "Here you are. I have split it in two."
   "What do you find there?"
   "Innumerable tiny seeds."
   "Then take one of the seeds and split it."
   "I have split the seed."
   "And what do you find there?"
   "Why, nothing, nothing at all."
   "Ah, dear son, but this great tree cannot possibly come from nothing. Even if you cannot see with your eyes that subtle something in the seed which produces this mighty form it is present none-

theless. That is the power, that is the spirit unseen which pervades everywhere and is in all things. Have faith! That is the spirit which lies at the root of all existence, and that also art thou, O Svetaketu."

(From the Chandogya Upanishad)

OLD LESSON

Anonymous

God made bees, and bees made honey,
God made man, and man made money;
Pride made the devil, and the devil made sin;
So God made a cole-pit to put the devil in.

NO LONGER MOURN FOR ME WHEN I AM DEAD

William Shakespeare

No longer mourn for me when I am dead
Than you shall hear the surly sullen bell
Give warning to the world that I am fled
From this vile world, with vilest worms to dwell:
Nay, if you read this line, remember not
The hand that writ it; for I love you so,
That I in your sweet thoughts would be forgot,
If thinking on me then should make you woe.
O, if, I say, you look upon this verse
When I perhaps compounded am with clay,
Do not so much as my poor name rehearse,
But let your love even with my life decay;
   Lest the wise world should look into your moan,
   And mock you with me after I am gone.

(From the Sonnets)

THE OLD CHISHOLM TRAIL

Anonymous

Come along, boys, and listen to my tale,
I'll tell you of my troubles on the old Chisholm trail.

Chorus
    Come ti yi youpy, youpy yea, youpy yea,
    Come ti yi youpy, youpy yea.

I started up the trail October twenty-third,
I started up the trail with the 2-U herd.

On a ten dollar hoss and a forty-dollar saddle,
And I'm goin' to punchin' Texas cattle.

I woke up one morning on the old Chisholm trail,
Rope in my hand and a cow by the tail.

I'm up in the mornin' afore daylight
And afore I sleep the moon shines bright.

My hoss throwed me off at the creek called Mud,
My hoss throwed me off round the 2-U herd.

Last time I saw him he was going 'cross the level
A-kicking up his heels and a-running like the devil.

It's cloudy in the west, a-lookin' like rain,
And my damned old slicker's in the wagon again.

No chaps, no slicker, and its pouring down rain,
And I swear, by God, I'll never night-herd again.

Last night I was on guard and the leader broke the ranks,
I hit my horse down the shoulders and I spurred him in the flanks.

The wind commenced to blow, and the rain began to fall,
Hit looked, by grab, like we was goin' to lose 'em all.

My slickers in the wagon and I'm gittin' mighty cold,
And these longhorn sons-o'-guns are gittin' hard to hold.

(219)

Saddle up, boys, and saddle up well,
For I think these cattle have scattered to hell.

With my blanket and my gun and my rawhide rope,
I'm a-slidin' down the trail in a long, keen lope.

I don't give a damn if they never do stop;
I'll ride as long as an eight-day clock.

We rounded 'em up and put 'em on the cars,
And that was the last of the old Two Bars.

Oh, its bacon and beans most every day—
I'd as soon be a-eatin' prairie hay.

I went to the boss to draw my roll,
He had it figgered out I was nine dollars in the hole.

I'll sell my outfit as soon as I can,
I won't punch cattle for no damned man.

With my knees in the saddle and my seat in the sky,
I'll quit punching cows in the sweet by and by.

Fare you well, old trail-boss, I don't wish you any harm,
I'm quittin' the business to go on the farm.

THE WOMAN TAKEN IN ADULTERY

Holy Bible, John 8:2–11

And early in the morning he came again into the temple, and all the people came unto him; and he sat down, and taught them.

And the scribes and Pharisees brought unto him a woman taken in adultery; and when they had set her in the midst,

They say unto him, Master, this woman was taken in adultery, in the very act.

Now Moses in the law commanded us that such should be stoned: but what sayest thou?

This they said, tempting him, that they might have to accuse him.

But Jesus stooped down, and with his finger, wrote on the ground, as though he heard them not.

So when they continued asking him, he lifted up himself, and said unto them, He that is without sin among you, let him first cast a stone at her.

And again he stooped down, and wrote on the ground.

And they which heard it, being convicted by their own conscience, went out one by one, beginning at the eldest, even unto the last: and Jesus was left alone, and the woman standing in the midst.

When Jesus had lifted up himself, and saw none but the woman, he said unto her, Woman, where are those thine accusers? hath no man condemned thee?

She said, No man, Lord. And Jesus said unto her, Neither do I condemn thee: go, and sin no more.

TO LUCASTA, ON GOING BEYOND THE SEAS

Richard Lovelace

If to be absent were to be
Away from thee;
Or that when I am gone
You or I were alone;
Then, my Lucasta, might I crave
Pity from blustering wind, or swallowing wave.

Though seas and land betwixt us both,
Our faith and troth,
Like separated souls,
All time and space controls:
Above the highest sphere we meet
Unseen, unknown, and greet as Angels greet.

So then we do anticipate
Our after-fate,
And are alive i' the skies,
If thus our lips and eyes
Can speak like spirits unconfined
In Heaven, their earthy bodies left behind.

WE ARE MADE FOR CO-OPERATION

Marcus Aurelius

(TRANSLATOR: Charles Long)

Begin the morning by saying to yourself, I shall meet with the busybody, the ungrateful, arrogant, deceitful, envious, unsocial. All these things happen to them by reason of their ignorance of what is good and evil. But I who have seen the nature of the good that it is beautiful, and of the bad that it is ugly, and the nature of him who does wrong, that it is akin to me, not only of the same blood and seed, but that it participates in the same intelligence and the same portion of divinity, I can neither be injured by any of them, for no one can fix on me what is ugly, nor can I be angry with my kinsman, nor hate him. For we are made for co-operation, like feet, like hands, like eyelids, like the rows of the upper and lower teeth. To act against one another is contrary to nature, and it is acting against one another to be vexed and to turn away.

AWAY

James Whitcomb Riley

I cannot say, and I will not say
That he is dead. He is just away!

With a cheery smile and a wave of the hand,
He has wandered into an unknown land,

And left us dreaming how very fair
It needs must be, since he lingers there.

And you—oh you, who the wildest yearn
For the old time step and the glad return—

Think of him faring on, as dear
In the love of There as the love of Here;

And loyal still, as he gave the blows
Of his warrior strength to his country's foes—

Mild and gentle, as he was brave,
When the sweetest love of his life he gave

To simple things; where the violets grew
Pure as the eyes they were likened to,

The touches of his hands have strayed
As reverently as his lips have prayed;

When the little brown thrush that harshly chirred
Was dear to him as the mocking bird;

And he pitied as much as a man in pain
A writhing honey-bee wet with rain.

Think of him still as the same, I say;
He is not dead—he is just—away!

A SOUTHERN GENERAL'S ACCOUNT OF PICKETT'S CHARGE AT GETTYSBURG

James Longstreet

I did not see General Lee that night. On the next morning he came to see me, and, fearing that he was still in his disposition to attack, I tried to anticipate him, by saying: "General, I have had my scouts out all night, and I find that you still have an excellent opportunity to move around to the right of Meade's army, and maneuvre him into attacking us." He replied, pointing with his fist at Cemetery Hill: "The enemy is there, and I am going to strike him." I felt that it was my duty to express my convictions; I said: "General, I have been a soldier all my life. I have been with soldiers engaged in fights by couples, by squads, companies, regiments, divisions, and armies, and should know, as well as any one, what soldiers can do. It is my opinion that no fifteen thousand men ever arrayed for battle can take that position," pointing to Cemetery Hill. General Lee, in reply to this, ordered me to prepare Pickett's Division for the attack. I should not have been so urgent had I not foreseen the hopelessness of the proposed assault. I felt that I must say a word against the sacrifice of my men; and then I felt that my record was such that General Lee would or could not misconstrue my motives.

I said no more, however, but turned away. The most of the morning was consumed in waiting for Pickett's men, and getting into position. The plan of assault was as follows: Our artillery was to be massed in a wood from which Pickett was to charge, and it was to pour a continuous fire upon the cemetery. Under cover of this fire, and supported by it, Pickett was to charge.

Our artillery was in charge of General E. P. Alexander, a brave, gifted officer. Colonel Walton was my chief of artillery; but Alexander, being at the head of the column, and being first in position, and being, besides, an officer of unusual promptness, sagacity, and intelligence, was given charge of the artillery. The arrangements were completed about one o'clock. General Alexander had arranged that a battery of seven eleven-pound howitzers, with fresh horses and full caissons, were to charge with Pickett, at the head of his line, but General Pendleton, from whom the guns had been borrowed, recalled them just before the charge was made, and thus deranged this wise plan. Never was I so depressed as upon that day. I felt that my men were to be sacrificed, and that I should have to order them to make a hopeless charge. I had instructed General Alexander, being unwilling to trust myself with the entire responsibility, to carefully observe the effect of the fire upon the enemy, and when it began to tell to notify Pickett to begin the assault. I was so much impressed with the hopelessness of the charge, that I wrote the following note to General Alexander: "If the artillery fire does not have the effect to drive off the enemy or greatly demoralize them, so as to make our efforts pretty certain, I would prefer that you should not advise General Pickett to make the charge. I shall rely a great deal on your judgment to determine the matter, and shall expect you to let Pickett know when the moment offers."

To my note the General replied as follows: "I will only be able to judge the effect of our fire upon the enemy by his return fire, for his infantry is but little exposed to view, and the smoke will obscure the whole field. If, as I infer from your note, there is an alternative to this attack, it should be carefully considered before opening our fire, for it will take all of the artillery ammunition we have left to test this one thoroughly; and, if the result is unfavorable, we will have none left for another effort; and, even if this is entirely successful, it can only be so at a very bloody cost." I still desired to save my men, and felt that if the artillery did not produce the desired effect, I would be justified in holding Pickett off. I wrote this note to Colonel Walton at exactly 1:30 P.M.: "Let the batteries open. Order great precision in firing. If the batteries at the peach orchard cannot be used against the point we intend attacking, let them open on the enemy at Rocky Hill." The cannonading which opened along both lines was grand. In a few moments a courier brought a note to General Pickett (who was standing near me) from Alexander, which, after reading, he handed to me. It was as follows: "If you are coming at all, you must come at once, or I cannot give you proper support; but the enemy's fire has not slackened at all; at least eighteen guns are still firing from the cemetery itself." After I had read the note, Pickett said to me: "General, shall I advance?" My feelings had so overcome me that I would not speak, for fear of betraying my want of confidence to him. I bowed affirmation, and turned to mount my horse. Pickett immediately said: "I shall lead my division forward, sir." I spurred my horse to the wood where Alexander was stationed with artillery. When I reached him, he told me of the disappearance of the seven guns which were to have led the charge with Pickett, and that his ammunition was so low that he could not properly support the charge. I at once ordered him to stop Pickett until the ammunition had been replenished. He informed me that he had no ammunition with which to replenish. I then saw that there was no help for it, and that Pickett must advance under his orders. He swept past our artillery in splendid style, and the men marched steadily and compactly down the slope. As they started up the ridge, over one hundred cannon from the breastworks of the Federals hurled a rain of canister, grape, and shell down upon them; still they pressed on until half way up the slope, when the crest of the hill was lit with a solid sheet of flame as the masses of infantry rose and fired. When the smoke cleared away, Pickett's Division was gone. Nearly two-thirds of his men lay dead on the field, and the survivors were sullenly retreating down the hill. Mortal man could not have stood that fire. In half an hour the contested field was cleared and the battle of Gettysburg was over.

THE CANDID PHYSICIAN

John C. Lettsom

When people's ill, they come to I,
    I physics, bleeds, and sweats 'em;
Sometimes they live, sometimes they die.
    What's that to I? I lets 'em.

CONCERNING THE U.S.A.

Thomas Babington Macaulay

Either some Caesar or Napoleon will seize the reins of government
with a strong hand, or your republic will be as fearfully plundered
and laid waste by barbarians in the Twentieth Century as the
Roman Empire was in the Fifth; with this difference, that the Huns
and Vandals who ravaged the Roman Empire came from without,
and that your Huns and Vandals will have been engendered within
your own country by your own institutions.

(From a letter to H. S. Randall, May 23, 1857)

THE EAGLE AND THE MOLE

Elinor Wylie

Avoid the reeking herd,
Shun the polluted flock,
Live like that stoic bird,
The eagle of the rock.

The huddled warmth of crowds
Begets and fosters hate;
He keeps, above the clouds,
His cliff inviolate.

When flocks are folded warm,
And herds to shelter run,
He sails above the storm,
He stares into the sun.

If in the eagle's track
Your sinews cannot leap,
Avoid the lathered pack,
Turn from the steaming sheep.

If you would keep your soul
From spotted sight or sound,
Live like the velvet mole;
Go burrow under ground.

And there hold intercourse
With roots of trees and stones,
With rivers at their source,
And disembodied bones.

A PLEA FOR JUDICIAL RESTRAINT

U.S. Supreme Court Justice Felix Frankfurter

One who belongs to the most vilified and persecuted minorities in history is not likely to be insensible to the freedoms guaranteed by our Constitution. Were my purely personal attitude relevant, I should whole-heartedly associate myself with the general libertarian views in the Court's opinion, representing as they do the thoughts and action of a lifetime. But as judges we are neither Jew nor Gentile, neither Catholic nor agnostic. We owe equal attachment to the Constitution and are equally bound by our judicial obligations, whether we derive our citizenship from the earliest or the latest immigrants to these shores. As a member of this Court I am not justified in writing my private opinions of policy into the Constittuion, no matter how deeply I may cherish them or how mischievous I may deem their disregard. The duty of a judge who must decide which of two claims before the Court shall prevail, that of a State to enact and enforce laws within its general competence or that of an individual to refuse obedience because of the demands of his conscience, is not that of the ordinary person. It can never be emphasized too much that one's own opinion about the wisdom or evil of a law should be excluded altogether when one is doing one's duty on the bench. The only opinion of our own even looking in that direction that is material is our opinion whether legislators could in reason have enacted such a law. . . .

When Mr. Justice Holmes, speaking for this Court, wrote that "it must be remembered that legislatures are ultimate guardian of the liberties and welfare of the people in quite as great a degree as the courts," he went to the very essence of our constitutional system and the democratic conception of our society. He did not mean that only for some phases of civil government this Court was not to supplant legislatures and sit in judgment upon the right or wrong of a challenged measure. He was stating the comprehensive judicial duty and role of this Court in our constitutional scheme whenever legislation is sought to be nullified on any ground, namely, that responsibility for legislation lies with legislatures, answerable as they are directly to the people, and this Court's only and very narrow function is to determine whether within the broad grant of authority vested in legislatures they have exercised a judgment for which reasonable justification can be offered. . . .

The uncontrollable power wielded by this Court brings it very close to the most sensitive areas of public affairs. As appeal from legislation to adjudication becomes more frequent, and its consequences more far reaching, judicial self-restraint becomes more and not less important, lest unwarrantably enter social and political domains wholly outside our concern. I think I appreciate fully the objections to the law before us. But to deny that it presents a question upon which men might reasonably differ appears to me to be intolerance. And since men may so reasonably differ, I deem it beyond my constitutional power to assert my view of the wisdom of this law against the view of the State of West Virginia.

(Dissenting Opinion, 1943)

TAKE MY LIFE AND LET IT BE

Frances R. Havergal

Take my life and let it be
Consecrated, Lord, to Thee;
Take my hands and let them move
At the impulse of Thy love,
At the impulse of Thy love.

Take my feet and let them be
Swift and beautiful for Thee;
Take my voice, and let me sing
Always, only, for my King.
Always, only, for my King.

Take my will and make it Thine
It shall be no longer mine;
Take my heart, it is Thine own.
It shall be Thy royal throne.
It shall be Thy royal throne.

(228)

THE COMPANY ONE KEEPS

Aimor R. Dickson

One night in late October,
When I was far from sober,
Returning with my load with manly pride,
My feet began to stutter
So I lay down in the gutter,
And a pig came near and lay down by my side,
A lady passing by was then heard plain to say,
"You can tell a man who boozes,
By the company he chooses."
At which the pig got up and slowly walked away.

THE MORNS ARE MEEKER THAN THEY WERE

Emily Dickinson

The morns are meeker than they were,
The nuts are getting brown;
The berry's cheek is plumper,
The rose is out of town.

The maple wears a gayer scarf,
The field a scarlet gown,
Lest I should be old-fashioned,
I'll put a trinket on.

When a true genius appears in the world you may know
him by this sign: that the dunces are all in confederacy
against him.

—Jonathan Swift

BEETHOVEN'S SIXTH SYMPHONY

Robert G. Ingersoll

This sound-wrought picture of the fields and woods, of flowering hedge and happy home, where thrushes build and swallows fly, and mothers sing to babes; this echo of the babbled lullaby of brooks that, dallying, wind and fall where meadows bare their daisied bosoms to the sun; this joyous mimicry of summer rain, the laugh of children, and the rhythmic rustle of the whispering leaves; this strophe of peasant life; this perfect poem of content and love.

TO MISTRESS MARGARET HUSSEY

John Skelton

> Merry Margaret,
> As midsummer flower,
> Gentle as falcon
> Or hawk of the tower;
> With solace and gladness,
> Much mirth and no madness,
> All good and no badness;
> So joyously,
> So maidenly,
> So womanly,
> Her demeaning;
> In everything
> Far far passing
> That I can indite
> Or suffice to write
> Of merry Margaret,
> As midsummer flower,
> Gentle as falcon
> Or hawk of the tower.
> As patient and as still
> And as full of good will,
> As the fair Isyphill,
> Coriander,
> Sweet pomander,
> Good Cassander;

Steadfast of thought,
Well made, well wrought.
Far may be sought
Ere ye can find
So courteous, so kind,
As merry Margaret,
This midsummer flower,
Gentle as falcon
Or hawk of the tower.

RHYMING RIDDLE

The beginning of eternity, the end of time and space,
The beginning of every end, and the end of every place.
                              (Answer: The Letter *E*)

TO AN ANXIOUS FRIEND

William Allen White

You tell me that law is above freedom of utterance. And I reply
that you can have no wise laws nor free enforcement of wise laws
unless there is free expression of the wisdom of the people—and,
alas, their folly with it. But if there is freedom, folly will die of its
own poison, and the wisdom will survive. That is the history of the
race. It is proof of man's kinship with God. You say that freedom
is not for time of stress, and I reply with the sad truth that only
in time of stress is freedom of utterance in danger. No one questions
it in calm days, because it is not needed. And the reverse is true also;
only when free utterance is suppressed it is needed, and when it is
needed, it is most vital to justice.

Peace is good. But if you are interested in peace through force
and without free discussion—that is to say, free utterance recently
and in order—your interest in justice is slight. And peace without
justice is tyranny, no matter how you may sugar-coat it with ex-
pedience. This state today is in no more danger from suppression
than from violence, because, in the end, suppression leads to violence.
Whoever pleads for justice helps to keep the peace; and whoever

(231)

tramples on the plea for justice temperately made in the name of peace only outrages peace and kills something fine in the heart of man which God put there when we got our manhood. When that is killed, brute meets brute on each side of the line.

So, dear friend, put fear out of your heart. This nation will survive, this state will prosper, the orderly business of life will go forward if only men can speak in whatever way given them to utter what their hearts hold—by voice, by posted card, by letter, or by press. Reason has never failed men. Only force and repression have made the wrecks in the world.

(Emporia Gazette, July 27, 1922)

THE BEST AND THE WORST

Anonymous

This is the best world that we live in,
To lend, and to spend, and to give in;
But to borrow, to beg, or to get a man's own,
It is the worst world that ever was known.

O NEVER STAR WAS LOST

Robert Browning

O never star
Was lost; here
We all aspire to heaven and there is heaven
Above us.
If I stoop
Into a dark tremendous sea of cloud,
It is but for a time; I press God's lamp
Close to my breast; its splendor soon or late
Will pierce the gloom. I shall emerge some day.

SAMUEL PEPYS DESCRIBES THE FIRE OF LONDON,
September, 1666

September 2nd (Lord's Day)—Some of our maids sitting up late last night to get things ready against our feast today. Jane called us about three in the morning, to tell us of a great fire they saw in the City. So I rose, and slipped on my night-gown, and went to her window, and thought it to be on the backside of Mark Lane at the farthest; but being unused to such fires as followed, I thought it far enough off; and so went to bed again, and to sleep. About seven arose to dress myself, and there looked out at the window, and saw the fire not so much as it was, and farther off. So to my closet to set things to right, after yesterday's cleaning.

By and by, Jane comes and tells me that she hears that above 300 houses have been burned down during tonight by the fire we saw, and that it is now burning down all Fish Street, by London Bridge. So I made myself ready presently and walked to the Tower; and there got up upon one of the high places, Sir J. Robinson's little son going up with me; and there I did see the houses at that end of the bridge all on fire, and an infinite great fire on this and the other side of the end of the bridge; which among other people, did trouble me for poor little Michell and our Sarah on the bridge.

So down, with my heart full of trouble, to the Lieutenant of the Tower, who tells me that it began this morning in the King's baker house in Pudding Lane, and that it hath burned down St. Magnus's Church and most part of Fish Street already. So I sat down by the waterside, and there got a boat, and through bridge, and there saw a lamentable fire. Poor Michell's house, as far as Old Swan, already burned that way, and the fire running farther, that in a very little time it got as far as the Steelyard, while I was there. Everybody endeavoring to remove their goods, and flinging into the river, or bringing them into lighters that lay off; poor people staying in their houses as long as till the very fire touched them and then running into boats or clambering from one pair of stairs, by the waterside, to another. And, among other things, the poor pigeons, I perceive, were loath to leave their houses, but hovered about their windows and balconies, till they burned their wings, and fell down.

Having stayed, and in an hour's time, seen the fire range every way; and nobody, to my sight, endeavoring to quench it, but to remove their goods, and leave all to the fire; and, having seen it get as far as the Steelyard, and the wind mighty high and driving it into the City; and everything, after so long a drought, providing combustile, even the very stones of the churches, and among other things, the poor steeple by which pretty Mrs. ———— lives, and whereof my old schoolfellow Elborough is parson, taken fire in the very top, and there burned till it fell down; I to Whitehall, with a gentleman with me, who desired to go off from the Tower, to see the fire, in my boat; and there up to the King's Closet in the Chapel, where people came about me, and I did give them an account dismayed them all, and word was carried in to the King. So I was called for, and did tell the King and the Duke of York what I saw; and that unless His Majesty did command houses to be pulled down, nothing could stop the fire.

They seemed much troubled, and the King commanded me to go to my Lord Mayor from him, and command him to spare no houses, but to pull down before the fire every way. The Duke of York bid me tell him that if he would have any more soldiers he shall; and so did my Lord Arlington afterwards, as a great secret. Here meeting with Captain Cocke, I in his coach, which he lent me, and Creed with me to Paul's; and there walked along Watling Street, as well as I could, every creature coming away Loaden with goods to save, and here and there sick people carried away in beds. Extraordinary good goods carried in carts and on backs.

At last met my Lord Mayor in Canning Street, like a man spent, with a handkerchief about his neck. To the King's message he cried, like a fainting woman, "Lord! what can I do? I am spent; people will not obey me. I have been pulling down houses; but the fire overtakes us faster than we can do it." That he needed no more soldiers; and that, for himself, he must go and refresh himself, having been up all night. So he left me, and I him, and walked home, seeing people all almost distracted, and no manner of means used to quench the fire. The houses, too, so very thick thereabouts, and full of matter for burning, as pitch and tar, in Thames Street; and warehouses of oil, and wines, and brandy, and other things.

Here I saw Mr. Isaac Houblon, the handsome man, prettily dressed and dirty, at his door at Dowgate, receiving some of his brother's things, whose houses were on fire; and, as he says, have been removed twice already; and he doubts (as it soon proved) that they must be in a little time removed from his house also, which was a sad consideration. And to see the churches all filling with goods by people who themselves should have been quietly there at this time. By this time it was about twelve o'clock; and so home, and there to find my guests, who were Mr. Wood and his wife Barbary Shelden, and also Mr. Moone; she mighty fine, and her husband, for aught I see, a likely man.

But Mr. Moone's design and mine, which was to look over my closet, and please him with the sight thereof, which he hath long desired, was wholly disappointed; for we were in great trouble and disturbance at this fire, not knowing what to think of it. However, we had an extraordinary good dinner, and as merry as at this time we could be. While at dinner, Mrs. Batelier came to inquire after Mr. Woolfe and Stanes, (whom it seems, are related to them) whose houses in Fish Street are all burned, and they in a sad condition. She would not stay in the fright.

Soon as dined, I and Moone away, and walked through the City, and the streets full of nothing but people and horses and carts loaden with goods, ready to run over one another, and removing goods from one burned house to another. They now removing out of Canning Street, (which received goods in the morning) into Lumbard-street, and further; and, among others, I now saw my little goldsmith, Stokes, receiving some friend's goods, whose house itself was burned out the day after. . . .

Having seen as much as I could now, I away to Whitehall by appointment, and there walked to St. James's Park, and there met my wife and Creed and Wood and his wife, and walked to my boat; and there upon the water again, and to the fire up and down, it still increasing, and the wind great. So near the fire as we could for smoke; and all over the Thames, with one's face in the wind, you were almost burned with a shower of fire-drops. This is very true; so as houses were burned by these drops and flakes of fire, three or four, nay, five or six houses, one from another. When we could endure no more upon the water, we to a little alehouse on the Bankside, over against the Three Cranes, and there stayed till it was dark almost, and saw the fire grow; and, as it grew darker, appeared more and more, and in corners and upon steeples, and between churches and houses, as far as we could see up the hill of the City, in a most horrid, malicious, bloody flame, not like the fine flame of an ordinary fire. . . .

We stayed till, it being darkish, we saw the fire as only one entire arch of fire from this to the other side of the bridge, and in a bow up the hill for an arch above a mile long; it made me weep to see it. The churches, houses, and all on fire and flaming at once; and a horrid noise the flames made, and the cracking of houses at their ruin.

So home with a sad heart, and there find everybody discoursing, and lamenting the fire; and poor Tom Hater come with some few of his goods saved out of his house, which was burned upon Fish Street Hill. I invited him in to lie at my house, and did receive his goods, but was deceived in his lying there, the news coming every moment of the growth of the fire, so we were forced to begin to pack up our own goods, and prepare for removal; and did by moon-shine (it being brave dry and moonshine and warm weather) carry much of my goods into the garden, and Mr. Hater and I did remove my money and iron chests into my cellar, as thinking that the safest place. And got my bags of gold into my office, ready to carry away, and my chief papers of account also there, and my tallies into a box by themselves. . . .

3rd. About four o'clock in the morning, my Lady Batten sent me a cart to carry away all my money, and plate, and best things, to Sir W. Rider's at Bednall-greene. Which I did, riding myself in my night-gown in the cart; and Lord to see how the streets and highways are crowded with people running and riding, and getting of carts at any rate to fetch away things. I find Sir W. Rider tired with being called up all night, and receiving things from several friends. His house full of goods, and much of Sir W. Batten's and Sir W. Pen's. I am eased at my heart to have my treasure so well secured. Then home, and with much ado to find a way, nor any sleep till this night to me nor my poor wife. But then all this day she and I, and all my people laboring to get away the rest of our things, and did get Mr. Tooker to get me a lighter to take them in, and we did carry them (myself some) over Tower Hill, which was by this time full of people's goods, bringing their goods thither; and down to the lighter which lay at the next quay, above the Tower Dock. . . .

4th. Up by break of day, to get away the remainder of my things; which I did by a lighter at the Iron Gate; and my hands so full, that it was the afternoon before we could get them all away. Sir W. Pen and I to the Tower street, and there met the fire burning three or four doors beyond Mr. Howell's, whose goods, poor man, his trays, and dishes, shovels, &c. were flung all along Tower street in the kennels, and people working therewith from one end to the other; the fire coming in on that narrow street, on both sides, with infinite fury. Sir W. Batten not knowing how to remove his wine, did dig a pit in the garden, and laid it in there; and I took the opportunity of laying all the papers of my office that I could not otherwise dispose of. And in the evening Sir W. Pen and I did dig another, and put our wine in it; and I my parmazan cheese, as well as my wine and some other things. . . . This night Mrs. Turner (who, poor woman, was removing her goods all this day, good goods into the garden, and knows not how to dispose of them), and her husband supped with my wife and me at night, in the office, upon a shoulder of mutton from the cook's, without any napkin, or any thing, in a sad manner, but were merry. Only now and then, walking into the garden, saw how horribly the sky looks, all on fire in the night, was enough to put us out of our wits; and, indeed, it was extremely dreadful, for it looks as if it was at us, and the whole heaven on fire. I after supper walked in the dark down to Tower street, and there saw it all on fire, at the Trinity House on that side, and the Dolphin Tavern on this side, which was very near us; and the fire with extraordinary vehemence. Now begins the practice of blowing up of houses in Tower street, those next the Tower, which at first did frighten people more than any thing; but it stopped the fire where it was done, it bringing down the houses to the ground in the same places they stood, and then it was easy enough to quench what little fire was in it, though it kindled nothing almost. . . .

5th. I lay down in the office again upon W. Hewer's quilt, being mighty weary, and sore in my feet with going till I was hardly able to stand. About two in the morning my wife calls me up, and tells me of new cries of fire, it being come to Barking Church, which is the bottom of our lane. I up; and finding it so, resolved presently to take her away, and did, and took my gold, which was about 2350 pounds. W. Hewer, and Jane, down by Proundy's boat to Woolwich; but Lord! what a sad sight it was by moon-light to see the whole City almost on fire, though you might see it plain at Woolwich, as if you were by it. There, when I come, I find the gates shut, but no guard kept at all; which troubled me, because of discourses now begun, that there is a plot in it, and that the French had done it. I got the gates open, and to Mr. Shelden's, where I locked up my gold, and charged my wife and W. Hewer never to leave the room without one of them in it, night or day. So back again, by the way seeing my goods well in the lighters at Deptford, and watched well by people. Home and whereas I expected to have seen our house on fire, it being now about seven o'clock, it was not. . . . Going to the fire, I find by the blowing up of houses, and the great help given by the workmen out of the King's yards, sent up by Sir W. Pen, there is a good stop given to it. . . . I up to the top of Barking steeple, and there saw the saddest sight of desolation that ever I saw; every where great fires, oil cellars, and brimstone, and other things burning. I became afraid to stay there long, and therefore got down again as fast as I could, the fire being spread as far as I could see it. . . . I walked into the town, and find Fanchurch street, Gracious street, and Lumbard-street, all in dust. The Exchange a sad sight, nothing standing there, of all the statues or pillars, but Sir Thomas Gresham's picture in the corner. Into Mooresfield, (our feet ready to burn, walking through the town among the hot coals), and find that full of people, and poor wretches carrying their goods there, and every body keeping his goods together by themselves; . . . So home at night, and find there good hopes of saving our office. . . .

6th. At home, did go with Sir W. Batten, and our neighbor, Knightly, (who, with one more, was the only man of any fashion left in all the neighborhood thereabouts, they all removing their goods, and leaving their houses to the mercy of the fire), to Sir R. Ford's, and there dined in an earthen platter—a fried breast of mutton; a great many of us, but very merry, and indeed a good meal, though as ugly a one, as ever I had in my life. Thence down to Deptford, and there with great satisfaction landed all my goods at Sir G. Carteret's safe, and nothing missed I could see or hear. This being done to my great content, I home, and to Sir W. Batten's, and there with Sir R. Ford, Mr. Knightly, and one Withers, a professed lying rogue, supped well, and mighty merry, and our fears over. . . .

7th. Up by five o'clock; and blessed be God! find all well; and by water to Pane's Wharf. Walked thence, and saw all the town burned, and a miserable sight. . . . To Sir W. Coventry, at St. James's, who lay without curtains, having removed all his goods; as the King at Whitehall and every body had done, and was doing. . . . Thence to the Swan, and there drank, and so home . . . and did give orders for my house to be made clean. . . . I home late to Sir W. Pen's, who did give me a bed; but without curtains or hangings, all being down. So here I went the first time into a naked bed, only my drawers on; and did sleep pretty well; but still both sleeping and waking had a fear of fire in my heart, that I took little rest.

EPITAPH

Anonymous

Here lies I and my three daughters,
Killed by drinking Cheltenham waters;
If we had stuck to epsom salts,
We'd not been a-lying in these here vaults.

CLEOPATRA DYING

Thomas Stephens Collier

Sinks the sun below the desert,
   Golden glows the sluggish Nile;
Purple flame crowns Spring and Temple,
   Lights up every ancient pile
Where the old gods now are sleeping;
   Isis and Osiris great,
Guard me, help me, give me courage
   Like a Queen to meet my fate.

"I am dying, Egypt, dying,"
   Let the Caesar's army come—
I will cheat him of his glory,
   Though beyond the Styx I roam,
Shall he drag this beauty with him—
   While the crowd his triumph sings?
No, no, never! I will show him
   What lies in the blood of Kings!

Though he holds the golden scepter,
   Rules the Pharaoh's sunny land,
Where old Nilus rolls resistless
   Through the sweeps of silvery sand—
He shall never say I met him
   Fawning, abject, like a slave—
I will foil him, though to do it
   I must cross the Stygian wave.

Oh, my hero, sleeping, sleeping—
   Shall I meet you on the shore
Of Plutonian shadows? Shall we
   In death meet and love once more?
See, I follow in your footsteps—
   Scorn the Caesar in his might;
For your love I will leap boldly
   Into realms of death and night.

Down below the desert sinking,
   Fades Apollo's brilliant car;
And from out the distant azure
   Breaks the bright beam of a star.

Venus, Queen of Love and Beauty,
  Welcomes me to death's embrace,
Dying, free, proud, and triumphant,
  The last sovereign of my race.

Dying, dying! I am coming,
  Oh, my hero, to your arms;
You will welcome me, I know it—
  Guard me from all rude alarms.
Hark! I hear the legions coming,
  Hear the cries of triumph swell,
But, proud Caesar, dead I scorn you—
  Egypt, Antony, farewell.

THE BATTLE OF THE ANTS

Henry David Thoreau

One day when I went out to my wood-pile, or rather my pile of stumps, I observed two large ants, the one red, the other much larger, nearly half an inch long, and black, fiercely contending with one another. Having once got hold they never let go, but struggled and wrestled and rolled on the chips incessantly.

Looking farther, I was surprised to find that the chips were covered with such combatants, that it was not a *duellum*, but a *bellum*, a war between two races of ants, the red always pitted against the black, and frequently two red ones to one black. The legions of these Myrmidons covered all the hills and vales in my wood-yard, and the ground was already strewn with the dead and dying, both red and black. It was the only battle which I have ever witnessed, the only battle-field I ever trod while the battle was raging; internecine war; the red republicans on the one hand, and the black imperialists on the other. On every side they were engaged in deadly combat, yet without any noise that I could hear, and human soldiers never fought so resolutely.

I watched a couple that were fast locked in each other's embraces, in a little sunny valley amid the chips, now at noonday prepared to fight till the sun went down, or life went out. The smaller red champion had fastened himself like a vise to his adversary's front, and through all the tumblings on that field never for an instant ceased to gnaw at one of his feelers near the root, having already caused the other to go by the board; while the stronger black one dashed him from side to side, and, as I saw on looking nearer, had already divested him of several of his members. They fought with more pertinacity than bulldogs. Neither manifested the least disposition to retreat. It was evident that their battle-cry was "Conquer or die."

In the meanwhile there came along a single red ant on the hillside of this valley, evidently full of excitement, who either had despatched his foe, or had not yet taken part in the battle; probably the latter, for he had lost none of his limbs; whose mother had charged him to return with his shield or upon it. Or perchance he was some Achilles, who had nourished his wrath apart, and had now come to avenge or rescue his Patroclus. He saw this unequal combat from afar—for the blacks were nearly twice the size of the red—he drew near with rapid pace till he stood on his guard within half an inch of the combatants; then, watching his opportunity, he sprang upon the black warrior, and commenced his operations near the root of his right fore leg, leaving the foe to select among his own members; and so there were three united for life, as if a new kind of attraction had been invented which put all other locks and cements to shame.

I should not have wondered by this time to find that they had their respective musical bands stationed on some eminent chip, and playing their national airs the while, to excite the slow and cheer the dying combatants. I was myself excited somewhat even as if they had been men. The more you think of it, the less the difference. And certainly there is not the fight recorded in Concord history, at least, if in the history of America, that will bear a moment's comparison with this, whether for the numbers engaged in it, or for the patriotism and heroism displayed. For numbers and for carnage it was an Austerlitz or Dresden. Concord Fight! Two killed on the patriot's side, and Luther Blanchard wounded! Why, here every ant was a Buttrick—"Fire! for God's sake, fire!"—and thousands shared the fate of Davis and Hosmer. There was not one hireling there. I have no doubt it was a principle they fought for, as much as our ancestors, and not to avoid a three-penny tax on their tea; and the result of this battle will be as important and memorable to those whom it concerns as those of the battle of Bunker Hill, at least.

I took up the chip on which the three I have particularly described were struggling, carried it into my house, and placed it under a tumbler on my window-sill, in order to see the issue. Holding a microscope to the first-mentioned red ant, I saw that, though he was assiduously gnawing at the near fore leg of his enemy, having severed his remaining feeler, his own breast was all torn away, exposing what vitals he had there to the jaws of the black warrior, whose breast-plate was apparently too thick for him to pierce; and the dark carbuncles of the sufferer's eyes shone with ferocity such as war only could excite. They struggled half an hour longer under the tumbler, and when I looked again the black soldier had severed the heads of his foes from their bodies, and the still living heads were hanging on either side of him like ghastly trophies at his saddle-bow, still apparently as firmly fastened as ever, and he was endeavoring with feeble struggles, being without feelers and with only the remnant of a leg, and I know not how many other wounds, to divest himself of them; which at length, after half an hour more, he accomplished.

I raised the glass, and he went off over the window-sill in that crippled state. Whether he finally survived that combat, and spent the remainder of his days in some Hotel des Invalides, I do not know; but I thought that his industry would not be worth much thereafter. I never learned which party was victorious, nor the cause of the war; but I felt for the rest of that day as if I had had my feelings excited and harrowed by witnessing the struggle, the ferocity and carnage, of a human battle before my door.

SING WHILE YOU DRIVE

Anonymous

At 45 miles per hour, sing—"Highways are Happy Ways."
At 55 miles, sing—"I'm But a Stranger Here, Heaven is My Home."
At 65 miles, sing—"Nearer, My God, to Thee!"
At 75 miles, sing—"When the Roll is Called Up Yonder, I'll Be There."
At 85 miles, sing—"Lord, I'm Coming Home."

I don't care what they call me as long as they mention my name.

—George M. Cohan

THE OCEAN OF LIFE

Henry Wadsworth Longfellow

Ships that pass in the night, and speak
    each other in passing;
Only a signal shown and a distant
    voice in the darkness;
So in the ocean of life we pass and
    speak one another,
Only a look and a voice; then darkness
    again and a silence.

ADMIRATION AND AWE

Immanuel Kant

Two things fill the mind with ever new and increasing admiration and awe, the oftener and more steadily we reflect on them: *the starry heavens above and the moral law within.* I have not to search for them and conjecture them as though they were veiled in darkness or were in the transcendent region beyond my horizon; I see them before me and connect them directly with the consciousness of my existence.

YOU, ANDREW MARVELL

Archibald MacLeish

And here face down beneath the sun
And here upon earth's noonward height
To feel the always coming on
The always rising of the night

To feel creep up the curving east
The earthy chill of dusk and slow
Upon those under lands the vast
And ever climbing shadow grow

(243)

And strange at Ecbatan the trees
Take leaf by leaf the evening strange
The flooding dark about their knees
The mountains over Persia change

And now at Kermanshah the gate
Dark empty and the withered grass
And through the twilight now the late
Few travelers in the westward pass

And Baghdad darken and the bridge
Across the silent river gone
And through Arabia the edge
Of evening widen and steal on

And deepen on Palmyra's street
The wheel rut in the ruined stone
And Lebanon fade out and Crete
High through the clouds and overblown

And over Sicily the air
Still flashing with the landward gulls
And loom and slowly disappear
The sails above the shadowy hulls

And Spain go under and the shore
Of Africa the gilded sand
And evening vanish and no more
The low pale light across that land

Nor now the long light on the sea

And here face downward in the sun
To feel how swift how secretly
The shadow of the night comes on . . .

TWENTY-YEAR-OLD QUEEN VICTORIA TELLS HER DIARY OF HER ENGAGEMENT AND MARRIAGE TO PRINCE ALBERT

April 10 [1839]. Talked of . . . Augusta, who I said was to go out everywhere, like any other girl; Lord M[elbourne] said that it was the first time a Princess of England did such a thing. "I don't think the King [George III] would have liked that," said Lord M. "If she goes out like any other girl, she runs the risk like any other girl of forming attachments," which is very true and awkward. "She may take a liking to somebody whom she couldn't marry," he added. . . .

April 15. Talked of some people, and Lord Melbourne said, "An Italian and an English make the finest animal in the world; it's the mixture of nations that makes the finest specimens of the human race." . . .

April 18. Lord M. then said, "Now, Ma'am for this other matter." I felt terrified. . . . Well, I mustered up courage, and said that my Uncle's great wish—was—that I should marry my Cousin Albert. . . . He said, "Cousins are not very good things," and "Those Coburgs are not popular abroad; the Russians hate them." I then said, who was there else? . . . I said I dreaded the thought of marrying; that I was so accustomed to have my own way, that I thought it was 10 to 1 that I shouldn't agree with any body. Lord M. said, "Oh! but you would have it still. . . ."

October 10, At ½ p. 7 I went to the top of the staircase to receive my 2 dear cousins Ernest and Albert—whom I found grown and changed, and embellished. It was with some emotion that I beheld Albert who is *beautiful*. I embraced them both and took them to Mamma. . . .

October 11. . . . Albert really is quite charming, and so excessively handsome, such beautiful blue eyes, an exquisite nose, and such a pretty mouth with delicate moustachios and slight but very slight whiskers; a beautiful figure, broad in the shoulders and a fine waist. At about ½ p. 10 dancing began. I danced 5 quadrilles . . . it is quite a pleasure to look at Albert when he gallops and valses, he does it so beautifully, holds himself so well with that beautiful figure of his. . . .

October 13. . . . I sat on the sofa with dearest Albert; Lord Melbourne sitting near me, Ernest playing at chess . . . I played 2 games at Tactics with dear Albert, and 2 at Fox and Geese. Stayed up till 20 m. p. 11. A delightful evening.

October. . . . At 1 came Lord Melbourne. . . . Talked of my Cousins' having gone out shooting. After a little pause I said to Lord M., that I had made up my mind (about marrying Albert) .—"You have?" he said; "well then, about the time?" Not for a year, I thought; which he said was too long. . . . "I think it's a very good thing, and you'll be much more comfortable; for a woman cannot stand alone for long, in whatever situation she is." . . . Then I asked, if I hadn't better tell Albert of my decision soon, in which Lord M. agreed. How? I asked, for that in general such things were done the other way,— which made Lord M. laugh. . . .

October 15. . . . At about ½ p. 12 I sent for Albert; he came to the Closet where I was alone, and after a few minutes I said to him, that I thought he must be aware *why* I wished them to come here,—and that it would make me too *happy* if he would consent to what I wished (to marry me) . We embraced each other, and he was *so* kind, *so* affectionate. I told him I was quite unworthy of him,—he . . . was so kind, and seemed so happy, that I really felt it was the happiest brightest moment in my life. I told him it was a great sacrifice,— which he wouldn't allow; I then told him of the necessity of keeping it a secret . . . and also that it was to be as early as the beginning of February. . . .

October 19. . . . My dearest Albert came to me at 10 m. to 12 and stayed with me till 20 m. p. 1. Such a pleasant happy time. He looked over my shoulder and watched me writing to the Duchess of Northumberland, and to the Duchess of Sutherland; and he scraped out some mistakes I had made. I told him I felt so grateful to him and would do everything to make him happy. I gave him a ring with the date of the ever so dear to me *15th* engraved in it. I also gave him a little seal I used to wear. I asked him if he would let me have a little of his dear hair. . . .

February 10 [1840]. Got up at ¼ to 9—well, having slept well; and breakfasted at ½ p. 9. Mamma came before me and brought me a Nosegay of orange flowers. . . . Wrote my journal, and to Lord M. Had my hair dressed and the wreath of orange flowers put on. Saw Albert for the *last* time *alone*, as my *Bridegroom*. Dressed. . . .

At ½ p. 12 I set off, dearest Albert having gone before. I wore a white satin gown with a very deep flounce of Honiton lace, imitation of old. I wore my Turkish diamond necklace and earrings, and Albert's beautiful sapphire brooch. Mamma and the Duchess of Sutherland went in the carriage with me. . . . When I arrived at St. James, I went into the dressing-room where my 12 young Train-bearers were, dressed all in white with white roses, which had a beautiful effect. Here I waited a little till dearest Albert's Procession had moved into the Chapel. I then went with my Train-bearers and ladies into the Throne-room, where the Procession formed; Lord

Melbourne in his fine new dress coat, bearing the Sword of State . . . Queen Anne's room was full of people, ranged on seats one higher than the other, as also in the Guard Room, and by the Staircase,— all very friendly; the Procession looked beautiful going downstairs. Part of the Colour Court was also covered in and full of people who were very civil. The Flourish of Trumpets ceased as I entered the Chapel, and the organ began to play, which had a beautiful effect. At the Altar, to my right, stood Albert. . . . The Ceremony was very imposing, and fine and simple, and I think OUGHT to make an everlasting impression on every one who promises at the Altar to *keep* what he or she promises. Dearest Albert repeated everything distinctly. I felt so happy when the ring was put on, and by Albert. As soon as the Service was over . . . I gave all the Train-bearers as a brooch a small *eagle* of turquoise. I then returned to Buckingham Palace alone with Albert; they cheered us most warmly and heartily; the crowd was immense. . . . I went and sat on the sofa in my dressing-room with Albert . . . then we went downstairs where all the Company was assembled and went into the dining-room . . . dearest Albert leading me in, and my train being borne by 3 Pages, Cowell, little Wemyss, and dear little Byng . . . Albert and I drank a glass of wine with Lord Melbourne, and to Lord Melbourne, whose fine coat I praised. . . . I went upstairs and undressed and put on a white silk gown trimmed with swansdown, and a bonnet with orange flowers. Albert went downstairs and undressed. . . . Dearest Albert came up and fetched me downstairs, where we took leave of Mamma and drove off at near 4; Albert and I alone.

I SHALL RETURN

General Douglas MacArthur

The President of the United States has ordered me to break through the Japanese lines and proceed from Corregidor to Australia for the purpose, as I understand it, of organizing the American offensive against Japan. A primary purpose of this is the relief of the Philippines. I came through and I shall return.

WALTZ ME AROUND AGAIN, WILLIE

Will D. Cobb

Willie Fitzgibbons who used to sell ribbons,
And stood up all day on his feet,
Grew very spooney on Madeline Mooney,
Who'd rather be dancing than eat.
Each evening she'd tag him, to some dance hall drag him,
And when the band started to play,
She'd up like a silly and grab tired Willie,
Steer him on the floor and she'd say:

"Waltz me around again, Willie, a-round, a-round, a-round,
The music it's dreamy, it's peaches and creamy,
Oh! don't let my feet touch the ground.
I feel like a ship on an ocean of joy,
I just want to holler out loud, 'Ship ahoy!'
Oh, waltz me around again, Willie, a-round, a-round, a-round."

Willie De Vere was a dry goods cashier,
At his desk he would sit all the day,
Till his doctor advised him to start exercising,
Or else he would soon fade away.
One night this poor looney met Madeline Mooney,
Fitzgibbons then shouted with joy,
"She's a good health regainer, you've got a great trainer,
Just wait till she hollers, my boy, *(Chorus.)*

COLLEGE AGE

Finley Peter Dunne

"If ye had a boy wud ye sind him to colledge?" asked Mr. Hennessy.

"Well," said Mr. Dooley, "at th' age whin a boy is fit to be in colledge I wudden't have him around th' house."

ORESTES SPEAKS OF RECOGNIZING A MAN'S WORTH

Euripides

(TRANSLATOR: Edward P. Coleridge)

Ah! there is no sure mark to recognize a man's worth; for human nature hath in it an element of confusion. For instance, I have seen ere now the son of a noble sire prove himself a worthless knave, and virtuous children spring from evil parents; likewise dearth in a rich man's spirit, and in a poor man's frame a mighty soul. By what standard then shall we rightly judge these things? By wealth? An evil test to use. By poverty then? Nay, poverty suffers from this, that it teaches a man to play the villain from necessity. To martial prowess must I turn? But who could pronounce who is the valiant man merely from the look of his spear? Better it is to leave these matters to themselves without troubling. For here is a man of no account in Argos, with no family reputation to boast, one of the common herd, proved a very hero. A truce to your folly! ye self-deceivers, swollen with idle fancies; learn to judge men by their converse, and by their habits decide who are noble. Such are those who rule aright both state and families; while those forms of flesh, devoid of intellect, are but figure-heads in the market-place. The strong arm, again, no more than the weak awaits the battle-shock, for this depends on natural courage.

(From *Electra*)

IN MEN WHOM MEN CONDEMN AS ILL

Joaquin Miller

In men whom men condemn as ill
I find so much of goodness still,
In men whom men pronounce divine
I find so much of sin and blot,
I do not dare to draw a line
Between the two, where God has not.

BALLAD OF TREES AND THE MASTER

Sidney Lanier

In the woods my Master went,
Clean forspent, forspent.
Into the woods my Master came,
Forspent with love and shame.
But the olives they were not blind to Him,
The little gray leaves were kind to Him:
The thorn-tree had a mind to Him
When into the woods He came.

Out of the woods my Master went,
And he was well content.
Out of the woods my Master came,
Content with death and shame.
When Death and Shame would woo Him last,
From under the trees they drew Him last:
'Twas on a tree they slew Him—last
When out of the woods He came.

RENEWING FRIENDSHIP

Samuel Johnson

I have often thought, that as longevity is generally desired, and
I believe, generally expected, it would be wise to be continually
adding to the number of our friends, that the loss of some may be
supplied by others. Friendship, "the vine of life," should, like a
well-stocked cellar, be thus continually renewed.

Human history becomes more and more a race between
education and catastrophe.

(H. G. Wells, 1920)

BLESS THIS HOUSE*

Mary H. Brahe and *Helen Taylor*

Bless this house, O Lord, we pray
Make it safe by night and day:
Bless these walls so firm and stout
Keeping want and trouble out;

Bless the roof and chimneys tall,
Let Thy peace lie over all:
Bless this door, that it may prove
Ever open to joy and love.

Bless these windows shining bright,
Letting in God's heavenly light:
Bless the hearth ablazing there,
With smoke ascending like a prayer:

Bless the people here within,
Keep them pure and free from sin;
Bless us all that we may be
Fit, O Lord, to dwell with thee.

AFTER MIDNIGHT IN LONDON

Oliver Goldsmith

The clock had just struck two, the expiring taper rises and sinks in the socket, the watchman forgets the hour in slumber, the laborious and the happy are at rest, and nothing wakes but meditation, guilt, revelry, and despair. The drunkard once more fills the destroying bowl, the robber walks his midnight round, and the suicide lifts his guilty arm against his own sacred person.

Let me no longer waste the night over pages of antiquity or the sallies of contemporary genius, but pursue the solitary walk, where

* From the song "Bless This House," music by Mary H. Brahe, words by Helen Taylor, copyright 1927, 1932, by Boosey and Co., Ltd.; renewed 1954, 1959. Reprinted by permission of Boosey and Hawkes, Inc.

(251)

Vanity, ever changing, but a few hours past walked before me—where she kept up the pageant, and now, like a forward child, seems hushed with her own importunities. What a gloom hangs all around! The dying lamp feebly emits a yellow gleam; no sound is heard but of the chiming clock, or the distant watch-dog. All the bustle of human pride is forgotten; an hour like this may well display the emptiness of human vanity. . . .

How few appear in those streets which but some few hours ago were crowded; and those who appear, now no longer wear their daily mask nor attempt to hide their lewdness or their misery.

But who are those who make the streets their couch, and find a short repose from wretchedness at the doors of the opulent? These are strangers, wanderers, and orphans, whose circumstances are too humble to expect redress, and their distresses are too great even for pity. Their wretchedness excites rather horror. Some are without the covering even of rags, and others emaciated with disease; the world has disclaimed them; society turns its back upon their distress, and has given them up to nakedness and hunger. These poor shivering females have once seen happier days, and been flattered into beauty. They have been sacrificed to the gay luxurious villain, and are now turned out to meet the severity of winter. Perhaps, now lying at the doors of their betrayers, they sue to wretches whose hearts are insensible, or debauchees who may curse, but will not relieve them.

Why, why was I born a man, and yet see the sufferings of wretches I cannot relieve! Poor houseless creatures! the world will give you reproaches, but will not give you relief. The slightest misfortune of the great, the most imaginary uneasiness of the rich, are aggravated with all the power of eloquence, and held up to engage our attention and sympathetic sorrow. The poor weep unheeded, persecuted by every subordinate species of tyranny; and every law which gives others security, becomes an enemy to them.

Why was this heart of mine formed with so much sensibility? or why was not my fortune adapted to its impulse? Tenderness, without a capacity of relieving, only makes the man who feels it more wretched than the object which sues for assistance.

PARENTS

Francis Bacon

The joys of parents are secret; and so are their griefs and fears. They cannot utter the one; nor will they utter the other. Children sweeten labors; but they make misfortunes more bitter. They increase the cares of life; but they mitigate the remembrance of death. The perpetuity by generation is common to beasts; but memory, merit, and noble works are proper to men.

TO KNOW ALL IS TO FORGIVE ALL

Nixon Waterman

If I knew you and you knew me—
If both of us could clearly see,
And with an inner sight divine
The meaning of your heart and mine—
I'm sure that we would differ less
And clasp our hands in friendliness;
Our thought would pleasantly agree
If I knew you, and you knew me.

If I knew you and you knew me,
As each one knows his own self, we
Could look each other in the face
And see therein a truer grace.
Life has so many hidden woes,
So many thorns for every rose;
The "Why" of things our hearts would see,
If I knew you and you knew me.

PRESIDENT KENNEDY TELLS CONGRESS
WE SHOULD SHOOT FOR THE MOON

Now is the time to take longer strides—time for a great new enterprise—time for this nation to take a clearly leading role in space achievements which, in many ways, may hold the key to our future on earth.

I believe we possess all the resources and talents necessary. But the facts of the matter are that we have never made the national decision or marshaled the national resources for such leadership. . . .

Recognizing the head start obtained by the Soviets with their large rocket engines, which gave them many months of lead time, and recognizing the likelihood that they will exploit this lead for some time to come, in still more impressive successes, we nevertheless are required to make new efforts of our own.

For while we cannot guarantee that we shall one day be first, we can guarantee that any failure to make this effort will make us last.

We take the additional risk of making it in full view of the world. . . .

But this is not merely a race. Space is open to us now. And our eagerness to share its meaning is not governed by the efforts of others. We got into space because whatever mankind must undertake, free men must fully share. . . .

I believe that this nation should commit itself to achieving the goal, before this decade is out, of landing a man on the moon and returning him safely to earth. No single space project in this period will be more impressive to mankind or more important for the long-range exploration of space. And none will be so difficult to accomplish. . . .

Let it be clear that this is a judgment which the members of the Congress must finally make. Let it be clear that I am asking the Congress and the country to accept a firm commitment to a new course of action. . . .

I believe we should go to the moon. . . .

This decision demands a major national commitment of scientific and technical manpower, material and facilities, and the possibility of their diversion from other important activities where they are already thinly spread. It means a degree of dedication, organization and discipline which have not always characterized our research and development efforts.

(May 25, 1961)

BLUE GIRLS

John Crowe Ransom

Twirling your blue skirts, traveling the sward
Under the towers of your seminary,
Go listen to your teachers old and contrary
Without believing a word.

Tie the white fillets then about your lustrous hair
And think no more of what will come to pass
Than bluebirds that go walking on the grass
And chattering on the air.

Practice your beauty, blue girls, before it fail;
And I will cry with my loud lips and publish
Beauty which all our power shall never establish,
It is so frail.

For I could tell you a story which is true:
I know a lady with a terrible tongue,
Blear eyes fallen from blue,
All her perfections tarnished—and yet it is not long
Since she was lovelier than any of you.

GEORGE WASHINGTON TO CONGRESS WHEN
HE RESIGNED HIS COMMISSION

Mr. President:

The great events on which my resignation depended having at
length taken place; I have now the honor of offering my sincere
Congratulations to Congress and of presenting myself before them
to surrender into their hands the trust committed to me, and to claim
the indulgence of retiring from the Service of my Country.

Happy in the confirmation of our Independence and Sovereignty
. . . I resign with satisfaction the Appointment I accepted with
diffidence. . . .

While I repeat my obligations to the Army in general, I should do
injustice to my own feelings not to acknowledge in this place the
peculiar Services and distinguished merits of the Gentlemen who
have been attached to my person during the War. It was impossible

the choice of confidential Officers to compose my family should have been more fortunate. . . .

I consider it an indispensable duty to close this last solemn act of my Official life, by commending the Interests of our dearest Country to the protection of Almighty God, and those who have the superintendence of them, to his holy keeping.

Having now finished the work assigned to me, I retire from the great theatre of Action; and bidding an Affectionate farewell to this August body under whose orders I have so long acted, I here offer my Commission, and take my leave of all the employments of Public office.

(December 23, 1783)

PORPHYRIA'S LOVER

Robert Browning

The rain set early in to-night,
    The sullen wind was soon awake,
It tore the elm-tops down for spite,
    And did its worst to vex the lake:
    I listened with heart fit to break.
When glided in Porphyria; straight
    She shut the cold out and the storm,
And kneeled and made the cheerless grate
    Blaze up, and all the cottage warm;
    Which done, she rose, and from her form
Withdrew the dripping cloak and shawl,
    And laid her soiled gloves by, untied
Her hat and let the damp hair fall,
    And, last, she sat down by my side
    And called me. When no voice replied,
She put my arm about her waist,
    And made her smooth white shoulder bare,
    And, stooping, made my cheek lie there,
    And spread o'er all, her yellow hair,
Murmuring how she loved me—she
    Too weak, for all her heart's endeavor,
To set its struggling passion free
    From pride, and vainer ties dissever,
    And give herself to me for ever.

But passion sometimes would prevail,
  Nor could to-night's gay feast restrain
A sudden thought of one so pale
  For love of her, and all in vain:
  So, she was come through wind and rain.
Be sure I looked up at her eyes
  Happy and proud; at last I knew
Porphyria worshipped me; surprise
  Made my heart swell, and still it grew
  While I debated what to do.
That moment she was mine, mine, fair,
  Perfectly pure and good: I found
A thing to do, and all her hair
  In one long yellow string I wound
  Three times her little throat around,
And strangled her. No pain felt she;
  I am quite sure she felt no pain.
As a shut bud that holds a bee,
  I warily oped her lids: again
  Laughed the blue eyes without a stain.
And I untightened next the tress
  About her neck; her cheeks once more
Blushed bright beneath my burning kiss:
  I propped her head up as before,
  Only, this time my shoulder bore
Her head, which droops upon it still:
  The smiling rosy little head,
So glad it has its utmost will,
  That all it scorned at once is fled,
  And I, its love, am gained instead!
Porphyria's love: she guessed not how
  Her darling one wish would be heard.
And thus we sit together now,
  And all night long we have not stirred,
  And yet God has not said a word!

MARRIAGE

Louis K. Anspacher

Marriage is that relation between man and woman in which the independence is equal, the dependence mutual, and the obligation reciprocal.

REFLECTIONS IN WESTMINSTER ABBEY

Joseph Addison

When I am in a serious humor I very often walk by myself in Westminster Abbey; where the gloominess of the place, and the use to which it is applied, with the solemnity of the building and the condition of the people who lie in it, are apt to fill the mind with a kind of melancholy, or rather thoughtfulness, that is not disagreeable. . . .

For my own part, though I am always serious, I do not know what it is to be melancholy; and can, therefore, take a view of nature in her deep and solemn scenes, with the same pleasure as in her most gay and delightful ones. By this means I can improve myself with those objects, which others consider with terror. When I look upon the tombs of the great, every emotion of envy dies in me; when I read the epitaphs of the beautiful, every inordinate desire goes out; when I meet with the grief of parents upon a tombstone, my heart melts with compassion; when I see the tomb of the parents themselves, I consider the vanity of grieving for those whom we must quickly follow. When I see kings lying by those who deposed them, when I consider rival wits placed side by side, or the holy men that divided the world with their contests and disputes, I reflect with sorrow and astonishment on the little competitions, factions, and debates of mankind.

HORSE SENSE

Anonymous

A horse can't pull while kicking.
This fact I merely mention.
And he can't kick while pulling,
    Which is my chief contention.

Let's imitate the good old horse
    And lead a life that's fitting;
Just pull an honest load, and then
    There'll be no time for kicking.

FATHER IN HEAVEN, WE THANK THEE

Ralph Waldo Emerson

For flowers that bloom about our feet,
For tender grass, so fresh and sweet,
For song of bird and hum of bee
For all things fair we hear or see—
    Father in heaven, we thank Thee!

For blue of stream, for blue of sky,
For pleasant shade of branches high,
For fragrant air and cooling breeze,
For beauty of the blowing trees—
    Father in heaven, we thank Thee!

For mother-love, for father-care,
For brothers strong and sisters fair,
For love at home and school each day,
For guidance lest we go astray—
    Father in heaven, we thank Thee!

For Thy dear, everlasting arms,
That bear us o'er all ills and harms,
For blessed words of long ago,
That help us now Thy will to know—
    Father in heaven, we thank Thee!

(259)

One, with God, is always a majority, but
many a martyr has been burned at the stake
while the votes were being counted.
—Thomas B. Reed

INWARD PEACE

Herman Melville

Consider the subtleness of the sea; how its most dreaded creatures glide under water, unapparent for the most part, and treacherous hidden beneath the loveliest tints of azure. Consider also the devilish brilliance and beauty of many of its most remorseless tribes, as the dainty embellished shape of many species of sharks. Consider, once more, the universal cannibalism of the sea; all whose creatures prey upon one another, carrying on eternal war since the world began.

Consider all this; and then turn to this green, gentle and most docile earth; consider them both, the sea and the land; and do you not find a strange analogy to something in yourself. For as this appalling ocean surrounds the verdant land, so in the soul of man there lies one insular Tahiti, full of peace and joy, but encompassed by all the horrors of the half-known life. God keep thee! Push not off from that isle, thou canst never return!

(From *Moby Dick*)

THE MARSHES OF GLYNN

Sidney Lanier

Glooms of the live-oaks, beautiful-braided and woven
With intricate shades of the vines that myriad-cloven
   Clamber the forks of the multiform boughs,—
     Emerald twilights,—
     Virginal shy lights,
Wrought of the leaves to allure to the whisper of vows,
When lovers pace timidly down through the green colonnades
   of the dim sweet woods, of the dear dark woods,
   Of the heavenly woods and glades,
That run to the radiant marginal stand-beach within
   The wide sea-marshes of Glynn;—

Beautiful glooms, soft dusks in the noon-day fire,—
Wildwood privacies, closets of lone desire,
Chamber from chamber parted with wavering arras of
    leaves,—
Cells for the passionate pleasure of prayer to the soul that
    grieves,
Pure with a sense of the passing of saints through the wood,
Cool for the dutiful weighing of ill with good;—
O braided dusks of the oak and woven shades of the vine,
While the riotous noon-day sun of the June-day long did shine
Ye held me fast in your heart and I held you fast in mine;
But now when the noon is no more, and riot is rest,
And the sun is a-wait at the ponderous gate of the West,
And the slant yellow beam down the wood-aisle doth seem
Like a lane into heaven that leads from a dream,—
Ay, now, when my soul all day hath drunken the soul of the
    oak,
And my heart is at ease from men, and the wearisome sound
    of the stroke
  Of the scythe of time and the trowel of trade is low,
  And belief overmasters doubt, and I know that I know,
  And my spirit is grown to a lordly great compass within,
That the length and the breadth and the sweep of the marshes
    of Glynn
Will work me no fear like the fear they have wrought me of
    yore
When length was fatigue, and when breath was but bitter-
    ness sore,
And when terror and shrinking and dreary unnamable pain
Drew over me out of the merciless miles of the plain,—

Oh, now, unafraid, I am fain to face
  The vast sweet visage of space.
To the edge of the wood I am drawn, I am drawn,
Where the gray beach glimmering runs, as a belt of the dawn,
  For a mete and a mark
    To the forest-dark:—
      So:
Affable live-oak, leaning low,—
Thus—with your favor—soft, with a reverent hand,
(Not lightly touching your person, Lord of the land!),
Bending your beauty aside, with a step I stand

On the firm-packed sand,
> Free

By a world of marsh that borders a world of sea.
  Sinuous southward and sinuous northward the shimmering band
  Of the sand-beach fastens the fringe of the marsh to the folds
    of the land.
Inward and outward to northward and southward the beach-lines
    linger and curl
As a silver-wrought garment that clings to and follows the firm
    sweet limbs of a girl
Vanishing, swerving, evermore curving again into sight,
Softly the sand-beach wavers away to a dim gray looping of light.
And what if behind me to westward the wall of the woods stand
    high?
The world lies east: how ample, the marsh and the sea and the sky!
A league and a league of marsh-grass, waist-high, broad in the
    blade,
Green, and all of a height, and unflecked with a light or a shade,
Stretch leisurely off, in a pleasant plain,
To the terminal blue of the main.
Oh, what is abroad in the marsh and the terminal sea?
  Somehow my soul seems suddenly free
From the weighing of fate and the sad discussion of sin,
By the length and the breadth and the sweep of the marshes of
    Glynn.

Ye marshes, how candid and simple and nothing-withholding and
    free
Ye publish yourselves to the sky and offer yourselves to the sea!
Tolerant plains, that suffer the sea and the rains and the sun,
Ye spread and span like the catholic man who hath mightily won
God out of knowledge and good out of infinite pain
And sight out of blindness and purity out of stain.
As the marsh-hen secretly builds on the watery sod,
Behold I will build me a nest on the greatness of God:
I will fly in the greatness of God as the marsh-hen flies
In the freedom that fills all the space 'twixt the marsh and
    the skies;
By so many roots as the marsh-grass sends in the sod
I will heartily lay me a-hold on the greatness of God:
Oh, like to the greatness of God is the greatness within
The range of the marshes, the liberal marshes of Glynn.

THE CURSE

(To A Sister Of An Enemy Of The Author's Who Disapproved Of "The Playboy")

J. M. Synge

Lord, confound this surly sister,
Blight her brow and blotch and blister,
Cramp her larynx, lung and liver,
In her guts a galling give her.

Let her live to earn her dinners
In Mountjoy with seedy sinners;
Lord, this judgment quickly bring,
And I'm your servant, J. M. Synge.

THE SOUND OF IMMORTAL SYMPHONIES

Victor Hugo

I feel within me the future life. I am like a forest that has once been razed; the new shoots are stronger and brisker. I shall most certainly rise towards the heavens. The sun's rays bathe my head. The earth gives me its generous sap, but the heavens illuminate me with the reflection of—of worlds unknown.

Some say the soul results merely from bodily powers. Why, then, does my soul become brighter when my bodily powers begin to waste away? Winter is above me, but eternal spring is within my heart. I inhale even now the fragrance of lilacs, violets, and roses just as I did when I was twenty.

The nearer my approach to the end, the plainer is the sound of immortal symphonies of worlds which invite me. It is wonderful, yet simple. It is a fairy tale; it is history.

For half a century I have been translating my thoughts into prose and verse; history, philosophy, drama, romance, tradition, satire, ode, and song; all of these have I tried. But I feel that I haven't given utterance to the thousandth part of what lies within me. When

I go to the grave I can say as others have said, "My day's work is done." But I cannot say, "My life is done." My day's work will recommence the next morning. The tomb is not a blind alley; it is a thoroughfare. It closes upon the twilight, but opens upon the dawn.

THE WIT OF JOHN F. KENNEDY

At a $100-a-plate Dinner, Salt Lake City, Utah, September, 1960:
I am deeply touched—not as deeply touched as you have been by coming to this dinner, but nevertheless, it is a sentimental occasion.

When asked by a little boy how he became a war hero:
It was absolutely involuntary. They sank my boat.

When he met Premier Khrushchev in Vienna and was told that the medal on the Russian's chest was the Lenin Peace Prize:
I hope you keep it.

During a White House Dinner honoring Nobel Prize Winners:
I think this is the most extraordinary collection of talent, of human knowledge, that has ever been gathered together at the White House—with the possible exception of when Thomas Jefferson dined alone.

May 27, 1961:
When we got into office, the thing that surprised me most was to find that things were just as bad as we'd been saying they were.

JEFFERSON'S SELF-WRITTEN EPITAPH

Here was buried
Thomas Jefferson
Author of the Declaration of American Independence,
Of the Statute of Virginia for Religious Freedom
And Father of the University of Virginia

MR. FLOOD'S PARTY

Edwin Arlington Robinson

Old Eben Flood, climbing alone one night
Over the hill between the town below
And the forsaken upland hermitage
That held as much as he should ever know
On earth again of home, paused warily.
The road was his with not a native near;
And Eben, having leisure, said aloud,
For no man else in Tilbury Town to hear:

"Well, Mr. Flood, we have the harvest moon
Again, and we may not have many more;
The bird is on the wing, the poet says,
And you and I have said it here before.
Drink to the bird." He raised up to the light
The jug that he had gone so far to fill,
And answered huskily: "Well, Mr. Flood,
Since you propose it, I believe I will."

Alone, as if enduring to the end
A valiant armor of scarred hopes outworn,
He stood there in the middle of the road
Like Roland's ghost winding a silent horn.
Below him, in the town among the trees,
Where friends of other days had honored him,
A phantom salutation of the dead
Rang thinly till old Eben's eyes were dim.

Then, as a mother lays her sleeping child
Down tenderly, fearing it may awake,
He set the jug down slowly at his feet
With trembling care, knowing that most things break;
And only when assured that on firm earth
It stood, as the uncertain lives of men
Assuredly did not, he paced away,
And with his hand extended paused again:

"Well, Mr. Flood, we have not met like this
In a long time; and many a change has come
To both of us, I fear, since last it was
We had a drop together. Welcome home!"

Convivially returning with himself,
Again he raised the jug up to the light;
And with an acquiescent quaver said.
"Well, Mr. Flood, if you insist, I might.

"Only a very little, Mr. Flood—
For auld lang syne. No more, sir; that will do."
So, for the time, apparently it did,
And Eben evidently thought so too;
For soon amid the silver loneliness
Of night he lifted up his voice and sang,
Secure, with only two moons listening,
Until the whole harmonious landscape range—

"For auld lang syne." The eary throat gave out,
The last word wavered, and the song was done.
He raised again the jug regretfully
And shook his head, and was again alone.
There was not much that was ahead of him,
And there was nothing in the town below—
Where strangers would have shut the many doors
That many friends had opened long ago.

PROPHECY

Horace Walpole

   The next Augustan age will dawn on the other side of the Atlantic.
There will, perhaps, be a Thucydides at Boston, a Xenophon at New
York, and, in time, a Virgil at Mexico, and a Newton at Peru. At
last some curious traveler from Lima will visit England and give
a description of the ruins of St. Paul's, like the editions of Balbec
and Palmyra.

(From *Letter to Horace Mann*, 1774)

THE MOUNTAIN AND THE SQUIRREL

Ralph Waldo Emerson

The mountain and the squirrel
Had a quarrel,
And the former called the latter
  "Little Prig";
Bun replied,
"You are doubtless very big;
But all sorts of things and weather
Must be taken in together,
To make up a year
And a sphere.
And I think it no disgrace
To occupy my place.
If I'm not so large as you,
You are not so small as I,
And not half so spry.
I'll not deny you make
A very pretty squirrel track;
Talents differ; all is well and wisely put;
If I cannot carry forests on my back,
Neither can you crack a nut."

WHY THEMISTOCLES' CHILD RULED THE WORLD

The child of Themistocles governed his mother;
The mother governed her husband;
The husband governed Athens;
Athens governed Greece;
Greece governed the world.
Therefore, Themistocles' child governed the world.

THE HEAVENS DECLARE THY GLORY, LORD!

Isaac Watts

The heavens declare thy glory, Lord!
    In every star thy wisdom shines;
But when our eyes behold thy word,
    We read thy name in fairer lines.

The rolling sun, the changing light,
    And nights and days thy power confess;
But the blest volume thou has writ
    Reveals thy justice and thy grace.

THE WORLD'S A BUBBLE

Francis Bacon

The world's a bubble, and the life of man
    Less than a span:
In his conception wretched, from the womb
    So to the tomb:
Curst from his cradle, and brought up to years
    With cares and fears.
Who then to frail mortality shall trust,
But limns on water, or but writes in dust.

Yet whilst with sorrow here we live opprest,
    What life is best?
Courts are but only superficial schools
    To dandle fools:
The rural parts are turn'd into a den
    Of savage men:
And where's a city from foul vice so free,
But may be term'd the worst of all the three?

Domestic cares afflict the husband's bed,
    Or pains his head:
Those that single live, take it for a curse,
    Or do things worse:

Some would have children; those that have them, moan
   Or wish them gone:
What is it, then, to have, or have no wife,
But single thraldom, or a double strife?

Our own affections still at home to please
   Is a disease:
To cross the seas to any foreign soil
   Peril and toil:
Wars with their noise affright us; when they cease,
   We're worse in peace;
What then remains, but that we still should cry
Not to be born, or being born, to die?

A PRAYER

Max Ehrmann

Let me do my work each day; and if the darkened hours of despair
overcome me, may I not forget the strength that comforted me in
the desolation of other times.

May I still remember the bright hours that found me walking
over the silent hills of my childhood, or dreaming, on the margin
of the quiet river, when a light glowed within me, and I promised
my early God to have courage amid the tempests of the changing
years. Spare me from bitterness and from the sharp passions of
unguarded moments. May I not forget that poverty and riches are
of the spirit. Though the world know me not, may my thoughts
and actions be such as shall keep me friendly with myself.

Lift my eyes from the earth, and let me not forget the uses of the
stars. Forbid that I should judge others lest I condemn myself. Let
me not follow the clamor of the world, but walk calmly in my path.

Give me a few friends who will love me for what I am; and keep
ever burning before my vagrant steps the kindly light of hope. And
though age and infirmity overtake me, and I come not within sight
of the castle of my dreams, teach me still to be thankful for life, and
for time's olden memories that are good and sweet; and may the
evening's twilight find me gentle still.

SOLOMON GRUNDY

Anonymous

Solomon Grundy,
Born on Monday,
Christened on Tuesday,
Married on Wednesday,
Took ill on Thursday,
Worse on Friday,
Died on Saturday,
Buried on Sunday;
This is the end
Of Solomon Grundy.

PRESIDENT KENNEDY TO THE NATION ON THE
CUBAN MISSILE CRISIS, OCTOBER 22, 1962

Within the past week unmistakable evidence has established the fact that a series of offensive missile sites is now in preparation on that imprisoned island.

The purpose of these bases can be none other than to provide a nuclear strike capability against the Western Hemisphere. . . .

Each of these missiles, in short, is capable of striking Washington, D.C., the Panama Canal, Cape Canaveral, Mexico City or any other city in the southeastern part of the United States, in Central America or in the Caribbean area.

Additional sites not yet completed appear to be designed for intermediate-range ballistic missiles capable of traveling more than twice as far, and thus capable of striking most of the major cities in the Western Hemisphere ranging as far north as Hudson's Bay, Canada, and as far south as Lima, Peru.

In addition, jet bombers, capable of carrying nuclear weapons, are now being uncrated and assembled in Cuba while the necessary air bases are being prepared.

This urgent transformation of Cuba into an important strategic base by the presence of these large long-range and clearly offensive weapons of sudden mass destruction constitutes an explicit threat to the peace and security of all the Americas in flagrant and deliberate defiance of the Rio Pact of 1947, the traditions of this nation and hemisphere, the joint resolution of the 87th Congress, the Charter of the United Nations and my own public warnings to the Soviets on September 4 and 13.

This action also contradicts the repeated assurances of Soviet spokesmen both publicly and privately delivered that the arms build-up in Cuba would retain its original defensive character and that the Soviet Union had no need or desire to station strategic missiles on the territory of any other nation.

The size of this undertaking makes clear that it had been planned for some months. . . .

But this secret, swift, extraordinary build-up of Communist missiles in an area well-known to have a special and historical relationship to the United States and the nations of the Western Hemisphere, in violation of Soviet assurances and in defiance of American and hemispheric policy—this sudden, clandestine decision to station strategic weapons for the first time outside of Soviet soil —is a deliberately provocative and unjustified change in the status quo which cannot be accepted by this country if our courage and our commitments are ever to be trusted again, by either friend or foe.

This nation is opposed to war. We are also true to our word.

Our unswerving objective, therefore, must be to prevent the use of these missiles against this or any other country; and to secure their withdrawal or elimination from the Western Hemisphere.

Our policy has been one of patience and restraint, as befits a peaceful and powerful nation which leads a world-wide alliance.

We have been determined not to be diverted from our central concerns by mere irritants, and fanatics. But now further action is required. And it is underway. And these actions may only be the beginning.

We will not prematurely or unnecessarily risk the course of world-wide nuclear war in which even the fruits of victory would be ashes in our mouth, but neither will we shrink from that risk at any time it must be faced.

Acting, therefore, in the defense of our own security and of the entire Western Hemisphere and under the authority entrusted to me by the Constitution as endorsed by the resolution of the Congress, I have directed that the following initial steps be taken immediately:

First, to halt this offensive build-up, a strict quarantine on all offensive military equipment under shipment to Cuba is being initiated. All ships of any kind bound for Cuba from whatever nation or port, where they are found to contain cargoes of offensive weapons, be turned back. This quarantine will be extended if needed to other types of cargo and carriers.

I have directed the armed forces to prepare for any eventualities, and I trust that in the interests of both the Cuban people and the Soviet technicians at the sites, the hazards to all concerned of continuing this threat will be recognized.

Third, it shall be the policy of this nation to regard any nuclear missile launched from Cuba against any nation in the Western Hemisphere as an attack by the Soviet Union on the United States requiring a full retaliatory response upon the Soviet Union.

Finally, I call Chairman Khrushchev to halt and eliminate this clandestine, reckless and provocative threat to world peace and to stable relations between our two nations.

I call upon him further to abandon this course of world domination and to join in an historic effort to end the perilous arms race and to transform the history of man.

He has an opportunity now to move the world back from the abyss of destruction by returning to his Government's own words that it had no need to station missiles outside its own territory, and withdrawing these weapons from Cuba; by refraining from any action which will widen or deepen the present crisis, and then by participating in a search for peaceful and permanent solutions.

We have no wish to war with the Soviet Union for we are a peaceful people who desire to live in peace with all other peoples.

But it is difficult to settle or even discuss these problems in an atmosphere of intimidation.

That is why this latest Soviet threat or any other threat which is made either independently or in response to our actions this week must and will be met with determination.

Any hostile move anywhere in the world against the safety and freedom of peoples to whom we are committed including in particular the brave people of West Berlin will be met by whatever action is needed.

My fellow citizens, let no one doubt that this is a difficult and dangerous effort on which we have set out. No one can foresee precisely what course it will take, or what course or casualties will be incurred.

Many months of sacrifice and self-discipline lie ahead, months in which both our patience and our will will be tested. Months in which many threats and denunciations will keep us aware of our dangers. But the greatest danger of all would be to do nothing.

The path we have chosen for the present is full of hazards, as all paths are. But it is the one most consistent with our character and courage as a nation and our commitments around the world.

The cost of freedom is always high, but Americans have always paid it.

And one path we shall never choose, and that is the path of surrender, or submission.

Our goal is not the victory of might, but the vindication of right; not peace at the expense of freedom, but both peace and freedom here in this hemisphere, and, we hope, around the world.

HOW FIRM A FOUNDATION

George Keith

How firm a foundation, ye saints of the Lord,
Is laid for your faith in His excellent Word!
What more can He say than to you He hath said,
To you who for refuge to Jesus have fled?
To you who for refuge to Jesus have fled.

"Fear not, I am with thee, O be not dismayed,
For I am thy God, I will still give thee aid;
I'll strengthen thee, help thee, and cause thee to stand,
Upheld by my gracious, omnipotent hand,
Upheld by my gracious, omnipotent hand.

When through the deep waters I call thee to go,
The rivers of sorrow shall not overflow;
For I will be with thee, thy trials to bless,
And sanctify to thee thy deepest distress,
And sanctify to thee thy deepest distress.

When through fiery trials thy path shall lie,
My grace all-sufficient, will be thy supply;
Then flames shall not hurt thee; I only design,
Thy dross to consume, and thy gold to refine,
Thy dross to consume, thy gold to refine."

AGATHON'S CONCLUSION

Plato

(TRANSLATOR: Benjamin Jowett)

I say of love that he is the fairest and best in himself, and the cause of what is fairest and best in all other things. And I have a mind to say of him in verse that he is the god who
  "Gives peace on earth and calms the stormy deep,
  Who stills the winds and bids the sufferer sleep."
He makes men to be of one mind at a banquet such as this, fulfilling them with affection and emptying them of disaffection. In sacrifices, banquets, dances, he is our lord—supplying kindness and banishing unkindness, giving friendship and forgiving enmity, the joy of the good, the wonder of the wise, the amazement of the gods; desired by those who have no part in him, and precious to those who have the better part in him; parent of delicacy, luxury, desire, fondness, softness, grace; careful of the good, uncareful of the evil. In every word, work, wish, fear—pilot, helper, defender, savior; glory of gods and men, leader best and brightest; in whose footsteps let every man follow, chanting a hymn and joining in that fair strain with which Love charms the souls of god and men.

(From *The Symposium*)

IN THE SHADE OF THE OLD APPLE TREE

Harry H. Williams

The oriole with joy was sweetly singing,
The little brook was babbling its tune,
The village bells at noon were gaily ringing,
The world seemed brighter than a harvest moon;
For there within my arms I gently pressed you,
And blushing red, you slowly turned away;
I can't forget the way I once caressed you;
I only pray we'll meet another day.

Chorus

In the shade of the old apple tree,
Where the love in your eyes I could see,
When the voice that I heard,
Like the song of the bird,
Seemed to whisper sweet music to me;
I could hear the dull buzz of the bee,
In the blossoms as you said to me,
With a heart that is true,
I'll be waiting for you,
In the shade of the old apple tree.

I've really come a long way from the city,
And though my heart is breaking, I'll be brave.
I've brought this bunch of flowers, I think they're pretty,
To place upon a fresh moulded grave;
If you will show me, father, where she's lying,
Or, if it's far, just point it out to me.
Said he, "She told us all when she was dying,
To bury her beneath the apple tree."

LAWYER ABRAHAM LINCOLN ADVISES A CLIENT

Yes, we can doubtless gain your case for you; we can set a whole neighborhood at loggerheads; we can distress a widowed mother and her six fatherless children, and thereby get for you six hundred dollars to which you seem to have a legal claim, but which rightfully belongs, it appears to me, as much to the woman and her children as it does to you. You must remember, however, that some things legally right are not morally right. We shall not take your case, but we will give you a little advice for which we will charge you nothing. You seem to be a sprightly, energetic man. We would advise you to try your hand at making six hundred dollars in some other way.

RESIGNATION

Walter Savage Landor

Why, why repine, my pensive friend,
  At pleasures slipp'd away?
Some the stern Fates will never lend,
  And all refuse to stay.

I see the rainbow in the sky
  The dew upon the grass;
I see them, and I ask not why
  They glimmer or they pass.

With folded arms I linger not
  To call them back; 'twere vain:
In this, or in some other spot,
  I know they'll shine again.

IF THE MAN

Samuel Johnson

If the man who turnips cries,
Cry not when his father dies,
'Tis a proof that he had rather
Have a turnip than a father.

LOVE ONE ANOTHER

Holy Bible, John 13:33–35

Little children, yet a little while I am with you. Ye shall seek me:
and as I said unto the Jews, Whither I go, ye cannot come: so now
I say to you.

A new commandment I give unto you, That ye love one another;
as I have loved you, that ye also love one another.

By this shall all men know that ye are my disciples, if ye love
one to another.

(276)

ELEGY IN A COUNTRY CHURCHYARD

G. K. Chesterton

The men that worked for England
They have their graves at home:
And bees and birds of England
About the cross can roam.

But they that fought for England,
Following a falling star,
Alas, alas for England
They have their graves afar.

And they that rule in England,
In stately conclave met,
Alas, alas for England
They have no graves as yet.

ROBERT E. LEE

Benjamin Harvey Hill

He was a foe without hate, a friend without treachery, a soldier without cruelty, and a victim without murmuring. He was a public officer without vices, a private citizen without wrong, a neighbor without reproach, a Christian without hypocrisy, and a man without guile. He was a Caesar without his ambition, a Frederick without his tyranny, a Napoleon without his selfishness, and a Washington without his reward.

UNIVERSAL DECLARATION OF HUMAN RIGHTS

(Adopted and proclaimed by the General Assembly of
the United Nations, on December 10, 1948)

1. All human beings are born free and equal in dignity and rights. They are endowed with reason and conscience and should act towards one another in a spirit of brotherhood.

2. Everyone is entitled to all rights and freedoms set forth in this Declaration, without distinction of any kind, such as race, color, sex, language, religion, political or other opinion, national or social origin, property, birth or other status. . . .

3. Everyone has the right to life, liberty and security of person.

4. No one shall be held in slavery or servitude; slavery and the slave trade shall be prohibited in all their forms.

5. No one shall be subjected to torture or to cruel, inhuman or degrading treatment or punishment.

6. Everyone has the right to recognition everywhere as a person before the law.

7. All are equal before the law and are entitled without any discrimination to equal protection of the law. . . .

8. Everyone has the right to an effective remedy by the competent national tribunals for acts violating the fundamental rights granted him by the constitution or by law.

9. No one shall be subjected to arbitrary arrest, detention or exile.

10. Everyone is entitled in full equality to a fair and public hearing by an independent and impartial tribunal, in the determination of his rights and obligations and of any criminal charge against him.

11. Everyone charged with a penal offense has the right to be presumed innocent until proved guilty according to law in a public trial at which he has had all the guarantees necessary for his defense. . . .

12. No one shall be subjected to arbitrary interference with his privacy, family, home or correspondence, nor to attacks upon his honor and reputation. . . .

13. Everyone has the right to freedom of movement and residence within the borders of each state.

Everyone has the right to leave any country, including his own, and to return to his country.

14. Everyone has the right to seek and to enjoy in other countries asylum from persecution.

This right may not be invoked in the case of prosecutions genuinely arising from non-political crimes or from acts contrary to the purposes and principles of the United Nations.

15. Everyone has the right to a nationality.

No one shall be arbitrarily deprived of his nationality nor denied the right to change his nationality.

16. Men and women of full age, without any limitation due to race, nationality or religion, have the right to marry and found a family. . . .

17. Everyone has the right to own property alone as well as in asso-

ciation with others. No one shall be aribitrarily deprived of his property.

18. Everyone has the right to freedom of thought, conscience and religion; this right includes freedom to change his religion or belief, and freedom, either alone or in community with others and in public or private, to manifest his religion or belief in teaching, practice, worship and observance.

19. Everyone has the right to freedom of opinion and expression; this right includes freedom to hold opinions without interference and to seek, receive and impart information and ideas through any media and regardless of frontiers.

20. Everyone has the right to freedom of peaceful assembly and association.

No one may be compelled to belong to an association.

21. Everyone has the right to take part in the government of his country, directly or through freely chosen representatives.

Everyone has the right of equal access to public service in his country.

The will of the people shall be the basis of the authority of government; this will shall be expressed in periodic and genuine elections which shall be by universal and equal suffrage and shall be held by secret vote or by equivalent free voting procedures.

22. Everyone, as a member of society, has the right to social security and is entitled to realize, through national effort and international co-operation and in accordance with the organization and resources of each State, of the economic, social and cultural rights indispensable for his dignity and the free development of his personality.

Everyone has the right to work, to free choice of employment, to just and favorable conditions of work and to protection against unemployment.

Everyone, without any discrimination, has the right to equal pay for equal work.

Everyone who works has the right to just and favorable remuneration ensuring for himself and his family an existence worthy of human dignity, and supplemented, if necessary, by other means of social protection.

Everyone has the right to form and to join trade unions for the protection of his interests.

24. Everyone has the right to rest and leisure, including reasonable limitation of working hours and periodic holidays with pay.

25. Everyone has the right to a standard of living adequate for the health and well-being of himself and of his family, including food, clothing, housing and medical care and necessary social services, and

the right to security in the event of unemployment, sickness, disability, widowhood, old age or other lack of livelihood in circumstances beyond his control.

Motherhood and childhood are entitled to special care and assistance. All children, whether born in or out of wedlock, shall enjoy the same social protection.

26. Everyone has the right to education. Education shall be free, at least in the elementary and fundamental stages. Elementary education shall be compulsory. Technical and professional education shall be made generally available and higher education shall be equally accessible to all on the basis of merit. . . .

Parents have a prior right to choose the kind of education that shall be given to their children.

27. Everyone has the right freely to participate in the cultural life of the community, to enjoy the arts and to share in the scientific advancement and its benefits.

Everyone has the right to the protection of the moral and material interests resulting from any scientific, literary or artistic production of which he is the author.

28. Everyone is entitled to a social and international order in which the rights and freedoms set forth in this Declaration can be fully realized.

29. Everyone has duties to the community in which the free and full development of his personality is possible.

In the exercise of his rights and freedoms, everyone shall be subject only to such limitations as are determined by law solely for the purpose of securing due recognition and respect for the rights and freedoms of others and of meeting the just requirements of morality, public order and the general welfare of a democratic society.

OF GARDENS

Francis Bacon

God Almighty first planted a garden. And indeed it is the purest of human pleasures. It is the greatest refreshment to the spirits of man. . . . I do hold . . . there ought to be gardens for all the months in the year; in which . . . things of beauty may be then in season.

SIX-YEAR-OLD MARJORY FLEMING PENS A POEM

Three turkeys fair their last have breathed,
And now this world forever leaved;
Their father, and their mother too,
They sigh and weep as well as you;
Indeed, the rats their bones have cranched,
Into eternity theire launched.
A direful death indeed they had,
As wad put any parent mad;
But she was more than usual calm,
She did not give a single dam.

(1809)

ONE DROP OF BLACK BLOOD

Langston Hughes

Negro blood is sure powerful—because just *one* drop of black blood makes a colored man. *One* drop—you are a Negro! Now, why is that? Why is Negro blood so much more powerful than any other kind of blood in the world? If a man has Irish blood in him, people will say, "He's *part* Irish." If he has a little Jewish blood, they'll say, "He's *half* Jewish." But if he has just a small bit of colored blood in him, BAM!—"He's a Negro." Not "He's *part* Negro." No, be it ever so little, if that blood is black, *"He's a Negro."* Now, that is what I do not understand—why our *one* drop is so powerful. Black is powerful. You can have 99 drops of white blood in your veins down South—but if that other *one* drop is black, shame on you. Even if you look white, you're black. That black is really powerful.

(From *Simple Takes a Wife*)

TO-MORROW

John Collins

In the downhill of life, when I find I'm declining,
   May my lot no less fortunate be
Than a snug elbow-chair can afford for reclining,
   And a cot that o'erlooks the wide sea;
With an ambling pad-pony to pace o'er the lawn,
   While I carol away idle sorrow,
And blithe as the lark that each day hails the dawn
   Look forward with hope for to-morrow.

       *   *   *   *

And when I at last must throw off this frail covering
   Which I've worn for three-score years and ten,
On the brink of the grave I'll not sink to keep hovering,
   Nor my thread wish to spin o'er again;
But my face in the glass I'll serenely survey,
   And with smiles count each wrinkle and furrow,
As this old worn-out stuff, which is thread-bare today
   May become everlasting to-morrow.

TENDER-HEARTEDNESS

Harry Graham

Billy, in one of his nice new sashes,
Fell in the fire and was burnt to ashes;
Now, although the room grew chilly,
I haven't the heart to poke poor Billy.

A man who has committed a mistake and does not correct
it is committing another mistake.
—Confucius

ODYSSEUS RETURNS TO HIS HOME

Homer

(TRANSLATOR: Andrew Lang)

Then Laertes answered him and spake, saying: "If thou are indeed Odysseus, mine own child, that art come hither, show me now a manifest token, that I may be assured."

Then Odysseus of many counsels answered him saying: . . . "But come, and I will even tell thee the trees through all the terraced garden, which thou gavest me once for mine own, and I was begging of thee this and that, being but a little child, and following thee through the garden. Through these very trees we were going, and thou didst tell me the names of each of them. Pear-trees thirteen thou gavest me and ten apple-trees and figs two-score, and, as we went, thou didst name the fifty rows of vines thou wouldst give me, whereof each one ripened at divers times, with all manners of clusters on their boughs, when the season of Zeus wrought mightily on them from on high."

So he spake, and straightway his knees were loosened, and his heart melted within him, as he knew the sure tokens that Odysseus showed him. About his dear son he cast his arms, and the steadfast goodly Odysseus caught him fainting to his breast.

(From *The Odyssey*)

CARL SANDBURG'S TRIBUTE TO ABRAHAM LINCOLN

Not often in the story of mankind does a man arrive on earth who is both steel and velvet, who is as hard as rock and soft as drifting fog, who holds in his heart and mind the paradox of terrible storm and peace unspeakable and perfect. Here and there across centuries come reports of men alleged to have these contrasts. And the incomparable Abraham Lincoln, born 150 years ago this day, is an approach if not a perfect realization of this character.

In the time of the April lilacs in the year 1865, on his death, the casket with his body was carried north and west a thousand miles; and the American people wept as never before; bells sobbed, cities wore crepe; people stood in tears and with hats off as the railroad burial car paused in the leading cities of seven states, ending its journey at Springfield, Ill., in the home town.

During the four years he was President he at times, especially in the first three months, took to himself the powers of a dictator; he commanded the most powerful armies till then assembled in modern warfare; he enforced conscription of soldiers for the first time in American history; under imperative necessity he abolished the right of habeas corpus; he directed politically and spiritually the wild, massive, turbulent forces let loose in civil war.

In the month the war began he told his secretary, John Hay, "My policy is to have no policy." Three years later in a letter to a Kentucky friend made public, he confessed plainly, "I have been controlled by events." His words at Gettysburg were sacred, yet strange with a color of the familiar: "We cannot consecrate—we cannot hallow—this ground. The brave men, living and dead, who struggled here, have consecrated it, far beyond our poor power to add or detract."

He could have said "the brave Union men." Did he have a purpose in omitting the word "Union"? Was he keeping himself and his utterance clear of the passion that would not be good to look at when the time came for peace and reconciliation? Did he mean to leave an implication that there were brave Union men and brave Confederate men, living and dead, who had struggled there? We do not know, of a certainty.

Was he thinking of the Kentucky father whose two sons died in battle, one in Union blue, the other in Confederate gray, the father inscribing on the stone over their double grave, "God knows which was right?" We do not know.

While the war winds howled he insisted that the Mississippi was one river meant to belong to one country, that railroad connection from coast to coast must be pushed through and the Union Pacific Railroad made a reality. While the luck of war wavered and broke and came again, as generals failed and campaigns were lost, he held enough forces of the North together to raise new armies and supply them, until generals were found who made war as victorious war has always been made, with terror, frightfulness, destruction, and on both sides, North and South, valor and sacrifice past words of man to tell.

In the mixed shame and blame of the immense wrongs of two crashing civilizations, often with nothing to say, he said nothing, slept not at all, and on occasions he was seen to weep in a way that made weeping appropriate, decent, majestic.

As he rode alone on horseback near Soldiers Home on the edge of Washington one night his hat was shot off; a son he loved died as he watched at the bed; his wife was accused of betraying information to the enemy, until denials from him were necessary.

(284)

An Indiana man at the White House heard him say, "Voorhees, don't it seem strange to you that I, who could never so much as cut off the head of a chicken, should be elected, or selected, into the midst of all this blood?"

Among the million words in the Lincoln utterance record, he interprets himself with a more keen precision than someone else offering to explain him. His simple opening of the House Divided speech serves for today:

"If we could first know where we are, and whither we are tending we could better judge what to do, and how to do it."

To his Kentucky friend, Joshua F. Speed, he wrote in 1855:

"Our progress in degeneracy appears to me to be pretty rapid. As a nation we began by declaring that 'all men are created equal except Negroes.' When the Know-Nothings get control, it will read 'All men are created equal except Negroes and foreigners and Catholics.' When it comes to this, I shall prefer emigrating to some country where they make no pretense of loving liberty."

Infinitely tender was his word from a White House balcony to a crowd on the White House lawn, "I have not willingly planted a thorn in any man's bosom," or to a military governor, "I shall do nothing through malice; what I deal with is too vast for malice."

He wrote for Congress to read on Dec. 1, 1862:

"In times like the present men would utter nothing for which they would not willingly be responsible through time and eternity."

Like an ancient psalmist he warned Congress:

"Fellow citizens, we cannot escape history. We will be remembered in spite of ourselves. No personal significance or insignificance can spare one or another of us. The fiery trial through which we pass will light us down in honor or dishonor to the latest generation."

Wanting Congress to break and forget past traditions his words came keen and flashing. "The dogmas of the quiet past are inadequate for the stormy present. We must think anew, we must act anew, we must disenthrall ourselves." They are the sort of words that actuated the mind and will of the men who created and navigated that marvel of the sea, the Nautilus, and her voyage from Pearl Harbor and under the North Pole icecap.

The people of many other countries take Lincoln now for their own. He belongs to them. He stands for decency, honest dealing, plain talk, and funny stories. "Look where he came from—don't he know all us strugglers and wasn't he a kind of tough struggler all his life right up to the finish?" Something like that you can hear in any near-by neighborhood and across the seas.

Millions there are who take him as a personal treasure. He had something they would like to see spread everywhere over the world. Democracy? We can't find words to say exactly what it is, but he had it. In his blood and bones he carried it. In the breath of his speeches and writing it is there. Popular government? Republican institutions? Government where the people have the say-so, one way or another telling their elected leaders what they want? He had the idea. It's there in the light and shadows of his personality, a mystery that can be lived but never fully spoken in words.

Our good friend the poet and playwright Mark Van Doren tells us:

"To me, Lincoln seems, in some ways, the most interesting man who ever lived. He was gentle, but his gentleness was combined with a terrific toughness, an iron strength."

How did Lincoln say he would like to be remembered? His beloved friend, Representative Owen Lovejoy of Illinois, had died in May of 1864 and friends wrote to Lincoln and he replied that the pressure of duties kept him from joining them in efforts for a marble monument to Lovejoy, the last sentence of his letter saying, "Let him have the marble monument along with the well-assured and more enduring one in the hearts of those who love liberty, unselfishly, for all men."

So perhaps we may say that the well assured and most enduring memorial to Lincoln is invisibly there, today, tomorrow and for a long time yet to come in the hearts of lovers of liberty, men and women who understand that wherever there is freedom there have been those who fought, toiled and sacrificed for it.

(Before a joint session of Congress, February 12, 1959)

GOD BLESS AMERICA

Irving Berlin

While the storm clouds gather
    Far across the sea,
Let us swear allegiance
    To a land that's free;
Let us all be grateful
    For a land so fair,
As we raise our voices
    In a solemn prayer.

God bless America,
Land that I love,
Stand beside her and guide her
Through the night with a
light from above;
From the mountains, to the prairies,
To the oceans white with foam,
God bless America
My home sweet home.

THE LATEST DECALOGUE

Arthur Hugh Clough

Thou shalt have one God only; who
Would be at the expense of two?
No graven image may be
Worshipped, except the currency.
Swear not at all; for, for thy curse
Thine enemy is none the worse.
At Church on Sunday to attend
Will serve to keep the world thy friend.
Honor thy parents; that it, all
From whom advancement may befall.
Thou shalt not kill; but needst not strive
Officiously to keep alive.
Do not adultery commit;
Advantage rarely comes of it.
Thou shalt not steal; an empty feat,
When it's so lucrative to cheat.
Bear not false witness; let the lie
Have time on its own wings to fly.
Thou shalt not covet, but tradition
Approves all forms of competition.

STANDING ALONE ON A HILL

Thomas Hardy

To persons standing alone on a hill during a clear mid-night such
as this, the roll of the world eastward is almost a palpable movement.
The sensation may be caused by the panoramic glide of the stars past
earthly objects, which is perceptible in a few minutes of stillness, or
by the better outlook upon space a hill affords, or by the wind, or by
the solitude; but whatever be its origin, the impression of riding
along is vivid and abiding. The poetry of motion is a phrase much in
use, and to enjoy the epic form of that gratification it is necessary to
stand on a hill at a small hour of the night, and, having first expanded
with a sense of difference from the mass of civilized mankind, who
are dreamwrapt and disregardful of all such proceedings at this time,
long and quietly watch your stately progress through the stars. After
such a nocturnal reconnoitre it is hard to get back to earth, and to
believe that the consciousness of such majestic speeding is derived
from a tiny human frame.

R-E-M-O-R-S-E

George Ade

The cocktail is a pleasant drink,
It's mild and harmless, I don't think.
When you've had one, you call for two,
And then you don't care what you do.
Last night I hoisted twenty-three
Of these arrangements into me;
My wealth increased, I swelled with pride;
I was pickled, primed and ossified.

RE-M-O-R-S-E!

Those dry martinis did the work for me;
Last night at twelve I felt immense;
Today I feel like thirty cents.
At four I sought my whirling bed,
At eight I woke with such a head!

(288)

It is no time for mirth or laughter—
The cold, gray dawn of the morning after.

If ever I want to sign the pledge,
It's the morning after I've had an edge;
When I've been full of the oil of joy
And fancied I was a sporty boy.
This world was one kaleidoscope
Of purple bliss, transcendent hope.
But now I'm feeling mighty blue—
Three cheers for the W. C. T. U.!

RE-M-O-R-S-E!

The water wagon is the place for me;
I think that somewhere in the game,
I wept and told my maiden name.
My eyes are bleared, my coppers hot;
I try to eat, but I can not;
It is no time for mirth or laughter—
The cold gray dawn of the morning after.

LOVE

William Shakespeare

What is love? 'tis not hereafter;
Present mirth hath present laughter;
    What's to come is still unsure:
In delay there lies no plenty;
Then come kiss me, sweet and twenty,
    Youth's a stuff will not endure.
                    (From *Twelfth Night*)

THE NAMES OF GOD

Friedrich A. Krummacher

When Alexander, the son of Philip, was at Babylon, he sent for a priest from every country and nation which he had vanquished and assembled them in his palace. Then he sat down on his throne and asked them (and there was a great number of them), saying: "Tell me, do you acknowledge and worship a supreme Being?"

Then all the priests bowed their heads and answered: "Yea, O king!"

Then the priest from India answered: "We call it Brahma, which signifieth the Great." The priest from Persia said: "We call it Ormus, that is, the Light." The priest from Judea said: "We call it Jehovah Adonai, the Lord which is, which was, and is to come."

Thus each priest had a peculiar name by which he designated the Supreme Being.

Then the king was wroth in his heart and said, "You have only one lord and king; henceforth you shall have only one God: Zeus is his name."

Then the priests were grieved at the saying of the king, and spake: "Our people always called him by the name we have proclaimed from their youth up. How then may we change it?"

But the king was yet more wroth. Then an old sage stood forth, a Brahmin, who had accompanied him to Babylon, and said, "Will it please my lord the king that I speak unto this assembly?"

Then he turned to the priests and said: "Doth not the celestial day-star, the source of earthly light, shine upon every one of you?"

Then all the priests bowed their heads and answered: "Yea!"

Then the Brahmin, asked them one by one: "How do you call it?"

And each priest told him a different word and a peculiar name, according to his own country and nation.

Then the Brahmin said to the king, "Shall they not henceforth call the day-star by one name? Helios is his name."

At these words the king was ashamed and said, "Let them use each his own word; for I perceive that the name and the image constitute not the being."

WHITE HOUSE BLESSING*

John Adams

I pray Heaven to bestow the best of blessings on this house, and all that shall hereafter inhabit it. May none but honest and wise men ever rule under this roof.

(In a letter from the White House, 1800.)

A REASONABLE AFFLICTION

Matthew Prior

On his death-bed poor Lubin lies;
　　His spouse is in despair;
With frequent sobs and mutual cries,
　　They both express their care.

"A different cause," says Parson Sly,
　　"The same effect may give:
Poor Lubin fears that he may die;
　　His wife, that he may live."

THE VOICE OF WISDOM

Holy Bible, Proverbs 8:22–31

The Lord possessed me in the beginning of his way, before his works of old.

I was set up from everlasting, from the beginning, or ever the earth was.

When there were no depths, I was brought forth: when there were no fountains abounding with water.

* Engraved on the fireplace of the White House State Dining Room by President Franklin D. Roosevelt.

Before the mountains were settled, before the hills was I brought forth:

While as yet he had not made the earth, nor the fields, nor the highest part of the dust of the world.

When he prepared the heavens, I was there: when he set a compass upon the face of the depth;

When he established the clouds above; when he strengthened the fountains of the deep;

When he gave to the sea his decree, that the waters should not pass his commandment; when he appointed the foundations of the earth:

Then I was by him, as one brought up with him, and I was daily his delight, rejoicing always before him;

Rejoicing in the habitable part of his earth: and my delights were with the sons of men.

THE SLAVE'S REQUEST

Sadi of Shiraz

(TRANSLATOR: Francis Gladwin)

One of the slaves of Umroolais having absconded, a person was sent in pursuit of him and brought him back. The vizier, being inimical to him, commanded him to be put to death, in order to deter other slaves from committing the like offense.

The slave prostrated himself before Umroolais and said, "Whatever may happen to me with your approval is lawful; what plea can the slave offer against the sentence of his lord? But seeing that I have been brought up under the bounties of your house, I do not wish at the resurrection you shall be charged with my blood. If you are resolved to kill your slave, do it comformably to the interpretation of the law, in order at the resurrection you may not suffer reproach."

The king asked, "After what manner shall I expound it?"

He replied: "Give me leave to kill the vizier and then, in retaliation for him, order me to be put to death, that you may kill me justly."

The king laughed and asked the vizier what was his advice on the occasion.

He replied: "O my lord, as an offering to the tomb of your father, liberate this rogue, in order that I also may not fall into calamity.

The crime is on my side, for not having observed the words of the sages, who say, 'When you combat with one who flings clods of earth, you break your own head by your folly; when you shoot at the face of your enemy, be careful that you sit out of his aim.' "

DAYS

Ralph Waldo Emerson

Daughters of Time, the hypocritic Days,
Muffled and dumb like barefoot dervishes,
And marching single in an endless file,
Bring diadems and fagots in their hands.
To each they offer gifts after his will,
Bread, kingdoms, stars, and sky that holds them all.
I, in my pleached garden, watched the pomp,
Forgot my morning wishes, hastily
Took a few herbs and apples, and the Day
Turned and departed silently. I, too late,
Under her solemn fillet saw the scorn.

JUST WORDS

Lewis Carroll

"I quite agree with you," said the Duchess, "and the moral of this is—'Be what you would seem to be'—or if you'd like it put more simply—Never imagine yourself not to be otherwise than what it might appear to others that that that you were or might have been was not otherwise than what you had been would have appeared to them to be otherwise."

ON THIS DAY I COMPLETE MY THIRTY-SIXTH YEAR

Lord Byron

'Tis time this heart should be unmoved,
  Since others it hath ceased to move:
Yet, though I cannot be beloved,
    Still let me love!

My days are in the yellow leaf;
  The flowers and fruits of love are gone;
The worm, the canker, and the grief
    Are mine alone!

The fire that on my bosom preys
  Is lone as some volcanic isle;
No torch is kindled at its blaze—
    A funeral pile.

The hope, the fear, the jealous care,
  The exalted portion of the pain
And power of love, I cannot share,
    But wear the chain.

But 't is not *thus*—and 't is not *here*—
  Such thoughts should shake my soul, nor *now*,
Where glory decks the hero's bier,
    Or binds his brow.

The sword, the banner, and the field,
  Glory and Greece, around me see!
The Spartan, borne upon his shield,
    Was not more free.

Awake! (not Greece—she *is* awake!)
  Awake, my spirit! Think through *whom*
Thy life-blood tracks its parent lake,
    And then strike home!

Tread those reviving passions down,
  Unworthy manhood!—unto thee
Indifferent should the smile or frown
    Of beauty be.

(294)

If thou regrett'st thy youth, *why live?*
  The land of honourable death
Is here:—up to the field, and give
  Away thy breath!

Seek out—less often sought than found—
  A soldier's grave, for thee the best;
Then look around, and choose thy ground,
  And take thy rest.

A VISIT WITH PRESIDENT LINCOLN

Nathaniel Hawthorne

Nine o'clock had been appointed as the time for receiving the deputation, and we were punctual to the moment; but not so the President, who sent us word that he was eating his breakfast and would come as soon as he could. His appetite, we were glad to think, must have been a pretty fair one; for we waited about half an hour in one of the antechambers, and then were ushered into a reception-room, in one corner of which sat the Secretaries of War and of the Treasury, expecting, like ourselves, the termination of the Presidential breakfast. During this interval there were several new additions to our group, one or two of whom were in a working-garb, so that we formed a very miscellaneous collection of people, mostly unknown to each other, and without any common sponsor, but all with an equal right to look our head-servant in the face.

By and by there was a little stir on the staircase and in the passage-way, and in lounged a tall, loose-jointed figure, of an exaggerated Yankee port and demeanor, whom (as being about the homeliest man I ever saw, yet by no means repulsive or disagreeable) it was impossible not to recognize as Uncle Abe.

Unquestionably, Western man though he be, and Kentuckian by birth, President Lincoln is the essential representative of all Yankees, and the veritable specimen, physically, of what the world seems determined to regard as our characteristic qualities. It is the strangest and yet the fittest thing in the jumble of human vicissitudes, that he, out of so many millions, unlooked for, unselected by any intelligible process that could be based upon his genuine qualities, unknown to those who chose him, and unsuspected of what endowments may adapt him for his tremendous responsibility, should have found the way open for him to fling his lank personality into the chair of state, —where, I presume, it was his first impulse to throw his legs on the council-table and tell the Cabinet Ministers a story. There is no describing his lengthy awkwardness nor the uncouthness of his movement; and yet it seemed as if I had been in the habit of seeing him daily, and had shaken hands with him a thousand times in some village street; so true was he to the aspect of the pattern American, though with a certain extravagance which, possibly, I exaggerated still further by the delighted eagerness with which I took it in. If put to guess his calling and livelihood, I should have taken him for a country schoolmaster as soon as anything else. He was dressed in a rusty black frock-coat and pantaloons, unbrushed, and worn so faithfully that the suit had adapted itself to the curves and angularities of his figure, and had grown to be an outer skin of the man. He had shabby slippers on his feet. His hair was black, still unmixed with gray, stiff, somewhat bushy, and had apparently been acquainted with neither brush nor comb that morning, after the disarrangement of the pillow; and as to a night-cap, Uncle Abe probably knows nothing of such effeminacies. His complexion is dark and sallow, betokening, I fear, an insalubrious atmosphere around the White House; he has thick black eyebrows and an impending brow; his nose is large, and the lines about his mouth are very strongly defined.

The whole physiognomy is as coarse a one as you would meet anywhere in the length and breadth of the States; but withal, it is redeemed, illuminated, softened, and brightened by a kindly, though serious look out of his eyes, and an expression of homely sagacity, that seems weighted with rich results of village experience. A great deal of native sense; no bookish cultivation, no refinement; honest at heart, and thoroughly so, and yet, in some sort, sly,—at least, endowed with a sort of tact and wisdom that are akin to craft, and would impel him, I think, to take an antagonist in flank, rather than to make a bull-run at him right in front. But, on the whole, I like this sallow, queer, sagacious visage, with the homely human sympathies that warmed it; and, for my small share in the matter, would as lief have Uncle Abe for a ruler as any man whom it would have been practicable to put in his place.

Immediately on his entrance the President accosted our member of Congress, who had us in charge, and, with a comical twist of his face, made some jocular remark about the length of his breakfast. He then greeted us all around, not waiting for an introduction, but shaking and squeezing everybody's hand with the utmost cordiality, whether the individual's name was announced to him or not. His manner towards us was wholly without pretense, but yet had a kind of natural dignity, quite sufficient to keep the forwardest of us from clapping him on the shoulder and asking him for a story.

THE WABASH CANNONBALL

Anonymous

From the great Atlantic Ocean
To the wide Pacific shore;
From the green of flowing mountains
To the southland by the shore,
She's mighty tall and handsome
And quite well-known by all,
She's the combination of the Wabash Cannonball.

Listen to the jingle,
The rumble and the roar,
As she glides along the woodland,
Through the hills and by the shore,
Hear the mighty rush of the engine,
Hear that lonesome hobo squall,
You're traveling through the jungles
On the Wabash Cannonball.

She come down from Birmingham
One cold December day,
As she rolled into the station,
You could hear the people say,
There's a girl from Birmingham,
She's long and she is tall
She come down from Birmingham
On the Wabash Cannonball.

Here's to Daddy Claxton,
May his name forever stand,
And always be remembered in
The courts of Alabam,
His earthly race is over
And the curtains round him fall,
We'll carry him home to victory on
The Wabash Cannonball.

CAUSE AND EFFECT

Anonymous

For want of a nail the shoe was lost;
For the want of a shoe the horse was lost;
For the want of a horse the rider was lost;
For the want of a rider the battle was lost;
For the want of a battle the kingdom was lost—
And all for the want of a horseshoe nail.

OPTIMIST AND PESSIMIST

McLandburgh Wilson

Twixt optimist and pessimist,
    The difference is droll;
The optimist sees the doughnut
    The pessimist sees the hole.

SUCCESS IS COUNTED SWEETEST

Emily Dickinson

Success is counted sweetest
By those who ne'er succeed.
To comprehend a nectar
Requires sorest need.

Not one of all the purple host
Who took the flag to-day
Can tell the definition,
So clear, of victory,

As he, defeated, dying,
On whose forbidden ear
The distant strains of triumph
Break, agonized and clear.

FOR YE SHALL GO OUT WITH JOY

Holy Bible, Isaiah 55:6–12

Seek ye the Lord while he may be found, call ye upon him while he is near.

Let the wicked forsake his way, and the unrighteous man his thoughts: and let him return unto the Lord, and he will have mercy upon him: and to our God, for he will abundantly pardon.

For my thoughts are not your thoughts, neither are your ways my ways, saith the Lord.

For as the heavens are higher than the earth, so are my ways higher than your ways, and my thoughts than your thoughts.

For as the rain cometh down, and the snow, from heaven and returneth not thither, but watered the earth, and maketh it bring forth and bud, that it may give seed to the sower, and bread to the eater:

So shall my word be that goeth forth out of my mouth: it shall not return unto me void; but it shall accomplish that which I please, and it shall prosper in the thing whereto I sent it.

For ye shall go out with joy, and be led forth with peace: the mountains and the hills shall break forth before you into singing, and all the trees of the field shall clap their hands.

THE BIG BEAR OF ARKANSAS

T. B. Thorpe

On a fine fall day, long time ago, I was trailing about for bar, and what should I see but fresh marks on the sassafras trees, about eight inches above any in the forest that I knew of. Says I, "them marks is a hoax, or it indicates the d——t bar that was ever grown." In fact, stranger, I couldn't believe it was real, and I went on. Again I saw the same marks, at the same height, and I *knew the thing lived*. That conviction came home to my soul like an earthquake. Says I, "here is something a-purpose for me: that bar is mine, or I give up the hunting business." The very next morning what should I see but a number of buzzards hovering over my cornfield. "The rascal has been there," said I, "for that sign is certain:" and, sure enough, on examining, I found the bones of what had been as beautiful a hog the day before, as was ever raised by a Buckeye. Then I tracked the critter out of the field to the woods, and all the marks he left behind, showed me that the was *the bar*.

Well, stranger, the first fair chase I ever had with that big critter, I saw him no less than three distinct times at a distance: the dogs run him over eighteen miles and broke down, my horse gave out, and I was as nearly used up as a man can be. That a bar runs at all, is puzzling; but how this one could tire down and bust up a pack of hounds and a horse, that were used to overhauling everything they started after in no time, was past my understanding. Well, stranger, that bar finally got so sassy, that he used to help himself to a hog off my premises whenever he wanted one; the buzzards followed after what he left, and so between *bar* and *buzzard* I rather think I was *out of pork*.

Well, missing that bar so often took hold of my vitals, and I wasted away. The thing had been carried too far, and it reduced me in flesh faster than an ager. I would see that bar in every thing I did; he *hunted me*, and that, too, like a devil, which I began to think he was. While in this fix, I made preparations to give him a last brush, and be done with it. Having completed every thing to my satisfaction, I started at sunrise, and to my great joy, I discovered from the way the dogs run, that they were near to him; finding his trail was nothing, for that had become as plain to the pack as a turnpike road. On we went, and coming to an open country, what should I see but the bar very leisurely ascending a hill, and the dogs close at his heels, either a match for him in speed, or else he did not care to get out of their way—I don't know which. But wasn't he a beauty, though? I loved him like a brother.

On he went, until he came to a tree, the limbs of which formed a crotch about six feet from the ground. Into this crotch he got and seated himself, the dogs yelling all around it; and there he sat eyeing them as quiet as a pond in low water. A green-horn friend of mine, in company, reached shooting distance before me, and blazed away, hitting the critter in the centre of his forehead. The bar shook his head as the ball struck it, and then walked down from that tree as gently as a lady would from a carriage. 'Twas a beautiful sight to see him do that—he was in such a rage that he seemed to be as little afraid of the dogs as if they had been sucking pigs; and the dogs warn't slow in making a ring around him at a respectful distance, I tell you; even Bowie-knife, himself, stood off. Then the way his eyes flashed—why the fire of them would have singed a cat's hair; in fact that bar was in a *wrath all over*. Only one pup came near him, and he was brushed out so totally with the bar's left paw, that he entirely disappeared; and that made the old dogs more cautious still. In the meantime, I came up, and taking deliberate aim as a man should do, at his side, just back of his foreleg, *if my gun did not snap*, call me a coward, and I won't take it personal. Yes, stranger, *it snapped*, and I could not find a cap about my person. While in this predicament, I turned round to my fool friend—says I, "Bill," says I, "you're an ass—you're a fool—you might as well have tried to kill that bar by barking the tree under his belly, as to have done it by hitting him in the head. Your shot has made a tiger of him, and blast me, if a dog gets killed or wounded when they come to blows, I will stick my knife into your liver, I will—" my wrath was up. I had lost my caps, my gun had snapped, the fellow with me had fired at the bar's head, and I expected every moment to see him close in with the dogs, and kill a dozen of them at least. In this thing I was mistaken, for the bar leaped over the ring formed by the dogs, and giving a fierce growl, was off—the pack, of course, in full cry after him.

The run this time was short, for coming to the edge of a lake the varmit jumped in, and swam to a little island in the lake, which it reached just a moment before the dogs. "I'll have him now," said I, for I had found my caps in the *lining of my coat*—so, rolling a log into the lake, I paddled myself across to the island, just as the dogs had cornered the bar in a thicket. I rushed up and fired—at the same time the critter leaped over the dogs and came within three feet of me, running like mad; he jumped into the lake, and tried to mount the log I had just deserted, but every time he got half his body on it, it would roll over and send him under; the dogs, too, got around him, and pulled him about, and finally Bowie-knife clenched with him, and they sunk into the lake together. Stranger, about this time, I was excited, and I stripped off my coat, drew my knife, and intended to have taken a part with Bowie-knife myself, when the bar rose to the surface. But the varmit staid under—Bowie-knife came up alone, more dead than alive, and with the pack came ashore. "Thank God," said I, "the old villain has got his deserts at last." Determined to have the body, I cut a grapevine for a rope, and dove down where I could see the bar in the water, fastened my queer rope to his leg, and fished him, with great difficulty, ashore. Stranger, may I be chawed to death by young alligators, if the thing I looked at wasn't a *she bar, and not the old critter after all*. The way matters got mixed on that island was unaccountably curious, and thinking of it made me more than ever convinced that I was hunting the devil himself. I went home that night and took to my bed—the thing was killing me. The entire team of Arkansaw in bar-hunting, acknowledged himself used up, and the fact sunk into my feelings like a snagged boat will in the Mississippi. I grew as cross as a bar with two cubs and a sore tail. The thing got out 'mong my neighbours, and I was asked how come on that individu-al that never lost a bar once started? and if that same individ-u-al didn't wear telescopes when he turned a she bar, of ordinary size, into an old he one, a little larger than a horse? "Perhaps," said I, "friends"—getting wrathy—"perhaps you want to call somebody a liar." "Oh, no," said they, "we only heard such things as being *rather common* of late, but we don't believe one word of it; oh, no,"—and then they would ride off and laugh like so many hyenas over a dead nigger.

It was too much, and I determined to catch that bar, go to Texas, or die,—and I made my preparations accordin'. I had the pack shut up and rested. I took my rifle to pieces and iled it. I put caps in every pocket about my person, for *fear of the lining*. I then told my neighbours, that on Monday morning—naming the day—I would start THAT bar, and bring him home with me, or they might divide my settlement among them, the owner having disappeared. Well, stranger, on the morning previous to the great day of my hunting expedition, I went into the woods near my house, taking my gun and Bowie-knife along, just *from habit*, and there sitting down also from habit, what should I see, getting over my fence, but *the bar*! Yes, the old varmit was within a hundred yards of me, and the way he walked *over that fence*—stranger, he loomed up like a *black mist*, he seemed so large, and he walked right towards me. I raised myself, took deliberate aim, and fired. Instantly the varmit wheeled, gave a yell, and *walked through the fence* like a falling tree would through a cobweb. I started after, but was tripped up by my inexpressibles, which either from habit, or the excitement of the moment, were about my heels, and before I had really gathered myself up, I heard the old varmit groaning in a thicket near by, like a thousand sinners, and by the time I reached him he was a corpse. Stranger, it took five niggers and myself to put the carcass on a mule's back, and old long-ears waddled under the load, as if he was foundered in every leg of his body, and with a common whopper of a bar, he would have trotted off, and enjoyed himself. 'Twould astonish you to know how big he was: I made a *bed-spread of his skin*, and the way it used to cover my bar mattress, and leave several feet on each side to tuck up, would have delighted you. It was in fact a creation bar, and if it had lived in Samson's time, and had met him, in a fair fight, it would have licked him in the twinkling of a dice-box. But, strangers, I never like the way I hunted, and *missed him*. There is something curious about it, I could never understand,—and I never was satisfied at his giving in so easy at last. Perhaps, he had heard of my preparations to hunt him the next day, so he jist come in, like Capt. Scott's coon, to save his wind to grunt with in dying; but that ain't likely. My private opinion is, that that bar was an *unhuntable bar, and died when his time come.*

(1841)

SPRING SONG

William Shakespeare

When daisies pied and violets blue
   And lady-smocks all silver-white
And cuckoo buds of yellow hue
   Do paint the meadows with delight,
The cuckoo then, on every tree,
Mocks married me: for thus sings he,
        Cuckoo;
Cuckoo, cuckoo: O world of fear,
Unpleasing to a married ear!

When shepherds pipe on oaten straws,
   And merry larks are ploughmen's clock,
When turtles tread, and rooks, and daws,
   And maidens bleach their summer smocks,
The cuckoo then, on every tree,
Mocks married men, for thus sings he,
        Cuckoo;
Cuckoo, cuckoo, O word of fear,
Unpleasing to a married ear!

(From *Love's Labour's Lost*)

There is only one class in the community that thinks more about money than the rich, and that is the poor.
—Oscar Wilde

THREE LITTLE MAIDS FROM SCHOOL

Sir William S. Gilbert

Three little maids from school are we,
Pert as a school girl well can be,
Filled to the brim with girlish glee,
　　Three little maids from school!

Everything is a source of fun.
Nobody's safe for we care for none!
Life is a joke that's just begun!
　　Three little maids from school!

Three little maids, who, all unwary,
Come from a ladies' seminary,
Freed from its genius tutelary—
　　Three little maids from school!

One little maid is a bride, Yum-Yum—
Two little maids in attendance come—
Three little maids is the total sum.
　　Three little maids from school!

From three little maids take one away.
Two little maids remain and they—
Won't have to wait very long, they say—
　　Three little maids from school!

Three little maids, who, all unwary,
Come from a ladies' seminary,
Freed from its genius tutelary—
　　Three little maids from school!

Bad officials are elected by good citizens who do not vote.
　　　　　　　　　　　　　　—George Jean Nathan

REFLECTIONS AFTER RETURNING FROM THE MOON

Neil A. Armstrong

We landed on the Sea of Tranquillity, in cool of the early lunar morning, when the long shadows would aid our perception.

The sun was only ten degrees above the horizon, while the earth turned through nearly a full day during our stay, the sun at Tranquillity Base rose barely eleven degrees—a small fraction of the month-long lunar day. There was a peculiar sensation of the duality of time—the swift rush of events that characterizes all our lives—and the ponderous parade which makes the aging of the universe.

Both kinds of time were evident—the first by the routine events of the flight—whose planning and execution were detailed to fractions of a second—the latter by rocks round us, unchanged throughout the history of man—whose three-billion-year-old secrets made them the treasure we sought. . . .

We came in peace for all mankind those nineteen hundred and sixty-nine years had constituted the majority of the age of Bisces—a twelfth of the great year that is measured by the thousand generaions the precession of the earth's axis required to scribe a giant circle in the heavens.

In the next twenty centuries, the age of Aquarius of the great year, the age for which our young people have such high hopes, humanity may begin to understand its most baffling mystery—where are we going? The earth is, in fact, traveling many thousands of miles per hour in the direction of the constellation Hercules—to some unknown destination in the cosmos. Man must understand his universe in order to understand his destiny.

Mystery creates wonder and wonder is the basis for man's desire to understand. Who knows what mysteries will be solved in our lifetime, and what new riddles will become the challenge of the new generations? Science has not mastered prophecy. We predict too much for the next year and yet far too little for the next ten. Responding to challenge is one of democracy's great strengths. Our success in space leads us to hope that this strength can be used in the next decade in the solution of many of our planet's problems.

(From Address to Congress, September 16, 1969)

FRANCESCA AND PAOLO, EXECUTED FOR THEIR ILLICIT LOVE, TELL THEIR SAD STORY TO DANTE ON HIS TRIP THROUGH HELL

(TRANSLATOR: Lord Byron)

"The land where I was born sits by the seas,
  Upon that shore to which the Po descends,
  With all his followers, in search of peace.
Love, which the gentle heart soon apprehends,
  Seized him for the fair person which was ta'en
  From me, and me even yet the mode offends.
Love, who to none beloved to love again
  Remits, seized me with wish to please, so strong,
  That, as thou seest, yet, yet it doth remain.
Love to one death conducted us along,
  But Caina waits for him our life who ended":
  These were the accents uttered by her tongue.—
Since I first listen'd to these souls offended,
  I bow'd my visage, and so kept it till—
  "What think'st thou?" said the bard; when I unbended,
And recommenced: "Alas! unto such ill
  How many sweet thoughts, what strong ecstasies,
  Led these their evil fortune to fulfil!"
And then I turn'd unto their side my eyes,
  And said, "Francesca, thy sad destinies
  Have made me sorrow till the tears arise.
But tell me, in the season of sweet sighs,
  By what and how thy love to passion rose,
  So as his dim desires to recognize?"
Then she to me: "The greatest of all woes
  Is to remind us of our happy days
  In misery, and that thy teacher knows.
But if to learn our passion's first root preys
  Upon thy spirit with such sympathy,
  I will do even as he who weeps and says.
We read one day for pastime, seated nigh,
  Of Lancilot, how love enchain'd him too.
  We were alone, quite unsuspiciously.
But oft our eyes met, and our cheeks in hue
  All o'er discolor'd by that reading were;
  But one point only wholly us o'erthrew;

When we read the long-sigh'd-for smile of her,
  To be thus kiss'd by such devoted lover,
  He who from me can be divid'd ne'er
Kiss'd my mouth, trembling in the act all over;
  Accursed was the book and he who wrote!
  That day no further leaf we did uncover."
While thus one spirit told us of their lot,
  The other wept, so that with pity's thralls
  I swoon'd, as if by death I had been smote,
And fell down even as a dead body falls.
          (From *The Divine Comedy*, "Inferno," Canto V)

NATIVE PERSONALITY

Walt Whitman

It is native personality, and that alone, that endows a man to stand before presidents or generals, or in any distinguish'd collection, with *aplomb*—and *not* culture, or any knowledge or intellect whatever.

GOOD THINGS

Francis Bacon

It was a high speech of Seneca (after the manner of the Stoics), that "The good things which belong to prosperity are to be wished, but the good things that belong to adversity are to be admired."

LOVE

George Herbert

Love bade me welcome; yet my soul drew back,
        Guilty of dust and sin,
But quick-ey'd Love, observing me grow slack
        From my first entrance in,
Drew nearer to me, sweetly questioning
        If I lack'd anything.

(307)

"A guest," I answer'd, "worthy to be here";
    Love said, "You shall be he."
"I, the unkind, ungrateful? Ah, my dear,
    I cannot look on Thee."
Love took my hand, and smiling did reply,
    "Who made the eyes but I?"

"Truth, Lord; but I have marr'd them; let my shame
    Go where it doth deserve."
"And know you not," says Love, "who bore the blame?"
    "My dear, then I will serve."
"You must sit down," says Love, "and taste My meat."
    So I did sit down and eat.

THE SECRET ISOLATED JOY OF THE THINKER

Oliver Wendell Holmes, Jr.

No man has earned the right to intellectual ambition until he
has learned to lay his course by a star which he has never seen—
to dig by the divining rod for springs which he may never reach.
In saying this, I point to that which will make your study heroic.
For I say unto you in all sadness of conviction, that to think great
thoughts you must be heroes as well as idealists. Only when you
have worked alone—when you have felt around you a black gulf
of solitude more isolating than that which surrounds the dying man,
and in hope and in despair have trusted to your own unshaken
will,—then only can you gain the secret isolated joy of the thinker,
who knows that, a hundred years after he is dead and forgotten,
men who had never heard of him will be moving to the measure
of his thought,—the subtle rapture of a postponed power, which the
world knows not because it has no external trappings, but which
to his prophetic vision is more real than that which commands an
army. And if this joy should not be yours, still it is only thus that
you can know that you have done what lay in you to do,—can say
that you have lived, and be ready for the end.

THE ROOF

Gelett Burgess

The Roof it has a Lazy Time
A-lying in the Sun;
The Walls they have to Hold Him Up;
They do not Have Much Fun!

FROM DOUGLAS MACARTHUR'S ADDRESS TO A JOINT MEETING OF CONGRESS

I do not stand here as advocate for any partisan cause, for the issues are fundamental and reach quite beyond the realm of partisan considerations. They must be resolved on the highest plane of national interest if our course is to prove sound and our future protected. . . .

The issues are global, and so interlocked that to consider the problems of one sector oblivious to those of another is to court disaster for the whole. While Asia is commonly referred to as the gateway to Europe, it is no less true that Europe is the gateway to Asia, and the broad influence of the one cannot fail to have its impact upon the other.

There are those who claim our strength is inadequate to protect on both fronts, that we cannot divide our effort. I can think of no greater expression of defeatism.

If a potential enemy can divide his strength on two fronts, it is for us to counter his efforts. The Communist threat is a global one. Its successful advance in one sector threatens the destruction of every other sector. You cannot appease or otherwise surrender to Communism in Asia without simultaneously undermining our efforts to halt its advance in Europe. . . .

I know war as few other men now living know it, and nothing to me is more revolting. I have long advocated its complete abolition, as its very destructiveness on both friend and foe has rendered it useless as a means of settling international disputes.

Indeed, on the second day of September, 1945, just following the surrender of the Japanese nation on the battleship *Missouri*, I formally cautioned as follows:

"Men since the beginning of time have sought peace. Various methods through the ages have been attempted to devise an international process to prevent or settle disputes between nations. From

(309)

the very start workable methods were found in so far as individual citizens were concerned, but the mechanics of an instrumentality of larger international scope have never been successful.

"Military alliances, balances of power, league of nations, all in turn failed, leaving the only path to be by way of the crucible of war. The utter destructiveness of war now blocks out this alternative. We have had our last chance. If we will not devise some greater and more equitable system, our Armageddon will be at our door. The problem basically is theological and involves a spiritual recrudescence, an improvement of human character that will synchronize with our almost matchless advances in science, art, literature and all material and cultural developments of the past 2,000 years. It must be of the spirit if we are to save the flesh.

But once war it forced upon us, there is no other alternative than to apply every available means to bring it to a swift end. War's very object is victory, not prolonged indecision.

In war there is no substitute for victory." . . .

I am closing my fifty-two years of military service. When I joined the Army, even before the turn of the century, it was the fulfillment of all my boyish hopes and dreams.

The world has turned over many times since I took the oath on the plains at West Point, and the hopes and dreams have long since vanished, but I still remember the refrain of one of the most popular barrack ballads of that day which proclaimed that old soldiers never die; they just fade away.

And like the old soldier of that ballad, I now close my military career and just fade away, an old soldier who tried to do his duty as God gave him the light to see that duty. Good-bye.

(April 19, 1951)

THESE ARE THE GIFTS I ASK

Henry van Dyke

These are the gifts I ask
Of Thee, Spirit serene:
Strength for the daily task,
Courage to face the road,
Good cheer to help me bear the traveler's load,
And, for the hours of rest that come between,
An inward joy of all things heard and seen.

(310)

These are the sins I fain
Would have Thee take away:
Malice and cold disdain,
Hot anger, sullen hate,
Scorn of the lowly, envy of the great,
And discontent that casts a shadow gray
On all the brightness of the common day.

AMERICA'S POSITION

Theodore Roosevelt

Much has been given to us, and much will rightfully be expected from us. We have duties to others and duties to ourselves; and we can shirk neither. We have become a great nation, forced by the fact of its greatness into relations with the other nations of the earth; and we must behave as beseems a people with such responsibilities. Toward all other nations, large and small, our attitude must be one of cordial and sincere friendship. We must show not only in our words but in our deeds that we are earnestly desirous of securing their good will by acting toward them in a spirit of just and generous recognition of all their rights. But justice and generosity in a nation, as in an individual, count most when shown not by the weak but by the strong. While ever careful to refrain from wronging others, we must be no less insistent that we are not wronged ourselves. We wish peace; but we wish the peace of justice, the peace of righteousness. We wish it because we think it is right and not because we are afraid. No weak nation can have cause to fear us, and no strong power should ever be able to single us out as a subject for insolent aggression.

(From *Inaugural Address*, March 4, 1905)

INSCRIPTION ON THE NATIONAL ARCHIVES BUILDING, WASHINGTON, D.C.

The heritage of the past is the seed that brings forth
the harvest of the future.

(311)

ON THE BANKS OF THE WABASH, FAR AWAY

Paul Dresser

'Round my Indiana homestead wave the corn fields,
In the distance loom the woodlands clear and cool,
Often times my thoughts revert to scenes of childhood,
Where I first received my lessons—Nature's school.
But one thing there is missing in the picture,
Without her face it seems so incomplete,—
I long to see my mother in the doorway,
As she stood there years ago, her boy to greet.

Chorus:
Oh, the moonlight's fair tonight along the Wabash,
From the fields there comes the breath of new-mown hay,
Through the sycamores the candelights are gleaming,
On the banks of the Wabash, far away.

Many years have passed since I strolled by the river
Arm in arm, with sweetheart Mary by my side.
It was there I tried to tell her that I loved her,
It was there I begged of her to be my bride.
Long years have passed since I strolled through the churchyard,
She's sleeping there, my angel, Mary dear;
I loved her but she thought I didn't mean it,
Still I'd give my future were she only here.

HOW I LEARNED THE MEANING OF LOVE

Helen Keller

The most important day I remember in all my life is the one on which my teacher, Anne Mansfield Sullivan, came to me. I am filled with wonder when I consider the immeasurable contrast between the two lives which it connects. It was the third of March, 1887, three months before I was seven years old.

On the afternoon of that eventful day, I stood on the porch, dumb, expectant. I guessed vaguely from my mother's signs and from the hurrying to and fro in the house that something unusual was about to happen, so I went to the door and waited on the steps. The afternoon sun penetrated the mass of honeysuckle that covered the porch, and fell on my upturned face. My fingers lingered almost unconsciously on the familiar leaves and blossoms which had just come forth to greet the sweet southern spring. I did not know what the future held of marvel or surprise for me. Anger and bitterness had preyed upon me continually for weeks. Then a languor had succeeded this passionate struggle.

Have you ever been at sea in a dense fog, when it seemed as if a tangible white darkness shut you in, and the great ship, tense and anxious, groped her way toward the shore with plummet and sounding-line, and you waited with beating heart for something to happen? I was like that ship before my education began, only I was without compass or sounding-line, and had no way of knowing how near the harbor was. "Light! give me light!" was the wordless cry of my soul, and the light of love shone on me.

I felt approaching footsteps. I stretched out my hand as I supposed to my mother. Some one took it, and I was caught up and held close in the arms of her who had come to reveal all things to me and, more than all things else, to love me.

The morning after my teacher came she led me into her room and gave me a doll. The little blind children at the Perkins Institute had sent it; but I did not know this until afterward. When I had played with it a little while, Miss Sullivan slowly spelled into my hand the word "d-o-l-l." I was at once interested in this finger play and tried to imitate it. When I finally succeeded in making the letters correctly I was flushed with childish pleasure and pride. Running downstairs to my mother I held up my hand and made the letters for doll. I did not know that I was spelling a word or even that words existed; I was simply making my fingers go in monkey-like imitation. In the days that followed I learned to spell in this uncomprehending way a great many words, among them pin, hat, cup and a few verbs like sit, stand, and walk. But my teacher had been with me several weeks before I understood that everything has a name.

One day, while I was playing with my new doll, Miss Sullivan put my big rag doll into my lap also, spelled "d-o-l-l" and tried to make me understand that "d-o-l-l" applied to both. Earlier in the day we had a tussle over the words "m-u-g" and "w-a-t-e-r." Miss Sullivan had tried to impress it upon me that "m-u-g" is mug and that "w-a-t-e-r" is water, but I persisted in confounding the two. In despair she had dropped the subject for the time, only to renew it at the first opportunity. I became impatient at her repeated attempts and, seizing the new doll, I dashed it upon the floor. I was keenly delighted when I felt the fragments of the broken doll at my feet. Neither sorrow nor regret followed my passionate outburst. I had not loved the doll. In the still, dark world in which I lived there was no strong sentiment or tenderness. I felt my teacher sweep the fragments to one side of the hearth, and I had a sense of satisfaction that the cause of my discomfort was removed. She brought me my hat, and I knew I was going out into the warm sunshine. This thought, if a wordless sensation may be called a thought, made me hop and skip with pleasure.

We walked down the path to the well-house, attracted by the fragrance of the honeysuckle with which it was covered. Some one was drawing water and my teacher placed my hand under the spout. As the cool stream gushed over one hand she spelled into the other the word water, first slowly, then rapidly. I stood still, my whole attention fixed upon the motions of her fingers. Suddenly I felt a misty consciousness as of something forgotten—a thrill of returning thought; and somehow the mystery of language was revealed to me. I knew then the "w-a-t-e-r" meant the wonderful cool something that was flowing over my hand. That living word awakened my soul, gave it light, hope, joy, set it free! There were barriers still, it is true, but barriers that could in time be swept away.

I left the well-house eager to learn. Everything had a name, and each name gave birth to a new thought. As we returned to the house every object which I touched seemed to quiver with life. That was because I saw everything with the strange, new sight that had come to me. On entering the door I remembered the doll I had broken. I felt my way to the hearth and picked up the pieces. I tried vainly to put them together. Then my eyes filled with tears; for I realized what I had done, and for the first time I felt repentance and sorrow.

I learned a great many new words that day. I do not remember what they all were; but I do know that mother, father, sister, teacher were among them—words that were to make the world blossom for me, "like Aaron's rod, with flowers." It would have been difficult to find a happier child than I was as I lay in my crib at the close of that eventful day and lived over the joys it had brought me, and for the first time longed for a new day to come.

I had now the key to all language, and I was eager to learn to use it. Children who hear acquire language without any particular effort; the words that fall from others' lips they catch on the wing, as it were, delightedly, while the little deaf child must trap them by a slow and often painful process. But whatever the process, the result is wonderful. Gradually from naming an object we advance step by step until we have traversed the vast distance between our first stammered syllable and the sweep of thought in a line of Shakespeare.

At first, when my teacher told me about a new thing I asked very few questions. My ideas were vague, and my vocabulary was inadequate; but as my knowledge of things grew, and I learned more and more words, my field of inquiry broadened, and I would return again and again to the same subject, eager for further information. Sometimes a new word revived an image that some earlier experience had engraved on my brain.

I remember the morning that I first asked the meaning of the word, "love." This was before I knew many words. I had found a few early violets in the garden and brought them to my teacher. She tried to kiss me; but at the time I did not like to have any one kiss me except my mother. Miss Sullivan put her arm gently around me and spelled into my hand, "I love Helen."

"What is love?" I asked.

She drew me closer to her and said, "It is here," pointing to my heart, whose beats I was conscious of for the first time. Her words puzzled me very much because I did not then understand anything unless I touched it.

I smelt the violets in her hand and asked, half in words, half in signs, a question which meant, "Is love the sweetness of flowers?"

"No," said my teacher.

Again I thought. The warm sun was shining on us.

"Is this not love?" I asked, pointing in the direction from which the heat came. "Is this not love?"

It seemed to me that there could be nothing more beautiful than the sun, whose warmth makes all things grow. But Miss Sullivan shook her head, and I was greatly puzzled and disappointed. I thought it strange that my teacher could not show me love.

A day or two afterward I was stringing beads of different sizes in symmetrical groups—two large beads, three small ones, and so on. I had made many mistakes, and Miss Sullivan had pointed them out again and again with gentle patience. Finally I noticed a very obvious error in the sequence and for an instant I concentrated my attention on the lesson and tried to think how I should have arranged the beads. Miss Sullivan touched my forehead and spelled with decided emphasis, "Think!"

In a flash I knew that the word was the name of the process that was going on in my head. This was my first conscious perception of an abstract idea.

For a long time I was still—I was not thinking of the beads in my lap, but trying to find a meaning for "love" in the light of this new idea. The sun had been under a cloud all day, and there had been brief showers; but suddenly the sun broke forth in all its southern splendor.

Again I asked my teacher, "Is this not love?"

"Love is something like the clouds that were in the sky before the sun came out," she replied. Then in simpler words than these, which at that time I could not have understood, she explained: "You cannot touch the clouds, you know, but you feel the rain and know how glad the flowers and the thirsty earth are to have it after a hot day. You cannot touch love either; but you feel the sweetness that it pours into everything. Without love you would not be happy or want to play."

The beautiful truth burst open my mind—I felt that there were invisible lines stretched between my spirit and the spirits of others.

From the beginning of my education Miss Sullivan made it a practice to speak to me as she would speak to any hearing child; the only difference was that she spelled the sentences into my hand instead of speaking them. If I did not know the words and idioms necessary to express my thoughts she supplied them, even suggesting conversation when I was unable to keep up my end of the dialogue.

This process was continued for several years; for the deaf child does not learn in a month, or even in two or three years, the numberless idioms and expressions used in the simplest daily intercourse. The little hearing child learns these from constant repetition and imitation. The conversation he hears in his home stimulates his mind and suggests topics and calls forth the spontaneous expression of his own thoughts. This natural exchange of ideas is denied to the deaf child. My teacher, realizing this, determined to supply the kinds of stimulus I lacked. This she did by repeating to me as far as possible, verbatim, what she heard, and by showing me how I could take part in the conversation. But it was a long time before I ventured to take the initiative and still longer before I could find something appropriate to say at the right time.

The deaf and the blind find it very difficult to acquire the amenities of conversation. How much more this difficulty must be augmented in the case of those who are both deaf and blind! They cannot distinguish the tone of the voice or, without assistance, go up and down the gamut of tones that give significance to words; nor can they watch the expression of the speaker's face, and a look is often the very soul of what one says.

PRONOUNS

Karle Wilson Baker

The Lord said,
"Say, 'we' ";
But I shook my head,
Hid my hands tight behind my back, and said,
Stubbornly,
"I."

The Lord said,
"Say, 'We' ";
But I looked upon them, grimy and all awry.
Myself in all those twisted shapes? Ah, no!
Distastefully I turned my head away,
Persisting,
"They."

The Lord said,
"Say, 'We' ";
And I,
At last,
Richer by a hoard
Of years
And tears,
Looked in their eyes and found the heavy word
That bent my neck and bowed my head:
Like a shamed schoolboy then I mumbled low,
"We,
Lord."

EPIGRAM

Sir William Watson

'Tis human fortune's happiest height, to be
  A spirit melodious, lucid, poised, and whole;
Second in order of felicity
  I hold it, to have walk'd with such a soul.

NEVER THE SPIRIT WAS BORN

Bhagavad Gita

(TRANSLATOR: Sir Edwin Arnold)

Never the spirit was born;
the spirit shall cease to be never;
Never was time it was not; End
and Beginning are dreams!
Birthless and deathless and changeless
remaineth the spirit for ever;
Death hath not touched it at all,
dead though the house of it seems!
Nay, but as when one layeth
his worn-out robes away,
And, taking new ones, sayeth,
"These will I wear today!"
So putteth by the spirit
lightly its garb of flesh,
And passeth to inherit
a residence afresh.

HORACE GREELEY TO THOMAS DEVYR, WHO ATTACKED HIM IN 1860 FOR ADVOCATING LINCOLN'S ELECTION

The only favor I shall ever ask of you is that you procure and read Benedict Arnold's letter to his betrayed countrymen after he escaped from West Point to the British camp, and then take a steady look at your own face in the mirror. I loathe you too much for your treason to the rights of man to speak to you, but for what you have said or may say about me I care nothing. I remain, glad that you have ceased personally to infest me,

—Horace Greeley

THE LIE

Sir Walter Raleigh

Go, Soul, the body's guest,
Upon a thankless arrant:
Fear not to touch the best;
The truth shall be thy warrant:
Go, since I needs must die,
And give the world the lie.

Say to the court, it glows
And shines like rotten wood;
Say to the church, it shows
What's good, and doth no good:
If church and court reply,
Then give them both the lie.

Tell potentates, they live
Acting by others' action;
Not loved unless they give,
Not strong but by a fraction:
If potentates reply,
Give potentates the lie.

Tell men of high condition,
That manage the estate,
Their purpose is ambition,
Their practice only hate:
And if they once reply,
Then give them all the lie.

Tell them that brave it most,
They beg for more by spending,
Who, in their greatest cost,
Seek nothing but commending:
And if they make reply,
Then give them all the lie.

Tell zeal it wants devotion;
Tell love it is but lust:
Tell time it is but motion;
Tell flesh it is but dust:
And wish them not reply,
For thou must give the lie.

Tell age it daily wasteth;
Tell honour how it alters;
Tell beauty how she blasteth;
Tell favour how it falters:
And as they shall reply,
Give every one the lie.

Tell wit how much it wrangles
In tickle points of niceness;
Tell wisdom she entangles
Herself in over-wiseness:
And when they do reply,
Straight give them both the lie.

Tell physic of her boldness;
Tell skill it is pretension;
Tell charity of coldness;
Tell law it is contention:
And as they do reply,
So give them still the lie.

Tell fortune of her blindness;
Tell nature of decay;
Tell friendship of unkindness;
Tell justice of delay:
And if they will reply,
Then give them all the lie.

Tell arts they have no soundness,
But vary by esteeming;
Tell schools they want profoundness,
And stand too much on seeming:
If arts and schools reply,
Give arts and schools the lie.

Tell faith it's fled the city,
Tell how the country erreth;
Tell manhood shakes off pity;
Tell virtue least preferreth:
And if they do reply,
Spare not to give the lie.

So when thou hast, as I
Commanded thee, done blabbing—
—Although to give the lie
Deserves no less than stabbing—
Stab at thee he that will,
No stab the soul can kill!

MY OWN MIND IS MY CHURCH

Thomas Paine

I believe in one God, and no more; and I hope for happiness beyond this life.

I believe in the equality of man; and I believe that religious duties consist in doing justice, loving mercy, and endeavoring to make our fellow-creatures happy. . . .

My own mind is my own church. . . .

It is necessary to the happiness of man, that he be mentally faithful to himself. Infidelity does not consist in believing, or in disbelieving; it consists in professing to believe what he does not believe. . . .

The belief of a God, so far from having anything of mystery in it, is of all beliefs the most easy, because it arises to us out of necessity. And the practice of moral truth, or, in other words, a practical imitation of the moral goodness of God, is no other than our acting toward each other as he acts benignly toward all. . . .

The only idea we can have of serving God, is that of contributing to the happiness of the living creation that God has made. This cannot be done by retiring ourselves from the society of the world and spending a recluse life in selfish devotion. . . .

I trouble not myself about the manner of future existence. I content myself with believing even to positive conviction, that the Power that gave me existence is able to continue it, in any form and manner he pleases, either with or without this body; and it appears more probable to me that I shall continue to exist hereafter, than that I should have had existence, as I now have, before that existence began.

(From *The Age of Reason*)

DON'T COPY CAT

Mark Twain

Don't, like the cat, try to get more out
of an experience than there is in it.
The cat, having sat upon a hot stove lid,
Will not sit upon a hot stove lid again.
Nor upon a cold stove lid.

HEALTH COUNSEL

Sir John Harrington

Use three physicians still: first Doctor Quiet,
Next Doctor Merry-man, and Doctor Diet.

Joy, Temperance and Repose
Slam the door on the doctor's nose.

THE FEAR OF DEATH

William Shakespeare

Ay, but to die, and go we know not where;
To lie in cold obstruction and to rot;
This sensible warm motion to become
A kneaded clod; and the delighted spirit
To bathe in fiery floods, or to reside
In thrilling region of thick-ribbed ice;
To be imprison'd in the viewless winds,
And blown with restless violence round about
The pendent world; or to be worse than worst
Of those that lawless and incertain thought
Imagine howling:—'tis too horrible!
The weariest and most loathed worldly life
That age, ache, penury, and imprisonment
Can lay on nature is a paradise
To what we fear of death.

(From *Measure for Measure*)

TOLERANCE

Thomas à Kempis

   Endeavor to be patient in bearing with the defects and infirmities of others, of what sort soever they be; for that thyself also has many failings which must be borne with by others. If thou canst not make thyself such an one as thou wouldst, how canst thou expect to have another in all things to thy liking?

POETRY

Marianne Moore

I, too, dislike it: there are things that are important
          beyond all this fiddle.
  Reading it, however, with a perfect contempt for it, one
          discovers in
it after all, a place for the genuine.
    Hands that can grasp, eyes
    that can dilate, hair that can rise
        if it must, these things are important not because a

high-sounding interpretation can be put upon them but be-
          cause they are
  useful. When they become so derivative as to become
          unintelligible,
  the same thing may be said for all of us, that we
    do not admire what
    we cannot understand: the bat
        holding on upside down or in quest of something to

eat, elephants pushing, a wild horse taking a roll, a tireless
          wolf under
  a tree, the immovable critic twitching his skin like a
          horse that feels a flea, the base-
  ball fan, the statistician—
    nor is it valid
        to discriminate against 'business documents and

school-books'; all these phenomena are important. One
     must make a distinction
   however: when dragged into prominence by half poets,
       the result is not poetry,
   nor till the poets among us can be
     'literalists of
     the imagination'—above
         insolence and triviality and can present

for inspection, imaginary gardens with real toads in them,
         shall we have
   it. In the meantime, if you demand on the one hand,
       the raw material of poetry in
   all its rawness and
   that which is on the other hand
       genuine, then you are interested in poetry.

CRITICISM

Samuel Johnson

Criticism is a study by which men grow important and formidable
at very small expense. The power of invention has been conferred
by nature upon few, and the labor of learning those sciences which
may, by mere labor, be obtained is too great to be willingly endured; but every man can exert such judgment as he has upon the
works of others; and he whom nature has made weak, and idleness
keeps ignorant, may yet support his vanity by the name of Critic. . . .
This profession has one recommendation peculiar to itself, that
it gives vent to malignity without real mischief. No genius was ever
blasted by the breath of critics. The poison which, if confined, would
have burst the heart, fumes away in empty hisses, and malice is set
at ease with very little danger to merit. The Critic is the only man
whose triumph is without another's pain, and whose greatness does
not rise upon another's ruin.

SWEET HOUR OF PRAYER

William W. Walford

Sweet hour of prayer, sweet hour of prayer,
That calls me from a world of care,
And bids me at my Father's throne
Make all my wants and wishes known;
In seasons of distress and grief,
My soul has often found relief,
And oft escaped the tempter's snare,
By thy return, sweet hour of prayer.

Sweet hour of prayer, sweet hour of prayer,
Thy wings shall my petition bear
To Him whose truth and faithfulness
Engage the waiting soul to bless;
And since He bids me seek His face,
Believe His word and trust His grace,
I'll cast on Him my every care,
And wait for thee, sweet hour of prayer,

Sweet hour of prayer, sweet hour of prayer,
May I thy consolation share,
Till, from Mount Pisgah's lofty height,
I view my home and take my flight;
This robe of flesh I'll drop and rise
To seize the everlasting prize;
And shout, while passing through the air,
Farewell, farewell, sweet hour of prayer.

CLOTHES

Henry David Thoreau

It is an interesting question how far men would retain their relative rank if they were divested of their clothes. Could you in such a case tell surely of any company of civilized men which belong to the respected class?

TWO SIDES OF WAR

Grantland Rice

All wars are planned by old men
  In council rooms apart,
Who plan for greater armament
  And map the battle chart.

But out along the shattered fields
  Where golden dreams turned gray,
How very young their faces were
  Where all the dead men lay.

Portly and solemn, in their pride
  The elders cast their vote
For this or that, or something else,
  That sounds the warlike note.

But where their sightless eyes stare out
  Beyond life's vanished joys,
I've noticed nearly all the dead
  Were hardly more than boys.

BENJAMIN FRANKLIN PROPOSES TO
MADAME HELVETIUS

Mortified at the barbarous resolution pronounced by you so positively yesterday evening, that you would remain single for the rest of your life as a compliment due to the memory of your husband, I retired to my chamber. Throwing myself upon my bed I dreamt that I was dead, and was transported to the blessed Elysian fields.
I was asked whether I wished to see any person in particular; to which I replied that I wished to see the philosophers. "There are two men who live here at hand in this garden; they are good neighbors and very friendly toward one another." "Who are they?" "Socrates and Helvetius." "I esteem them both highly; but let me see Helvetius first, because I understand a little French but not a word of Greek." I was conducted to him; he received me with much courtesy, having known me, he said, by character some time past.

He asked me a thousand questions relative to the war, the present state of religion, of liberty, of the government in France.

"You do not inquire, then," said I, "after your dear friend, Madame Helvetius; yet she loves you exceedingly. I was in her company not more than an hour ago." "Ah," said he, "you make me recur to my past happiness, which ought to be forgotten in order to be happy here. For many years I could think of nothing but her, though at length I am consoled. I have taken another wife, the most like her that I could find; she is not, indeed, altogether so handsome, but she has a great fund of wit and good sense, and her whole study is to please me. She is at this moment gone to fetch the nectar and ambrosia to regale me; stay awhile and see her."

"I perceive," said I, "that your former friend is more faithful to you than you are to her; she has had several good offers, but has refused them all. I will confess to you that I love her extremely, but she was cruel to me and rejected me peremptorily for your sake." "I pity you sincerely," said he, "for she is an excellent woman, handsome and amiable. But do not the Abbe de la R— and the Abbe M— visit her?" "Certainly they do; not one of your friends has dropt her acquaintance." "If you had gained the Abbe M— with a bribe of good coffee and cream perhaps you would have succeeded; for he is as deep a reasoner as Dun Scotus or St. Thomas; he arranges and methodizes his arguments in such a manner that they are almost irresistible. Or if by a fine edition of some old classic you had gained the Abbe de la R— to speak against you, that would have been still better, as I always observed that when he recommended anything to her, she had a great inclination to do exactly the contrary."

As he finished these words the new Madame Helvetius entered with the nectar and I recognized her as my former American friend, Mrs. Franklin! I reclaimed her, but she answered me coldly, "I was a good wife to you for forty-nine years and four months, nearly half a century; let that content you. I have formed a new condition here, which will last to eternity."

Indignant at this refusal of my Eurydice, I immediately resolved to quit those ungraceful shades and return to this good world again, to behold the sun and you. Here am I, let us *avenge ourselves*.

THE WOODSPURGE

Dante Gabriel Rossetti

The wind flapped loose, the wind was still,
Shaken out dead from tree and hill:
I had walked on at the wind's will,—
I sat now, for the wind was still.

Between my knees my forehead was,—
My lips, drawn in, said not Alas!
My hair was over in the grass,
My naked ears heard the day pass.

My eyes, wide open, had the run
Of some ten weeds to fix upon;
Among those few, out of the sun,
The woodspurge flowered, three cups in one.

From perfect grief there need not be
Wisdom or even memory:
One thing then learnt remains to me,—
The woodspurge has a cup of three.

SOCRATES' PRAYER

(TRANSLATOR: Benjamin Jowett)

Beloved Pan, and all ye other gods who haunt this place, give me
beauty in the inward soul; and may the outward and inward man
be at one. May I reckon the wise to be the wealthy, and may I have
such a quantity of gold as a temperate man and he only can bear.
(From Plato's *Phaedrus*)

ALL TIMES ARE HIS SEASONS

John Donne

We ask our daily bread, and God never says, You should have come yesterday. He never says, You must come again tomorrow. But "today if you will hear His voice," today He will hear you. If some king of the earth have so large an extent of dominion in north and south as that he hath winter and summer together in his dominions, so large an extent of east and west as that he hath day and night together in his dominions, much more hath God mercy and judgment together. He brought light out of darkness, not out of a lesser light. He can bring thy summer out of winter though thou have no spring. Though in the ways of fortune, or misunderstanding, or conscience, thou have been benighted till now, wintered and frozen, clouded and eclipsed, damp and benumbed, smothered and stupefied till now, now God comes to thee, not as in the dawning of the day, not as in the bud of the spring, but as the sun at noon, to banish all shadows; as the sheaves in harvest, to fill all penuries. All occasions invite His mercies, and all times are His seasons.

God made sun and moon to distinguish seasons, and day and night; and we cannot have the fruits of the earth but in their seasons. But God hath made no decrees to distinguish the seasons of His mercies. In Paradise the fruits were ripe the first minute, and in Heaven it is always autumn, His mercies are ever in their maturity.

O COME QUICKLY!

Thomas Campion

Never weather-beaten sail more willing bent to shore,
Never tired Pilgrim's limbs affected slumber more,
Than my wearied spirit now longs to fly out of my troubled breast.
O come quickly, sweetest Lord, take my soul to rest.

Ever-blooming are the joys of heav'n's high paradise,
Cold age deafs not there our ears, nor vapour dims our eyes:
Glory there the sun outshines, whose beams the blessèd only see;
O come quickly, glorious Lord, and raise my spirit to thee.

MEMORABILIA

Robert Browning

Ah, did you once see Shelley plain,
    And did he stop and speak to you,
And did you speak to him again?
    How strange it seems and new!

But you were living before that,
    And also you are living after;
And the memory I started at—
    My starting moves your laughter!

I crossed a moor, with a name of its own
    And a certain use in the world no doubt,
Yet a hand's-breadth of it shines alone
    'Mid the blank miles round about:

For there I picked up on the heather
    And there I put inside my breast
A molted feather, an eagle-feather!
    Well, I forget the rest.

MAKE BIG PLANS

Daniel Burnham

Make no little plans; they have no magic to stir men's blood and probably in themselves will not be realized. Make big plans; aim high in hope and work, remembering that a noble, logical diagram once recorded will never die, but long after we are gone will be a living thing, asserting itself with ever-growing intensity. Remember that our sons and grandsons are going to do things that would stagger us. Let your watchword be order and your beacon beauty.

STRANGE COINCIDENCES

Both Presidents Lincoln and Kennedy were concerned with the issue of Civil Rights. Lincoln was elected in 1860, Kennedy in 1960. Both were slain on Friday and in the presence of their wives. Both were shot from behind and in the head. Their successors, both named Johnson, were Southern Democrats, and both were in the Senate. Andrew Johnson was born in 1808 and Lyndon Johnson was born in 1908. John Wilkes Booth was born in 1839; Lee Harvey Oswald was born in 1939. Booth and Oswald were Southerners favoring unpopular ideas. Booth and Oswald were both assassinated before going to trial. Both Presidents' wives lost children through death while in the White House. Lincoln's secretary, whose name was Kennedy, advised him not to go to the theatre; Kennedy's secretary, whose name was Lincoln, advised him not to go to Dallas. Booth shot Lincoln in a theatre and ran to a warehouse. Oswald shot Kennedy from a warehouse and ran to a theatre. The names, Lincoln and Kennedy, each contain seven letters. The names, Andrew Johnson and Lyndon Johnson, each contain thirteen letters. The names John Wilkes Booth and Lee Harvey Oswald, each contain fifteen letters. Both Johnsons were opposed for re-election by men whose names started with G.

WRITTEN IN EARLY SPRING

William Wordsworth

I heard a thousand blended notes
    While in a grove I sat reclined,
In that sweet mood when pleasant thoughts
    Bring sad thoughts to the mind.

To her fair works did Nature link
    The human soul that through me ran;
And much it grieved my heart to think
    What man has made of man.

Through primrose tufts, in that green bower,
    The periwinkle trail'd its wreaths;
And 'tis my faith that every flower
    Enjoys the air it breathes.

The birds around me hopp'd and play'd,
   Their thoughts I cannot measure—
But the least motion which they made
   It seem'd a thrill of pleasure.

The budding twigs spread out their fan
   To catch the breezy air;
And I must think, do all I can,
   That there was pleasure there.

If this belief from heaven be sent,
   If such be Nature's holy plan,
Have I not reason to lament
   What man has made of man?

SENECA CHIEF RED JACKET TO CHRISTIAN MISSIONARIES, 1805

Brother, you say there is but one way to worship and serve the Great Spirit. If there is but one religion, why do you white people differ so much about it? Why are not all agreed, as you can all read the Book?

Brother, we do not understand these things. We are told that your religion was given to your forefathers and has been handed down from father to son. We also have a religion which was given to our forefathers and has been handed down to us, their children. We worship in that way. It teaches us to be thankful for all the favors we receive, to love each other, and to be united. We never quarrel about religion.

Brother, the Great Spirit has made us all, but He has made a great difference between His white and His red children. He has given us different complexions and different customs. To you He has given the arts. To these, He has not opened our eyes. We know these things to be true. Since He has made so great a difference between us in other things, why may we not conclude that He has given us a different religion according to our understanding? The Great

Spirit does right. He knows what is best for His children; we are satisfied.

Brother, we do not wish to destroy your religion or take it from you. We only want to enjoy our own.

THE BELLS OF HEAVEN

Ralph Hodgson

'Twould ring the bells of Heaven
The wildest peal for years,
If Parson lost his senses
And people came to theirs,
And he and they together
Knelt down with angry prayers
For tamed and shabby tigers
And dancing dogs and bears,
And wretched, blind pit ponies,
And little hunted hares.

OATH TAKEN BY THE PRESIDENT OF
THE UNITED STATES

I do solemnly swear that I will faithfully execute the office of President of the United States, and will, to the best of my ability, preserve, protect and defend the Constitution of the United States.

LOVELIEST OF TREES

A. E. Housman

Loveliest of trees, the cherry now
Is hung with bloom along the bough,
And stands about the woodland ride
Wearing white for Eastertide.

Now, of my threescore years and ten,
Twenty will not come again,
And take from seventy springs a score,
It only leaves me fifty more.

And since to look at things in bloom
Fifty springs are little room,
About the woodlands I will go
To see the cherry hung with snow.

LOVE THE BEAUTIFUL

Moses Mendelssohn

Love the beautiful,
Seek out the true,
Wish for the good,
And the best do.

TO ONE WHO HAS BEEN LONG IN CITY PENT

John Keats

To one who has been long in city pent,
  'Tis very sweet to look into the fair
  And open face of heaven,—to breathe a prayer
Full in the smile of the blue firmament.
Who is more happy, when, with heart's content,
  Fatigued he sinks into some pleasant lair
  Of wavy grass, and reads a debonair
And gentle tale of love and languishment?
Returning home at evening, with an ear
  Catching the notes of Philomel,—an eye
Watching the sailing cloudlet's bright career,
  He mourns that day so soon has glided by:
E'en like the passage of an angel's tear
  That falls through the clear ether silently.

PRAYER OF AN UNKNOWN CONFEDERATE SOLDIER

I asked God for strength, that I might achieve,
I was made weak, that I might learn humbly to obey . . .
I asked for health, that I might do greater things,
I was given infirmity, that I might do better things . . .
I asked for riches, that I might be happy,
I was given poverty that I might be wise . . .
I asked for power, that I might have the praise of men,
I was given weakness, that I might feel the need of God . . .
I asked for all things, that I might enjoy life,
I was given life, that I might enjoy all things . . .
I got nothing that I asked for—but everything that I had hoped for.
Almost despite myself, my unspoiled prayers were answered.
I am among all men, most richly blessed.

REST

John Sullivan Dwight

Rest is not quitting
    The busy career,
Rest is the fitting
    Of self to its sphere.

'Tis the brook's motion,
    Clear without strife,
Fleeing to ocean
    After its life.

'Tis loving and serving
    The Highest and Best!
'Tis onwards! unswerving,
    And that is true rest.

THOMAS BAILEY ALDRICH WRITES A LETTER TO PROFESSOR EDWARD S. MORSE

My Dear Morse: It was very pleasant to receive a letter from you the other day. Perhaps I should have found it pleasanter if I had been able to decipher it. I don't think I mastered anything beyond the date, which I knew, and the signature, at which I guessed. There is a singular and perpetual charm in a letter of yours; it never grows old, and it never loses its novelty. One can say every morning, as one looks at it: "Here's a letter of Morse's I haven't read yet. I think I shall take another shy at it today; and maybe I shall be able in the course of years to make out what he means by those "t's" that look like "w's" and those "i's" that haven't any eyebrows." Other letters are read, and thrown away and forgotten; but yours are kept forever—unread. One of them will last a reasonable man a lifetime.

THE CREED OF OUR POLITICAL FAITH

Thomas Jefferson

Equal and exact justice to all men, of whatever state or persuasion, religious or political; peace, commerce, and honest friendship with all nations, entangling alliances with none. . . . Freedom of religion; freedom of the press, and freedom of person under the protection of the *habeas corpus*, and trial by juries impartially selected. These principles form the bright constellation which has gone before us, and guided our steps through an age of revolution and reformation. The wisdom of our sages and the blood of our heroes have been devoted to their attainment. They should be the creed of our political faith, the text of civil instruction, the touchstone by which we try the services of those we trust; and should we wander from them in moments of error or alarm, let us hasten to retrace our steps and to regain the road which alone leads to peace, liberty, and safety.

(From *First Inaugural Address*, 1801)

THE GAME OF LIFE

Thomas H. Huxley

The chess board is the world, the pieces are the phenomena of the universe, the rules of the game are what we call the laws of Nature. The player on the other side is hidden from us. We know that his play is always fair, just, and patient. But we also know, to our cost, that he never overlooks a mistake, or makes the smallest allowance for ignorance.

EPITAPH ON THE POLITICIAN

Hilaire Belloc

Here, richly, with ridiculous display,
The Politician's corpse was laid away.
While all of his acquaintance sneered and slanged,
I wept: for I had longed to see him hanged.

SPRING

Alfred,Lord Tennyson

Now fades the last long streak of snow,
   Now burgeons every maze of quick
   About the flowering squares, and thick
By ashen roots the violets blow.

Now rings the woodland loud and long,
   The distance takes a lovelier hue,
   And drown'd in yonder living blue
The lark becomes a sightless song.

Now dance the lights on lawn and lea,
   The flocks are whiter down the vale,
   And milkier every milky sail,
On winding stream or distant sea;

Where now the seamew pipes, or dives
In yonder greening gleam, and fly
The happy birds, that change their sky
To build and brood, that live their lives

From land to land; and in my breast
Spring wakens too; and my regret
Becomes an April violet,
And buds and blossoms like the rest.
(From *In Memoriam*)

INTELLECTS

Oliver Wendell Holmes, M.D.

There are one-story intellects, two-story intellects, and three-story intellects with skylights. All fact collectors, who have no aim beyond their facts, are one-story men. Two-story men compare, reason, generalize, using the labors of the fact collectors as well as their own. Three-story men idealize, imagine, predict; their best illumination comes from above, through the skylight.

THE SOMNAMBULIST RIVER PILOT

Mark Twain

There used to be an excellent pilot on the river, a Mr. X., who was a somnambulist. It was said that if his mind was troubled about a bad piece of river, he was pretty sure to get up and walk in his sleep and do strange things. He was once a fellow-pilot for a trip or two with George Ealer, on a great New Orleans passenger packet. During a considerable part of the first trip George was uneasy, but got over it by and by, as X. seemed content to stay in his bed when asleep. Late one night the boat was approaching Helena, Ark.; the water was low, and the crossing above the town in a very blind and tangled condition. X. had seen the crossing since Ealer had, and as the night was particularly drizzly, sullen, and dark, Ealer was considering whether he had not better have X. called to assist in running the place, when the door opened and X. walked in. Now, on very dark nights, light is a deadly enemy to piloting; you are aware that if you stand in a lighted room, on such a night, you cannot see things in the street to any purpose; but if you put out the lights and stand in the gloom you can make out objects in the street pretty well. So, on very dark nights, pilots do not smoke; they allow no fire in the pilot-house stove, if there is a crack which can allow the least ray to escape; they order the furnaces to be curtained with huge tarpaulins from the boat, and the skylights to be closely blinded. Then no light whatever issues from the boat. The undefinable shape that now entered the pilothouse had Mr. X.'s voice. This said:

"Let me take her, George; I've seen this place since you have, and it is so crooked that I reckon I can run it myself easier than I could tell you how to do it."

"It is kind of you, and I swear I am willing. I haven't got another drop of perspiration left in me. I have been spinning around and around the wheel like a squirrel. It is so dark I can't tell which way she is swinging till she is coming around like a whirligig."

So Ealer took a seat on the bench, panting and breathless. The black phantom assumed the wheel without saying anything, steadied the waltzing steamer with a turn or two, and then stood at ease, coaxing here a little to this side and then to that, as gently and as sweetly as if the time had been noonday. When Ealer observed this marvel of steering, he wished he had not confessed! He stared, and wondered, and finally said:

"Well, I thought I knew how to steer a steamboat, but that was another mistake of mine."

X. said nothing, but went serenely on with his work. He rang for the leads; he rang to slow down the steam; he worked the boat carefully and neatly into invisible marks, then stood at the center of the wheel and peered blandly out into the blackness, fore and aft, to verify his position; as the leads shoaled more and more, he stopped the engines entirely, and the dead silence and suspense of "drifting" followed; when the shoalest water was struck, he cracked down on the steam, carried her handsomely over, and then began to work her warily into the next system of shoal-marks; the same patient, heedful use of leads and engines followed, the boat slipped through without touching bottom, and entered upon the third and last intricacy of the crossing; imperceptibly she moved through the gloom, crept by inches into her marks, drifted tediously till the shoalest water was cried, and then, under a tremendous head of steam, went swinging over the reef and away into deep water and safety!

Ealer let his long-pent breath pour out into a great relieving sigh, and said:

"That's the sweetest piece of piloting that was ever done on the Mississippi River! I wouldn't believe it could be done, if I hadn't seen it."

There was no reply, and he added:

"Just hold her five minutes longer, partner, and let me run down and get a cup of coffee."

A minute later Ealer was biting into a pie, down there in the "texas," and comforting himself with coffee. Just then the night watchman happened in, and was about to happen out again, when he noticed Ealer, and exclaimed:

"Who is at the wheel, sir?"

"X."

"Dart for the pilot-house, quicker than lightning!"

The next moment both men were flying up the pilot-house companionway, three steps at a jump! Nobody there! The great steamer was whistling down the middle of the river at her own sweet will! The watchman shot out of the place again; Ealer seized the wheel, set an engine back with power, and held his breath while the boat reluctantly swung away from a "towhead," which she was about to knock into the middle of the Gulf of Mexico!

By and by the watchman came back and said:

"Didn't that lunatic tell you he was asleep, when he first came up here?"

"No."

"Well, he was. I found him walking along on top of the railings, just as unconcerned as another man would walk a pavement; and I put him to bed; now just this minute there he was again, away astern, going through that sort of tight-rope deviltry the same as before."

"Well, I think I'll stay by the next time he has one of those fits. But I hope he'll have them often. You just ought to have seen him take this boat through Helena crossing. I never saw anything so gaudy before. And if he can do such gold-leaf, kid-glove, diamond-breast-pin piloting when he is sound asleep, what couldn't he do if he was *dead*!"

CREDO

Edwin Arlington Robinson

I cannot find my way: there is no star
In all the shrouded heavens anywhere;
And there is not a whisper in the air
Of any living voice but one so far
That I can hear it only as a bar
Of lost, imperial music, played when fair
And angel fingers wove, and unaware,
Dead leaves to garlands where no roses are.
No, there is not a glimmer, nor a call,
For one that welcomes, welcomes when he fears,
The black and awful chaos of the night;
But through it all,—above, beyond it all—
I know the far-sent message of the years,
I feel the coming glory of the Light!

THE BIG ROCK CANDY MOUNTAIN

Anonymous

One ev'ning as the sun went down
And the jungle fire was burning,
Down the track came a hobo, humming,
And he said, "Boys, I'm not turning.
I'm headed for a land that's far away,
Beside the crystal fountain.
I'll see you all this coming fall
In the Big Rock Candy Mountain.

Chorus:
"In the Big Rock Candy Mountain,
There's a land that's fair and bright,
Where the handouts grow on bushes
And you sleep out ev'ry night,
Where the boxcars all are empty
And the sun shines ev'ry day—

Oh, the birds and bees and the cigaret trees,
The rock and rye springs where the whangdoodle sings,
In the Big Rock Candy Mountain.

On the Big Rock Candy Mountain,
All the cops have wooden legs,
And the bulldogs all have rubber teeth,
And the hens lay softboiled eggs.
The farmers' trees are full of fruit,
And the barns are full of hay.
Oh, I'm bound to go where there ain't no snow,
Where the sleet don't fall and the wind don't blow,
In the Big Rock Candy Mountain.

On the Big Rock Candy Mountain,
You never change your socks,
And the little stream of alkyhol
Comes trickling down the rocks.
The shacks all have to tip their hats
And the railroad bulls are blind,
There's a lake of stew and of whisky, too,
You can paddle all around in a big canoe,
On the Big Rock Candy Mountain.

On the Big Rock Candy Mountain,
The jails are made of tin,
And you can bust right out again
As soon as they put you in.
There ain't no shorthandled shovels,
No axes, saws or picks—
I'm a-going to stay there where you sleep all day—
Oh, they boiled in oil the inventor of toil
In the Big Rock Candy Mountain.

Oh, come with me, and we'll go see
The Big Rock Candy Mountain."

AN ELEGY ON THAT GLORY OF HER SEX, MRS. MARY BLAIZE

Oliver Goldsmith

Good people all, with one accord,
    Lament for Madame Blaize,
Who never wanted a good word—
    From those who spoke her praise.

The needy seldom pass'd her door,
    And always found her kind;
She freely lent to all the poor,—
    Who left a pledge behind.

She strove the neighbourhood to please,
    With manners wond'rous winning,
And never followed wicked ways,—
    Unless when she was sinning.

At church, in silks and satins new,
    With hoops of monstrous size,
She never slumber'd in her pew,—
    But when she shut her eyes.

Her love was sought, I do aver,
    By twenty beaux and more;
The king himself has followed her,—
    When she has walk'd before.

But now her wealth and finery fled,
    Her hangers-on cut short all;
The doctors found, when she was dead,—
    Her last disorder mortal.

Let us lament, in sorrow sore,
    For Kent-street well may say,
That had she lived a twelve-month more,—
    She had not died today.

INSCRIPTION ON PLYMOUTH ROCK MONUMENT

This monument marks the first burying ground in Plymouth of the passengers of the Mayflower. Here, under cover of darkness, the fast dwindling company laid their dead, leveling the earth above them lest the Indians should learn how many were the graves. History records no nobler venture for faith and freedom than of this Pilgrim band. In weariness and painfulness, in watching, often in hunger and cold, they laid the foundation of a state wherein every man through countless ages should have liberty to worship God in his own way. May their example inspire thee to do thy part in perpetuating and spreading the lofty ideals of our republic throughout the world.

ODE TO EVENING

William Collins

If aught of oaten stop or pastoral song
May hope, O pensive Eve, to soothe thine ear,
    Like thy own brawling springs,
    Thy springs, and dying gales;

O Nymph reserved,—while now the bright-hair'd sun
Sits in yon western tent, whose cloudy skirts
    With brede ethereal wove,
    O'erhang his wavy bed:

Now air is hush'd, save where the weak-ey'd bat
With short shrill shriek flits by on leathern wing,
    Or where the beetle winds
    His small but sullen horn,

As oft he rises 'midst the twilight path,
Against the pilgrim borne in heedless hum,—
    Now teach me, maid composed,
    To breathe some soften'd strain,

Whose numbers, stealing through thy dark'ning vale,
May not unseemly with its stillness suit;
    As musing slow I hail
    Thy genial loved return.

For when thy folding-star arising shows
His paly circlet, at his warning lamp
        The fragrant Hours, and Elves
        Who slept in buds the day,

And many a Nymph who wreathes her brows with sedge
And sheds the freshening dew, and lovelier still
        The pensive Pleasures sweet,
        Prepare thy shadowy car.

Then let me rove some wild and heathy scene;
Or find some ruin midst its dreary dells,
        Whose walls more awful nod
        By thy religious gleams.

Of if chill blustering winds or driving rain
Prevent my willing feet, be mine the hut
        That, from the mountain's side,
        Views wilds and swelling floods,

And hamlets brown, and dim-discover'd spires;
And hears their simple bell; and marks o'er all
        Thy dewy fingers draw
        The gradual dusky veil.

While Spring shall pour his showers, as oft he wont,
And bathe thy breathing tresses, meekest Eve!
        While Summer loves to sport
        Beneath thy lingering light;

While sallow Autumn fills thy lap with leaves;
Or Winter, yelling through the troublous air,
        Affrights thy shrinking train
        And rudely rends thy robes;

So long, regardful of thy quiet rule,
Shall Fancy, Friendship, Science, smiling Peace,
        Thy gentlest influence own,
        And love thy favourite name!

LINES WRITTEN ON THE ANTIQUITY OF MICROBES

Strickland Gillilan

Adam
Had 'em.

O MISTRESS MINE

William Shakespeare

O mistress mine, where are you roaming?
O, stay and hear; your true love's coming,
    That can sing both high and low:
Trip no further, pretty sweeting;
Journeys end in lovers meeting,
    Every wise man's son doth know.
                    (From *Twelfth Night*)

THE UNITED STATES

Thomas Jefferson

. . . soul, its climate, its equality, liberty, laws, people and manners.
My God! how little do my countrymen know what precious blessings
they are in possession of, and which no other people on earth enjoy!
                    (From a letter to Monroe, June 17, 1785)

The louder he talked of his honor, the faster we counted
our spoons.
                    —Ralph Waldo Emerson

EMPEROR HADRIAN'S DYING ADDRESS TO HIS SOUL

Soul of mine, pretty one, flitting one,
    Guest and partner of my clay,
    Whither wilt thou hie away—
Pallid one, rigid one, naked one,
    Never to play again, never to play?

AMERICA IS GREAT BECAUSE—

I sought for the greatness
and genius of America
in her commodious harbors
and her ample rivers,
and it was not there;

in the fertile fields
and boundless prairies,
and it was not there;

in her rich mines
and her vast world commerce,
and it was not there.

Not until I went
into the churches of America
and heard her pulpits
aflame with righteousness,
did I understand the secret
of her genius and power.

America is great
because she is good,
and if America ever ceases to be good,
America will cease to be great.
        —Attributed to de Tocqueville
         but not found in his works.

(347)

I HAVE A GOODLY HERITAGE

Holy Bible, Psalm 16:5–9

The Lord is the portion of mine inheritance and of my cup: thou maintainest my lot.

The lines are fallen unto me in pleasant places; yea, I have a goodly heritage.

I will bless the Lord, who hath given me counsel; my reins also instruct me in the night seasons.

I have set the Lord always before me: because he is at my right hand, I shall not be moved.

Therefore my heart is glad, and my glory rejoiceth: my flesh also shall rest in hope.

A GOOD WIFE

Agada

(TRANSLATOR: Samuel Taylor Coleridge)

Rabbi Meir . . . sat during the whole of one Sabbath in the public school, and instructed the people. During his absence from his house, his two sons, both of them of uncommon beauty, and enlightened in the law, died. His wife bore them to his bed-chamber, laid them upon the marriage-bed, and spread a white covering over their bodies.

Toward evening, Rabbi Meir came home.

"Where are my beloved sons," he asked, "that I may give them my blessing?"

"They are gone to the school," was the answer.

"I repeatedly looked round the school," he replied, "and I did not see them there."

She reached him a goblet; he praised the Lord at the going out of the Sabbath, drank, and again asked,

"Where are my sons, that they may drink of the cup of blessing?"

"They will not be far off," she said, and placed food before him, that he might eat.

He was in a gladsome and genial mood, and when he had said

grace after the meal, she thus addressed him: "Rabbi, with thy permission, I would fain propose to thee one question."

"Ask it, then, my love!" he replied.

"A few days ago, a person entrusted some jewels to my custody, and now he demands them again: should I give them back again?"

"This is a question," said Rabbi Meir, "which my wife should not have thought it necessary to ask. What! wouldst thou hesitate or be reluctant to restore to everyone his own?"

"No," she replied, "but yet I thought it best not to restore them without acquainting thee therewith."

She then led him to their chamber, and, stepping to the bed, took the white covering from their bodies.

"Ah, my sons! my sons!" thus loudly lamented the father: "My sons! the light of mine eyes, and the light of my understanding; I was your father, but ye were my teachers in the law!"

The mother turned away, and wept bitterly. At length, she took her husband by the hand, and said,

"Rabbi, didst thou not teach me that we must not be reluctant to restore that which was entrusted to our keeping? See, the Lord gave, and the Lord has taken away, and blessed be the name of the Lord!"

"Blessed be the name of the Lord," echoed Rabbi Meir, "and blessed be His name for thy sake, too. For well it is written, 'He that hath found a virtuous woman, hath a greater treasure than costly pearls. She openeth her mouth with wisdom, and on her tongue is the instruction of kindness.'"

LAUGH AND BE MERRY

John Masefield

Laugh and be merry, remember, better the world with a song,
Better the world with a blow in the teeth of a wrong.
Laugh, for the time is brief, a thread the length of a span.
Laugh and be proud to belong to the old proud pageant of man.

Laugh and be merry; remember, in olden time,
God made Heaven and Earth for joy He took in a rhyme,
Made them, and filled them full with the strong red wind of His mirth,
The splendid joy of the stars: the joy of the earth.

(349)

So we must laugh and drink from the deep blue cup of the sky,
Join the jubilant song of the great stars sweeping by,
Laugh, and battle, and work, and drink of the wine outpoured
In the dear green earth, the sign of the joy of the Lord.

Laugh and be merry together, like brothers akin,
Guesting awhile in the rooms of a beautiful inn,
Glad till the dancing stops, and the lilt of the musics ends.
Laugh till the game is played; and be you merry, my friends.

FAMILY PRAYER

Book of Common Prayer

O Lord, support us all the day long, until the shadows lengthen
and the evening comes, and the busy world is hushed, and the fever
of life is over, and our work is done. Then in Thy mercy grant us a
safe lodging, and a holy rest, and peace at the last.

FOR A DEAD LADY

Edwin Arlington Robinson

No more with overflowing light
Shall fill the eyes that now are faded,
Nor shall another's fringe with night
Their woman-hidden world as they did.
No more shall quiver down the days
The flowing wonder of her ways,
Whereof no language may requite
The shifting and the many-shaded.

The grace, divine, definitive,
Clings only as a faint forestalling;
The laugh that love could not forgive
Is hushed, and answers to no calling;

The forehead and the little ears
Have gone where Saturn keeps the years;
The breast where roses could not live
Has done with rising and with falling.

The beauty, shattered by the laws
That have creation in their keeping,
No longer trembles at applause,
Or over children that are sleeping;
And we who delve in beauty's lore
Know all that we have known before
Of what inexorable cause
Makes Time so vicious in his reaping.

JOHN F. KENNEDY STATES HIS POSITION ON CHURCH AND STATE

I believe in an America where the separation of church and state is absolute—where no Catholic prelate would tell the President (should he be a Catholic) how to act, and no Protestant minister would tell his parishioners for whom to vote—where no church or church school is granted any public funds or political preference. . . . an America that is officially neither Catholic, Protestant nor Jewish— where no public official either requests or accepts instructions on public policy from . . . any . . . ecclesiastical source . . . where there is no Catholic vote, no anti-Catholic vote, no bloc voting of any kind . . . and where religious liberty is so indivisible that an act against one church is treated as an act against all. . . . I am not the Catholic candidate for President. I am the Democratic Party's candidate for President who happens also to be a Catholic. I do not speak for my church on public matters, and the church does not speak for me.

(Houston, Texas, September, 1959)

OBITUARY

William Allen White

Frank Munsey, the great publisher, is dead. Frank Munsey contributed to the journalism of his day the great talents of a meat packer, the morals of a money changer and the manners of an undertaker. He and his kind have about succeeded in transforming a once noble profession into an eight per cent security. May he rest in trust.

(*Emporia Gazette*, December 23, 1925)

SWEET CONTENT

Thomas Dekker

Art thou poor, yet hast thou golden slumbers?
                    O sweet content!
Art thou rich, yet is thy mind perplexed?
                    O punishment!
Dost thou laugh to see how fools are vexed
To add to golden numbers, golden numbers?
O sweet content! O sweet, O sweet content!
   Work apace, apace, apace, apace;
   Honest labour bears a lovely face;
Then hey nonny, nonny, hey nonny nonny!

Canst drink the waters of the crispéd spring?
                    O sweet content!
Swimm'st thou in wealth, yet sink'st in thine own tears?
                    O punishment!
Then he that patiently want's burden bears,
No burden bears, but is a king, a king!
O sweet content! O sweet, O sweet content!
   Work apace, apace, apace, apace;
   Honest labour bears a lovely face;
Then hey nonny, nonny, hey nonny nonny!

DUTY, HONOR, COUNTRY

General Douglas MacArthur

At West Point, New York, May 12, 1962

As I was leaving the hotel this morning, a doorman asked me, "Where are you headed for, General? And when I replied, "West Point," he remarked, "Beautiful place. Have you ever been there before?"

No human being could fail to be deeply moved by such a tribute as this. Coming from a profession I have served so long, and a people I have loved so well, it fills me with an emotion I cannot express. . . .

Duty-Honor-Country. Those three hallowed words reverently dictate what you ought to be, what you can be, and what you will be. They are your rallying points: to build courage when courage seems to fail; to regain faith when there seems to be little cause for faith; to create hope when hope becomes forlorn. . . .

The unbelievers will say they are but words, but a slogan, but a flamboyant phrase. Every pedant, every demagogue, every cynic, every hypocrite, every trouble maker, and, I am sorry to say, some others of an entirely different character, will try to downgrade them even to the extent of mockery and ridicule.

But these are some of the things they do.

They build your basic character, they mold you for your future roles as the custodians of the nation's defense, they make you strong enough to know when you are weak, and brave enough to face yourself when you are afraid. They teach you to be proud and unbending in honest failure, but humble and gentle in success; not to substitute words for actions, nor to seek the path of comfort, but to face the stress and spur of difficulty and challenge; to learn to stand up in the storm but to have compassion on those who fail; to master yourself before you seek to master others; to have a heart that is clean, a goal that is high; to learn to laugh yet never forget how to weep; to reach into the future yet never neglect the past; to be serious yet never to take yourself too seriously; to be modest so that you will remember the simplicity of true greatness, the open mind of true wisdom, the meekness of true strength. They give you a temper of the will, a quality of the imagination, a vigor of the emotions, a freshness of the deep springs of life, a temperamental predominance of courage over timidity, an appetite for adventure over love of ease. They create in your heart the sense of wonder, the unfailing hope of what next,

(353)

and the joy and inspiration of life. They teach you in this way to be an officer and a gentleman.

And what sort of soldiers are those you are to lead? Are they reliable, are they brave, are they capable of victory? Their story is known to all of you; it is the story of the American man-at-arms. My estimate of him was formed on the battlefield many, many years ago, and has never changed. I regarded him then as I regard him now— as one of the world's noblest figures, not only as one of the finest military characters but also as one of the most stainless. . . .

In twenty campaigns, on a hundred battlefields, around a thousand campfires, I have witnessed that enduring fortitude, that patriotic self-abnegation, and that invincible determination which have carved his statue in the hearts of his people. From one end of the world to the other he has drained deep the chalice of courage.

As I listened to those songs of the glee club, in memory's eye I could see those staggering columns of the First World War, bending under soggy packs, on many a weary march from dripping dusk to drizzling dawn, slogging ankle deep through the mire of shell-shocked roads, to form grimly for the attack, blue-lipped, covered with sludge and mud, chilled by the wind and rain; driving home to their objective, and for many, to the judgment seat of God.

I do not know the dignity of their birth but I do know the glory of their death. They died unquestioning, uncomplaining, with faith in their hearts, and on their lips the hope that we would go on to victory. Always for them—Duty-Honor-Country; always their blood and sweat and tears as we sought the way and the light and the truth.

And twenty years after, on the other side of the globe, again the filth of murky foxholes, the stench of ghostly trenches, the slime of dripping dugouts; those boiling suns of relentless heat, those torrential rains of devastating storm; the loneliness and utter desolation of jungle trails, the bitterness of long separation from those they loved and cherished, the deadly pestilence of tropical disease, the horror of stricken areas of war; their resolute and determined defense, their swift and sure attack, their indomitable purpose, their complete and decisive victory—always victory—always through the bloody haze of their last reverberating shot, the vision of gaunt, ghastly men reverently following your password of Duty-Honor-Country.

The code which those words perpetuate embraces the highest moral laws and will stand the test of any ethics or philosophies ever promulgated for the uplift of mankind. Its requirements are for the things that are right, and its restraints are from the things that are wrong.

The soldier, above all other men, is required to practice the greatest act of religious training—sacrifice. In battle and in the face of danger and death, he discloses those Divine attributes which his Maker gave when He created man in His own image. No physical courage and no brute instinct can take the place of the Divine help which alone can sustain him. . . .

You now face a new world—a world of change. The thrust into outer space of the satellite, spheres and missiles marked the beginning of another epoch in the long story of mankind—the chapter of the space age. In the five or more billions of years the scientists tell us it has taken to form the earth, in the three or more billion years of development of the human race, there has never been a greater, a more abrupt or staggering evolution. We deal now not with things of this world alone, but with the illimitable distances and as yet unfathomed mysteries of the universe. We are reaching out for a new and boundless frontier.

We speak in strange terms: of harnessing the cosmic energy; of making winds and tides work for us; . . . of mining ocean floors for new fields of wealth and food; of disease preventatives to expand life into the hundreds of years; of controlling the weather for a more equitable distribution of heat and cold, of rain and shine; of space ships to the moon; of the primary target in war, no longer limited to the armed forces of an enemy, but instead to include his civil populations; of ultimate conflict—between a united human race and the sinister forces of some other planetary galaxy; of such dreams and fantasies as to make life the most exciting of all time.

And through all this welter of change and development, your mission remains fixed, determined, inviolable—it is to win our wars. Everything else in your professional career is but a corollary to this vital dedication. . . . Yours is the profession of arms—the will to win, the sure knowledge that in war there is no substitute for victory; that if you lose, the nation will be destroyed; that the very obsession of your public service must be Duty-Honor-Country.

Others will debate the controversial issues, national and international, which divide men's minds; but serene, calm, aloof, you stand as the nation's war guardian, as its lifeguard from the raging tides of international conflict, as its gladiator in the arena of battle. For a century and a half you have defended, guarded, and protected its hallowed tradition of liberty and freedom, of right and justice. Let civilian voices argue the merits or demerits of our processes of government. . . . These great national problems are not for your professional participation or military solution. Your guidepost stands out like a ten-fold beacon in the night—Duty-Honor-Country.

You are the leaven which binds together the entire fabric of our national system of defense. From your ranks come the great captains who hold the nation's destiny in their hands the moment the war tocsin sounds. The long Gray Line has never failed us. Were you to do so, a million ghosts in olive drab, in brown khaki, in blue and gray, would rise from their white crosses thundering those magic words—Duty-Honor-Country. This does not mean that you are war mongers.

On the contrary, the soldier, above all other people, prays for peace, for he must suffer and bear the deepest wounds and scars of war. But always in our ears ring the ominous words of Plato, that wisest of all philosophers; "Only the dead has seen the end of War."

The shadows are lengthening for me. The twilight is here. My days of old have vanished tone and tint; they have gone glimmering through the dreams of things that were. Their memory is one of wondrous beauty, watered by tears, and coaxed and caressed by the smiles of yesterday.

I listen vainly, but with thirsty ear, for the witching melody of faint bugles blowing reveille, of far drums beating the long roll. In my dreams I hear again the crash of guns, the rattle of musketry, the strange, mournful mutter of the battlefield.

But in the evening of my memory, always I come back to West Point. Always there echoes and re-echoes Duty-Honor-Country.

Today marks my final roll call with you, but I want you to know that when I cross the river my last conscious thought will be The Corps—and The Corps—and The Corps—and The Corps.

I bid you farewell.

LOVE'S PHILOSOPHY

Percy Bysshe Shelley

The fountains mingle with the river
And the rivers with the ocean,
The winds of heaven mix for ever
With a sweet emotion;
Nothing in the world is single,
All things by a law divine
In another's being mingle—
Why not I with thine?

See the mountains kiss high heaven,
And the waves clasp one another;
No sister flower would be forgiven
If it disdained its brother;
And the sunlight clasps the earth,
And the moonbeams kiss the sea—
What are all these kissings worth,
If thou kiss not me?

HUEY LORD COMPARES HOOVER AND ROOSEVELT

Hoover is a hoot owl. Roosevelt is a scrootch owl. A hoot owl bangs into the roost and knocks the hen clear off and catches her while she's flying. But a scrootch owl slips into the roost and scrootches up to the hen and talks softly to her. And the hen just falls in love with him, and the next thing you know, there ain't no hen.

AFTERWARDS

Thomas Hardy

When the Present has latched its postern behind my tremulous
    stay,
  And the May month flaps its glad green leaves like wings,
Delicate-filmed as new-spun silk, will the neighbors say,
  'He was a man who used to notice such things'?

If it be in the dusk when, like an eyelid's soundless blink,
    The dewfall-hawk comes crossing the shades to alight
Upon the wind-warped upland thorn, a gazer may think,
  'To him this must have been a familiar sight.'

If I pass during some nocturnal blackness, mothy and warm,
    When the hedgehog travels furtively over the lawn,
One may say, 'He strove that such innocent creatures should come to
    no harm,
  But he could do little for them; and now he is gone.'

If, when hearing that I have been stilled at last, they stand at the
      door,
  Watching the full-starred heavens that winter sees
Will this thought rise on those who will meet my face no more,
  'He was one who had an eye for such mysteries'?

And will any say when my bell of quittance is heard in the gloom,
  And a crossing breeze cuts a pause in its outrollings,
Till they rise again, as they were a new bell's boom,
    'He hears it not now, but used to notice such things'?

H. L. MENCKEN'S FAMOUS HOAX HISTORY
OF THE BATHTUB

(Titled "A Neglected Anniversary," and first printed in the *New York Evening Mail* on December 28, 1917, this hoax was widely accepted and reprinted as sober truth, and eventually found its way into medical literature and standard reference books. Although Mencken repeatedly and publicly stated it was a hoax without any truth whatsoever, it is still regarded in some places as accurate history.)

On December 20 there flitted past us, absolutely without public notice, one of the most important profane anniversaries in American history, to wit, the seventy-fifth anniversary of the introduction of the bathtub into These States. Not a plumber fired a salute or hung out a flag. Not a governor proclaimed a day of prayer. Not a newspaper called attention to the day.

True enough, it was not entirely forgotten. Eight or nine months ago one of the younger surgeons connected with the Public Health Service in Washington happened upon the facts while looking into the early history of public hygiene, and at his suggestion a committee was formed to celebrate the anniversary with a banquet. But before the plan was perfected Washington went dry [with introduction of war time prohibition], and so the banquet had to be abandoned. As it was, the day passed wholly unmarked, even in the capital of the *nation*.

Bathtubs are so common today that it is almost impossible to imagine a world without them. They are familiar to nearly everyone in all incorporated towns; in most of the large cities it is unlawful to build a dwelling house without putting them in; even on the farm they have begun to come into use. And yet the first American bathtub was installed and dedicated so recently as December 20, 1842, and for all I know to the contrary, it may be still in existence and in use.

Curiously enough, the scene of its setting was Cincinnati, then a squalid frontier town, and even today surely no leader in culture. But Cincinnati, in those days as in these, contained many enterprising merchants, and one of them was a man named Adam Thompson, a dealer in cotton and grain. Thompson shipped his grain by steamboat down the Ohio and Mississippi to New Orleans, and from there sent it to England in sailing vessels. This trade frequently took him to England, and in that country, during the 30's, he acquired the habit of bathing.

The bathtub was then still a novelty in England. It had been introduced in 1828 by Lord John Russell and its use was yet confined to a small class of enthusiasts. Moreover, the English bathtub, then as now, was a puny and inconvenient contrivance—little more, in fact, than a glorified dishpan—and filling it and emptying it required the attendance of a servant. Taking a bath, indeed, was a rather heavy ceremony, and Lord John in 1835 was said to be the only man in England who had yet come to doing it every day.

Thompson, who was of inventive fancy—he later devised the machine that is still used for bagging hams and bacon—conceived the notion that the English bathtub would be much improved if made large enough to admit the whole body of an adult man, and if its supply of water, instead of being hauled to the scene by a maid, were admitted by pipes from a central reservoir and run off by the same means. Accordingly, early in 1842 he set about building the first modern bathroom in his Cincinnati home—a large house with Doric pillars, standing near what is now the corner of Monastery and Orleans streets.

There was then, of course, no city water supply, at least in that part of the city, but Thompson had a large well in his garden, and he installed a pump to lift its water to the house. This pump, which was operated by six Negroes, much like an old time fire engine, was connected by a pipe with a cypress tank in the garret of the house, and here the water was stored until needed. From the tank two other pipes ran to the bathroom. One, carrying cold water, was a direct line. The other, designed to provide hot water, ran down a great chimney of the kitchen, and was coiled inside it like a giant spring.

The tub itself was of new design, and became the grandfather of all the bathtubs of today. Thompson had it made by James Cullness, the leading Cincinnati cabinetmaker of those days, and its material was Nicaragua mahogany. It was nearly seven feet long and fully four feet wide. To make it watertight, the interior was lined with sheet lead, carefully soldered at the joints. The whole contraption weighed about 1,750 pounds, and the floor of the room in which it was placed had to be reinforced to support it. The exterior was elaborately polished.

In this luxurious tub Thompson took two baths on December 20, 1842—a cold one at 8 A.M., and a warm one some time during the afternoon. The warm water, heated by the kitchen fire, reached a temperature of 105 degrees. On Christmas day, having a party of gentlemen to dinner, he exhibited the new marvel to them and gave an exhibition of its use, and four of them, including a French visitor, Col. Duchanel, risked plunges into it. The next day all Cincinnati— then a town of 100,000 people—had heard of it, and the local newspapers described it at length and opened their columns to violent discussions of it.

The thing, in fact, became a public matter, and before long there was a bitter and double-headed opposition to the new invention, which had been promptly imitated by several other wealthy Cincinnatians. On the one hand it was denounced as an epicurean and obnoxious toy from England, designed to corrupt the democratic simplicity of the Republic, and on the other hand it was attacked by the medical faculty as dangerous to health and a certain inviter of "phthistic, rheumatic fevers, inflammation of the lungs and the whole category of zymotic diseases." (I quote from the *Western Medical Repository* of April 23, 1843.)

The noise of the controversy soon reached other cities, and in more than one place medical opposition reached such strength that it was reflected in legislation. Late in 1843, for example, the Philadelphia Common Council considered an ordinance prohibiting bathing between November 1 and March 15, and it failed of passage by but two votes. During the same year the legislature of Virginia laid a tax of $30 a year on all bathtubs that might be set up, and in Hartford, Providence, Charleston and Wilmington (Del.) special and very heavy water rates were levied upon those who had them. Boston, early in 1845, made bathing unlawful except upon medical advice, but the ordinance was never enforced and in 1862 it was repealed.

This legislation, I suspect, had some class feeling in it, for the Thompson bathtub was plainly too expensive to be owned by any save the wealthy; indeed, the common price for installing one in New York in 1854 was $500. Thus the low caste politicians of the time made capital by fulminating against it, and there is even some suspicion of political bias in many of the early medical denunciations. But the invention of the common pine bathtub, lined with zinc, in 1847, cut off this line of attack, and thereafter the bathtub made steady progress.

The zinc tub was devised by John F. Simpson, a Brooklyn plumber, and his efforts to protect it by a patent occupied the courts until 1855. But the decisions were steadily against him, and after 1848 all the plumbers of New York were equipped for putting in bathtubs. According to a writer in the *Christian Register* for July 17, 1857, the first one in New York was opened for traffic on September 12, 1847, and by the beginning of 1850 there were already nearly 1,000 in use in the big town.

After this, medical opposition began to collapse, and among other eminent physicians Dr. Oliver Wendell Holmes declared for the bathtub, and vigorously opposed the lingering movement against it in Boston. The American Medical Association held its annual meeting in Boston in 1849, and a poll of the members in attendance showed that nearly 55 per cent of them now regarded bathing as harmless, and that more than 20 per cent advocated it as beneficial. At its meeting in 1850 a resolution was formally passed giving the imprimatur of the faculty to the bathtub. The homeopaths followed with a like resolution in 1853.

But it was the example of President Millard Fillmore that, even more than the grudging medical approval, gave the bathtub recognition and respectability in the United States. While he was still Vice-President, in March, 1850, he visited Cincinnati on a stumping tour, and inspected the original Thompson tub. Thompson himself was now dead, but his bathroom was preserved by the gentlemen who had bought his house from the estate. Fillmore was entertained in this house and, according to Chamberlain, his biographer, took a bath in the tub. Experiencing no ill effects, he became an ardent advocate of the new invention and on succeeding to the Presidency at Taylor's death, July 9, 1850, he instructed his secretary of war, Gen. Charles M. Conrad, to invite tenders for the construction of a bathtub in the White House.

This action, for a moment, revived the old controversy, and its opponents made much of the fact that there was no bathtub at Mount Vernon, or at Monticello, and that all the Presidents and other magnificoes of the past had got along without any such monarchical luxuries. The elder Bennett, in the New York *Herald*, charged that Fillmore really aspired to buy and install in the White House a porphyry and alabaster bath that had been used by Louis Philippe at Versailles. But Conrad, disregarding all this clamor, duly called for bids, and the contract was presently awarded to Harper and

Gillespie, a firm of Philadelphia engineers, who proposed to furnish a tub of thin cast iron capable of floating the largest man.

This was installed early in 1851, and remained in service in the White House until the first Cleveland administration, when the present enameled tub was substituted. The example of the President soon broke down all that remained of the old opposition, and by 1860, according to the newspaper advertisements of the time, every hotel in New York had a bathtub, and some had two and even three. In 1862 bathing was introduced into the Army by General Mc-Clellan, and in 1870 the first prison bathtub was set up at Moyamensing Prison, in Philadelphia.

So much for the history of the bathtub in America. One is astonished, on looking into it, to find that so little of it has been recorded. The literature, in fact, is almost nil. But perhaps this brief sketch will encourage other inquirers and so lay the foundation for an adequate celebration of the centennial in 1942.

LISTEN TO THE MOCKING-BIRD

Septimus Winner

I'm dreaming now of Hally, sweet Hally, sweet Hally,
I'm dreaming now of Hally,
For the thought of her is one that never dies;
She's sleeping in the valley, the valley, the valley,
She's sleeping in the valley,
And the mocking-bird is singing where she lies.

Refrain:
Listen to the mocking-bird,
Listen to the mocking-bird,
The mocking-bird still singing o'er her grave,
Listen to the mocking-bird,
Listen to the mocking-bird,
Still singing where the weeping willows wave.

Ah! well I yet remember, remember, remember,
Ah! well I yet remember
When we gathered in the cotton side by side;
'Twas in the mild September, September, September,
'Twas in the mild September,
And the mocking-bird was singing far and wide.

When the charms of spring awaken, awaken, awaken,
When the charms of spring awaken,
And the mocking-bird is singing on the bough,
I feel like one forsaken, forsaken, forsaken,
I feel like one forsaken,
Since my Hally is no longer with me now.

LIBERTY

John Milton

Give me the liberty to know, to utter and to argue freely according to conscience above all liberties. And though all the winds of doctrine were let loose to play upon the earth, so Truth be in the field, we do injuriously, by licensing and prohibiting, to misdoubt her strength. Let her and Falsehood grapple; who ever knew Truth put to the worse, in a free and open encounter?

PRAYER

Hartley Coleridge

Be not afraid to pray—to pray is right.
Pray, if thou canst, with hope; but ever pray,
Though hope be weak, or sick with long delay;
Pray in the darkness, if there be no light. . . .
Whate'er is good to wish, that ask of Heaven,
Though it be what thou canst not hope to see:
Pray to be perfect, though material leaven
Forbid the spirit so on earth to be:
But if for any wish thou darest not pray,
Then pray to God to cast that wish away.

JOY, SHIPMATE, JOY!

Walt Whitman

Joy, shipmate, joy!
  (Pleased to my soul at death I cry;)
  Our life is closed, our life begins;
The long, long, anchorage we leave,
The ship is clear at last, she leaps!
She swiftly courses from the shore;
Joy, shipmate, joy!

THE BURNING BABE

Robert Southwell

As I in hoary winter's night stood shivering in the snow,
Surprised I was with sudden heat which made my heart to glow;
And lifting up a fearful eye to view what fire was near,
A pretty Babe all burning bright did in the air appear;
Who, scorched with excessive heat, such floods of tears did shed,
As though his flood should quench his flames which with his tears
    were fed.
"Alas!" quoth he, "but newly born in fiery heats I fry,
Yet none approach to warm their hearts or feel my fire but I.
My faultless breast the furnace is, the fuel wounding thorns;
Love is the fire, and sighs the smoke, the ashes shame and scorns;
The fuel justice layeth on, and mercy blows the coals;
The metal in this furnace wrought are men's defiled souls:
For which, as now on fire I am to work them to their good,
So will I melt into a bath to wash them in my blood."
With this he vanished out of sight and swiftly shrunk away,
And straight I called unto mind that it was Christmas day.

THE MALTHUSIAN LAW

T. R. Malthus

I see no way by which man can escape from the weight of this law which pervades all animated nature. No fancied equality, no agrarian regulations, in their utmost extent, could remove the pressure of it even for a single century. And it appears, therefore, to be decisive against the possible existence of society. . . . Famine seems to be the last, the most dreadful resource of nature. The power of population is so superior to the power in the earth to produce subsistence for man, that premature death must in some shape or other visit the human race. The vices of mankind are active and able ministers of depopulation. They are the precursors in the great army of destruction; and often finish the dreadful work themselves. But should they fail in this war of extermination, sick seasons, epidemics, pestilence, and plague, advance in terrific array, and sweep off their thousands and ten thousands. Should success be still incomplete, gigantic, inevitable, famine stalks in the rear, and with one mighty blow levels the population with the food of the world.

(1798)

FRIENDSHIP IS LOVE WITHOUT HIS WINGS

Lord Byron

Why should my anxious breast repine,
　Because my youth is fled?
Days of delight may still be mine;
　Affection is not dead.
In tracing back the years of youth,
One firm record, one lasting truth
　Celestial consolation brings;
Bear it, ye breezes, to the seat
Where first my heart responsive beat,—
　"Friendship is Love without his wings!"

NOW IS THE DAY

Phillips Brooks

You who are letting miserable misunderstandings run from year to year, meaning to clear them up someday; you who are keeping wretched quarrels alive because you cannot quite make up your minds that now is the day to sacrifice your pride and kill them; you who are passing men sullenly upon the street, not speaking to them out of some silly spite, and yet knowing that it would fill you with shame and remorse if you heard that one of them were dead to-morrow morning; you who are letting your neighbor starve, till you hear that he is dying of starvation; or letting your friend's heart ache for a word of appreciation or sympathy, which you mean to give him someday; if you could only know and see and feel, all of a sudden, that "the time is short," how it would break the spell! How you would go instantly and do the thing which you might never have another chance to do!

A MOTTO FREQUENTLY FOUND ON
OLD CHURCH BELLS

Death tales I tell, The wind dispell, Ill feelings quell,
The slothful shake, the storm clouds break, the Sabbath wake.

THE FALCONER OF GOD

William Rose Benét

I flung my soul to the air like a falcon flying.
I said: "Wait on, wait on, while I ride below!
   I shall start a heron soon
   In the marsh beneath the moon—
A strange white heron rising with silver on its wings,
     Rising and crying
   Wordless, wondrous things;
  The secret of the altars, of the world's heart-strings,
   The answer to their woe.
Then stoop thou upon him, and grip and hold him so!"

My wild soul waited on as falcons hover.
I beat the reedy fens as I trampled past
   I heard the mournful loon
   In the marsh beneath the moon.
And then, with feathery thunder, the bird of my desire
      Broke from the cover
    Flashing silver fire.
  High up among the stars I saw his pinions spire.
     The pale clouds gazed aghast
As my falcon stooped upon him, and gripped and held him fast.

My soul dropped through the air—with heavenly plunder?—
Gripping the dazzling bird my dreaming knew?
   Nay! but a piteous freight,
   A dark and heavy weight
Despoiled of silver plumage, its voice forever stilled—
     All of the wonder
    Gone that ever filled
  Its guise with glory. O bird that I have killed,
     How brilliantly you flew
Across my rapturous vision when first I dreamed of you—

Yet I fling my soul on high with new endeavor,
And I ride the world below with a joyful mind.
   I shall start a heron soon
   In the marsh beneath the moon—
A wondrous silver heron its inner darkness fledges!
     I beat forever
    The fens and the sedges.
  The pledge is still the same—for all disastrous pledges,
     All hopes resigned!
My soul still flies above me for the quarry it shall find!

WISDOM FROM WILLIAM PENN

They that love beyond the world cannot be separated by it.
Death cannot kill what never dies.
Nor can spirits ever be divided, that love and live in the same
principle: the root and record of their friendship.
If absence be not death, neither is theirs.

Death is but crossing the world, as friends do the seas; they live in one another still.

For they must needs be present, that love and live in that which is omnipresent.

In this divine glass they see face to face; and their converse is free.

This is the comfort of friends, that though they may be said to die, yet their friendship and society are, in the best sense, ever present, because immortal.

THE TABLE AND THE CHAIR

Edward Lear

Said the Table to the Chair,
"You can hardly be aware
How I suffer from the heat
And from chilblains on my feet.

"If we took a little walk,
We might have a little talk;
Pray let us take the air,"
Said the Table to the Chair.

Said the Chair unto the Table,
"Now you *know* we are not able:
How foolishly you talk,
When you know we *cannot* walk!"

Said the Table with a sigh,
"It can do no harm to try.
I've as many legs as you:
Why can't we walk on two?"

So they both went slowly down,
And walked about the town
With a cheerful bumpy sound
And they toddled round and round;

And everybody cried,
As they hastened to their side,
"See! the Table and the Chair
Have come out to take the air!"

But in going down an alley
To a castle in the valley
They completely lost their way,
And wandered all the day;

Till to see them safely back,
They paid a Ducky-quack,
And a beetle, and a Mouse,
Who took them to their house.

Then they whispered to each other,
"O delightful little brother,
What a lovely walk we've taken!
Let us dine on beans and bacon!"

So the Ducky and the leetle
Browny-Mousy and the Beetle
Dined and danced upon their heads
Till they toddled to their beds.

LESSON OF THE BUMBLEBEE

Anonymous

According to the theory of aerodynamics and as may be readily demonstrated through wind tunnel experiments, the bumblebee is unable to fly. This is because the weight, size and shape of his body in relation to the total wingspread makes flying impossible.

BUT THE BUMBLEBEE, BEING IGNORANT OF THESE SCIENTIFIC TRUTHS, GOES AHEAD AND FLIES ANYWAY —AND MAKES A LITTLE HONEY EVERY DAY.

To recommend thrift to the poor is both grotesque and insulting. It is advising a man who is starving to eat less.
—Oscar Wilde

CODE OF CONDUCT FOR MEMBERS OF
U.S. ARMED FORCES

Promulgated by President Eisenhower, August, 1955

1. I am an American fighting man, I serve in the forces which guard my country and our way of life. I am prepared to give my life in their defense.

2. I will never surrender of my own free will. If in command I will never surrender my men while they still have the means to resist.

3. If I am captured I will continue to resist by all means available. I will make every effort to escape and aid others to escape. I will accept neither parole nor special favors from the enemy.

4. If I become a prisoner of war, I will keep faith with my fellow prisoners. I will give no information or take part in any action which might be harmful to my comrades. If I am senior, I will take command. If not I will obey the lawful orders of those appointed over me and will back them up in every way.

5. When questioned, should I become a prisoner of war, I am bound to give only name, rank, service number, and date of birth. I will evade answering further questions to the utmost of my ability. I will make no oral or written statements disloyal to my country and its allies or harmful to their cause.

6. I will never forget that I am an American fighting man, responsible for my actions, and dedicated to the principles which made my country free. I will trust in my God and in the United States of America.

(The above is not to be confused with the Uniform Code of Military Justice, violation of which could lead to court-martial proceedings.)

A HYMN—O GOD OF EARTH AND ALTAR

G. K. Chesterton

O God of earth and altar,
  Bow down and hear our cry,
Our earthly rulers falter,
  Our people drift and die;

The walls of gold entomb us.
  The swords of scorn divide,
Take not thy thunder from us,
  But take away our pride.

From all that terror teaches,
  From lies of tongue and pen,
From all the easy speeches
  That comfort cruel men,
For sale and profanation
  Of honour and the sword,
From sleep and from damnation,
  Deliver us, good Lord!

Tie in a living tether
  The prince and priest and thrall,
Bind all our lives together,
  Smite us and save us all;
In ire and exultation
  Aflame with faith, and free,
Lift up a living nation,
  A single sword to thee.

THE GIFT OF A LOVELY THOUGHT

Anonymous

If instead of a jewel, or even a flower, we could cast the gift of a lovely thought into the heart of another, that would be giving as the angels must give.

SWEETEST LOVE, I DO NOT GO

John Donne

Sweetest love, I do not go
  For weariness of thee,
Nor in hope the world can show
  A fitter Love for me;

But since that I
At the last must part, 'tis best,
Thus to use myself in jest
   By feigned deaths to die.

Yesternight the sun went hence
   And yet is here today;
He hath no desire nor sense,
   Nor half so short a way;
      Then fear not me,
But believe that I shall make
Speedier journeys, since I take
   More wings and spurs than he.

Oh, how feeble is man's power,
   That, if good fortune fall,
Cannot add another hour,
   Nor a lost hour recall!
      But come bad chance,
And we join it to our strength,
And we teach it art and length,
   Itself o'er us to advance.

When thou sigh'st, thou sigh'st not wind,
   But sigh'st my soul away;
When thou weep'st, unkindly kind,
   My life's blood doth decay.
      It cannot be
That thou lov'st me as thou say'st,
If in thine my life thou waste,
   That art the best of me.

Let not thy divining heart
   Forethink me any ill;
Destiny may take thy part,
   And may thy fears fulfill.
      But think that we
Are but turned aside to sleep;
They who one another keep
   Alive, ne'er parted be.

SCREWTAPE, AN EXECUTIVE DEVIL IN HELL, ADVISES WORMWOOD, ONE OF HIS TEMPTERS ON EARTH

C. S. Lewis

My dear Wormwood,

I note what you say about guiding your patient's reading and taking care that he sees a good deal of his materialist friend. But are you not being a trifle *naïf*? It sounds as if you supposed that *argument* was the way to keep him out of the Enemy's clutches. That might have been so if he had lived a few centuries earlier. At that time the humans still knew pretty well when a thing was proved and when it was not; and if it was proved they really believed it. They still connected thinking with doing and were prepared to alter their way of life as the result of a chain of reasoning. But what with the weekly press and other such weapons, we have largely altered that. Your man has been accustomed, ever since he was a boy, to having a dozen incompatible philosophies dancing about together inside his head. He doesn't think of doctrines as primarily "true" or "false," but as "academic" or "practical," "outworn" or "contemporary," "conventional" or "ruthless." Jargon, not argument, is your best ally in keeping him from the Church. Don't waste time trying to make him think materialism is *true*! Make him think it is strong or stark or courageous—that it is the philosophy of the future. That's the sort of thing he cares about. . . .

By the very act of arguing you awake the patient's reason; and once it is awake, who can forsee the result? Even if a particular train of thought can be twisted so as to end in our favor, you will find that you have been strengthening in your patient the fatal habit of attending to universal issues and withdrawing his attention from the stream of immediate sense experience. Your business is to fix his attention on the stream. Teach him to call it "real life" and don't let him ask what he means by "real."

Lawyers are the only persons in whom ignorance of the law is not punished.

—Jeremy Bentham

WISE WASTING OF DAYS

Thomas Dekker

To awaken each morning with a smile brightening my face, to greet the day with reverence, for the opportunities it contains; to approach my work with a clean mind; to hold ever before me, even in the doing of little things, the Ultimate Purpose toward which I am working; to meet men and women with laughter on my lips and love in my heart, to be gentle, kind and courteous through all the hours; to approach the night with weariness that ever woos sleep and the joy that comes from work well done—this is how I desire to waste wisely my days.

INSCRIPTION ON THE CROSS

Holy Bible, John 19:19–22

And Pilate wrote a title, and put it on the cross. And the writing was JESUS OF NAZARETH THE KING OF THE JEWS.

This title then read many of the Jews; for the place where Jesus was crucified was nigh to the city: and it was written in Hebrew, and Greek, and Latin.

Then said the chief priests of the Jews to Pilate, Write not, The King of the Jews; but that he said, I am the King of the Jews.

Pilate answered, What I have written I have written.

GRATITUDE

Charles Kingsley

Thank God every morning when you get up that you have something to do which must be done, whether you like it or not. Being forced to work, and forced to do your best, will breed in you temperance and self-control, diligence and strength of will, cheerfulness and content, and a hundred virtues which the idle never know.

WHERE THE BEE SUCKS, THERE SUCK I

William Shakespeare

Where the bee sucks, there suck I:
In a cowslip's bell I lie;
There I couch when owls do cry.
On the bat's back I do fly
After summer merrily.
Merrily, merrily shall I live now
Under the blossom that hangs on the bough.
(From *The Tempest*)

THE LAST TEMPTATION

T. S. Eliot

Now is my way clear, now is the meaning plain:
Temptation shall not come in this kind again.
The last temptation is the greatest treason:
To do the right deed for the wrong reason.
(From *Murder in the Cathedral*)

TOLERANCE

Jeremy Taylor

When Abraham sat at his tent door, according to his custom, waiting to entertain strangers, he espied an old man, stooping and leaning on his staff, weary with age and travail, coming towards him, who was a hundred years of age; he received him kindly, washed his feet, provided supper, caused him to sit down; but, observing that the old man ate and prayed not, nor begged a blessing on his meat, he asked him why he did not worship the God of heaven. The old man told him that he worshipped the fire only, and acknowledged no other God. At which answer Abraham grew so zealously angry, that he threw the old man out of his tent, and exposed him to all the evils

(375)

of the night and an unguarded condition. When the old man was gone, God called Abraham, and asked him where the stranger was. "I thrust him away, because he did not worship thee." God answered him, "I have suffered him these hundred years, though he dishonored me; and wouldst thou not endure him one night, when he gave thee no trouble?"

RENOUNCEMENT

Alice Meynell

I must not think of thee; and, tired yet strong,
I shun the thought that lurks in all delight—
The thought of thee—and in the blue Heaven's height,
And in the dearest passage of a song.
Oh, just beyond the fairest thoughts that throng
This breast, the thought of thee waits, hidden yet bright;
But it must never, never come in sight;
I must stop short of thee the whole day long.
But when sleep comes to close each difficult day,
When night gives pause to the long watch I keep,
And all my bonds I needs must loose apart,
Must doff my will as raiment laid away,—
With the first dream that comes with the first sleep
I run, I run, I am gathered to thy heart.

ABRAHAM LINCOLN ANNOUNCES HIS FIRST TRY FOR PUBLIC OFFICE

I have no wealth or popular relations to recommend me. My case is thrown exclusively upon the independent voters of this county, and if elected they will have conferred a favor upon me, for which I shall be unremitting in my labors to compensate. But if the good people in their wisdom shall see fit to keep me in the background, I have been too familiar with disappointments to be very much chagrined.

(Announcing his candidacy for the Illinois legislature in the columns of the Illinois *Sangamo Journal*, March 9, 1832)

AS BROTHERS LIVE TOGETHER

Henry Wadsworth Longfellow

Down the rivers, o'er the prairies,
Came the warriors of the nations,
Came the Delawares and Mohawks,
Came the Choctaws and Camanches,
Came the Shoshonies and Blackfeet,
Came the Pawnees and Omahas,
Came the Mandans and Dacotahs,
Came the Hurons and Ojibways,
All the warriors drawn together
By the signal of the Peace-Pipe,
To the Mountains of the Prairie,
To the great Red Pipe-stone Quarry
   And they stood there on the meadow,
With their weapons and their war-gear,
Painted like the leaves of Autumn,
Painted like the sky of morning,
Wildly glaring at each other;
In their faces stern defiance,
In their hearts the feuds of ages,
The hereditary hatred,
The ancestral thirst of vengeance.
   Gitche Manito, the mighty,
The creator of the nations,
Looked upon them with compassion,
With paternal love and pity;
Looked upon their wrath and wrangling
But as quarrels among children,
   Over them he stretched his right hand
To subdue their stubborn natures,
To allay their thirst and fever,
By the shadow of his right hand;
Spake to them with voice majestic
As the sound of far-off waters,
Falling into deep abysses,
Warning, chiding, spake in this wise:—
   "O my children! my poor children!
Listen to the words of wisdom,
Listen to the words of warning,

From the lips of the Great Spirit,
From the Master of Life, who made you!
  "I have given you lands to hunt in,
I have given you streams to fish in,
I have given you bear and bison,
I have given you roe and reindeer,
I have given you brant and beaver,
Filled the marshes full of wild-fowl,
Filled the river full of fishes;
Why then are you not contented?
Why then will you hunt each other?
  "I am weary of your quarrels,
Weary of your wars and bloodshed,
Weary of your prayers for vengeance,
Of your wranglings and dissensions;
All your strength is in your union,
All your danger is in discord;
Therefore be at peace henceforward
And as brothers live together.
  "I will send a prophet to you,
A Deliverer of the nations,
Who shall guide you and shall teach you,
Who shall toil and suffer with you.
If you listen to his counsels,
You will multiply and prosper;
If his warnings pass unheeded,
You will fade away and perish!
  "Bathe now in the stream before you,
Wash the war-paint from your faces,
Wash the blood-stains from your fingers,
Bury your war-clubs and your weapons,
Break the red stone from this quarry,
Mould and make it into Peace-Pipes,
Take the reeds that grow beside you,
Deck them with your brightest feathers,
Smoke the calumet together,
And as brothers live henceforward!"
  Then upon the ground the warriors
Threw their cloaks and shirts of deer-skin,
Threw their weapons and their war-gear,
Leaped into the rushing river,
Washed the war-paint from their faces.
Clear above them flowed the water,

Clear and limpid from the footprints
Of the Master of Life descending;
Dark below them flowed the water,
Soiled and stained with streaks of crimson,
As if blood were mingled with it!
   From the river came the warriors,
Clean and washed from all their war-paint;
On the banks their clubs they buried,
Buried all their warlike weapons,
Gitche Manito, the mighty,
The Great Spirit, the Creator,
Smiled upon his helpless children!
   And in silence all the warriors
Broke the red stone of the quarry,
Smoothed and formed it into Peace-Pipes,
Broke the long reeds by the river,
Decked them with their brightest feathers,
And departed each one homeward,
While the Master of Life, ascending,
Through the opening of cloud-curtains,
Through the doorways of the heaven,
Vanished from before their faces,
In the smoke that rolled about him,
The Pulwana of the Peace-Pipe!
                    (From *The Song of Hiawatha*)

HOPE

Oliver Goldsmith

Hope, like a gleaming taper's light,
   Adorns and cheers our way;
And still, as darker grows the night,
   Emits a brighter ray.

THE BLUE-TAIL FLY

Anonymous

When I was young I used to wait
On my master and hand him his plate,
And pass the bottle when he got dry,
And brush away the blue-tail fly.

Chorus: Jimmy crack corn and I don't care,
Jimmy crack corn and I don't care,
Jimmy crack corn and I don't care,
My master's gone away!

And when he'd ride in the afternoon,
I'd follow after with a hickory broom;
The pony being like to shy
When bitten by a blue-tail fly.

One day he ride around the farm,
The flies so numerous, they did swarm.
One chanced to bite him on the thigh;
The devil take the blue-tail fly!

The pony run, he jump, he pitch;
He threw my master in the ditch.
He died—and the jury wondered why—
The verdict was the blue-tail fly.

They laid him under a 'simmon tree:
His epitaph is there to see:
"Beneath this stone I'm forced to lie,
A victim of the blue-tail fly."

Opinion is a species of property that I am always desirous
of sharing with my friends.

—Charles Lamb

THE GOLD RUSH

Mark Twain

Look history over and you will see. The missionary comes after the whiskey—I mean, he arrives after the whiskey has arrived. Next comes the poor immigrant with ax and hoe and rifle; next, the trader, next the miscellaneous rush; next the gambler, the desperado, the highwayman, and all their kindred in sin of both sexes; and next the smart chap who has bought up an old grant that covers all the land; this brings in the lawyer tribe; the vigilance committe brings the undertaker. All these interests bring the newspaper; the newspaper starts up politics and a railroad; all hands turn to and build a church and a jail—and behold, civilization is established forever in the land.

LIPS THAT TOUCH LIQUOR

George W. Young

You are coming to woo me, but not as of yore,
When I hastened to welcome your ring at the door;
For I trusted that he who stood waiting me then,
Was the brightest, the truest, the noblest of men,
Your lips, on my own, when they printed "Farewell,"
Had never been soiled by the "beverage of hell";
But they come to me now with the bacchanal sign,
And the lips that touch liquor must never touch mine.

Conclusion of THE COMMUNIST MANIFESTO

Karl Marx and Friedrich Engels

The Communists disdain to conceal their views and aims. They openly declare that their ends can be attained only by the forcible overthrow of all existing social conditions. Let the ruling classes tremble at a communistic revolution. The proletarians have nothing to lose but their chains. They have a world to win.

Workingmen of the world, unite!

(1848)

THE MIRACLE

Sir Thomas Browne

Now for my life, it is a miracle—which to relate were not a History, but a piece of Poetry, and would sound to common ears like a Fable; for the World, I count it not an Inn, but an Hospital; and a place not to live, but to die in. The world that I regard is myself; it is the Microcosm of my own frame that I cast mine eye on; for the other, I use it but like my Globe, and turn it round sometimes for my recreation. Men that look upon my outside, perusing only my condition and Fortunes, do err in my Altitude; for I am above Atlas his shoulders. The earth is a point, not only in respect of the Heavens above us, but that of the Heavenly, and celestial part within us; that mass of flesh that circumscribes me, limits not my mind; that surface that tells the Heavens it hath an end, cannot persuade me that I have any; I take my circle to be above three hundred and sixty; though the number of the Arc do measure my body, it comprehendeth not my mind; while I study to find how I am a Microcosm or little world, I find myself something more than great. There is surely a piece of Divinity in us; something that was before the Elements, and owes no homage unto the Sun.

BILL NYE'S OBSERVATIONS ON SPACE

Space is very large. It is immense, very immense. A great deal of immensity exists in space. Space has no top, no bottom. In fact, it is bottomless both at the bottom and at the top. Space extends as far backwards as it does forward, and *vice versa*. There is no compass of space, nor points of the compass, and no boxing of the compass. A billion million of miles traveled in space won't bring a man any nearer than one mile or one inch. Consequently, in space, it's better to stay where you are, and let well enough alone.

OLD ENGLISH PRAYER

Anonymous

Take time to work—
   It is the price of success.
Take time to think—
   It is the source of power.
Take time to play—
   It is the secret of perpetual youth.
Take time to read—
   It is the fountain of wisdom.
Take time to be friendly—
   It is the road to happiness.
Take time to dream—
   It is hitching your wagon to a star.
Take time to love and to be loved—
   It is the privilege of the gods.
Take time to look around—
   It is too short a day to be selfish.
Take time to laugh—
   It is the music of the soul.

I ADMIRE THE HUMAN RACE

Roger William Riis

I admire the human race. I do, indeed. Everybody is busy running us down, these days, for the mess they say we have made here and there and everywhere. Pshaw! That's short-range stuff, a worm's eye view of our world. Over the marching and abundant centuries, we haven't made any mess. Far from it!

We have done and are doing a better job than anyone has any right to expect. We're all right!

From the beginning, we found ourselves alone in a vast universe, and not only alone but the only living thing on this planet which could realize its loneness. We realized it, gave it a good close look, and then turned our attention to making something practical and useful out of an unprecedented situation.

First of all, we found for ourselves a Light, a God, and we got a

(383)

sense of direction, a goal to work toward. This was pretty clever of us, if you think of it carefully.

We proceeded to set up standards for our living together. Early in our experience we made the revolutionary discovery that gentleness and kindliness were more practical than brute strength. No other species has ever found that out and used it as a model and practical code of conduct.

We have in actual fact no one we need answer to, beyond ourselves, and yet we observe our ideal standards in remarkable degree. We are honest and trustworthy one with another so that it is the exception, it is news, when we commit a theft. We are decent 99 per cent of the time, when we could easily be vile.

With silence and mystery behind us and ahead of us, we make up gay little songs and whistle them, and our feet keep jig time to them. We look life and fate in the eye, and smile. I like that, and I admire the people who do it.

Alone among all living things, we have discovered Beauty, and we cherish it, and create it for eye and ear. Alone among living things, we have the power to look at our environment and criticize it and improve it.

Finding it necessary to live together by the millions, we created for ourselves governing systems covering vast geographical spaces. Now we actually have the thrilling and terrific idea of a world government, a global government to bring justice to white and black, to Eskimo and Afrikander, rich and poor, not because any tribe is powerful and can exact justice, but because we have conceived and created the ideal of justice and plan it for all men. This is great. This is not the act of a little animal, or a mean animal. This is possible only to a great animal. We think in global terms. We inhabit a star, and we know it.

Finding that we have to work to stay alive, we work with ability beyond imagining. Out of the earth we take food, and improve that food year by year; we take heat, and light, so that darkness which lay upon the face of the earth is dispelled by man-made light. We enjoy all the myriad products of our unparalleled ingenuity.

Every morning the necessity for the day's work faces us. And we go and do a day's work, with an overall average effectiveness and perseverance that is amazing, considering many of the jobs.

Of a persistence, a daring and ingenuity impossible to surpass, we find ways to move easily under the water and through the air. Now we speculatively eye our neighboring planets. It should astound no one if man one day begins to move among these planets. How shall I not admire such a creature? Daunted by nothing, his horizons constantly recede, the territories of his possession and use expand and expand.

Whenever he comes to an impassable obstacle, an apparently final barrier, he goes to work at it and, in due time, surpasses it. If he has limits, I do not see where they are. I do not think he has limits. I think he is a child of the universe who inherits eternity. I think he is wonderful, I am his devoted partisan, and I am proud indeed to be one of him.

THE GARDEN YEAR

Sara Coleridge

January brings the snow,
Makes our feet and fingers glow.

February brings the rain,
Thaws the frozen lake again.

March brings breezes, loud and shrill,
To stir the dancing daffodil.

April brings the primrose sweet,
Scatters daisies at our feet.

May brings flocks of pretty lambs,
Skipping by their fleecy dams.

June brings tulips, lilies, roses,
Fills the children's hands with posies.

Hot July brings cooling showers,
Apricots, and gillyflowers.

August brings the sheaves of corn,
Then the harvest home is borne.

Warm September brings the fruit;
Sportsmen then begin to shoot.

Fresh October brings the pheasant;
Then to gather nuts is pleasant.

Dull November brings the blast;
Then the leaves are whirling fast.

Chill December brings the sleet,
Blazing fire, and Christmas treat.

DOWN IN THE VALLEY

Anonymous

Down in the valley, the valley so low,
Hang your head over, hear the wind blow.

Hear the wind blow, dear, hear the wind blow,
Hang your head over, hear the wind blow.

If you don't love me, love whom you please;
Throw your arms 'round me, give my heart ease.

Write me a letter, send it by mail,
Send it in care of Birmingham jail.

Throw your arms 'round me, before it's too late;
Throw yours 'round me, feel my heart break.

Writing this letter, containing three lines,
Answer my question: "Will you be mine?"

"Will you be mine, dear, Will you be mine?"
Answer my question: "Will you be mine?"

Go build me a castle forty feet high;
So I can see him, as he goes by.

As he goes by, dear; as he goes by;
So I can see him, as he goes by.

Roses love sunshine, violets love dew,
Angels in heaven know I love you.

JESUS' PARABLE OF THE SOWER

Holy Bible, Luke 8:5–15

A sower went out to sow his seed: and as he sowed, some fell by the wayside; and it was trodden down, and the fowls of the air devoured it.

And some fell upon a rock; and as soon as it was sprung up, it withered away, because it lacked moisture.

And some fell among thorns; and the thorns sprang up with it, and choked it.

And other fell on good ground, and sprang up, and bare fruit an hundredfold. And when he said these things, he cried, He that hath ears to hear, let him hear.

And his disciples asked him, saying, What might this parable be?

And he said, Unto you it is given to know the mysteries of the kingdom of God: but to others in parables; that seeing they might not see, and hearing they might not understand.

Now the parable is this: The seed is the word of God.

Those by the way side are they that hear; them cometh the devil, and taketh away the word out of their hearts, lest they should believe and be saved.

They on the rock are they, which, when they hear, receive the word with joy; and these have no root, which for a while believe, and in time of temptation fall away.

And that which fell among thorns are they, which, when they have heard, go forth, and are choked with cares and riches and pleasures of this life, and bring no fruit to perfection.

But that on the good ground are they, which, in an honest and good heart, having heard the word, keep it, and bring forth fruit with patience.

CIVIL LIBERTY

Edmund Burke

Men are qualified for civil liberty in exact proportion to their disposition to put moral chains upon their own appetites. . . . Society cannot exist unless a controlling power upon will and appetite be placed somewhere, and the less of it there is within, the more there must be without. It is ordained in the eternal constitution of things that men of intemperate minds cannot be free. Their passions forge their fetters.

ACCORDING TO JOSH BILLINGS:

The quickest way to take the starch out of a man who is always blaming himself, is to agree with him. This ain't what he is looking for.

Q. How fast does sound travel?

A. This depends a good deal upon the nature of the noise you are talking about. The sound of a dinner horn, for instance, travels a half mile in a second, while an invitation to get up in the morning I have known to be three quarters of an hour going up two pairs of stairs, and then not have strength enough left to be heard.

I am a poor man, but I have this consolation: I am poor by accident, not design.

It is a wise man who profits by his own experience—but it is a good deal wiser one, who lets the rattlesnake bite the other fellow.

Take all the fools out of this world, and there wouldn't be any fun, nor profit, living in it.

Lasting reputations are of a slow growth; the man who wakes up famous some morning, is very apt to go to bed some night and sleep it all off.

Never take the bull by the horns, young man, but take him by the tail, then you can let go when you want to.

PETRUCHIO IS UNDAUNTED BY KATHARINA

William Shakespeare

Gremio: But will you woo this wild-cat? . . .
Petruchio: Why came I hither but to that intent?
Think you a little din can daunt mine ears?
Have I not in my time heard lions roar?
Have I not heard the sea puff'd up with winds
Rage like an angry boar chafed with sweat?
Have I not heard great ordnance in the field,

And heaven's artillery thunder in the skies?
Have I not in a pitched battle heard
Loud 'larums, neighing steeds, and trumpets clang?
And do tell me of a woman's tongue,
That gives not half so great a blow to hear
As will a chestnut in a farmer's fire?
Tush, tush! fear boys with bugs.

(From The Taming of the Shrew)

CALLICLES' EXHORTATION

Plato

(TRANSLATOR: Benjamin Jowett)

Now I, Callicles, am persuaded of the truth of these things, and I consider how I shall present my soul whole and undefiled before the judge in that day. Renouncing the honors at which the world aims, I desire only to know the truth, and to live as well as I can, and, when I die, to die as well as I can. And to the utmost of my power, I exhort all other men to do the same. And, in return for your exhortation of me, I exhort you also to take part in the great combat, which is the combat of life, and greater than every other earthly conflict.

(From Gorgias)

OBSERVE THE WHOLE OF IT

Thomas Wolfe

There where the hackles of the Rocky Mountains
Blaze in the blank and naked radiance of the moon,
Go—
Make your resting-stool upon the highest peak.
Can you not see us now?

The continental wall juts sheer and flat,
Its huge black shadow on the plain,
And the plain sweeps out against the East,

(389)

Two thousand miles away.
The great snake that you see there
Is the Mississippi River.

Behold
The gem-strung towns and cities
Of the good, green East,
Flung like star-dust through the field of night.
That spreading constellation to the north
Is called Chicago,
And that giant wink that blazes in the moon
Is the pendant lake that it is built upon.
Beyond, close-set and dense as a clenched fist,
Are all the jeweled cities of the eastern seaboard.
There's Boston,
Ringed with the bracelet of its shining little towns,
And all the lights that sparkle
On the rocky indentations of New England.

Here, southward and a little to the west,
And yet still coasted to the sea,
Is our intensest ray,
The splintered firmament of the towered island
Of Manhattan.
Round about her, sown thick as grain,
Is the glitter of a hundred towns and cities.

The long chain of lights there
Is the necklace of Long Island and the Jersey shore.
Southward and inland, by a foot or two,
Behold the duller glare of Philadelphia.
Southward further still,
The twin constellations—Baltimore and Washington.
Westward, but still within the borders
Of the good, green East,

That night-time glow and smolder of hell-fire
Is Pittsburgh.
Here, St. Louis, hot and humid
In the cornfield belly of the land,
And bedded on the mid-length coil and fringes
Of the snake.
There at the snake's mouth,

Southward six hundred miles or so,
You see the jeweled crescent of old New Orleans.
Here, west and south again,
You see the gemmy glitter
Of the cities on the Texas border.

Turn now, seeker,
On your resting-stool atop the Rocky Mountains,
And look another thousand miles or so
Across moon-blazing fiend-worlds of the Painted Desert
And beyond Sierra's ridge.
That magic congeries of lights
There to the west,
Ringed like a studded belt
Around the magic setting of its lovely harbor,
Is the fabled town of San Francisco.
Below it, Los Angeles
And all the cities of the California shore.
A thousand miles to north and west,
The sparkling towns of Oregon and Washington.

Observe the whole of it,
Survey it as you might survey a field.
Make it your garden, seeker,
Or your backyard patch.
Be at ease in it.
It's your oyster—yours to open if you will.

O THOU WHO ART OUR AUTHOR AND OUR END

Sir John Beaumont

O Thou Who art our Author and our End,
On Whose large mercy chains of hope depend;
Lift me to Thee by Thy propitious hand:
For lower I can find no place to stand.

HELEN OF KIRCONNELL

Anonymous

I wish I were where Helen lies,
Night and day to me she cries;
O that I were where Helen lies,
  On fair Kirconnell lea!

Curst be the heart that thought the thought,
And curst the hand that fired the shot,
When in my arms burd Helen dropt,
  And died to succour me!

O think na ye my heart was sair,
When my Love dropp'd and spak nae mair!
There did she swoon wi' meile care,
  On fair Kirconnell lea.

As I went down the water side,
None but my foe to be my guide,
None but my foe to be my guide,
  On fair Kirconnell lea;

I lighted down my sword to draw,
I hacked him in pieces sma',
I hacked him in pieces sma',
  For her sake that died for me.

O Helen fair, beyond compare!
I'll mak a garland o' thy hair,
Shall bind my heart for evermair,
  Until the day I die!

O that I were where Helen lies!
Night and day on me she cries;
Out of my bed she bids me rise,
  Says, "Haste, and come to me!"

O Helen fair! O Helen chaste!
If I were with thee, I'd be blest,
Where thou lies low and taks thy rest,
  On fair Kirconnell lea.

I wish my grave were growing green,
A winding-sheet drawn o'er me e'en,
And I in Helen's arms lying,
    On fair Kirconnell lea.

I wish I were where Helen lies!
Night and day on me she cries;
And I am weary of the skies,
    For her sake that died for me.

CHOOSE LIFE

Holy Bible, Deuteronomy 30:15–19

See, I have set before thee this day life and good, and death and evil:
In that I command thee this day to love the Lord thy God, to walk
in his ways, and to keep his commandments and his statutes and his
judgments, that thou mayest live and multiply: and the Lord thy
God shall bless thee in the land whither thou goest to possess it.

But if thine heart turn away, so that thou wilt not hear, but shalt
be drawn away, and worship other gods, and serve them:

I denounce unto you this day, that ye shall surely perish, and that
ye shall not prolong your days upon the land, whither thou passest
over Jordan to go to possess it.

I call heaven and earth to record this day against you, that I have
set before you life and death, blessing and cursing: therefore choose
life, that both thou and thy seed may live.

PLUTARCH RELATES HOW ANTONY FELL UNDER THE SPELL OF CLEOPATRA

(TRANSLATOR: John Dryden)

The last and crowning mischief that could befall him [Antony]
came in the love of Cleopatra, to awaken and kindle to fury passions
that as yet lay still and dormant in his nature, and to stifle and finally
corrupt any elements that yet made resistance in him of goodness and
a sound judgment. He fell into the snare thus. When making preparation for the Parthian war, he sent to command her to make her

(393)

personal appearance in Cilicia, to answer an accusation, that she had given great assistance, in the late wars, to Cassius. Dellius, who was sent on this message, had no sooner seen her face, and remarked her adroitness and subtlety in speech, but he felt convinced that Antony would not so much as think of giving any molestation to a woman like this; on the contrary, she would be the first in favor with him. So he set himself at once to pay his court to the Egyptian, and gave her his advice, "to go," in the Homeric style, to Cilicia, "in her best attire," and bade her fear nothing from Antony, the gentlest and kindest of soldiers. She had some faith in the words of Dellius, but far more in her own attractions; which, having formerly recommended her to Caesar and the young Cnaeus Pompey, she did not doubt might prove yet more successful with Antony. Their acquaintance was with her when a girl, young and ignorant of the world, but she was to meet Antony in the time of life when women's beauty is most splendid, and their intellects are in full maturity. She made great preparations for her journey, of money, gifts, and ornaments of value, such as so wealthy a kingdom might afford, but she brought with her, her surest hopes in her own magic arts and charms.

She received several letters, both from Antony and from his friends, to summon her, but she took no account of these orders; and at last, as if in mockery of them, she came sailing up the river Cydnus, in a barge with gilded stern and outspread sails of purple, while oars of silver beat time to the music of flutes and fifes and harps. She herself lay all alone under a canopy of cloth of gold, dressed as Venus in a picture, and beautiful young boys, like painted Cupids, stood on each side to fan her. Her maids were dressed like sea nymphs and graces, some steering at the rudder, some working at the ropes. The perfumes diffused themselves from the vessel to the shore, which was covered with multitudes, part following the galley up the river on either bank, part running out of the city to see the sight. The market-place was quite emptied, and Antony was at last left alone, sitting upon the tribunal; while the word went through all the multitude that Venus was come to feast with Bacchus, for the common good of Asia. On her arrival, Antony sent to invite her to supper. She thought it fitter he should come to her; so, willing to show his good-humor and courtesy, he complied, and went. He found the preparations to receive him magnificent beyond expression, but nothing so admirable as the great number of lights; for on a sudden there was let down altogether so great a number of branches with lights in them so ingeniously disposed, some in squares, and some in circles, that the whole thing was a spectacle that has seldom been equalled for beauty.

The next day Antony invited her to supper, and was very desirous to outdo her in magnificence as well as contrivance; but he found he was altogether beaten in both, and was so well convinced of it that he was himself the first to jest and mock at his poverty of wit and his rustic awkwardness. She perceiving that his raillery was broad and gross, and savored more of the soldier than the courtier, rejoined in the same taste, and fell into it at once, without any sort of reluctance or reserve. For her actual beauty, it is said, was not in itself so remarkable that none could be compared with her, or that no one could see her without being struck by it, but the contact of her presence, if you lived with her, was irresistible; the attraction of her person, joining with the charm of her conversation, and the character that attended all she said or did, was something bewitching. It was a pleasure merely to hear the sound of her voice, with which, like an instrument of many strings, she could pass from one language to another; so that there were few of the barbarian nations that she answered by an interpreter; to most of them she spoke herself, as to the Ethiopians, Troglodytes, Hebrews, Arabians, Syrians, Nedes, Parthians, and many others, whose languages she had learnt; which was all the more surprising because most of the kings, her predecessors, scarcely gave themselves the trouble to acquire the Egyptian tongue, and several of them quite abandoned the Macedonian.

Antony was so captivated by her that, while Fulvia his wife maintained his quarrels in Rome against Caesar by actual force of arms, and the Parthian troops, commanded by Lebienus (the king's general having made him commander-in-chief), were assembled in Mesopotamia, and ready to enter Syria, he could yet suffer himself to be carried away by her to Alexandria, there to keep holiday, like a boy, in play and diversion, squandering and fooling away in enjoyments that most costly, as Antiphon says, of all valuables, time. . . .

To return to Cleopatra. Plato admits four sorts of flattery, but she had a thousand. Were Antony serious or disposed to mirth, she had at any moment some new delight or charm to meet his wishes; at every turn she was upon him, and let him escape her neither by day nor by night. She played at dice with him, drank with him, hunted with him; and when he exercised in arms, she was there to see. At night she would go rambling with him to disturb and torment people at their doors and windows, dressed like a servant-woman, for Antony also went in servant's disguise, and from these expeditions he often came home very scurvily answered, and sometimes even beaten severely, though most people guessed who it was. However, the Alexandrians in general liked it all well enough, and joined good-humoredly and kindly in his frolics and play, saying they were much obliged to Antony for acting his tragic parts at Rome, and keeping his comedy for them. It would be trifling without end to be particular in his follies, but his fishing must not be forgotten. He went out one day to angle with Cleopatra, and being so unfortunate as to catch nothing in the presence of his mistress, he gave secret orders to the fishermen to dive under water, and put fishes that had already been taken upon his hooks; and these he drew so fast that the Egyptian perceived it. But, feigning great admiration, she told everybody how dexterous Antony was, and invited them next day to come and see him again. So, when a number of them had come on board the fishing boats, as soon as he had let down his hook, one of her servants was beforehand with his divers, and fixed upon his hook a salted fish from Pontus. Antony, feeling his line give, drew up the prey, and when, as may be imagined, great laughter ensued, "Leave," said Cleopatra, "the fishing-rod, general, to us poor sovereigns of Pharos and Canopus; your game is cities, provinces, and kingdoms."

VIRTUE

George Herbert

Sweet day, so cool, so calm, so bright,
The bridal of the earth and sky;
The dew shall weep thy fall tonight,
      For thou must die.

Sweet rose, whose hue, angry and brave,
Bids the rash gazer wipe his eye;
Thy root is ever in its grave,
      And thou must die.

Sweet spring, full of sweet days and roses,
A box where sweets compacted lie;
My music shows ye have your closes,
      And all must die.

Only a sweet and virtuous soul,
Like seasoned timber, never gives;
But though the whole world turn to coal,
      Then chiefly lives.

A POLICEMAN'S LOT

Sir William S. Gilbert

When a felon's not engaged in his employment,
   Or maturing his felonious little plans,
His capacity for innocent enjoyment
   Is just as great as any honest man's.
Our feelings we with difficulty smother
   When constabulary duty's to be done.
Ah, take one consideration with another,
   A policeman's lot is not a happy one.

When the enterprising burglar's not a-burgling,
   When the cut-throat isn't occupied in crime,
He loves to hear the little brook a-gurgling,
   And listen to the merry village chime.
When the coster's finished jumping on his mother,
   He loves to lie a-basking in the sun.
Ah, take one consideration with another,
   A policeman's lot is not a happy one.

POLITICAL SKILL

Abraham Lincoln, asked what he thought was the best attribute for a politician, said he thought it "would be the ability to raise a cause which would produce an effect and then fight the effect."

THE HAPPIEST MAN

Seneca

The longest space of time exhibits only what may be found in one day—light and darkness, with their vicissitudes and alternations. Every day should be therefore so ordered and disposed, as if it closed the series, and were the measure and completion of our existence. . . .

He is the happiest man—the secure possessor of himself, who waits for the morrow without solicitude;—he who can go to bed at night saying, "I have lived," in the full sense of the phrase, rises every morning with a day gained.

THE TRUE TEACHER

James A. Garfield

I am not willing that this discussion should close without mention of the value of a true teacher. Give me a log hut, with only a simple bench, Mark Hopkins on one end and I on the other, and you may have all the buildings, apparatus and libraries without him.

MUSEE DES BEAUX ARTS

W. H. Auden

About suffering they were never wrong,
The Old Masters: how well they understood
Its human position; how it takes place
While someone else is eating or opening a window or just
        walking dully along;
How, when the aged are reverently, passionately waiting
For the miraculous birth, there always must be
Children who did not specially want it to happen, skating
On a pond at the edge of the wood:
They never forgot
That even the dreadful martyrdom must run its course
Anyhow in a corner, some untidy spot
Where the dogs go on with their doggy life and the torturer's
        horse
Scratches its innocent behind on a tree.

In Brueghel's *Icarus*, for instance: how everything turns away
Quite leisurely from the disaster; the ploughman may
Have heard the splash, the forsaken cry,
But for him it was not an important failure; the sun shone
As it had to on the white legs disappearing into the green
Water; and the expensive delicate ship that must have seen
Something amazing, a boy falling out of the sky,
Had somewhere to get to and sailed calmly on.

DOCTOR FELL

Thomas Brown

I do not love thee, Doctor Fell,
The reason why I cannot tell,
But this one thing I know full well:
I do not love thee, Doctor Fell.

THE PROCURATOR OF JUDAEA*

Anatole France

(TRANSLATOR: John Chapman)

Laelius Lamia, born in Italy of illustrious parents, amid a circle of youthful wastrels abandoned himself to licentious courses. But being accused of engaging in criminal relations with the wife of a man of consular rank, and being found guilty, he was exiled by Tiberius Caesar. At that time he was just entering his twenty-fourth year. During the eighteen years that his exile lasted he traversed Syria, Palestine, Cappadocia and Armenia, and made prolonged visits to Antioch, Caesarea and Jerusalem. When Caius was raised to the purple, Lamia obtained permission to return to Rome. He even regained a portion of his possessions. Adversity had taught him wisdom.

He avoided all intercourse with the wives and daughters of Roman citizens, made no efforts toward obtaining office, held aloof from public honors, and lived a secluded life. In his sixty-second year, being afflicted with an illness which proved in no slight degree troublesome, he decided to have recourse to the waters at Baiae. The coast at that point was the resort of the wealthy Roman, greedy of pleasure. For a week Lamia lived alone, without a friend in the brilliant crowd. Then one day, after dinner, he ascended the incline which, covered with vines that resembled bacchantes, looked out upon the waves.

He seated himself by the side of a path beneath a terebinth, and let his glances wander over the lovely landscape. To his left, livid

* Abridged

and bare, the Phlegraean plain stretched out toward the ruins of Cumae. On his right, Cape Misenum plunged its abrupt spur beneath the Tyrrhenian Sea. Beneath his feet luxurious Baiae, following the graceful outline of the coast, displayed its gardens, its villas thronged with statues, its porticos, its marble terraces along the shores of the blue ocean where the dolphins sported. On the extreme horizon Vesuvius looked forth smiling.

Lamia drew from a fold in his toga a scroll containing the *Treatise upon Nature*, extended himself upon the ground, and began to read. But the warning cries of a slave necessitated his rising to allow of the passage of a litter which was being carried along the narrow pathway through the vineyards. The litter being uncurtained, Lamia could see stretched upon the cushions the figure of an elderly man of immense bulk who, supporting his head on his hand, gazed out with a gloomy and disdainful expression. His nose, which was aquiline, and his chin, which was prominent, seemed desirous of meeting across his lips, and his jaws were powerful.

Lamia was convinced that the face was familiar to him. He hesitated a moment before the name came to him. Then suddenly hastening toward the litter with a display of surprise and delight—

"Pontius Pilate!" he cried. "The gods be praised who have permitted me to see you once again!"

The old man gave a signal to the slaves to stop, and cast a keen glance upon the stranger.

"Pontius, my dear host," resumed the latter, "have twenty years so far whitened my hair and hollowed my cheeks that you no longer recognize your friend Laelius Lamia?"

At this name Pontius Pilate dismounted from the litter as actively as the weight of his years permitted him, and embraced Laelius Lamia again and again.

"Gods! what a treat it is to me to see you once more! But, alas, you call up memories of those long-vanished days when I was Procurator of Judaea in the province of Syria. Why, it must be thirty years ago that I first met you. It was at Caesarea, whither you came to drag out your weary term of exile. I was fortunate enough to alleviate it a little, and out of friendship, Lamia, you followed me to that depressing place Jerusalem, where the Jews filled me with bitterness and disgust. You remained for more than ten years my guest and my companion, and in converse about Rome and things Roman we both of us managed to find consolation—you for your misfortunes, and I for my burdens of State."

Lamia embraced him afresh.

"Pontius, tell me, have the gods fulfilled your desires? Tell me about your family, your fortunes, your health."

"I have withdrawn to Sicily, where I possess estates, and where I cultivate wheat for the market. My eldest daughter, my best-beloved Pontia, who has been left a widow, lives with me, and directs my household. The gods be praised, I have preserved my mental vigor; my memory is not in the least degree enfeebled. But old age always brings in its train a long procession of griefs and infirmities. I am cruelly tormented with gout. And at this very moment you find me on my way to the Phlegraean plain in search of a remedy for my sufferings. From that burning soil, whence at night flames burst forth, proceed acrid exhalations of sulphur, which, so they say, ease the pains and restore suppleness to the joints. At least, the physicians assure me that it is so.

"The fumes are more powerful when the ground is still warm beneath the sun's rays. I must hasten on. Adieu! But now that I have rediscovered a friend, I should wish to take advantage of my good fortune. Do me the favor, Laelius Lamia, to give me your company at supper at my house tomorrow. My house stands on the seashore, at the extreme end of the town in the direction of Misenum.

"Till tomorrow, Lamia," he repeated, as he climbed once more into his litter. "Tomorrow we will talk about Judaea."

The following day at the supper hour Lamia presented himself at the house of Pontius Pilate. Two couches only were in readiness for occupants. Creditably but simply equipped, the table held a silver service in which were set out beccaficos in honey, thrushes, oysters from the Lucrine lake, and lampreys from Sicily. As they proceeded with their repast, Pontius and Lamia exchanged inquiries about their ailments.

After a time they turned to the subject of the great engineering feats that had been accomplished in the country; the prodigious bridge constructed by Caius between Puteoli and Baiae, and the canals which Augustus excavated to convey the waters of the ocean to Lake Avernus and the Lucrine lake.

"I also," said Pontius, with a sigh, "I also wished to set afoot public works of great utility. When, for my sins, I was appointed Governor of Judaea, I conceived the idea of furnishing Jerusalem with an abundant supply of pure water by means of an aqueduct. The elevation of the levels, the gradient for the brazen reservoirs to which the distribution pipes were to be fixed—I had gone into every detail, and decided everything for myself with the assistance of mechanical experts. But far from viewing with satisfaction the construction of

(401)

that conduit, which was intended to carry to their town upon its massive arches not only water but health, the inhabitants of Jerusalem gave vent to lamentable outcries. They gathered tumultuously together, exclaiming against the sacrilege and impiousness and, hurling themselves upon the workmen, scattered the foundation stones. Can you picture to yourself, Lamia, a filthier set of barbarians? Nevertheless, Vitellius decided in their favor, and I received orders to put a stop to the work."

"It is a knotty point," said Lamia, "how far one is justified in devising things for the common weal against the will of the populace."

Pontius Pilate continued as though he had not heard this interruption.

"Refuse an aqueduct! What madness! But whatever is of Roman origin is distasteful to the Jews. In their eyes we are an unclean race, and our very presence appears a profanation to them.

"They fear us and they despise us. Yet is not Rome the mother and warden of all those peoples who nestle smiling upon her venerable bosom? Those whom we have subdued we look on as our friends, and we leave those conquered races, nay, we secure to them the permanence of their customs and their laws. Did Syria, rent asunder by its rabble of petty kings, ever even begin to taste of peace and prosperity until it submitted to the armies of Pompey? And when Rome might have reaped a golden harvest as the price of her good will, did she lay hands on the hoards that swell the treasuries of barbaric temples? Did she despoil the shrine of Cybele at Pessinus, or the Morimene and Cilician sanctuaries of Jupiter, or the temple of the Jewish god at Jerusalem? The Jews alone hate and withstand us. They withhold their tribute till it is wrested from them."

"The Jews," replied Lamia, "are profoundly attached to their ancient customs. They suspected you, unreasonably I admit, of a desire to abolish their laws and change their usages. Do not resent it, Pontius, if I say that you did not always act in such a way as to disperse their unfortunate illusion. It gratified you, despite your habitual self-restraint, to play upon their fears, and more than once have I seen you betray in their presence the contempt with which their beliefs and religious ceremonies inspired you. One must admit that though they have never risen like us to an appreciation of things divine, the Jews celebrate rites which their very antiquity renders venerable."

Pontius Pilate shrugged his shoulders.

"They have very little knowledge of the nature of the gods," he said. "They worship Jupiter, yet abstain from naming him or erecting a statue of him. They do not even adore him under the semblance of a rude stone, as certain of the Asiatic peoples do. They know nothing of Apollo, of Neptune, of Mars, nor of Pluto, nor of any goddess. . . . Why are you laughing, Lamia?"

"I was laughing," said Lamia, "at an amusing idea which just occurred to me. I was thinking that perchance some day the Jupiter of the Jews might come to Rome and vent his fury upon you. Why should he not? Asia and Africa have already enriched us with a considerable number of gods. We have seen temples in honor of Isis and the dog-faced Anubis erected in Rome. Beware, Pontius, lest the invisible Jupiter of the Jews disembark some day on the quay at Ostia!"

At the idea of a god coming out of Judaea, a fleeting smile played over the severe countenance of the Procurator. Then he replied gravely—

"How would the Jews manage to impose their sacred law on outside peoples, when they are in a perpetual state of tumult amongst themselves as to the interpretation of that law? You have seen them yourself, Lamia, in the public squares, split up into twenty rival parties, with staves in their hands, abusing each other and clutching one another by the beard. You have seen them on the steps of the temple, tearing their filthy garments as a symbol of lamentation, with some wretched creature in a frenzy of prophetic exaltation in their midst. Since the genius of Rome has towered over them, capital sentences pronounced by their own tribunals can only be carried out with the sanction of the proconsul or the procurator, they harry the Roman magistrate at any hour to procure his signature to their baleful decrees, they besiege the pretorium with their cries of 'Death!' A hundred times, at least, have I known them, mustered, rich and poor together, all united under their priests, make a furious onslaught on my ivory chair, seizing me by the skirts of my robe, by the thongs of my sandals, and all to demand of me—nay, to exact from me—the death sentence on some unfortunate whose guilt I failed to perceive, and as to whom I could only pronounce that he was as mad as his accusers."

Lamia exerted himself to lead the conversation back to a less acrimonious note.

"Pontius," he said, "it is not difficult for me to understand your long-standing resentment. Truly, what you have experienced of the character of the Jews is nothing to their advantage. But I lived in Jerusalem as an interested onlooker, and mingled freely with the people, and I succeeded in detecting certain obscure virtues in these

(403)

rude folk which were altogether hidden from you. I have met Jews who were all mildness, whose simple manners and faithfulness of heart recalled to me what our poets have related concerning the Spartan lawgiver. And you yourself, Pontius, have seen perish beneath the cudgels of your legionaries simple-minded men who have died for a cause they believed to be just without revealing their names. Such men do not deserve our contempt.

"And the Jewesses I found extremely pleasing. I was young then, and the Syrian women stirred all my senses to response. Their ruddy lips, their liquid eyes that shone in the shade, their sleepy gaze pierced me to the very marrow. Painted and stained, smelling of nard and myrrh, steeped in odors, their physical attractions are both rare and delightful.

"With what languorous grace they dance, those Syrian women! I knew a Jewess at Jerusalem who used to dance in a poky little room, on a threadbare carpet, by the light of one smoky little lamp, waving her arms as she clanged her cymbals. Her loins arched, her head thrown back and, as it were, dragged down by the weight of her heavy red hair, her eyes swimming with voluptuousness, eager, languishing, compliant, she would have made Cleopatra herself grow pale with envy. I was in love with her barbaric dances, her voice—a little raucous and yet so sweet—her atmosphere of incense, the semisomnolescent state in which she seemed to live. I followed her everywhere. I mixed with the vile rabble of soldiers, conjurers, and extortioners with which she was surrounded.

"One day, however, she disappeared, and I saw her no more. Long did I seek her in disreputable alleys and taverns. It was more difficult to learn to do without her than to lose the taste for Greek wine. Some months after I lost sight of her, I learned by chance that she had attached herself to a small company of men and women who were followers of a young Galilean thaumaturgist. His name was Jesus; he came from Nazareth, and he was crucified for some crime, I don't quite know what. Pontius, do you remember anything about the man?"

Pontius Pilate contracted his brows and his hand rose to his forehead in the attitude of one who probes the deeps of memory. Then after a silence of some seconds—

"Jesus?" he murmured, "Jesus of Nazareth? I cannot call him to mind."

COUNT THAT DAY LOST

George Eliot

If you sit down at set of sun
And count the acts that you have done,
  And, counting, find
One self-denying deed, one word
That eased the heart of him who heard,
  One glance most kind
That fell like sunshine where it went—
Then you may count that day well spent.

But if, through all the livelong day,
You've cheered no heart, by yea or nay—
  If, through it all
You've nothing done that you can trace
That brought the sunshine to one face—
  No act most small
That helped some soul and nothing cost—
Then count that day as worse than lost.

THE PROPHET

Horace Traubel

He said, "I see." And they said: "He's crazy; crucify him." He still said: "I see." And they said: "He's an extremist." And they tolerated him. And he continued to say: "I see." And they said: "He's eccentric." And they rather liked him, but smiled at him. And he stubbornly said again: "I see." And they said: "There's something in what he says." And they gave him half an ear. But he said as if he'd never said it before: "I see." And at last they were awake; and they gathered about him and built a temple in his name. And yet he only said: "I see." And they wanted to do something for him. "What can we do to express to you our regret?" He only smiled. He touched them with the ends of his fingers and kissed them. What could they do for him? "Nothing more than you have done," he answered. And what was that? they wanted to know. "You see," he said, "that's reward enough; you see, you see."

THE BOOK OF BOOKS

Sir Walter Scott

Within this ample volume lies
The mystery of mysteries.
Happiest they of human race
To whom their God has given grace
To read, to fear, to hope, to pray,
To lift the latch, to force the way;
But better had they ne'er been born
That read to doubt or read to scorn.

WOMAN'S WILL

John G. Saxe

Men dying make their wills—but wives
Escape a work so sad;
Why should they make what all their lives
The gentle dames have had?

GEORGE WASHINGTON TO THE AMERICAN TROOPS BEFORE THE BATTLE OF LONG ISLAND

The time is now near at hand which must probably determine whether Americans are to be freemen or slaves; whether they are to have any property they can call their own; whether their houses and and farms are to be pillaged and destroyed, and themselves consigned to a state of wretchedness from which no human efforts will deliver them. The fate of unborn millions will now depend, under God, on the courage and conduct of this army. Our cruel and unrelenting enemy leaves us only the choice of a brave resistance, or the most abject submission. We have, therefore, to resolve to conquer or to die. . . .

The eyes of all our countrymen are now upon us; and we shall have their blessings and praises, if happily we are the instruments of saving them from the tyranny meditated against them. Let us, therefore, animate and encourage each other, and show the whole world that a freeman contending for liberty on his own ground is superior to any slavish mercenary on earth.

Liberty, property, life and honor, are all at stake. Upon your courage and conduct rest the hopes of our bleeding and insulted country. Our wives, children and parents, expect safety from us only; and they have every reason to believe that Heaven will crown with success so just a cause. The enemy will endeavor to intimidate by show and appearance; but remember they have been repulsed on various occasions by a few brave Americans. Their cause is bad—their men are conscious of it; and if opposed with firmness and coolness on their first onset, with our advantage of works, and knowledge of the ground, the victory is most assuredly ours. Every good soldier will be silent and attentive, wait for orders, and reserve his fire until he is sure of doing execution.

(July, 1776)

GREAT THINGS

Thomas Hardy

Sweet cyder is a great thing,
  A great thing to me,
Spinning down to Weymouth town
  By Ridgway thirstily,
And maid and mistress summoning
  Who tend the hostelry;
O cyder is a great thing,
  A great thing to me!

The dance it is a great thing,
  A great thing to me,
With candles lit and partners fit
  For night-long revelry;
And going home when day-dawning
  Peeps pale upon the lea:
O dancing is a great thing,
  A great thing to me!

Love is, yea, a great thing,
  A great thing to me,
When having dreams across the lawn
  In darkness silently,

A figure flits like one a-wing
  Out from the nearest tree:
O love is, yea, a great thing,
  A great thing to me!

Will these be always great things,
  Great things to me? . . .
Let it befall that One will call,
  "Soul, I have need of thee":
What then? Joy-jaunts, impassioned flings,
  Love, and its ecstasy,
Will always have been great things,
  Great things to me!

OATH TAKEN BY THOSE ENTERING THE U.S. ARMED FORCES

I, ..., do solemnly swear (or affirm) that I will bear true faith and allegiance to the United States of America; that I will serve them honestly and faithfully against all their enemies whomsoever; and that I will obey the orders of the President of the United States and the orders of the officers appointed over me, according to the regulations and the Uniform Code of Military Justice.

THE SONG OF THE UNGIRT RUNNERS

Charles Hamilton Sorley

We swing ungirded hips,
  And lightened are our eyes,
The rain is on our lips,
  We do not run for prize.
We know not whom we trust
  Nor whitherward we fare,
But we run because we must
  Through the great wide air.

The waters of the sea
   Are troubled as by storm.
The tempest strips the trees
   And does not leave them warm.
Does the tearing tempest pause?
   Do the tree-tops ask it why?
So we run without a cause
   'Neath the big bare sky.

The rain is on our lips,
   We do not run for prize.
But the storm the water whips
   And the wave howls to the skies.
The winds arise and strike it
   And scatter it like sand,
And we run because we like it
   Through the broad bright land.

THE WIT OF SYDNEY SMITH

Macaulay was a book in breeches; he not only overflowed with learning but stood in the slops; he was laying society waste with his waterspouts of talk; people in his company burst for want of an opportunity of dropping in a word; he confounded soliloquy and colloquy. The great use of the raised center, revolving on a round table, would be to put Macaulay on it and distribute his talk fairly to the company. *When Smith called on Macaulay and found him ill in bed, he said later that he was* more agreeable than I have ever seen him. There were some gorgeous flashes of silence.

Luttrell is remarkably well, considering that he has been remarkably well for so many years.

Philosopher Malthus came here last week. I got an agreeable party for him of unmarried people. There was only one lady who had a child; but he is a good-natured man, and, if there are no appearances of approaching fertility, is civil to every lady.

The observances of the Church concerning feasts and fasts are tolerably well kept upon the whole, since the rich keep the feasts and the poor the fasts.

THE TIDE RISES, THE TIDE FALLS

Henry Wadsworth Longfellow

The tide rises, the tide falls,
The twilight darkens, the curlew calls;
Along the sea-sands damp and brown
The traveller hastens toward the town,
 And the tide rises, the tide falls.

Darkness settles on roofs and walls,
But the sea, the sea in the darkness calls;
The little waves, with their soft, white hands,
Efface the footprints in the sands,
 And the tide rises, the tide falls.

The morning breaks; the steeds in their stalls
Stamp and neigh, as the hostler calls;
The day returns, but nevermore
Returns the traveller to the shore.
 And the tide rises, the tide falls.

NAMING THE NEW LAND

Martin Waldseemüller

But now that these parts have been more extensively examined, and another fourth part has been discovered by Amerigo Vespucci . . . I do not see why any one should by right object to name it America . . . after its discoverer, Americus, a man of sagacious mind, since both Europe and Asia took their names from women.

(From *Cosmographia Introductio*, 1507)

We should all be concerned about the future because we will have to spend the rest of our lives there.

—Charles F. Kettering

THE EARTH IS THE LORD'S

Holy Bible, Psalm 24

The earth is the Lord's, and the fulness thereof; the world, and that they that dwell therein:

For he hath founded it upon the seas, and established it upon the floods.

Who shall ascend into the hill of the Lord? or who shall stand in his holy place?

He that hath clean hands, and a pure heart; who hath not lifted up his soul unto vanity, nor sworn deceitfully.

He shall receive the blessing from the Lord, and righteousness from the God of his salvation.

This is the generation of them that seeks him, that seek thy face, O Jacob, Selah.

Lift up your heads, O ye gates: and be ye lift up, ye everlasting doors; and the King of glory shall come in.

Who is this King of glory? The Lord strong and mighty, the Lord mighty in battle.

Lift up your heads, O ye gates; even lift them up, ye everlasting doors; and the King of glory shall come in.

Who is this King of glory? The Lord of hosts, he is the King of glory. Selah.

PERILS OF DARKNESS

William Shakespeare

>   ... know'st thou not
> That when the searching eye of heaven is hid,
> Behind the globe, that lights the lower world,
> Then thieves and robbers range abroad unseen
> In murders and in outrage, boldly here;
> But when from under this terrestrial ball
> He fires the proud tops of the eastern pines
> And darts his light through every guilty hole,
> Then murders, treasons and detested sins,
> The cloak of night being pluck'd from off their backs,
> Stand bare and naked, trembling at themselves?
>   (From *King Richard II*)

THE TWELVE DAYS OF CHRISTMAS

Anonymous

The first day of Christmas,
My true love sent to me
A partridge in a pear tree.

The second day of Christmas,
My true love sent to me
Two turtle doves, and
A partridge in a pear tree.

The third day of Christmas,
My true love sent to me
Three French hens,
Two turtle doves, and
A partridge in a pear tree.

The fourth day of Christmas,
My true love sent to me
Four colly birds,
Three French hens,
Two turtle doves, and
A partridge in a pear tree.

The fifth day of Christmas,
My true love sent to me
Five gold rings,
Four colly birds,
Three French hens,
Two turtle doves, and
A partridge in a pear tree.

The sixth day of Christmas,
My true love sent to me
Six geese a-laying,
Five gold rings,
Four colly birds,
Three French hens,
Two turtle doves, and
A partridge in a pear tree.

The seventh day of Christmas
My true love sent to me
Seven swans a-swimming,
Six geese a-laying,
Five gold rings,
Four colly birds,
Three French hens,
Two turtle doves, and
A partridge in a pear tree.

The eighth day of Christmas
My true love sent to me
Eight maids a-milking,
Seven swans a-swimming,
Six geese a-laying,
Five gold rings,
Four colly birds,
Three French hens,
Two turtle doves, and
A partridge in a pear tree.

The ninth day of Christmas
My true love sent to me
Nine drummers drumming,
Eight maids a-milking,
Seven swans a-swimming,
Six geese a-laying,
Five gold rings,
Four colly birds,
Three French hens,
Two turtle doves, and
A partridge in a pear tree.

The tenth day of Christmas
My true love sent to me
Ten pipers piping,
Nine drummers drumming,
Eight maids a-milking,
Seven swans a-swimming,
Six geese a-laying,
Five gold rings,
Four colly birds,
Three French hens,

Two turtle doves, and
A partridge in a pear tree.

The eleventh day of Christmas
My true love sent to me
Eleven ladies dancing,
Ten pipers piping,
Nine drummers drumming,
Eight maids a-milking,
Seven swans a-swimming,
Six geese a-laying,
Five gold rings,
Four colly birds,
Three French hens,
Two turtle doves, and
A partridge in a pear tree.

The twelfth day of Christmas
My true love sent to me
Twelve lords a-leaping,
Eleven ladies dancing,
Ten pipers piping,
Nine drummers drumming,
Eight maids a-milking,
Seven swans a-swimming,
Six geese a-laying,
Five gold rings,
Four colly birds,
Three French hens,
Two turtle doves, and
A partridge in a pear tree.

THE KING CAN DO NO WRONG

Sir William Blackstone

That the king can do no wrong, is a necessary and fundamental principle of the English constitution: meaning only that in the first place, whatever may be amiss in the conduct of public affairs is not chargeable personally on the king: nor is he, but his ministers, accountable for it to the people; and secondly, that the prerogative of the crown extends not to do an injury; for being created for the benefit of the people, it cannot be exerted to their prejudice. Whenever therefore it happens that, by misinformation or inadvertence, the crown hath been induced to invade the private rights of any of its subjects, though no action will lie against the sovereign (for who shall command the king?), yet the law hath furnished the subject with a decent and respectful mode of removing that invasion, by informing the king of the true state of the matter in dispute: and as it presumes that to know of any injury and to *redress* it are inseparable in the royal breast, it then issues as of course, in the king's own name, his orders to his judges to do justice to the party aggrieved.

WHEN I HEARD THE LEARN'D ASTRONOMER

Walt Whitman

When I heard the learn'd astronomer,
When the proofs, the figures, were ranged in columns before me,
When I was shown the charts and diagrams, to add, divide, and
    measure them,
When I sitting heard the astronomer where he lectured with much
    applause in the lecture-room,
How soon unaccountable I became tired and sick,
Till rising and gliding out I wander'd off by myself,
In the mystical moist night-air, and from time to time,
Look'd up in perfect silence at the stars.

THE AMERICAN EAGLE

Benjamin Franklin

I wish that the bald eagle had not been chosen as the representative of our country; he is a bird of bad moral character; he does not get his living honestly. He is never in good case; but, like those among men who live by sharping and robbing, he is generally poor, and often very lousy. Besides he is a rank coward; the little *king-bird*, not bigger than a sparrow, attacks him boldly and drives him out of the district.

FOR THIS IS WISDOM

Laurence Hope

For this is Wisdom; to love, to live,
To take what Fate, or the Gods, may give,
To ask no question, to make no prayer,
To kiss the lips and caress the hair,
Speed passion's ebb as you greet its flow,—
To have,— to hold,— and,— in time,— let go!

HERE MEN FROM THE PLANET EARTH
FIRST SET FOOT ON THE MOON.
JULY 1969 A.D.
WE CAME IN PEACE FOR ALL MANKIND.
(Inscription on a stainless steel plaque attached
to the landing vehicle left on the moon)

CAPTAIN JOHN SMITH RELATES HOW POCAHONTAS SAVED HIS LIFE

At last they brought him [Smith] to Werowocomoco, where was Powhatan, their emperor. Here more than two hundred of those grim courtiers stood wondering at him, as he had been a monster; till Powhatan and his train had put themselves in their greatest braveries. Before a fire upon a seat like a bedstead, he sat covered with a great robe, made of raccoon skins and all the tails hanging by. On either hand did sit a young wench of sixteen or eighteen years, and along on each side the house, two rows of men, and behind them as many women, with all their heads and shoulders painted red, many of their heads bedecked with the white down of birds, but every one with something, and a great chain of white beads about their necks. At his entrance before the king, all the people gave a great shout. The queen of Appamatuck was appointed to bring him water to wash his hands, and another brought him a bunch of feathers, instead of a towel to dry them. Having feasted him after their best barbarous manner they could, a long consultation was held, but the conclusion was, two great stones were brought before Powhatan: then as many as could lay hands upon him, dragged him to them, and thereon laid his head, and being ready with their clubs to beat out his brains, Pocahontas, the king's dearest daughter, when no entreaty could prevail, got his head in her arms, and laid down her own upon his to save his from death: whereat the emperor was contented he should live to make him hatchets, and her bells, beads, and copper; for they thought him as well of all occupations as themselves.

(1624)

RESPICE FINEM

Frances Quarles

My soul, sit thou a patient looker-on;
Judge not the play before the play is done;
Her plot hath many changes; every day
Speaks a new scene; the last act crowns the play.

THE THUNDER OF IMPERIAL NAMES

Thomas Wolfe

First for the thunder of imperial names, the names of men and battles, the names of places and great rivers, the mighty names of the states. The name of The Wilderness; and the names of Antietam, Chancellorsville, Shiloh, Bull Run, Fredricksburg, Cold Harbor, the Wheat Fields, Ball's Bluff, and the Devil's Den; the names of Cowpens, Brandywine, and Saratoga; of Death Valley, Chickamauga, and the Cumberland Gap. The names of the Nantahalas, the Bad Lands, the Painted Desert, the Yosemite, and the Little Big Horn; the names of Yancey and Cabarrus counties; and the terrible name of Hatteras.

Then, for the continental thunder of the states: the names of Montana, Texas, Arizona, Colorado, Michigan, Maryland, Virginia and the two Dakotas, the names of Oregon and Indiana, of Kansas and the rich Ohio; the powerful name of Pennsylvania, and the name of Old Kentucky; the undulance of Alabama; the names of Florida and North Carolina.

In the red-oak thickets at the break of day long hunters lay for bear—the rattle of arrows in laurel leaves, the war cries round the painted buttes, and the majestical names of the Indian Nations: the Pawnees, the Algonquins, the Iroquois, the Comanches, the Black Feet, the Seminoles, the Cherokees, the Sioux, the Hurons, the Mohawks, the Navahos, the Utes, the Omahas, the Onandagas, the Chippewas, the Crees, the Chickasaws, the Arapohoes, the Catawbas, the Dakotas, the Apaches, the Croatans, and the Tuscaroras; the names of Powhatan and Sitting Bull, and the name of the Great Chief, Rain-In-The-Face. . . .

The rails go westward in the dark. Brother, have you seen starlight on the rails? Have you heard the thunder of the fast express?

Of wandering forever, and the earth again—the names of the mighty rails that bind the nation, the wheeled thunder of the names that net the continent: The Pennsylvania, the Union Pacific, the Sante Fe, the Baltimore and Ohio, the Chicago and Northwestern, the Southern, the Louisiana and Northern, the Seaboard Air Line, the Chicago, Milwaukee and St. Paul; the Lackawanna; the New York, New Haven and Hartford, the Florida East Coast; the Rock Island; and the Denver and Rio Grande. . . .

The names of the great tramps who range the nation on the fastest trains: the names of the great tramps Oklahoma, Red Fargo Pete, Dixie Joe, Iron Mike, The Frisco Kid, Nigger Dick, Red Chi, Ike the Kike, and the Jersey Dutchman. . . .

By the waters of life, by time, by time: the names of the mighty rivers, the alluvial gluts, the chains of the continent, the throats that drink America (Sweet Thames, flow gently, till I end my song) . The names of the men who pass and the myriad names of the earth that abides forever: the names of the men who are doomed to wander and the name of that immense and lonely land on which they wander, to which they return, in which they will be buried—America! The immortal earth which waits forever, the trains that thunder on the continent, the men who wander and the women who cry out "Return."

Finally, the names of the great rivers that are flowing in the darkness (Sweet Thames, flow gently till I end my song).

By the waters of life, by time, by time: the names of great mouths, the mighty maws, the vast wet coiling never glutted and unending snakes that drink the continent. Where, sons of men, and in what other land will you find others like them, and where can you match the mighty music of their names?—The Monongahela, the Colorado, the Rio Grande, the Columbia, the Tennessee, the Hudson (Sweet Thames!) ; the Kennebec, the Rappahannock, the Delaware, the

Penobscot, the Wabash, the Chesapeake, the Swannanoa, the Indian River, the Niagara (Sweet Afton!); the Saint Lawrence, the Susquehanna, the Tombigbee, the Nantahala, the French Broad, the Chattahoochee, the Arizona, and the Potomac (Father Tiber!) — these are a few of their princely names, these are a few of their great proud glittering names, fit for the immense and lonely land that they inhabit.

PROTECTION FROM PROTECTORS

Henry David Thoreau

I went to the store the other day to buy a bolt for our front door, for as I told the storekeeper, the Governor was coming here. "Aye," said he, and the Legislature too." "Then I will take two bolts," said I. He said that there had been a steady demand for bolts and locks of late, for our protectors were coming.

A MIND DISEASED

William Shakespeare

Macbeth: How does your patient, doctor?
Doctor: Not so sick, my lord,
As she is troubled with thick-coming fancies,
That keep her from her rest.
Macbeth: Cure her of that.
Canst thou not minister to a mind diseased,
Pluck from the memory a rooted sorrow,
Raze out the written troubles of the brain,
And with some sweet oblivious antidote
Cleanse the stuff'd bosom of that perilous stuff
Which weighs upon the heart?
Doctor: Therein the patient
Must minister to himself.

(From *Macbeth*)

(419)

OLD COLLEGE SONG WITH VARIANT LINES TO SUIT

Anonymous

"Don't send my boy to Harvard," the dying mother said,
"Don't send him to Michigan, I'd rather see him dead.
Don't send him to Columbia, though it's better than Cornell,
And rather than in Yale, I would rather see my boy in the evening,
By the moonlight."

THE LIFE OF MAN ON EARTH

Anonymous

You remember, it may be, O king, that which sometimes happens in
winter when you are seated at table with your earls and thanes. Your
fire is lighted, and your hall warmed, and without is rain and snow
and storm. Then comes a swallow flying across the hall; he enters by
one door, and leaves by another. The brief moment while he is
within is pleasant to him; he feels not rain nor cheerless winter
weather; but the moment is brief—the bird flies away in the
twinkling of an eye, and he passes from winter to winter. Such, me
thinks, is the life of man on earth, compared with the uncertain time
beyond. It appears for a while; but what is the time which comes
after—the time which was before? We know not. If, then, this new
doctrine may teach us somewhat of greater certainty, it were well
that we should regard it.

> *(Attributed to a chief of the North-
> umbrians, speaking in the presence of
> nobles who had declared that the old
> gods were powerless. This took place at
> the turn of the seventh century, when
> Christian missionaries came to Great
> Britain after the Saxon invasion.)*

WHAT MUST GOD THINK?

Abraham Lincoln

We, on our side, are praying to Him to give us victory, because we believe we are right; but those on the other side pray to Him, look for victory, believing they are right. What must He think of us?

YOUR MISSION

Ellen M. H. Gates

If you cannot on the ocean,
  Sail among the swiftest fleet,
Rocking on the highest billows,
  Laughing at the storms you meet,
You can stand among the sailors,
  Anchored yet within the bay;
You can lend a hand to help them,
  As they launch their boats away.

If you are too weak to journey
  Up the mountain, steep and high,
You can stand within the valley,
  While the multitude go by.
You can chant in happy measure,
  As they slowly pass along;
Though they may forget the singer,
  They will not forget the song.

If you have not gold and silver
  Ever ready to command,
If you cannot toward the needy
  Reach an ever-open hand,
You can visit the afflicted,
  O'er the erring you can weep;
You can be a true disciple,
  Sitting at the Saviour's feet.

If you cannot in a conflict
   Prove yourself a soldier true,
If where the fire and smoke are thickest
   There's no work for you to do,
When the battle field is silent,
   You can go with careful tread;
You can bear away the wounded,
   You can cover up the dead.

Do not stand then idly waiting
   For some greater work to do;
Fortune is a lazy goddess,
   She will never come to you.
Go and toil in any vineyard,
   Do not fear to do or dare;
If you want a field of labor,
   You can find it anywhere.

THE NOBLE NATURE

Ben Jonson

It is not growing like a tree
   In bulk, doth make Man better be;
Or standing long an oak, three hundred year,
To fall a log at last, dry, bald, and sere:
     A lily of a day
     Is fairer far in May,
   Although it fall and die that night;
   It was the plant and flower of Light.
In small proportions we just beauties see;
And in short measures life may perfect be.

If you lend a friend five dollars and never see him again,
it's worth it.

                         —Anonymous

THE UNKNOWN SOLDIER

Heywood Broun

They call him "the unknown hero." It is enough, it is better that we should know him as "the unknown soldier." "Hero" suggests a superman and implies somebody exalted above his fellows. This man was one of many. We do not know what was in his heart when he died. It is entirely possible that he was a fearful man. He may even have gone unwillingly into the fight. That does not matter now. The important thing is that he was alive and is dead.

He was drawn from a far edge of the world by the war and in it he lost his identity. War may have been well enough in the days when it was a game for heroes, but now it sweeps into the combat everything and every man within a nation. The unknown soldier stands for us as symbol of this blind and far-reaching fury of modern conflict. His death was in vain unless it helps us to see that the whole world is our business. No one is too great to be concerned with the affairs of mankind, and no one too humble.

The unknown soldier was a typical American and it is probable that once upon a time he used to speak of faraway folks as "those foreigners." He thought they were no kin of his, but he died in one of the distant lands. His blood and the blood of all the world mingled in a common stream.

The body of the unknown soldier has come home, but his spirit will wander with his brothers. There will be no rest for his soul until the great democracy of death has been translated into the unity of life.

THE ARTIST

Anonymous

During the great age of ancient Greece a certain sculptor was chided because of the exquisite care he took in fashioning and embellishing the head or uppermost part of the columns of a lofty temple.

"Why spend so much time on the details of a section that human eyes cannot possibly see?" asked a government official.

The old artist put down his hammer and chisel, glared with amazement at his questioner, and said fervently, "But the gods will see it!"

DEMOCRACY OF DEATH

John Donne

The ashes of an Oak in the Chimney, are no Epitaph of that Oak, to tell me how high or how large that was; It tells me not what flocks it sheltered while it stood, nor what men it hurt when it fell. The dust of great persons' graves is speechless too, it says nothing, it distinguishes nothing . . . When a whirl-wind hath blown the dust of the Church-yard into the Church, and the man sweeps out the dust of the Church into the Church-yard, who will undertake to sift those dusts again, and to pronounce, This is the patrician, this is the noble flower, and this is the yeomanly, this the Plebeian class.

FATIGUE

Hilaire Belloc

I'm tired of Love: I'm still more tired of Rhyme.
But Money gives me pleasure all the time.

IMAGINED HOMESTEADS

Henry David Thoreau

At a certain season of our life we are accustomed to consider every spot as the possible site for a house. I have thus surveyed the country on every side within a dozen miles of where I live. In imagination I have bought all the farms in succession, for all were to be bought, and I knew their price. I walked over each farmer's premises, tasted his wild apples, discoursed on husbandry with him, took his farm at his price, at any price, mortgaging it to him in my mind; even put a higher price on it—took everything but a deed of it—took his word for his deed, for I dearly love to talk—cultivated it, and him too to some extent, I trust, and withdrew when I had enjoyed it long enough, leaving him to carry it on. This experience entitled me to be regarded as a sort of real-estate broker by my friends. Wherever I sat, there I might live, and the landscape radiated from me accordingly. I discovered many a site for a house not likely to be soon improved, which some might have thought too far from the village, but to my eyes the village was too far from it. Well, there I might live, I said; and there I did live, for an hour, a summer and a winter life; saw how I could let the years run off, buffet the winter through, and see the spring come in. The future inhabitants of this region, wherever they may place their houses, may be sure that they have been anticipated. An afternoon sufficed to lay out the land into orchard, woodlot, and pasture, and to decide what fine oaks or pines should be left to stand before the door, and when each tree could be seen to the best advantage; and then I let it lie, fallow perchance, for a man is rich in proportion to the number of things which he can afford to let alone.

THE EAGLE

Alfred Tennyson

He clasps the crag with crooked hands:
Close to the sun in lonely lands,
Ringed with the azure world, he stands.

The wrinkled sea beneath him crawls;
He watches from his mountain walls,
And like a thunderbolt he falls.

ON TAKING UP ONE'S CROSS

Holy Bible, Luke 9:23–26

And he said to them all, If any man will come after me, let him deny himself, and take up his cross daily, and follow me.

For whosoever will save his life, shall lose it: but whosoever will lose his life for my sake, the same shall save it.

For what is a man advantaged, if he gain the whole world, and lose himself or be cast away?

For whosoever shall be ashamed of me and of my words, of him shall the Son of man be ashamed, when he shall come in his own glory, and in his Father's, and of the holy angels.

SWEET BETSEY FROM PIKE

Anonymous

Oh, don't you remember sweet Betsey from Pike,
Who crossed the big mountains with her lover Ike,
With two yoke of cattle, a large yellow dog,
A tall shanghai rooster and one spotted hog.

One evening quite early they camped on the Platte,
'Twas near by the road on a green shady flat,
Where Betsey, sore-footed, lay down to repose—
With wonder Ike gazed on that Pike County rose.

Their wagon broke down with a terrible crash,
And out on the prairie rolled all kinds of trash;
A few little baby clothes done up with care—
'Twas rather suspicious, though all on the *square*.

The shanghai ran off, and their cattle all died;
That morning the last piece of bacon was fried;
Poor Ike was discouraged, and Betsey got mad,
The dog drooped his tail and looked wondrously sad.

They stopped at Salt Lake to inquire the way,
When Brigham declared that sweet Betsey should stay;
But Betsey got frightened and ran like a deer,
While Brigham stood pawing the ground like a steer.

They soon reached the desert, where Betsey gave out,
And down in the sand she lay rolling about;
While Ike, half distracted, looked on with surprise,
Saying, "Betsey, get up, you'll get sand in your eyes."

Sweet Betsey got up in a great deal of pain,
Declared she'd go back to Pike County again;
But Ike gave a sigh, and they fondly embraced,
And they travelled along with his arm round her waist.

They suddenly stopped on a very high hill,
With wonder looked down upon old Placerville;
Ike sighed when he said, and he cast his eyes down,
"Sweet Betsey, my darling, we've got to Hangtown."

Long Ike and sweet Betsey attended a dance;
Ike wore a pair of his Pike County pants;
Sweet Betsey was covered with ribbons and rings;
Says Ike, "You're an angel, but where are your wings?"

A miner said, "Betsey, will you dance with me?"
"I will that, old hoss, if you don't make too free;
But don't dance me hard; do you want to know why?
Dog on you! I'm chock full of strong alkali!"

This Pike County couple got married of course,
And Ike became jealous—obtained a divorce;
Sweet Betsey, well satisfied, said with a shout,
"Good-by, you big lummox, I'm glad you've backed out!"

THERE IS AMERICA

Edmund Burke

Young man, there is America—which at this day serves for little more than to amuse you with stories of savage men and uncouth manners; yet shall, before you taste of death, show itself equal to the whole of that commerce which now attracts the envy of the world.

(From a speech, 1775)

SLOW ME DOWN, LORD!

Orin L. Crane

Slow me down, Lord!
Ease the pounding of my heart by the quieting of my mind.
Steady my hurried pace,
With a vision of the eternal reach of time.
Give me, amidst the confusion of my day,
The calmness of the everlasting hills.
Break the tension of my nerves

(427)

With the soothing music of the singing streams
That live in my memory.
Help me to know the magical restoring power of sleep.
Teach me the art of taking minute vacations of slowing down.
To look at a flower;
To chat with an old friend or make a new one;
To pat a stray dog; to watch a spider build a web;
To smile at a child; or to read from a good book.
Remind me each day
That the race is not always to the swift;
That there is more to life
Than increasing its speed.

WHAT A FRIEND WE HAVE IN JESUS

Joseph Scriven

What a friend we have in Jesus,
  All our sins and griefs to bear;
What a privilege to carry
  Everything to God in prayer.
Oh, what peace we often forfeit,
  Oh, what needless pain we bear—
All because we do not carry
  Everything to God in prayer.

Have we trials and temptations?
  Is there trouble anywhere?
We should never be discouraged,
  Take it to the Lord in prayer.
Can we find a Friend so faithful,
  Who will all our sorrows share?
Jesus knows our every weakness,
  Take it to the Lord in prayer.

Are we weak and heavy laden,
  Cumbered with a load of care?
Precious Saviour, still our refuge,—
  Take it to the Lord in prayer.

Do thy friends despise, forsake thee?
Take it to the Lord in prayer:
In his arms he'll take and shield thee,
Thou wilt find a solace there.

FAME

Anonymous

The halls of fame are open wide
And they are always full;
Some go in by the door called "push,"
And some by the door called "pull."

ONE YEAR

William Drummond of Hawthorden

One year is sufficient to behold all the Magnificence of Nature, nay, even one Day and Night; for more is but the same brought again. This Sun, that Moon, these Stars, the varying Dance of the Spring, Summer, Autumn, Winter, is that very same which the Golden Age did see. They which have the longest time lent them to live in, have almost no Part of it at all, measuring it either by the Space of Time which is past, when they were not, or by that which is to come. Why shouldst thou then care, whether thy Days be many or few, which, when prolonged to the uttermost, prove, paralleled with Eternity, as a Tear is to the Ocean? To die young, is to do that soon, and in some fewer days, which once thou must do; it is but the giving over of a Game, that after never so many Hazards, must be lost.

A MORNING PRAYER

Robert Louis Stevenson

The day returns and brings us the petty round of irritating concerns and duties. Help us to play the man, help us to perform them with laughter and kind faces, let cheerfulness abound with industry. Give us to go blithely on our business all this day, bring us to our resting beds weary and content and undishonored, and grant us in the end the gift of sleep.

WINSTON CHURCHILL TELLS HOW HE TOOK CHARGE

The morning of the tenth of May [1940] dawned, and with it came the tremendous news. Boxes with telegrams poured in from the Admiralty, the War Office and the Foreign Office. The Germans had struck their long-awaited blow. Holland and Belgium were both invaded. Their frontiers had been crossed at numerous points. The whole movement of the German Army upon the invasion of the Low Countries and of France had begun. . . .

In the splintering crash of this vast battle, the quiet conversations we had had in Downing Street faded or fell back in one's mind. However, I remember being told that Mr. Chamberlain had gone, or was going, to see the King, and that was naturally to be expected. Presently a message arrived summoning me to the Palace at six o'clock. It only takes two minutes to drive there from the Admiralty along the Mall. . . .

I was taken immediately to the King. His Majesty received me most graciously and bade me sit down. He looked at me searchingly and quizzically for some moments, and then said: "I suppose you don't know why I have sent for you?" Adopting his mood, I replied, "Sir, I simply couldn't imagine why." He laughed and said: "I want to ask you to form a Government." I said I would certainly do so. . . .

I told the King that I would immediately send for the leaders of the Labour and Liberal Parties, that I proposed to form a War Cabinet of five or six Ministers, and that I hoped to let him have at least five names before midnight. . . .

Thus, then, on the night of the tenth of May, at the outset of the mighty battle, I acquired the chief power in the State, which henceforth I wielded in ever-growing measure for five years and three months of world war, at the end of which time, all our enemies having surrendered unconditionally, or being about to do so, I was immediately dismissed by the British electorate from all further conduct of their affairs.

During these last crowded days of the political crisis, my pulse had not quickened at any moment. I took it all as it came. But I cannot conceal from the reader of this truthful account that as I went to bed at about 3 A.M. I was conscious of a profound sense of relief. At last I had the authority to give directions over the whole scene. I felt as if I were walking with Destiny, and that all my past life had been but a preparation for this hour and for this trial. Eleven years in the political wilderness had freed me from ordinary party antagonisms. My warnings over the last six years had been so numerous, so detailed, and were now so terribly vindicated, that no one could gainsay me. I could not be reproached either for making the war or for want of preparation for it. I thought I knew a good deal about it all, and I was sure I should not fail. Therefore, although impatient for the morning, I slept soundly and had no need for cheering dreams. Facts are better than dreams.

LUKE HAVERGAL

Edwin Arlington Robinson

Go to the western gate, Luke Havergal,
There where the vines cling crimson on the wall,
And in the twilight wait for what will come.
The leaves will whisper there of her, and some,
Like flying words, will strike you as they fall;
But go, and if you listen, she will call.
Go to the western gate, Luke Havergal—
Luke Havergal.

No, there is not a dawn in eastern skies
To rift the fiery night that's in your eyes;
But there, where western glooms are gathering,
The dark will end the dark, if anything:
God slays himself with every leaf that flies,
And hell is more than half of paradise.
No, there is not a dawn in eastern skies—
In eastern skies.

Out of a grave I come to tell you this,
Out of a grave I come to quench the kiss
That flames upon your forehead with a glow
That blinds you to the way that you must go.
Yes, there is yet one way to where she is,
Bitter, but one that faith may never miss.
Out of a grave I come to tell you this—
To tell you this.

There is the western gate, Luke Havergal,
There are the crimson leaves upon the wall.
Go, for the winds are tearing them away,—
Nor think to riddle the dead words they say,
Nor any more to feel them as they fall;
But go, and if you trust her she will call.
There is the western gate, Luke Havergal—
Luke Havergal.

GENERALIZATION

Joseph Capp

As a rule, man's a fool.
When it's hot, he wants it cool.
When it's cool, he wants it hot,
Always wanting what is not,
Never liking what he's got.
I maintain, as a rule,
Man's a fool.

MRS. MALAPROP SAID:

Oh, there's nothing to be hoped for from her! she's as headstrong as
an allegory on the banks of the Nile.

There, sir, an attack upon my language! what do you think of that?—
an aspersion upon my parts of speech! was ever such a brute! Sure, if

I reprehend anything in this world it is the use of my oracular tongue, and a nice derangement of epitaphs!

Come girls! this gentleman will exhort us.—come, sir, you're our envoy—lead the way, and we'll precede.

(From Richard Brinsley Sheridan's play *The Rivals*, 1775)

NEW FRIENDS AND OLD FRIENDS

Joseph Parry

Make new friends, but keep the old;
Those are silver, these are gold.
New-made friendships, like new wine,
Age will mellow and refine.
Friendships that have stood the test—
Time and change—are surely best;
Brow may wrinkle, hair grow gray;
Friendship never knows decay.
For 'mid old friends, tried and true,
Once more we our youth renew.
But old friends, alas! may die;
New friends must their place supply.
Cherish friendship in your breast—
New is good, but old is best;
Make new friends, but keep the old;
Those are silver, these are gold.

Thrice is he armed that hath his quar-
    rel just;
And four times he who gets his fist in
    fust.
                                    —Josh Billings

THOMAS JEFFERSON UPHOLDS THE VALUE
OF NEWSPAPERS

I am persuaded myself that the good sense of the people will always be found to be the best army. They may be led astray for the
moment, but will soon correct themselves. The people are the only
censors of their governors; and even their errors will tend to keep
these to the true principles of their institution. To punish these
errors too severely would be to suppress the only safeguard of the
public liberty. The way to prevent these irregular interpositions of
the people, is to give them full information of their affairs through
the channel of the public papers, and to contrive that those papers
should penetrate the whole mass of the people. The basis of our
government being the opinion of the people, the very first object
would be to keep that right; and were it left to me to decide whether
we should have a government without newspapers, or newspapers
without a government, I should not hesitate to prefer the latter.

(1787)

THE SNOW-STORM

Ralph Waldo Emerson

Announced by all the trumpets of the sky,
Arrives the snow, and, driving o'er the fields,
Seems nowhere to alight: the whited air
Hides hills and woods, the river and the heaven,
And veils the farm-house at the garden's end.
The sled and traveller stopped, the courier's feet
Delayed, all friends shut out, the housemates sit
Around the radiant fireplace, enclosed
In a tumultuous privacy of storm.
Come see the north wind's masonry.
Out of an unseen quarry evermore
Furnished with tile, the fierce artificer
Curves his white bastions with projected roof
Round every windward stake, or tree, or door.
Speeding, the myriad-handed, his wild work
So fanciful, so savage, nought cares he
For number or proportion. Mockingly,

On coop or kennel he hangs Parian wreaths;
A swan-like form invests the hidden thorn;
Fills up the farmer's lane from wall to wall,
Maugre the farmer's sighs; and at the gate
A tapering turret overtops the work.
And when his hours are numbered, and the world
Is all his own, retiring, as he were not,
Leaves, when the sun appears, astonished Art
To mimic in slow structures, stone by stone,
Built in an age, the mad wind's night-work,
The frolic architecture of the snow.

LOVE'S PURSUIT

Robert Browning

Escape me?
Never—
Beloved!
While I am I, and you are you,
   So long as the world contains us both,
   Me the loving and you the loth,
While the one eludes, must the other pursue.

SPOONERISMS

Reverend W. A. Spooner (1844–1930), the Warden of New College, was famous for his habitual metathesis—transposing the initial sound of words so as to form some laughable combination. These are some of the best that are attributed to him.

Upon dismissing a student: You have deliberately tasted two worms; you can leave Oxford by the town drain.
We all know what it is to have a half-warmed fish within us [for "half-formed wish"].
Yes, indeed, the Lord is a shoving leopard.
Rebuking his congregation for its small attendance, and meaning to refer to the weary benches, *he said:* I am tired of addressing these beery wenches.

Sir, I believe you are under the affluence of incahol.

Now, Rabbabbas was a bobber.

He referred to a blushing crow *instead of a* crushing blow.

It is kisstomary to cuss the bride.

And perhaps most famous of all, he said, Mardon me, Padam, but I am afraid that you are occupewing the wrong pie. May I sew you to another sheet?

THE BALLAD OF WILLIAM SYCAMORE
(1790–1871)

Stephen Vincent Benét

My father, he was a mountaineer,
His fist was a knotty hammer;
He was quick on his feet as a running deer,
And he spoke with a Yankee stammer.

My mother, she was merry and brave,
And so she came to her labor,
With a tall green fir for her doctor grave
And a stream for her comforting neighbor.

And some are wrapped in linen fine,
And some are like a godling's scion;
But I was cradled on twigs of pine
In the skin of a mountain lion.

And some remember a white, starched lap
And a ewer with silver handles;
But I remember a coonskin cap
And the smell of bayberry candles.

The cabin logs, with the bark still rough,
And my mother who laughed at trifles,
And the tall, lank visitors, brown as snuff,
With their long, straight squirrel-rifles.

I can hear them dance, like a foggy song,
Through the deepest one of my slumbers,
The fiddle squeaking the boots along
And my father calling the numbers.

The quick feet shaking the puncheon-floor,
And the fiddle squealing and squealing,
Till the dried herbs rattled above the door
And the dust went up to the ceiling.

There are children lucky from dawn to dusk,
But never a child so lucky!
For I cut my teeth on "Money Musk"
In the Bloody Ground of Kentucky!

When I grew tall as the Indian corn,
My father had little to lend me,
But he gave me his great, old powder-horn
And his woodsman's skill to befriend me.

With a leather shirt to cover my back,
And a redskin nose to unravel
Each forest sign, I carried my pack
As far as a scout could travel.

Till I lost my boyhood and found my wife,
A girl like a Salem clipper!
A woman straight as a hunting-knife
With eyes as bright as the Dipper!

We cleared our camp where the buffalo feed,
Unheard-of streams were our flagons;
And I sowed my sons like the apple-seed
On the trail of the Western wagons.

They were right, tight boys, never sulky or slow,
A fruitful, a goodly muster.
The eldest died at the Alamo.
The youngest fell with Custer.

The letter that told it burned my hand.
Yet we smiled and said, "So be it!"
But I could not live when they fenced the land,
For it broke my heart to see it.

I saddled a red, unbroken colt
And rode him into the day there;
And he threw me down like a thunderbolt
And rolled on me as I lay there.

(437)

The hunter's whistle hummed in my ear
As the city-men tried to move me,
And I died in my boots like a pioneer
With the whole wide sky above me.

Now I lie in the heart of the fat, black soil,
Like the seed of a prairie thistle;
It has washed my bones with honey and oil
And picked them clean as a whistle.

And my youth returns, like the rains of Spring,
And my sons, like the wild-geese flying;
And I lie and hear the meadow-lark sing
And have much content in my dying.

Go play with the towns you have built of blocks,
The towns where you would have bound me!
I sleep in my earth like a tired fox,
And my buffalo have found me.

THE LORD IS MY LIGHT AND MY SALVATION

Holy Bible, Psalm 27:1, 4, 14

The Lord is my light and my salvation; whom shall I fear? the Lord is the strength of my life; of whom shall I be afraid? . . .

One thing have I desired of the Lord, that will I seek after; that I may dwell in the house of the Lord all the days of my life, to behold the beauty of the Lord, and to inquire in his temple. . . .

Wait on the Lord; be of good courage, and he shall strengthen thine heart: wait, I say, on the Lord.

The only thing necessary for the triumph of evil is for good men to do nothing.

—Edmund Burke

IN THE SWEET BY AND BY

S. F. Bennett

There's a land that is fairer than day,
And by faith we can see it afar;
For the Father there waits over the way,
To prepare us a dwelling-place there.

Chorus
In the sweet by and by,
We shall meet on that beautiful shore,
In the sweet by and by,
We shall meet on that beautiful shore.

We shall sing on that beautiful shore,
The melodious songs of the blest,
And our spirits shall sorrow no more,
Not a sigh for the blessing of rest.

To our bountiful Father above,
We will offer our tribute of praise,
For the glorious gift of His love,
And the blessings that hallow our days.

NEW ENGLAND SPRING

Mark Twain

There is a sumptuous variety about the New England weather that
compels the stranger's admiration—and regret. The weather is always doing something there; always attending strictly to business;
always getting up new designs and trying them on people to see how
they will go. But it gets through more business in Spring than in any
other season. In the Spring I have counted one hundred and thirty-
six different kinds of weather inside of twenty-four hours. Probable
nor'-east to sou'-west winds, varying to the southard and westard
and eastard and points between; high and low barometer, sweeping
round from place to place; probable areas of rain, snow, hail, and
drought, succeeded or preceded by earthquakes with thunder and
lightning.

ONE SOLITARY LIFE

Anonymous

Here is a man who was born in an obscure village, the child of a peasant woman. He grew up in another obscure village. He worked in a carpenter shop until he was thirty, and then for three years he was an itinerant preacher.

He never wrote a book. He never held an office. He never owned a home. He never had a family. He never went to college. He never traveled two hundred miles from the place where he was born. He never did one of the things that usually accompany greatness. . . . While still a young man, the tide of popular opinion turned against him. His friends ran away. One of them denied him. He was turned over to his enemies. He went through the mockery of a trial. He was nailed upon a cross between two thieves. His executioners gambled for the only piece of property he had on earth while he was dying—his coat. When he was dead he was taken down and laid in a borrowed grave through the pity of a friend.

Nineteen wide centuries have come and gone; today he is the centerpiece of the human race and the Leader of the column of progress.

I am far within the mark when I say that all the armies that ever marched, and all the navies that ever were built, and all the parliaments that ever sat, and all the kings that ever reigned, put together, have not affected the life of man upon this earth as powerfully as has that one solitary life.

EFFECTIVE PRAYER

Holy Bible, Luke 11:9–13

And I say unto you, Ask, and it shall be given you; seek and ye shall find; knock and it shall be opened unto you.

For every one that asketh receiveth; and he that seeketh findeth; and to him that knocketh it shall be opened.

If a son shall ask bread of any of you that is a father, will he give him a stone? or if he ask a fish, will he for a fish give him a serpent?

Or if he shall ask an egg, will he offer him a scorpion?

If ye then, being evil, know how to give good gifts unto your children; how much more shall your heavenly Father give the Holy Spirit to them that ask him?

MY OBJECT ALL SUBLIME

Sir William S. Gilbert

A more humane Mikado never
　Did in Japan exist;
　　To nobody second,
　　I'm certainly reckoned
A true philanthropist.
It is my very humane endeavor
　To make, to some extent,
　　Each evil liver
　　A running river
Of harmless merriment.

　　　My object all sublime
　　　I shall achieve in time—
　To let the punishment fit the crime—
　　　　The punishment fit the crime;
　　　And make each prisoner pent
　　　Unwillingly represent
　A source of innocent merriment—
　　　　Of innocent merriment!

All prosy dull society sinners,
　Who chatter and bleat and bore,
　　Are sent to hear sermons
　　From mystical Germans
Who preach from ten to four:
The amateur tenor, whose vocal villainies
　All desire to shirk,
　　Shall, during off-hours,
　　Exhibit his powers
To Madame Tussaud's waxwork:

The lady who dyes a chemical yellow,
　　Or stains her grey hair puce,
　　　Or pinches her figger,
　　　Is blacked like a nigger
With permanent walnut juice:
The idiot who, in railway carriages,
　　Scribbles on window panes,
　　　We only suffer
　　　To ride on a buffer
In Parliamentary trains.

The advertising quack who wearies
　　With tales of countless cures,
　　　His teeth, I've enacted,
　　　Shall all be extracted
By terrific amateurs:
The music-hall singer attends a series
　　Of masses and fugues and "ops"
　　　By Bach, interwoven
　　　With Spohr and Beethoven,
At classical Monday Pops:
The billiard sharp whom any one catches
　　His doom's extremely hard—
　　　He's made to dwell
　　　In a dungeon cell
On a spot that's always barred;
And there he plays extravagant matches
　　In fitless finger-stalls,
　　　On a cloth untrue
　　　With a twisted cue,
And elliptical billiard balls!

DARE TO DO OUR DUTY

Abraham Lincoln

　Neither let us be slandered from our duty by false accusations against us, nor frightened from it by menaces of destruction to the government, nor of dungeons to ourselves. Let us have faith that right makes might, and in that faith let us to the end dare to do our duty as we understand it.

(1860)

A THANKSGIVING TO GOD FOR HIS HOUSE

Robert Herrick

Lord, Thou hast given me a cell
   Wherein to dwell,
A little house whose humble roof
   Is weather-proof. . . .
Low is my porch, as is my fate,
   Both void of state;
And yet the threshold of my door
   Is worn by th' poor,
Who hither come and freely get
   Good words, or meat. . . .
'Tis Thou that crown'st my glittering hearth
   With guileless mirth. . . .
All these and better Thou dost send
   Me, to this end,
That I should render, for my part,
   A thankful heart.

WALT WHITMAN DESCRIBES THE PEOPLE IN WASHINGTON JUST PRIOR TO THE CIVIL WAR

They were, seven-eighths of them, the meanest kind of bawling and blowing officeholders, office-seekers, pimps, malignants, conspirators, murderers, fancy-men, customhouse clerks, contractors, kept-editors, spaniels well trained to carry and fetch, jobbers, infidels, disunionists, terrorists, mail-riflers, slave-catchers, pushers of slavery, creatures of the President, creatures of would-be Presidents, spies, bribers, compromisers, lobbyers, spongers, ruined sports, expelled gamblers, policy-backers, monte-leaders, duelists, carriers of concealed weapons, deaf men, pimpled men, and scarred inside with vile disease, gaudy outside with gold chains made from people's money and harlot's money, twisted together; crawling, serpentine men, the lousy combings and born freedom-sellers of the earth.

THE WOMEN SPEAK OUT IN DEFENSE OF THEMSELVES

Aristophanes

(TRANSLATOR: B. B. Rogers)

Men never speak a good word,
            never one, for the feminine gender,
Every one says we're a Plague,
            the source of all evil to man,
War, dissension, and strife.
            Come, answer me this, if you can:
Why, if we're *really* a Plague,
            you're so anxious to have us for wives;
And charge us not to be peeping,
            nor to stir out of doors for our lives.
Isn't it silly to guard
            a Plague with such scrupulous care?
Zounds! how you rave, coming home,
            if your poor little wife isn't there.
Should you not rather be glad,
            and rejoice all the days of your life.
Rid of a *Plague,* you know,
            the source of dissension and strife?
If on a visit we sport,
            and sleep when the sporting is over,
O, how you rummage about;
            what a fuss, your lost Plague to discover.
Every one stares at your Plague
            if she happens to look on the street:
Stares all the more if your Plague
            thinks proper to blush and retreat.
Is it not plain, then, I ask,
            that Women are really the best? . . .
Is there a man who can equal,
            in matters of glory and war,
Lady Victoria, Mistress
            of Marathon, queen of the Sea?
Is not Prudence a Woman,
            and who is so clever as she?
Certainly none of your statesmen,
            who only a twelvemonth ago

Gave up their place and their duty.
              Would women demean themselves so?
Women don't ride in their coaches,
              as Men have been doing of late,
Pockets and purses distended
              with cash they have filched from the State.
We, at the very outside,
              steal a wee little jorum of corn,
Putting it back in the even,
              whatever we took in the morn.
But this is a true description of you.
Are ye not gluttonous, vulgar, perverse,
Kidnappers, housebreakers, footpads, and worse?
And we in domestic economy too
Are thriftier, shiftier, wiser than you.
                        (From *The Thesmophoriazusae*)

SAIL, DON'T DRIFT

Oliver Wendell Holmes, M.D.

I find the greatest thing in this world not so much where we stand, *as in what direction we* are moving. To reach the port of heaven, we must sail sometimes with the wind, and sometimes against it, but we sail, and not drift, nor live at anchor.

IN MEMORIAM
Margaritae Sorori

William Ernest Henley

A late lark twitters from the quiet skies;
And from the west,
Where the sun, his day's work ended,
Lingers as in content,
There falls on the old, grey city
An influence luminous and serene,
A shining peace.

(445)

The smoke ascends
In a rosy-and-golden haze. The spires
Shine, and are changed. In the valley
Shadows rise. The lark sings on. The sun,
Closing his benediction,
Sinks, and the darkening air
Thrills with a sense of the triumphing night—
Night with her train of stars
And her great gift of sleep.

So be my passing!
My task accomplished and the long day done,
My wages taken, and in my heart
Some late lark singing,
Let me be gathered to the quiet west,
The sundown splendid and serene,
Death.

A PROPHETIC UTTERANCE

Leo Szilard

The first bomb that is detonated over Japan will be spectacular
enough to start a race in atomic armaments between us and other
nations . . . The strong position of the United States in the world
in the past thirty years has been due to the fact that the U. S. could
out-produce every other country in heavy armaments. The existence
of the atomic bomb means the end of the strong position of the
United States in this respect.

> (From a letter to President Roosevelt, written on
> April 12, 1945, the day the President died.)

I never knew a man in my life who could not bear
another's misfortune perfectly like a Christian.

—Alexander Pope

ALL SERVICE RANKS THE SAME WITH GOD

Robert Browning

All service ranks the same with God:
If now, as formerly he trod
Paradise, his presence fills
Our earth, each only as God wills
Can work—God's puppets, best and worst,
Are we; there is no last or first.

ECONOMIC SYSTEMS

Anonymous

Free Enterprise: You furnish your own ladder, the government merely stands by to steady it as you climb.

Socialism: The government furnishes you a ladder for free—but with no rungs.

Communism: The Comrades, finding you already well up on the ladder, jerk it from under you, break it up and beat you to death with the pieces.

GROWING OLD

R. J. Wells

A little more tired at the close of day,
A little less anxious to have our way;
A little less anxious to scold and blame,
And so we are nearing the journey's end,
Where Time and Eternity meet and blend.

A little less care for bonds and gold,
A little more zest in the days of old;
A broader view and a saner mind,
And a little more love for all mankind;
And so we are faring adown the way
That leads to the gates of a better day.

(447)

A little more love for the friends of youth,
A little less zeal for established truth;
A little more charity in our views,
A little less thirst for the daily news;
And so we are folding our tents away
And passing in silence, at close of day.

A little more leisure to sit and dream,
A little more real the things unseen;
A little nearer to those ahead,
With visions of those long-loved and dead;
And so we are going, where all must go,
To the place the living may never know.

A little more laughter, a few more tears,
And we shall have told our increasing years;
The book is closed, and the prayers are said,
And we are a part of the countless dead.
Thrice happy, if then some soul can say,
"I live because he has passed my way."

DIRCE

Walter Savage Landor

Stand close around, ye Stygian set,
   With Dirce in one boat convey'd!
Or Charon, seeing, may forget
   That he is old and she a shade.

SO WE SAUNTER TOWARD THE HOLY LAND

Henry David Thoreau

The sun sets on some retired meadow, where no house is visible, with all the glory and splendor that is lavished on cities, and, perchance, as it has never set before—where there is but a solitary marsh-hawk to have his wings gilded by it, or only a musquash looks out from his cabin, and there is some little black-veined brook in the midst of the marsh, just beginning to meander, winding slowly round a decaying stump. We walked in so pure and bright a light, gilding the withered grass and leaves, so softly and serenely bright, I thought I had never bathed in such a golden flood, without a ripple or a murmur to it. The west side of every wood and rising ground gleamed like a boundary of Elysium, and the sun on our backs seemed like a gentle herdsman driving us home at evening.

So we saunter toward the Holy Land, till one day the sun shall shine more brightly than ever he has done, shall perchance shine into our minds and hearts, and light up our whole lives with a great awakening light, as warm and serene and golden as on a bank-side in autumn.

THE DARKLING THRUSH

Thomas Hardy

I leant upon a coppice gate
  When Frost was spectre-gray,
And Winter's dregs made desolate
  The weakening eye of day.
The tangled bine-stems scored the sky
  Like strings of broken lyres,
And all mankind that haunted nigh
  Had sought their household fires.

The land's sharp features seemed to be
  The Century's corpse outleant,
His crypt the cloudy canopy,
  The wind his death-lament.
The ancient pulse of germ and birth
  Was shrunken hard and dry,
And every spirit upon earth
  Seemed fervourless as I.

At once a voice arose among
  The bleak twigs overhead
In a full-hearted evensong
  Of joy illimited;
An aged thrush, frail, gaunt, and small,
  In blast-beruffled plume,
Had chosen thus to fling his soul
  Upon the growing gloom.

So little cause for carolings
    Of such ecstatic sound
Was written on terrestrial things
    Afar or nigh around,
That I could think there trembled through
    His happy good-night air
Some blessed Hope, whereof he knew
    And I was unaware.

MYSTERY ENGENDERS RELIGION

Albert Einstein

The most beautiful experience we can have is the mysterious. It is the fundamental emotion which stands at the cradle of true art and true science. Whoever does not know it and can no longer wonder, no longer marvel, is as good as dead, and his eyes are dimmed. It was the experience of mystery—even if mixed with fear—that engendered religion. A knowledge of the existence of something we cannot penetrate, our perceptions of the profoundest reason and the most radiant beauty, which only in their most primitive forms are accessible to our minds—it is this knowledge and this emotion that constitute true religiosity; in this sense, and in this alone, I am a deeply religious man.

THE UTMOST IN FRIENDSHIP

John E. McCann

"I would go up to the gates of hell with a friend,
    Through thick and thin."
The other said, as he bit off a concha's end,
    "I would go in."

(450)

GOD IS OUR REFUGE AND STRENGTH

Holy Bible, Psalm 46:1–6, 10–11

God is our refuge and strength, a very present help in trouble.

Therefore will we not fear, though the earth be removed, and though the mountains be carried into the midst of the sea;

Though the waters thereof roar and be troubled, though the mountains shake with the swelling thereof. Selah.

There is a river, the streams whereof shall make glad the city of God, the holy place of the tabernacles of the Most High.

God is in the midst of her; she shall not be moved: God shall help her, and that right early. . . .

Be still, and know that I am God; I will be exalted among the heathen, I will be exalted in the earth.

The Lord of hosts is with us; the God of Jacob is our refuge. Selah.

AT THE ROUND EARTH'S IMAGIN'D CORNERS

John Donne

At the round earth's imagin'd corners, blow
Your trumpets, Angels, and arise, arise
From death, you numberless infinities
Of souls, and to your scatter'd bodies go,
All whom the flood did, and fire shall o'erthrow,
All whom war, dearth, age, agues, tyrannies,
Despair, law, chance, hath slain, and you whose eyes,
Shall behold God, and never taste death's woe.
But let them sleep, Lord, and me mourn a space,
For, if above all these, my sins abound,
'Tis late to ask abundance of thy grace,
When we are there; here on this lowly ground,
Teach me how to repent; for that's as good
As if thou hadst seal'd my pardon, with thy blood.

PEACE

Victor Hugo

Have courage for the great sorrows of life and patience for the small ones; and when you have laboriously accomplished your daily tasks, go to sleep in peace. God is awake.

BENJAMIN FRANKLIN'S LETTER OF INTRODUCTION FOR ONE LEAVING EUROPE FOR THE UNITED STATES

Sir:—the bearer of this, who is going to America, presses me to give him a letter of recommendation, though I know nothing of him, not even his name. This may seem extraordinary, but I assure you it is not uncommon here. Sometimes, indeed, one unknown person brings another equally unknown, to recommend him; and sometimes they recommend one another!

As to this gentleman, I must refer you to himself for his character and merits, with which he is certainly better acquainted than I can possibly be. I recommend him, however, to those civilities which every stranger, of whom one knows no harm, has a right to; and I request you will do him all the favor that, on further acquaintance, you shall find him to deserve. I have the honor, to be etc.—

(Paris, April 2, 1777)

HABEAS CORPUS

That every Englishman who is imprisoned by any authority what-soever, has an undoubted right, by his agents, or friends, to apply for, and obtain a write of *habeas corpus,* in order to procure his liberty by due course of law.

(Resolution of The House of Lords, 1679)

THE PHARISEE AND THE PUBLICAN

Holy Bible, Luke 18:9–14

And he spake this parable unto certain which trusted in them-selves that they were righteous, and despised others:

Two men went up into the temple to pray; one a Pharisee, and the other a publican.

The Pharisee stood and prayed thus with himself: God, I thank thee that I am not as other men are, extortioners, unjust, adulterers, or even as this publican:

I fast twice in the week, I give tithes of all that I possess.

And the publican, standing afar off, would not lift up so much as his eyes unto heaven, but smote his breast, saying, God be merciful to me a sinner.

I tell you, this man went down to his house justified rather than the other: for every one that exalteth himself shall be abased; and he that humbleth himself shall be exalted.

WILL YOU LOVE ME IN DECEMBER
AS YOU DO IN MAY?

James J. Walker

Now in the summer of life, sweetheart,
You say you love but me,
Gladly I give all my heart to you,
Throbbing with ecstasy.
But last night I saw while a-dreaming,
The future old and gray,
And I wondered if you'll love me then dear,
Just as you do today.

Chorus
Will you love me in December as you do in May,
Will you love me in the good old fashioned way?
When my hair has all turned gray,
Will you kiss me then, and say,
That you love me in December as you do in May?

(453)

You say the glow on my cheek, sweetheart,
Is like the rose so sweet;
But when the bloom of fair youth has flown,
Then will our lips still meet?
When life's setting sun fades away dear,
And all is said and done,
Will your arms still entwine and caress me,
Will our hearts beat as one?

GOD WITH US

Anonymous

God be in my head,
And in my understanding;
God be in mine eyes,
And in my looking;
God be in my mouth
And in my speaking;
God be in my heart,
And in my thinking;
God be at my end and at my departing.

NEW YORK CITY

Irvin S. Cobb

There is this to be said for New York City; It is the one densely
inhabited locality—with the possible exception of Hell—that has
absolutely not a trace of local pride.

Old men are fond of giving good advice to console themselves for their inability to give bad examples.
—La Rochefoucauld

PAST RUIN'D ILION HELEN LIVES

Walter Savage Landor

Past ruin'd Ilion Helen lives;
    Alcestis rises from the shades;
Verse calls them forth; 'tis verse that gives
    Immortal youth to mortal maids.
Soon shall Oblivion's deepening veil
    Hide all the peopled hills you see,
The gay, the proud, while lovers hail
    These many summers you and me.

THE BRITISH SPIRIT OF RESISTANCE

Winston S. Churchill

What a triumph of life these battered cities is over the worst that fire and bomb can do! What a vindication of the civilized and decent way of living we have been trying to work for and work toward in our island! What a proof of the virtues of free institutions! What a test of the quality of our local authorities and of customs and societies so steadily built!

This ordeal by fire has, in a certain sense, even exhilarated the manhood and the womanhood of Britain. The sublime but also terrible, somber experiences and emotions of the battlefield, which for centuries had been reserved for the soldiers and sailors, are now shared for good or ill by the entire population. All are proud of being under fire of the enemy.

Old men, little children, the crippled, veterans of former wars, aged women, the ordinary hard-pressed citizens—or subject of the King as he likes to call himself—the sturdy workmen who swing the hammers or load the ships, the skillful craftsmen, the members of every kind of A. R. P. service are proud to feel that they stand in the lines together with our fighting men when one of the greatest causes is being fought out. And fought out it will be to the end. This indeed is the grand, heroic period of our history and the light of glory shines on all.

(April 27, 1941)

(455)

DO YOU FEAR THE WIND?

Hamlin Garland

Do you fear the force of the wind,
The slash of the rain?
Go face them and fight them,
Be savage again.
Go hungry and cold like the wolf,
  Go wade like the crane;
The palms of your hands will thicken,
The skin of your cheek will tan,
You'll grow ragged and weary and swarthy,
  But you'll walk like a man!

GATHER YE ROSES

Robert Louis Stevenson

Gather ye roses while ye may,
  Old time is still a-flying;
A world where beauty fleets away
  Is no world for denying.
Come lads and lasses, fall to play
  Lose no more time in sighing.

The very flowers you pluck to-day
  To-morrow will be dying;
  And all the flowers are crying,
And all the leaves have tongues to say,—
Gather ye roses while ye may.

ALL MEN SHOULD WORK

Abraham Lincoln

I hold that if the Almighty had ever made a set of men that should do all the eating and none of the work, He would have made them with mouths only and no hands; and if He had ever made another class that He intended should do all the work and no eating, He would have made them with hands only and no mouths.

THE OLD STOIC

Emily Brontë

Riches I hold in light esteem,
    And Love I laugh to scorn;
And lust of fame was but a dream
    That vanished with the morn:

And, if I pray, the only prayer
    That moves my lips for me
Is, "Leave the heart that now I bear,
    And give me liberty!"

Yea, as my swift days near their goal,
    'Tis all that I implore:
    In life and death a chainless soul
With courage to endure.

THE MARRIED LOVER

Coventry Patmore

Why, having won her, do I woo?
    Because her spirit's vestal grace
Provokes me always to pursue,
    But, spirit-like, eludes embrace;
Because her womanhood is such
    That, as on court-days subjects kiss
The Queen's hand, yet so near a touch
    Affirms no mean familiarness;
Nay, rather marks more fair the height
    Which can with safety so neglect
To dread, as lower ladies might,
    That grace could meet with disrespect;
Thus she with happy favour feeds
    Allegiance from a love so high
That thence no false conceit proceeds
    Of difference bridged, or state put by;

Because, although in act and word
　　As lowly as a wife can be,
Her manner, when they call me lord,
　　Remind me 'tis by courtesy;
Not with her least consent of will.
　　Which would my proud affection hurt,
But by the noble style that still
　　Imputes an unattained desert;
Because her hair and lofty brows,
　　When all is won which hope can ask,
Reflect a light of hopeless snows
　　That bright in virgin ether bask;
Because, though free of the outer court
　　I am, this Temple keeps its shrine
Sacred to heaven; because, in short,
　　She's not and never can be mine.

BOUNDING THE UNITED STATES

John Fiske

　The United States—bounded on the north by the Aurora Borealis, on the south by the precession of the equinoxes, on the east by the primeval chaos and on the west by the Day of Judgment.

AT DAY'S END

Anonymous

Now that day doth end,
My spirit I commend,
To Thee, my Lord, my Friend.
Into Thy hands, yea, Thine,
Those glorious hands benign,
Those human hands divine
My spirit I resign.

BILL NYE ACCEPTS APPOINTMENT AS POSTMASTER OF LARAMIE, WYOMING

Office of *Daily Boomerang*, Laramie City, Wy.
August 9, 1882

MY DEAR GENERAL:

I have received by telegraph the news of my nomination by the President and my confirmation by the Senate, as postmaster at Laramie, and wish to extend my thanks for same.

I have ordered an entirely new set of boxes and post office outfit, including new corrugated cuspidors for the lady clerks.

I look upon the appointment, myself, as a great triumph of eternal truth over error and wrong. It is one of the epochs, I may say, in the Nation's onward march toward political purity and perfection. I do not know when I have noticed any stride in the affairs of state which so thoroughly impressed me by its wisdom.

Now that we are co-workers in the same department, I trust that you will not feel shy or backward in consulting me at any time relative to matters concerning post office affairs. Be perfectly frank with me, and feel perfectly free to just bring anything of that kind right to me. Do not feel reluctant because I may at times appear haughty and indifferent, cold or reserved. Perhaps you do not think I know the difference between a general delivery and a three-m quad, but that is a mistake. My general information is far beyond my years.

With profound regard, and a hearty endorsement of the policy of the President and the Senate, whatever it may be,

I remain, sincerely yours,
BILL NYE, P. M.

Gen. Frank Hatton, Washington, D.C.

IN ALL THESE TURNING LIGHTS I FIND NO CLUE

Maxwell Anderson

The following is the conclusion of the play "Winterset." Miriamne and Mio, poor young lovers, have just been murdered by gangsters, Miriamne deliberately exposing herself to the murderer's gun. Esdras, a venerable rabbi and Miriamne's father, witnessed the crime.

(459)

ESDRAS: Miriamne—Miriamne—yes, and Mio,
one breath shall call you now—forgive us both—
forgive this ancient evil of the earth
that brought you here—
GARTH: Why must she be a fool?
ESDRAS: Well, they were wiser than you and I. To die
when you are young and untouched, that's beggary
to a miser of years, but the devils locked in synod
shake and are daunted when men set their lives
at hazard for the heart's love, and lose. And these,
who were yet children, will weigh more than all
a city's elders when the experiment
is reckoned up in the end. Oh Miriamne,
and Mio—Mio, my son—know this where you lie,
this is the glory of earthborn men and women,
not to cringe, never to yield, but standing,
take defeat implacable and defiant,
die unsubmitting. I wish that I'd died so,
long ago; before you're old you'll wish
that you had died as they have. On this star,
in this hard star-adventure, knowing not
what the fires mean to right and left, not whether
a meaning was intended or presumed,
man can stand up, and look out blind, and say:
in all these turning lights I find no clue,
only a masterless night, and in my blood
no certain answer, yet is my mind my own,
yet is my heart a cry toward something dim
in distance, which is higher than I am
and makes me emperor of the endless dark
even in seeking! What odds and ends of life
men may live otherwise, let them live, and then
go out, as I shall go, and you. Our part
is only to bury them. Come, take her up.
They must not lie here.

THE HOUSE ON THE HILL

Edwin Arlington Robinson

They are all gone away,
 The House is shut and still,
There is nothing more to say.

Through broken walls and gray
 The winds blow bleak and shrill;
They are all gone away.

Nor is there one today
 To speak them good or ill:
There is nothing more to say.

Why is it then we stray
 Around that sunken sill?
They are all gone away,

And our poor fancy-play
 For them is wasted skill:
There is nothing more to say.

There is ruin and decay
 In the House on the Hill:

They are all gone away,
There is nothing more to say.

BROTHERHOOD

Holy Bible, First John 2:9–11; 4:20–21

He that saith he is in the light, and hateth his brother, is in darkness even until now.

He that loveth his brother abideth in the light, and there is none occasion of stumbling in him.

But he that hateth his brother is in darkness, and walketh in darkness, and knoweth not whither he goeth, because that darkness hath blinded his eyes. . . .

If a man say, I love God, and hateth his brother, he is a liar: for he that loveth not his brother whom he hath seen, how can he love God whom he hath not seen?

And this commandment have we from him, That he who loveth God love his brother also.

WHO READS AN AMERICAN BOOK?

Sydney Smith

In the four quarters of the globe, who reads an American book? or goes to an American play? or looks at an American statue or picture? What does the world yet owe to American physicians or surgeons? What new substances have their chemists discovered, or what old ones have they analyzed? What new constellations have been discovered by telescopes of Americans? What have they done in mathematics? Who drinks out of American glasses? or eats from American plates? Or wears American coats or gowns? or sleeps in American blankets?

(1820)

NIGHT

William Blake

The sun descending in the west,
  The evening star does shine;
The birds are silent in their nest.
  And I must seek for mine.
    The moon, like a flower
    In heaven's high bower,
    With silent delight
    Sits and smiles on the night.

Farewell, green fields and happy grove,
  Where flocks have took delight:
Where lambs have nibbled, silent move
  The feet of angels bright;

Unseen they pour blessing
And joy without ceasing
On each bud and blossom
On each sleeping bosom.

They look in every thoughtless nest
  Where birds are cover'd warm;
They visit caves of every beast,
  To keep them all from harm:
    If they see any weeping
    That should have been sleeping,
    They pour sleep on their head,
    And sit down by their bed.

When wolves and tigers howl for prey,
  They pitying stand and weep,
Seeking to drive their thirst away
  And keep them from the sheep.
    But, if they rush dreadful,
    The angels, most heedful,
    Receive each mild spirit,
    New worlds to inherit.

And there the lion's ruddy eyes
  Shall flow with tears of gold:
And pitying the tender cries,
  And walking round the fold:
    Saying, "Wrath by His meekness,
    And, by His health, sickness,
    Are driven away
    From our immortal day.

"And now beside thee, bleating lamb,
  I can lie down and sleep,
Or think on Him who bore thy name,
  Graze after thee, and weep.
    For, wash'd in life's river,
    My bright mane for ever
    Shall shine like the gold
    As I guard o'er the fold."

(463)

PLAY REVIEW

Eugene Field

Last night Mr. Creston Clarke played King Lear at the Tabor Grand. All through the five acts of that Shakespearean tragedy he played the King as though under momentary apprehension that someone else was about to play the Ace.

(Denver Tribune, 1880 or 1881)

THE VAGABOND

Robert Louis Stevenson

Give to me the life I love,
  Let the lave go by me,
Give the jolly heaven above
  And the byway nigh me.
Bed in the bush with stars to see,
  Bread I dip in the river—
There's the life for a man like me,
  There's the life for ever.

Let the blow fall soon or late,
  Let what will be o'er me;
Give the face of earth around
  And the road before me.
Wealth I seek not, hope nor love,
  Nor a friend to know me;
All I seek the heaven above
  And the road below me.

Or let autumn fall on me
  Where afield I linger,
Silencing the bird on tree,
  Biting the blue finger:
White as meal the frosty field—
  Warm the fireside haven—
Not to autumn will I yield,
  Not to winter even!

Let the blow fall soon or late,
    Let what will be o'er me;
Give the face of earth around,
    And the road before me.
Wealth I ask not, hope nor love,
    Nor a friend to know me.
All I ask the heaven above,
    And the road below me.

THE PAST

Finley Peter Dunne

"But Hinnissy, th' past always looks betther thin it was. It's only pleasant because it isn't here."

EVERYDAY WILL BE SUNDAY

Anonymous

A young fellow who did not much enjoy working, did do some work figuring out that eventually every day will be Sunday.
Every year has 365 days.
If you sleep eight hours a day it equals 122 days.
This leaves 243 days.
If you rest eight hours a day it equals another 122 days.
This leaves 121 days.
There are 52 Sundays, thus leaving 69 days.
If you have a half-day on Saturday, this equals 26 days, and leaves 43 days.
If you have 1½ hour for lunch every work day, this equals 28 days, leaving 15 days.
Two weeks vacation equals 14 days.
This leaves only one day.
And on Labor Day nobody works.

From SLEEP AND POETRY

John Keats

Stop and consider! life is but a day,
A fragile dewdrop on its perilous way
From a tree's summit; a poor Indian's sleep
While his boat hastens to the monstrous steep
of Montmorenci. Why so sad a moan?
Life is the rose's hope while yet unblown;
The reading of an ever-changing tale;
The light uplifting of a maiden's veil;
A pigeon tumbling in clear summer air;
A laughing school-boy, without grief or care,
Riding the springy branches of an elm.

BENJAMIN FRANKLIN'S RELIGIOUS BELIEFS

I believe in one God, the Creator of the universe. That he governs
it by his providence. That he ought to be worshipped. That the most
acceptable service we render him is doing good to his other children.
That the soul of man is immortal, and will be treated with justice in
another life respecting its conduct in this.

GOE, AND CATCHE A FALLING STARRE

John Donne

Goe, and catche a falling starre,
　Get with child a mandrake roote,
Tell me, where all past yeares are,
　Or who cleft the Divel's foot,
Teach me to heare Mermaides singing,
　Or to keep off envies stinging
　　　　And finde
　　　　What winde
Serves to advance an honest minde.

If thou be'st borne to strange sights,
  Things invisible go see,
Ride ten thousand daies and nights,
  Till age snow white haires on thee,
Thou, when thou return'st, wilt tell mee
All strange wonders that befell thee,
          And sweare
          No where
Lives a woman true, and faire.

If thou find'st one, let mee know,
  Such a Pilgrimage were sweet;
Yet doe not; I would not goe,
  Though at next doore wee might meet,
Though shee were true when you met her,
At last till you write your letter,
          Yet shee
          Will bee
False, ere I come, to two or three.

ST. JAMES INFIRMARY

Anonymous

It was down in old Joe's barroom,
On a corner by the square;
The drinks were served as usual,
And the usual crowd was there.

On my left stood Joe McKennedy,
His eyes were bloodshot red;
He turned to the crowd around him,
These were the very words he said:

"I went down to the St. James Infirmary,
I saw my baby there,
Stretched out on a long white table,
So sweet, so cold, so fair."

(467)

Chorus:
"Let her go, let her go, God bless her!
Wherever she may be:
She may search this wide world over,
Never find as sweet a man as me."

"When I die please bury me
In my high-top Stetson hat;
Put a twenty-dollar gold-piece on my watch-chain,
So the gang'll know I'm standing pat.

"I want six crap-shooters for pall-bearers,
A chorus girl to sing me a song;
Put a jazz band on my hearse-wagon
To raise hell as we roll along.

"And now that you've heard my story,
I'll take another shot of booze.
If anyone should happen to ask you,
Well, I've got those gambler's blues."

EXCEPT THE LORD BUILD THE HOUSE

Holy Bible, Psalm 127

Except the Lord build the house, they labor in vain that build it;
except the Lord keep the city, the watch waketh but in vain.

It is vain for you to rise up early, to sit up late, to eat the bread
of sorrows: for so he giveth his beloved sleep.

Lo, children are an heritage of the Lord: and the fruit of the
womb is his reward.

As arrows are in the hand of a mighty man; so are children of the
youth.

Happy is the man that hath his quiver full of them: they shall not
be ashamed, but they shall speak with the enemies in the gate.

IN THE GARDEN

Emily Dickinson

A bird came down the walk:
He did not know I saw;
He bit an angle-worm in halves
And ate the fellow raw.

And then he drank a dew
From a convenient grass,
And then hopped sidewise to the wall
To let a beetle pass.

He glanced with rapid eyes
That hurried all abroad—
They looked like frightened beads, I thought;
He stirred his velvet head

Like one in danger; cautious,
I offered him a crumb,
And he unrolled his feathers
And rowed him softer home

Than oars divide the ocean,
Too silver for a seam,
Or butterflies, off banks of noon,
Leap, plashless, as they swim.

LOOK TO THYSELF

Epictetus

(TRANSLATOR: Elizabeth Carter)

Men are disturbed, not by things, but by the notions they form concerning things. Death, for example, is not in itself terrible; for it did not appear so to Socrates; the terror resides only in our opinion. When therefore we are hindered, or disturbed, or grieved, let us seek the cause rather in ourselves than elsewhere. It is the action of an uninstructed person to lay the fault of his own bad condition upon others; of a partly instructed person, to lay the fault on himself; and of one perfectly instructed, neither on others, nor on himself.

LINCOLN'S LETTER TO MAJOR RAMSEY

Executive Mansion
October 17, 1861

My Dear Sir:
The lady bearer of this says she has two sons who want to work. Set them at it if possible. Wanting to work is so rare a want that it should be encouraged.

Yours truly,
A. LINCOLN

DEAR LORD! KIND LORD!

James Whitcomb Riley

Dear Lord! Kind Lord!
    Gracious Lord! I pray
Thou wilt look on all I love
    Tenderly today!

Weed their hearts of weariness,
    Scatter every care
Down a wake of angel-wings
    Winnowing the air.

And with all the needy
    O divide, I pray,
This vast treasure of content
    That is mine today.

DREAM AND REALITY

Henry David Thoreau

If one advances confidently in the direction of his dreams, and endeavors to live the life which he imagined, he will meet with a success unexpected in common hours. . . . In proportion as he simplifies his life, the laws of the universe will appear less complex, and solitude will not be solitude, nor poverty poverty, nor weakness weakness. If you have built castles in the air, your work need not be lost; that is where they should be. Now put foundations under them.

PERSEVERANCE

Anonymous

If a task is once begun
Never leave it till it's done.
Be the labor great or small,
Do it well or not at all.

TO WOMAN

Mark Twain

Human intelligence cannot estimate what we owe to woman, sir. She sews on our buttons; she mends our clothes; she ropes us in at the church fairs; she confides in us; she tells us whatever she can find out about the little private affairs of the neighbors; she gives us good advice, and plenty of it; she soothes our aching brows; she bears our children—ours as a general thing.

I repeat, sir, that in whatever position you place a woman she is an ornament to society and a treasure to the world. As a sweetheart she has few equals and no superiors; as a cousin, she is convenient; as a wealthy grandmother with an incurable distemper, she is precious;

as a wet nurse, she has no equal among men. What sir, would the people of the earth be without woman? They would be scarce, sir, almighty scarce.

THE SOUND OF THE SEA

Henry Wadsworth Longfellow

The sea awoke at midnight from its sleep,
And round the pebbly beaches far and wide
I heard the first wave of the rising tide
Rush onward with uninterrupted sweep;
A voice out of the silence of the deep,
A sound mysteriously multiplied
As of a cataract from the mountain's side,
Or roar of winds upon a wooded steep.
So comes to us at times, from the unknown
And inaccessible solitudes of being,
The rushing of the sea-tides of the soul;
And inspirations, that we deem our own,
Are some divine foreshadowing and foreseeing
Of things beyond our reason or control.

OUR COMMON NATURE

Ralph Waldo Emerson

In all conversation between two persons, tacit reference is made as to a third party, to a common nature. That third party or common nature is not social; it is impersonal; it is God.

Men are not hanged for stealing horses, but that horses may not be stolen.
—George Savile, Marquess of Halifax

ALL FOR LOVE

Lord Byron

O talk not to me of a name great in story;
The days of our youth are the days of our glory;
And the myrtle and ivy of sweet-two-and-twenty
Are worth all your laurels, though ever so plenty.

What are garlands and crowns to the brow that is wrinkled?
'Tis but as a dead flower with May-dew besprinkled:
Then away with all such from the head that is hoary—
What care I for the wreaths that can only give glory?

O Fame!—If I e'er took delight in thy praises,
'Twas less for the sake of thy high-sounding phrases,
Than to see the bright eyes of the dear one discover
She thought that I was not unworthy to love her.

There chiefly I sought thee, there only I found thee;
Her glance was the best of the rays that surround thee;
When it sparkled o'er aught that was bright in my story,
I knew it was love, and I felt it was glory.

MY OWN EPITAPH

John Gay

Life is a jest and all things show it;
I thought so once, but now I know it.

WHEN THE LAMP IS SHATTER'D

Percy Bysshe Shelley

When the lamp is shatter'd
The light in the dust lies dead—
When the cloud is scatter'd,
The rainbow's glory is shed.

(473)

When the lute is broken,
Sweet tones are remember'd not;
When the lips have spoken,
Loved accents are soon forgot.

As music and splendour
Survive not the lamp and the lute,
The heart's echoes render
No song when the spirit is mute—
No song but sad dirges,
Like the wind through a ruin'd cell,
Or the mournful surges
That ring the dead seaman's knell.

When hearts have once mingled,
Love first leaves the well-built nest;
The weak one is singled
To endure what it once possess'd.
O Love! who bewailest
The frailty of all things here,
Why choose you the frailest
For your cradle, your home, and your bier?

Its passions will rock thee
As the storms rock the ravens on high;
Bright reason will mock thee
Like the sun from a wintry sky.
From thy nest every rafter
Will rot, and thine eagle home
Leave thee naked to laughter,
When leaves fall and cold winds come.

THINK ON THESE THINGS

Holy Bible, Phillippians 4:8

Finally, brethren, whatsoever things are true, whatsoever things
are honest, whatsoever things are just, whatsoever things are pure,
whatsoever things are lovely, whatsoever things are of good report;
if there be any virtue, and if there be any praise, think on these
things.

I AM AN AMERICAN

Elias Lieberman

I am an American.
My father belongs to the Sons of the
    Revolution;
My mother, to the Colonial Dames.
One of my ancestors pitched tea
    overboard in Boston Harbor;
Another stood his ground with Warren;
Another hungered with Washington at
    Valley Forge.
My forefathers were America in the making:
They spoke in her council halls;
They died on her battle-fields;
They commanded her ships;
They cleared her forests.
Dawn reddened and paled.
Stanch hearts of mine beat fast
    at each new star
In the nation's flag.
Keen eyes of mine foresaw her
    greater glory:
The sweep of her seas,
The plenty of her plains,
The man-hives in her billion-wired cities.
Every drop of blood in me holds a
    heritage of patriotism.
I am proud of my past.
I am an American.
I am an American.
My father was an atom of dust,
My mother a straw in the wind,
To His serene majesty.
One of my ancestors died in the
    mines of Siberia;
Another was crippled for life by
    twenty blows of the *knout.*
Another was killed defending his
    home during the massacres.
The history of my ancestors is a
    trail of blood

To the palace-gate of the Great
    White Czar.
But then the dream came—
The dream of America.
In the light of the Liberty torch
The atom of dust became a man
And the straw in the wind became
    a woman
For the first time.
"See," said my father, pointing
    to the flag that fluttered near,
"That flag of stars and stripes is yours;
It is the emblem of the promised land,
It means, my son, the hope of humanity.
Live for it—die for it!"
Under the open sky of my new
    country I swore to do so;
And every drop of blood in me
    will keep that vow.
I am proud of my future.
I am an American.

TO BE MISUNDERSTOOD

Ralph Waldo Emerson

Misunderstood! It is a right fool's word. Is it so bad then to be misunderstood? Pythagoras was misunderstood, and Socrates and Jesus,
and Luther, and Copernicus, and Galileo and Newton and every
pure and wise spirit that ever took flesh. To be great is to be
misunderstood.

WISHES TO HIS SUPPOSED MISTRESS

Richard Crashaw

Whoe'er she be—
That not impossible She
Thou shall command my heart and me:

Where'er she lie,
Lock'd up from mortal eye
In shady leaves of destiny:

Till that ripe birth
Of studied Fate stand forth,
And teach her fair steps to our earth:

Till that divine
Idea take a shine
Of crystal flesh, through which to shine:

Meet you her, my Wishes,
Bespeak her to my blisses,
And be ye call'd my absent kisses.

I wish her store
Of worth may leave her poor
Of wishes; and I wish—no more.

Now, if Time knows
That Her, whose radiant brows
Weave them a garland of my vows;

Her, whose just bays
My future hopes can raise,
A trophy to her present praise;

Her, that dares be
What these lines wish to see;
I seek no further, it is She.

'Tis She, and here,
Lo! I unclothe and clear
My Wishes' cloudy character.

May she enjoy it
Whose merit dare apply it,
But modesty dares still deny it!

Such worth as this is
Shall fix my flying Wishes,
And determine them to kisses.

Let her full glory,
My fancies, fly before ye;
Be ye my fictions—but her story.

THE MAN WHO TALKED PROSE

Molière

M. JOURDAIN—I must tell you something in complete confidence.
   I am in love with a woman of great quality, and I'd like you to
   help me write a small note which I can drop at her feet.
THE PROFESSOR—Very well. You wish to send her some verses?
M. JOURDAIN—No,—no verses.
THE PROFESSOR—Just prose, then?
M. JOURDAIN—Neither prose nor verses.
THE PROFESSOR—It must be one or the other.
M. JOURDAIN—Why so?
THE PROFESSOR—Simply because to express oneself, one must do
   it in either verse or prose.
M. JOURDAIN—There's nothing but verse or prose?
THE PROFESSOR—No, sir. Everything that is not prose is verse,
   and everything that is not verse is prose.
M. JOURDAIN—What is it then when we speak?
THE PROFESSOR—Prose.
M. JOURDAIN—What! When I say "Nicole, bring me my slippers
   and give me my night-cap"—is that prose?
THE PROFESSOR—Yes, sir.
M. JOURDAIN—Upon my word! Here I have been speaking prose
   for more than forty years, and never knew it till now!

(From The Bourgeois Gentleman, 1670)

MR. DOOLEY ON TAXES

Finley Peter Dunne

"An' so th' war is over?" asked Mr. Hennessy.

"On'y part iv it," said Mr. Dooley. "Th' part that ye see in th' pitcher pa-apers is over, but th' tax collector will continyoo his part iv th' war with relentless fury. Cav'lry charges are not th' only wans in a rale war."

PRESIDENT JOHNSON ADDRESSES CONGRESS ON THE CIVIL RIGHTS LAW, MARCH, 1965

I speak tonight for the dignity of man and the destiny of democracy. I urge every member of both parties, Americans of all religions and of all colors, from every section of this country, to join me in that cause. . . .

For the cries of pain and the hymns and protests of oppressed people, have summoned into convocation all the majesty of this great government of the greatest nation on earth.

Our mission is at once the oldest and the most basic of this country: to right wrong, to do justice, to serve man.

In our time we have come to live with moments of great crisis. Our lives have been marked with debate about great issues, issues of war and peace, issues of prosperity and depression. But rarely in any time does an issue lay bare the secret heart of America itself. Rarely are we met with a challenge, not to our growth or abundance, or our welfare or our security, but rather to the values and the purpose and the meaning of our beloved nation.

The issue of equal rights for American Negroes is such an issue. And should we defeat every enemy, and should we double our wealth and conquer the stars and still be unequal to this issue, then we will have failed as a people and as a nation.

There is no Negro problem. There is no Southern problem. There is no Northern problem. There is only an American problem. And we are met here tonight as Americans, not as Democrats or Republicans, we are met here as Americans to solve that problem. . . .

Many of the issues of civil rights are very complex and most difficult. But about this there can be and should be no argument. Every American citizen must have an equal right to vote. There is no reason which can excuse the denial of that right. There is no duty which weighs more heavily on us than the duty we have to ensure that right.

Yet the harsh fact is that in many places in this country men and women are kept from voting simply because they are Negroes. . . .

We cannot, we must not refuse to protect the right of every American to vote in every election that he may desire to participate in. And we ought not, we must not wait another eight months before we get a bill. We have already waited a hundred years and more and the time for waiting is gone. . . .

The time of justice has now come. I tell you that I believe sincerely that no force can hold it back. It is right in the eyes of man and God that it should come. And when it does, I think that day will brighten the lives of every American.

For Negroes are not the only victims. How many white children have gone uneducated, how many white families have lived in stark poverty, how many white lives have been scarred by fear because we wasted our energy and our substance to maintain the barriers of hatred and terror.

So I say to all of you here and all in the nation tonight, that those who appeal to you to hold on to the past do so at the cost of denying you your future. . . .

This is the richest and most powerful country which ever occupied this globe. The might of past empires is little compared to ours.

But I do not want to be the President who built empires, or sought grandeur, or extended dominion. I want to be the President who educated young children to the wonders of their world. I want to be the President who helped to feed the hungry and prepare them to be taxpayers instead of taxeaters. I want to be the President who helped the poor to find their own way and who protected the right of every citizen to vote in every election. I want to be the President who helped to end hatred among his fellow men and who prompted love among the people of all races and all regions and all parties. I want to be the President who helped to end war among the brothers of this earth.

WHO LOVE THE RAIN

Frances Wells Shaw

Who loves the rain,
And loves his home,
And looks on life with quiet eyes,
Him will I follow through the storm;
And at his hearth-fire keep me warm;
Nor hell nor heaven shall that soul surprise,
Who loves the rain,
And loves his home,
And looks on life with quiet eyes.

THE HOUSE BEAUTIFUL

Anonymous

The Crown of the house is Godliness.
The Beauty of the house is Order.
The Glory of the house is Hospitality.
The Blessing of the house is Contentment.

COURAGE

Mark Twain

Courage is resistance to fear, mastery of fear—not absence of fear. Except a creature be part coward it is not a compliment to say it is brave; it is merely a loose misapplication of the word. Consider the flea!—incomparably the bravest of all the creatures of God, if ignorance of fear were courage. Whether you are asleep or awake he will attack you, caring nothing for the fact that in bulk and strength you are to him as are the massed armies of the earth to a sucking child; he lives both day and night and all days and nights in the very lap of peril and the immediate presence of death, and yet is no more afraid than is the man who walks the streets of a city that was

(481)

threatened by an earthquake ten centuries before. When we speak of Clive, Nelson and Putnam as men who "didn't know what fear was," we ought always to add the flea—and put him at the head of the procession.

THE PURIST

Ogden Nash

I give you now Professor Twist,
A conscientious scientist.
Trustees exclaimed, "He never bungles!"
And sent him off to distant jungles.
Camped on a tropic riverside,
One day he missed his loving bride.
She had, the guide informed him later,
Been eaten by an alligator.
Professor Twist could not but smile.
"You mean," he said, "a crocodile."

A CONVERSATION ABOUT A FUTURE LIFE

Leo N. Tolstoy

(TRANSLATOR: Constance Garnett)

Pierre interrupted him. "Do you believe in a future life?" he asked.
"In a future life?" repeated Prince Andrey.
But Pierre did not give him time to answer, and took this repetition as a negative reply, the more readily as he knew Prince Andrey's atheistic views in the past. "You say that you can't see the dominion of good and truth on the earth. I have not seen it either, and it cannot be seen if one looks out upon our life as the end of everything. On earth, this earth here" (Pierre pointed to the open country), "there is no truth—all this deception and wickedness. But in the world, the whole world, there is a dominion of truth, and we are now the children of earth, but eternally the children of the whole universe. Don't I feel in my soul that I am a part of that vast, harmon-

ious whole? Don't I feel that in that vast, innumerable multitude of beings, in which is made manifest the Godhead, the higher power—what you choose to call it—I constitute one grain, one step upward from lower beings to higher ones? If I see, see clearly that ladder that rises up from the vegetable to man, why should I suppose that ladder breaks off with me and does not go on further and further? I feel that I cannot disappear as nothing does disappear in the universe, that indeed I always shall be and always have been. I feel that beside me, above me, there are spirits, and that in their world there is truth."

"Yes, that's Herder's theory," said Prince Andrey. "But it's not that, my dear boy, convinces me; but life and death are what have convinced me. What convinces me is seeing a creature dear to me, and bound up with me, to whom one has done wrong, and hoped to make it right" (Prince Andrey's voice shook and he turned away), "and all at once that creature suffers, is in agony, and ceases to be. . . . What for? It cannot be that there is no answer! And I believe there is. That's what convinces me, that's what has convinced me," said Prince Andrey.

"Just so, just so," said Pierre; "isn't that the very thing I'm saying?"

"No. I only say that one is convinced of the necessity of a future life, not by argument, but when one goes hand-in-hand with some one, and all at once that some one slips away *yonder into nowhere*, and you are left facing that abyss and looking down into it. And I have looked into it . . ."

"Well, that's it then! You know there is a *yonder* and there is *some one. Yonder* is the future life; *Some One* is God."

Prince Andrey did not answer. The coach and horses had long been taken across to the other bank, and had been put back into the shafts, and the sun had half sunk below the horizon, and the frost of evening was starring the pools at the fording-place; but Pierre and Andrey, to the astonishment of the footmen, coachmen, and ferry-men, still stood in the ferry and were still talking.

"If there is a God and there is a future life, then there is truth and there is goodness; and the highest happiness of man consists in striving for their attainment. We must live, we must love, we must believe," said Pierre, "that we are not only living today on this clod of earth, but have lived and will live for ever there in everything" (he pointed to the sky). Prince Andrey stood with his elbow on the rail of the ferry, and as he listened to Pierre he kept his eyes fixed on the red reflection of the sun on the bluish stretch of water. Pierre ceased speaking. There was perfect stillness. The ferry had long since come to a standstill, and only the eddies of the current flapped with a faint sound on the bottom of the ferry boat. It seemed to Prince Andrey that the lapping of the water kept up a refrain to Pierre's words: "It's the truth, believe it."

"Yes, if only it were so!" he said. "Let us go and get in, though," added Prince Andrey, and as he got out of the ferry he looked up at the sky, to which Pierre had pointed him, and for the first time since Austerlitz he saw the lofty, eternal sky, as he had seen it lying on the field of Austerlitz, and something that had long been slumbering, something better that had been in him, suddenly awoke with a joyful, youthful feeling in his soul. That feeling vanished as soon as Prince Andrey returned again to the habitual conditions of life, but he knew that that feeling—though he knew not how to develop it—was still within him. Pierre's visit was for Prince Andrey an epoch, from which there began, though outwardly unchanged, a new life in his inner world.

(From *War and Peace*, Part V, Chapter XII)

THIRTY WORDS

The Ten Most Beautiful Words in English, as suggested by Wilfred Funk:
>   dawn, lullaby, hush, luminous, murmuring, tranquil,
>   mist, chimes, golden, melody.

The Ten Ugliest Words, as suggested by The National Association of Teachers of Speech:
>   phlegmatic, crunch, flatulent, cacophony, treachery, sap,
>   jazz, plutocrat, gripe, plump.

The Ten Most Over-Worked Words, as suggested by Wilfred Funk:
>   okay, terrific, lousy, contact, definitely, gal,
>   racket, swell, impact, honey.

THE WOODPECKER

Coleman Cox

Even the woodpecker owes his success to the fact that he uses his head and keeps pecking away until he finishes the job he starts.

WITH SNOW WHITE VEIL

Henry Wadsworth Longfellow

With snow-white veil and garments as of flame,
    She stands before thee, who so long ago
    Filled thy young heart with passion and the woe
    From which thy song and all its splendors came;
And while with stern rebuke she speaks thy name,
    The ice about thy heart melts as the snow
    On the mountain heights, and in swift overflow
    Comes gushing from thy lips in sobs of shame.
Thou makest full confession; and a gleam,
    As of the dawn on some dark forest cast,
    Seems on thy lifted forehead to increase;
Lethe and Eunoë—the remembered dream
    And the forgotten sorrow—bring at last
    That perfect pardon which is perfect peace.

HELEN OF TROY

William Shakespeare

She's bitter to her country: hear me, Paris:
For every false drop in her bawdy veins
A Grecian's life hath sunk; for every scruple
Of her contaminated carrion weight,
A Trojan hath been slain: since she could speak,
She hath not given so many good words breath
As for her Greeks and Trojans suffer'd death.
             (From *Troilus and Cressida*)

All sorts of allowances are made for the illusions of youth; and none, or almost none, for the disenchantment of age.

             —Robert Louis Stevenson

ABRAHAM LINCOLN MEDITATES ON
THE WILL OF GOD

The will of God prevails. In great contests each party claims to act in accordance with the will of God. Both *may* be and one *must* be wrong. God cannot be *for* and *against* the same thing at the same time. In the present civil war it is quite possible that God's purpose is something different from the purpose of either party; and yet the human instrumentalities, working just as they do, are ready to say that this is probably true; that God wills this contest, and wills that it shall not end yet. By His mere great power on the minds of the now contestants, He could have either *saved* or *destroyed* the Union without a human contest. Yet the contest began. And having begun, He could give the final victory to either side any day. Yet the contest proceeds.

(September 30, 1862)

DAVID GARRICK, THE ACTOR, TO SIR JOHN HILL,
A PHYSICIAN WHO WROTE PLAYS

> For physic and farces,
> Thy equal there scarce is:
> Thy farces are physic,
> Thy physic a farce is.

A TOWN'S TRIBUTE TO ITS FRIEND

William Allen White

The other day in Emporia [Kansas], the longest funeral procession that has formed in ten years followed the Rev. John Jones three long miles in the hot July sun out to Dry Creek Cemetery. Now, a funeral procession may mean little or much. When a rich and powerful man dies, the people play politics and attend his funeral for various reasons. But here was the body of a meek, gentle little old man—a man "without purse or scrip." It won't take twenty minutes to settle his estate in probate court. He was a preacher of the gospel—but preachers have been buried before this in Emporia without much show of sorrow.

The reason so many people lined up behind the hearse that held the kind old man's mortality was simple: they loved him. He devoted his life to helping people. In a very simple way, without money or worldly power, he gave of the gentleness of his heart to all around him. . . . When others gave money—which was of their store—he gave prayers and hard work and an inspiring courage. He helped. In his sphere he was a power. And so when he lay down to sleep hundreds of friends trudged out to bid him good-by with moist eyes and with cramped throats to wish him sweet slumber.

A FOREIGN RULER

Walter Savage Landor

He says, *My reign is peace,* so slays
   A thousand in the dead of night.
Are you all happy now? he says,
   And those he leaves behind cry *quite.*
He swears he will have no contention,
   And sets all nations by the ears;
He shouts aloud, *No intervention!*
   Invades, and drowns them all in tears.

KING LEAR CONDEMNS HIS DAUGHTER

William Shakespeare

Hear, nature, hear; dear goddess, hear!
Suspend thy purpose, if thou didst intend
To make this creature fruitful:
Into her womb convey sterility:
Dry up in her the organs of increase,
And from her derogate body never spring
A babe to honor her! If she must teem,
Create her child of spleen, that it may live
And be a thwart disnatured torment to her.

(487)

Let it stamp wrinkles in her brow of youth;
With cadent tears fret channels in her cheeks;
Turn all her mother's pains and benefits
To laughter and contempt; that she may feel
How sharper than a serpent's tooth it is
To have a thankless child! Away, Away!

(From *King Lear*)

MY WILD IRISH ROSE

Chauncey Olcott

If you listen, I'll sing you a sweet little song
Of a flower that's now drooped and dead,
Yet dearer to me, yes, than all of its mates,
Though each holds aloft its proud head.
'Twas given to me by a girl that I know;
Since we've met, faith, I've known no repose,
She is dearer by far than the world's brightest star,
And I call her my wild Irish rose.

Chorus
My wild Irish rose,
The sweetest flower that grows,
You may search everywhere,
But none can compare
With my wild Irish rose.
My wild Irish rose,
The dearest flower that grows,
And some day for my sake
She may let me take
The bloom from my wild Irish rose.

They may sing of their roses which by other names,
Would smell just as sweetly, they say,
But I know that my Rose would never consent
To have that sweet name taken away.
Her glances are shy when e'er I pass by
The bower where my true love grows.
And my one wish has been that some day I may win
The heart of my wild Irish rose.

THE WIT OF ADLAI STEVENSON

Man does not live by words alone, despite the fact that sometimes he has to eat them.

On Taxes: There was a time when a fool and his money were soon parted, but now it happens to everybody.

Do you know the difference between a beautiful woman and a charming one? A beauty is a woman you notice, a charmer is one who notices you.

The relationship of the toastmaster to speaker should be the same as that of the fan to the fan dancer. It should call attention to the subject without making any particular effort to cover it.

Eggheads unite—you have nothing to lose but your yolks.

I have sometimes said that flattery is all right—if you don't inhale.

You know how it is in an election year. They pick a President and then for four years they pick on him.

I have finally figured out what the Republican orators mean by what they call "moderate progressivism." All they mean is: "Don't just do something. Stand there."

In 1956, after losing a Presidential election for the second time: I think I missed my calling. As a matter of fact, I think I missed it twice.

Winter lingered so long in the lap of Spring that it occasioned a great deal of talk.

—Bill Nye

THE WINDHOVER
To Christ our Lord

Gerard Manley Hopkins

I caught this morning morning's minion, king-
dom of daylight's dauphin, dapple-dawn-drawn Falcon, in his riding
Of the rolling level underneath him steady air, and striding
High there, how he rung upon the rein of a wimpling wing
In his ecstasy! then off, off forth on swing,
As a skate's heel sweeps smooth on a bow-bend: the hurl and gliding
Rebuffed the big wind. My heart in hiding
Stirred for a bird,—the achieve of, the mastery of the thing!

Brute beauty and valour and act, oh, air, pride, plume, here
Buckle! AND the fire that breaks from thee then, a billion
Times told lovelier, more dangerous, O my chevalier!
No wonder of it: shéer plód makes plough down sillion
Shine, and blue-bleak embers, ah my dear,
Fall, gall themselves, and gash gold-vermilion.

THE STERN PARENT

Harry Graham

Father heard his children scream,
So he threw them in the stream,
Saying, as he drowned the third,
"Children should be seen, *not* heard!"

Liquor talks mighty loud when it gets loose from the jug.
—Joel Chandler Harris

THE HERO AND THE SAINT

Felix Adler

The hero is one who kindles a great light in the world, who sets up blazing torches in the dark streets of life for men to see by. The saint is the man who walks through the dark paths of the world, himself a "light".

A LITTLE SONG OF LIFE

Lizette Woodworth Reese

Glad that I live am I;
That the sky is blue;
Glad for the country lanes,
And the fall of dew.

After the sun the rain,
After the rain the sun;
This is the way of life,
Till the work be done.

All that we need to do,
Be we low or high,
Is to see that we grow
Nearer the sky.

WILLIAM FAULKNER'S RESIGNATION AS POSTMASTER

As long as I live under the capitalistic system I expect to have my life influenced by the demands of moneyed people. But I will be damned if I propose to be at the beck and call of every itinerant scoundrel who has two cents to invest in a postage stamp. This, sir, is my resignation.

ASTROPHEL TO STELLA

Sir Philip Sidney

Loving in truth, and fain in verse my love to show,
    That she, dear she, might take some pleasure of my pain;
Pleasure might cause her read, reading might make her know,
    Knowledge might pity win, and pity grace obtain:
I sought fit words to paint the blackest face of woe;
    Studying inventions fine, her wits to entertain,
Oft turning others' leaves to see if thence would flow
    Some fresh and fruitful showers upon my sun-burned brain.
But words came halting forth, wanting Invention's stay;
    Invention, Nature's child, fled step-dame Study's blows,
And others' feet still seemed but strangers in my way.
    Thus, great with child to speak, and helpless in my throes,
    Biting my truant pen, beating myself for spite:
    "Fool," said my Muse to me, "look in thy heart and write!"

THE GOOD-MORROW

John Donne

I wonder by my troth, what thou, and I
Did, till we lov'd? were we not wean'd till then?
But suck'd on countrey pleasures, childishly?
Or snorted we in the Seven Sleepers den?
T'was so; But this, all pleasures fancies bee.
If ever any beauty I did see
Which I desir'd, and got, t'was but a dreame of thee.

And now good morrow to our waking soules,
Which watch not one another out of feare;
For love all love of other sights controules,
And makes one little roome an every where.
Let sea-discoverers to new worlds have gone,
Let Maps to other, worlds on worlds have showne,
Let us possesse one world; each hath one, and is one.

My face in thine eye, thine in mine appeares,
And true, plaine hearts doe in the faces rest;
Where can we finde two fitter hemispheares
Without sharpe North, without declining West?
Whatever dyes, was not mixt equally;
If our two loves be one, or, thou and I
Love so alike that none doe slacken, none can die.

LAWYER LINCOLN ANSWERS AN INQUIRY CONCERNING THE FINANCIAL STANDING OF A FELLOW TOWNSMAN

First of all, he has a wife and baby; together they ought to be worth $500,000 to any man. Secondly, he has an office in which there is a table worth $1.50, and three chairs, worth, say $1.00. Last of all, there is in one corner a large rathole, which will bear looking into.

Respectfully,

A. Lincoln

THE ROSE OF TRALEE

C. Mordaunt Spencer

The pale moon was rising above the green mountain,
The sun was declining beneath the blue sea,
When I strayed with my love to the pure crystal fountain
That stands in the beautiful vale of Tralee;
She was lovely and fair as the rose of the summer,
Yet 'twas not her beauty alone that won me.
Oh, no! 'Twas the truth in her eye ever dawning,
That made me love Mary, The Rose of Tralee.

The cool shades of evening their mantle were spreading,
And Mary all smiling was listening to me.
The moon through the valley her pale rays was shedding,
When I won the heart of The Rose of Tralee;
Though lovely and fair as the rose of the summer,
Yet 'twas not her beauty alone that won me.
Oh, no! 'Twas the truth in her eye ever dawning,
That made me love Mary, The Rose of Tralee.

(493)

JUDGMENT

Anonymous

Before God's footstool to confess
A poor soul knelt, and bowed his head;
"I failed," he cried. The Master said,
"Thou didst thy best—that is success!"

ANYTHING GOD, BUT HATE

Anonymous

Anything, God, but hate;
I have known it in my day,
And the best it does is scar your soul
And eat your heart away.
Man must know more than hate,
As the years go rolling on;
For the stars survive and the spring survives,
Only man denies the dawn.
God, if I have but one prayer
Before the cloud-wrapped end,
I'm sick of hate and the waste it makes.
Let me be my brother's friend.

THE FARMER AND THE FOX

Aesop

A farmer, having a long grievance against a fox for robbing from his chicken yard, caught the fox at last, and was determined to take full revenge on him. He tied a cloth soaked in oil to the fox's tail, and then set it on fire. The fox, by a strange fatality, rushed through the fields of the farmer. It was the time of the wheat harvest, and the flaming tail of the fox set the wheat on fire, and it was all destroyed. The farmer reaped nothing that year.

COMMONPLACE

Susan Coolidge

"A commonplace life," we say, and we sigh,
But why should we sigh as we say?
The commonplace sun in the commonplace sky
Makes up the commonplace day;
The moon and the stars are commonplace things,
And the flower that blooms, and the bird that sings,
But dark were the world, and sad our lot,
If the flowers failed, and the sun shone not;
And God, who studies each separate soul,
Out of commonplace lives makes His beautiful whole.

ONE DAY AT A TIME

Ralph Waldo Emerson

Finish every day and be done with it. You have done what you could. Some blunders and absurdities no doubt crept in; forget them as soon as you can. Tomorrow is a new day; begin it well and serenely and with too high a spirit to be cumbered with your old nonsense. This day is all that is good and fair. It is too dear, with its hopes and invitations, to waste a moment on the yesterdays.

REMEMBRANCE

Emily Brontë

Cold in the earth—and the deep snow piled above thee,
Far, far removed, cold in the dreary grave!
Have I forgot, my only Love, to love thee,
Severed at last by Time's all-severing wave?

Now, when alone, do my thoughts no longer hover
Over the mountains, on that northern shore,
Resting their wings where heath and fern-leaves cover
The noble heart for ever, ever more?

Cold in the earth—and fifteen wild Decembers,
From those brown hills, have melted into spring:
Faithful, indeed, is the spirit that remembers
After such years of change and suffering!

Sweet love of youth, forgive, if I forget thee,
While the world's tide is bearing me along;
Other desires and other hopes beset me,
Hopes which obscure, but cannot do thee wrong!

No other sun has lightened up my heaven,
No other star has ever shone for me;
All my life's bliss from thy dear life was given,
All my life's bliss is in the grave with thee.

But, when the days of golden dreams had perished,
And even Despair was powerless to destroy;
Then did I learn how existence could be cherished,
Strengthened and fed without the aid of joy.

Then did I check the tears of useless passion—
Weaned my young soul from yearning after thine;
Sternly denied its burning wish to hasten
Down to that tomb already more than mine.

And, even yet, I dare not let it languish,
Dare not indulge in memory's rapturous pain;
Once drinking deep of that divinest anguish,
How could I seek the empty world again?

After reading the epitaphs in the cemetery, you wonder
where they bury the sinners.

—Anonymous

(496)

A FATEFUL MESSAGE AND AN ANNOUNCEMENT
THAT SHOOK THE WORLD

August 6, 1945

TO THE PRESIDENT
FROM THE SECRETARY OF WAR

Big bomb dropped on Hiroshima August 5 at 7.15 P.M. Washington time. First reports indicate complete success which was even more conspicuous than earlier test.

Hiroshima bombed visibly with only one tenth cover at 052315A. There was no fighter opposition and no flak. Parsons reports 15 minutes after drop as follows: "Results clear cut successful in all respects. Visible effects greater than in any test. Conditions normal in airplane following delivery."

HARRY S TRUMAN ANNOUNCES THE FIRST
ATOMIC BOMB

Sixteen hours ago an American airplane dropped one bomb on Hiroshima. . . . It is a harnessing of the basic power of the universe. The force from which the sun draws its powers has been loosed against those who brought war to the Far East. We have spent two billion dollars on the greatest scientific gamble in history—and won.

(August 6, 1945)

PRESIDENT TRUMAN TO CONGRESS, JANUARY 7, 1953

Recently in the thermonuclear tests at Eniwetok, we have entered another stage in the world-shaking development of atomic energy. From now on man moves into a new era of destructive power, capable of creating explosions of a new order of magnitude, dwarfing the mushroom clouds of Hiroshima and Nagasaki.

A TRANQUIL CONSCIENCE

Thomas à Kempis

Great tranquillity of heart hath he that careth neither for praises nor the fault-finding of men. He will easily be content and pacified whose conscience is pure. Thou art not the more holy, if thou art praised; nor the more worthless, if thou art found fault with. What thou art, that thou art; neither by words canst thou be made greater than what thou art in the sight of God.

I THOUGHT ONCE HOW THEOCRITUS HAD SUNG

Elizabeth Barrett Browning

I thought once how Theocritus had sung
Of the sweet years, the dear and wished-for years,
Who each one in a gracious hand appears
To bear a gift for mortals, old or young:
And, as I mused it in his antique tongue,
I saw, in gradual vision through my tears,
The sweet, sad years, the melancholy years,
Those of my own life, who by turns had flung
A shadow across me. Straightway I was 'ware,
So weeping, how a mystic Shape did move
Behind me, and drew me backward by the hair;
And a voice said in mastery, while I strove,—
"Guess now who holds thee?"—"Death," I said. But, there,
The silver answer rang—"Not Death, but Love."

JESUS AND THE WOMAN AT THE WELL

Holy Bible, John 4:5–26

Then cometh he to a city of Samaria, which is called Sychar, near to the parcel of ground that Jacob gave to his son Joseph.

Now Jacob's well was there. Jesus therefore, being wearied with his journey, sat thus on the well: and it was about the sixth hour.

There cometh a woman of Samaria to draw water: Jesus saith unto her, Give me to drink.

(For his disciples were gone away unto the city to buy meat.)

Then saith the woman of Samaria unto him, How is it that thou, being a Jew, askest drink of me, which am a woman of Samaria? for the Jews have no dealings with the Samaritans.

Jesus answered and said unto her, If thou knewest the gift of God, and who it is that saith to thee, Give me to drink: thou wouldest have asked of him, and he would have given thee living water.

The woman saith unto him, Sir, thou hast nothing to draw with, and the well is deep: from whence then hast thou that living water?

Art thou greater than our father Jacob, which gave us the well, and drank thereof himself, and his children, and his cattle?

Jesus answered and said unto her, Whosoever drinketh of this water shall thirst again:

But whosoever drinketh of the water that I shall give him shall never thirst; but the water that I shall give him shall be in him a well of water springing up into everlasting life.

The woman saith unto him, Sir, give me this water, that I thirst not, neither come hither to draw.

Jesus saith unto her, Go, call thy husband and come hither.

The woman answered and said, I have no husband. Jesus said unto her, Thou hast well said, I have no husband:

For thou hast had five husbands; and he whom thou now hast is not thy husband: in that saidst thou truly.

The woman said unto him, Sir, I perceive that thou art a prophet.

Our fathers worshipped in this mountain; and ye say, that in Jerusalem is the place where men ought to worship.

Jesus saith unto her, Woman, believe me, the hour cometh, when ye shall neither in this mountain, nor yet at Jerusalem, worship the Father.

Ye worship ye know not what: we know what we worship: for salvation is of the Jews.

But the hour cometh, and now is, when the true worshippers shall worship the Father in spirit and in truth: for the Father seeketh such to worship him.

God is a Spirit: and they that worship him must worship him in spirit and in truth.

The woman saith unto him, I know that Messias cometh, which is called Christ: when he is come, he will tell us all things.

Jesus saith unto her, I that speak unto thee am he.

WEDDING SIGNS

Anonymous

Married in white, you have chosen all right.
Married in gray, you will go far away.
Married in black, you will wish yourself back.
Married in red, you will wish yourself dead.
Married in green, ashamed to be seen.
Married in blue, he will always be true.
Married in pearl, you will live in a whirl.
Married in yellow, ashamed of your fellow.
Married in brown, you will live out of town.
Married in pink, your fortune will sink.

I THINK CONTINUALLY OF THOSE WHO WERE TRULY GREAT

Stephen Spender

I think continually of those who were truly great
Who, from the womb, remembered the soul's history
Through corridors of light where the hours are suns,
Endless and singing. Whose lovely ambition
Was that their lips, still touched with fire,
Should tell of the spirit clothed from head to foot in song.
And who hoarded from the spring branches
The desires falling across their bodies like blossoms.

What is precious is never to forget
The delight of the blood drawn from ageless springs
Breaking through rocks in worlds before our earth;
Never to deny its pleasure in the simple morning light,
Nor its grave evening demand for love;
Never to allow gradually the traffic to smother
With noise and fog the flowering of the spirit.

Near the snow, near the sun, in the highest fields
See how these names are feted by the waving grass,
And by the streamers of white cloud,

(500)

And whispers of wind in the listening sky;
The names of those who in their lives fought for life,
Who wore at their hearts the fire's center.
Born of the sun they traveled a short while towards the sun,
And left the vivid air signed with their honour.

WHAT CAN I DO?

Horace Traubel

What can I do? I can talk out when others are silent. I can say man when others say money. I can stay up when others are asleep. I can keep on working when others have stopped to play. I can give life big meanings when others give life little meanings. I can say love when others say hate. I can say every man when others say one man. I can try events by a hard test when others try it by an easy test.

What can I do? I can give myself to life when other men refuse themselves to life.

I HOLD HIM HAPPIEST

Menander

I hold him happiest
Who, before going quickly whence he came,
Hath looked ungrieving on these majesties,
The world-wide sun, the stars, waters and clouds
And fire. Live, Parmeno, a hundred years
Or a few weeks, these thou wilt always see,
And never, never, any greater thing.

BLACK IS THE COLOR OF MY TRUE LOVE'S HAIR

Anonymous

Black, black, black is the color of my true love's hair,
Her lips are like some rosy fair,
The prettiest face and the neatest hands,
I love the ground whereon she stands.

I love my love and well she knows,
I love the grass whereon she goes,
If she on earth no more I see,
I can't serve her as she has me.

I go to Troublesome to mourn and weep,
But satisfied I never could sleep.
I'll write to you in a few little lines.
I'll suffer death ten thousand times.

So fare you well, my own true love,
The time has passed and I wish you well.
But still I hope the time will come
When you and I will be one.

BE PRESENT AT OUR TABLE, LORD

John Cennick

Be present at our table, Lord;
Be here and everywhere adored;
Thy creatures bless and grant that we
May feast in paradise with Thee.

LET ME LIVE BUT FROM YEAR TO YEAR

Henry van Dyke

Let me but live from year to year,
    With forward face and unreluctant soul;
    Not hurrying to, nor turning from the goal;
Not mourning for the things that disappear
In the dim past, nor holding back in fear
    From what the future veils; but with a whole
    And happy heart, that pays its toll
To Youth and Age, and travels on with cheer.

So let the way wind up the hill or down
 O'er rough or smooth, the journey will be joy;
 Still seeking what I sought when but a boy,
New friendship, high adventure, and a crown,
 My heart will keep the courage of the quest,
 And hope the road's last turn will be the best.

GUESTS AT A GROUND-BREAKING

H. I. Phillips

"I didn't see your picture in the paper," we said to the Unknown Soldier, commenting on recent ceremonies marking the beginning of work on the United Nations' new home on the East River, New York.

"No," replied the Unknown Warrior. "But I was there."

Of course he was there. We should have known it. The Unknown Soldiers of all the great nations were there, with the countless dead of 10,000 battlefields and campaigns through the centuries. Colin Kelly was there, and Meyer Levin. Ernie Pyle sat on a mound of freshly turned earth watching attentively. There were GI Joes, and Marines and sailors and airmen. . . . Men from the armies of Caesar, Napoleon, Haig, Foch, Washington, Grant, Lee, Scott and Eisenhower. . . . Ghostly figures come out of Thermopylae, Troy, the Alamo, Balaklava, Waterloo, Gettysburg, Château Thierry, Guadalcanal and Bastogne.

They were there with skepticism in their faces, but with a prayer on their lips. . . . One common prayer, "Please, Lord, make it come out right this time!"

There were women, too, watching and praying and hoping . . . Nurse Cavell, Clara Barton, Joan of Arc, and the spirits of the great hosts of Gold Star mothers, countless orphans and widows. . . .

Photographers rushed around heedlessly, snapping mayors and diplomats. They missed the people that really counted. . . . They didn't plead "Another smile, a big, wide one!" with the dead come back from Iwo Jima, Salerno and Cassino. . . . They didn't say "Hold your hand up, waving" to any delegates from the hells of Pearl Harbor, the Coral Sea, Soissons, Mons, Harpers Ferry, Khartoum, Crecy, Blenheim.

Unphotographed and unnoticed too by the photographers and

reporters stood an odd group: Lincoln, Grant, Lee, Pickett, Pompey, Hannibal and Joe Doakes.

As dusk settled over the steam shovels a striking apparition was seen. . . . It was that of a Man on a Cross. . . . And a voice said to those who would hear, "Blessed are they which do hunger and thirst after righteousness; for they shall be filled. . . . Blessed are the merciful for they shall obtain mercy. . . . Blessed are the peace-makers, for they shall be called the Children of God."

THOU EASER OF ALL WOES

John Fletcher and Francis Beaumont

Care-charming sleep, thou easer of all woes,
Brother to Death, sweetly thyself dispose
On this afflicted prince. Fall, like a cloud,
In gentle showers; give nothing that is loud
Or painful to his slumbers; easy, sweet,
And as a purling stream, thou son of Night,
Pass by his troubled senses; sing his pain,
Like hollow murmuring wind, or silver rain;
Into this prince, gently, oh, gently slide,
And kiss him into slumbers, like a bride!

FREE TRADE IN IDEAS

Justice Oliver Wendell Holmes

But when men have realized that time has upset many fighting faiths, they may come to believe even more than they believe the very foundations of their own conduct that the ultimate good desired is better reached by free trade in ideas—that the best test of truth is the power of the thought to get itself accepted in the competition of the market, and that truth is the only ground upon which their wishes safely can be carried out. That at any rate is the theory of our Constitution. It is an experiment, as all life is an experiment.

(1919)

RUMORS

Reginald Arkell

Actual evidence I have none,
But my aunt's charwoman's sister's son
Heard a policeman, on his beat,
Say to a housemaid in Downing Street
That he had a brother, who had a friend,
Who knew when the war was going to end.

HUCK FINN'S OLD MAN CONDEMNS THE GOVERNMENT

Mark Twain

While I was cooking supper the old man took a swig or two and got sort of warmed up, and went to ripping again. He had been drunk over in town, and laid in the gutter all night, and he was a sight to look at. A body would have thought he was Adam—he was just all mud. Whenever his liquor began to work he most always went for the government! This time he says:

"Call this a govment! why just look at it and see what it's like. Here's the law a-standing ready to take a man's son away from him—a man's own son, which he has had all the trouble and all the anxiety and all the expense of raising. Yes, just as that man has got that son raised at last, and ready to go to work and begin to do sumthin' for *him* and give him a rest, the law up and goes for him. And they call *that* govment! That ain't all, nuther. The law backs that old Judge Thatcher up and helps him to keep me out o' my property. Here's what the law does: The law takes a man worth six thousand dollars and up'ards, and jams him into an old trap of a cabin like this, and lets him go round in clothes that ain't fitten for a hog. They call that govment! A man can't get his rights in a govment like this. Sometime's I've a mighty notion to just leave the country for good and all. Yes, and I *told* 'em so; I told old Thatcher so to his face. Lots of 'em heard me, and can tell what I said. Says I, for two cents I'd leave the blamed country and never come a-near it ag'in. Them's the very words. I says, look at my hat—if you call it a hat—but the lid raises up and the rest of it goes down till it's below my chin, and then it ain't rightly a hat at all, but more like my head

(505)

was shoved up through the jint o' stove-pipe. Look at it, says I—such a hat for me to wear—one of the wealthiest men in this town if I could git my rights.

"Oh, yes, this is a wonderful govment, wonderful. Why looky here. There was a free nigger there from Ohio—a mulateer, most as white as a white man. He had the whitest shirt on you ever see, too, and the shinest hat; and there ain't a man in that town that's got as fine clothes as what he had; and he had a gold watch and chain, and a silver-headed cane—the awfulest old gray-headed nabob in the state. And what do you think? They said he was a p'fessor in a college, and could talk all kinds of languages, and knowed everything. And that ain't the wust. They said he could *vote* when he was at home. Well, that let me out. Thinks I, what is the country a-coming to? It was 'lection day, and I was about to go and vote myself if I warn't too drunk to get there; but when they told me there was a state in this country where they'd let that nigger vote, I drawed up. I says I'll never vote ag'in. Them's the very words I said; they all heard me; and the country may rot for all me—I'll never vote ag'in as long as I live. And to see the cool way of that nigger—why he wouldn't a' give me the road if I hadn't shoved him out o' the way. I says to the people, why ain't this nigger put up at auction and sold?—that's what I want to know. And what do you reckon they said? Why they said he couldn't be sold till he's been in the state six months, and he hadn't been there that long yet. There, now—that's a specimen. They call that a govment that can't sell a free nigger till he's been in the state six months. Here's a govment that calls itself a govment, and lets on to be a govment, and thinks it is a govment, and yet's got to set stock still for six whole months before it can take a-hold of a prowling, thieving, infernal, white-shirted free nigger, and—"

Pap was a-going on so he never noticed where his old limber legs were taking him to, so he went head over heels over the tub of salt pork and barked both shins, and the rest of his speech was all the hottest kind of language—mostly hove at the nigger and the govment, though he give the tub some too, all along, here and there.

FAITH

Blaise Pascal

It is the heart which experiences God, and not the reason. This, then, is faith: God felt by the heart, not by the reason.

Faith is a gift of God; do not believe that we said it was a gift of reasoning. Other religions do not say this of their faith. They only give reasoning in order to arrive at it, and yet it does not bring them to it.

VALEDICTION FORBIDDING MOURNING

John Donne

As virtuous men pass mildly away,
   And whisper to their souls to go,
Whilst some of their sad friends do say,
   "The breath goes now," and some say "No";

So let us melt and make no noise,
   No tear-floods nor sigh-tempests move;
'Twere profanation of our joys
   To tell the laity our love.

Moving of th' earth brings harms and fears;
   Men reckon what it did and meant;
But trepidation of the spheres,
   Though greater far, is innocent.

Dull sublunary lovers' love
   (Whose soul is sense) cannot admit
Absence, because it doth remove
   Those things which elemented it.

But we by a love so much refined
   That ourselves know not what it is,
Inter-assurèd of the mind,
   Careless eyes, lips, and hands to miss.

Our two souls, therefore, which are one,
  Though I must go, endure not yet
A breach, but an expansion,
  Like gold to airy thinness beat.

If they be two, they are two so
  As stiff twin compasses are two;
Thy soul, the fixt foot, makes no show
  To move, but both do if the other do.

And though it in the center sit,
  Yet when the other far doth roam,
It leans and harkens after it,
  And grows erect as that comes home.

Such wilt thou be to me, who must
  Like th' other foot, obliquely run;
Thy firmness makes my circle just,
  And makes me end, where I begun.

IDA, SWEET AS APPLE CIDER

Eddie Leonard

In the region where the roses always bloom,
Breathing out upon the air their sweet perfume,
Lives a dusky maid I long to call my own,
For I know my love for her will never die;
When the sun is sinking in the golden West,
Little Robin Red Breasts gone to seek their nests,
Then I sneak down to the place I love the best,
Every evening there alone I sigh.

Chorus
Ida! sweet as apple cider,
Sweeter than all I know,
Come out, in the silvery moonlight,
Of love we'll whisper, so soft and low!
Seems I can't live without you,
Listen, Oh! Honey, do!
Ida! I idolize yer,
I love you, Ida, indeed I do.

(508)

When the moon comes stealing up behind the hill,
Everything around seems so calm and still;
Save the gentle calling of the whip-poor-will,
Then I long to hold her little hand in mine,
Through the trees the winds are sighing soft and low;
Seems to come and whisper that your love is true;
Come and be my own now, Sweetheart, do, oh do!
Then my life will seem almost divine.

KING LEAR PLEDGES REVENGE

William Shakespeare

You see me here, you gods, a poor old man,
As full of grief as age; wretched in both:
If it be you that stirs these daughters' hearts
Against their father, fool me not so much
To bear it tamely; touch me with noble anger,
And let not women's weapons, water-drops,
Stain my man's cheeks! No, you unnatural hags,
I will have such revenge on you both
That all the world shall—I will do such things,—
What they are, yet I know not, but they shall be
The terrors of the earth. You think I'll weep;
No, I'll not weep:
I have full cause of weeping; but this heart
Shall break into a hundred thousand flaws,
Or ere I'll weep, O fool, I shall go mad!

(From *King Lear*)

THE DONKEY

G. K. Chesterton

When fishes flew and forests walked
    And figs grew upon thorn,
Some moment when the moon was blood
    Then surely I was born;

(509)

With monstrous head and sickening cry
   And ears like errant wings,
The devil's walking parody
   Of all four-footed things.

The tattered outlaw of the earth,
   Of ancient crooked will;
Starve, scourge, deride me: I am dumb,
   I keep my secret still.

Fools! For I also had my hour;
   One far fierce hour and sweet:
There was a shout about my ears,
   And palms before my feet.

OSCAR WILDE WRITES FROM PRISON

If after I am free a friend gave a feast, and did not invite me to it,
I should not mind a bit. I can be perfectly happy by myself. With
freedom, flowers, books, and the moon, who could not be perfectly
happy! . . . But if after I am free a friend of mine had a sorrow and
refused to allow me to share it, I should feel it more bitterly. If he
shut the door of the house of mourning against me, I would come
back again and again and beg to be admitted, so that I might share
in what I was entitled to share in. If he thought me unworthy, unfit
to weep with him, I should feel it as the most poignant humiliation,
as the most terrible mode in which disgrace could be inflicted on me.

From AUGURIES OF INNOCENCE

William Blake

A robin redbreast in a cage
Puts all heaven in a rage. . . .
He who shall hurt the little wren
Shall never be beloved by men.
He who the ox to wrath has moved
Shall never be by woman loved.

(510)

The wanton boy that kills the fly
Shall feel the spider's enmity . . .
The harlot's cry from street to street
Shall weave Old England's winding-sheet. . . .
Every night and every morn
Some to misery are born,
Every morn and every night
Some are born to sweet delight.
Some are born to sweet delight
Some are born to endless night.

IDEALS

Carl Schurz

Ideals are like stars; you will not succeed in touching them with
your hands. But like the seafaring man on the desert of waters, you
choose them as your guides, and following them you will reach your
destiny.

LIGHT IN DARKNESS

Talmud

When Adam saw for the first time the sun go down, and an ever-
deepening gloom enfold creation, his mind was filled with terror.
God then took pity on him, and endowed him with the divine in-
tuition to take two stones—the name of one was Darkness and the
name of the other Shadow of Death—and rub them against each
other, and so discover fire. Thereupon Adam exclaimed with grateful joy: "Blessed be the Creator of Light."

JOHN ANDERSON

Robert Burns

John Anderson my jo, John,
   When we were first acquent
Your locks were like the raven,
   Your bonnie brow was brent;
But now your brow is beld, John,
   Your locks are like the snaw;
But blessings on your frosty pow,
   John Anderson my jo.

John Anderson my jo, John,
   We clamb the hill thegither,
And monie a canty day, John,
   We've had wi' ane anither:
Now we maun totter down, John,
   But hand in hand we'll go,
And sleep thegither at the foot,
   John Anderson my jo.

BROTHERHOOD

Abraham Lincoln

Let us at all times remember that all
American citizens are brothers of a
common country, and should dwell together
in bonds of fraternal feeling.

MEETING AT NIGHT

Robert Browning

The grey sea and the long black land;
And the yellow half-moon large and low;
And the startled little waves that leap
In fiery ringlets from their sleep,
As I gain the cove with pushing prow,
And quench its speed i' the slushy sand

Then a mile of warm sea-scented beach;
Three fields to cross till a farm appears;
A tap at the pane, the quick sharp scratch
And blue spurt of a lighted match,
And a voice less loud, thro' its joys and fears,
Than the two hearts beating each to each!

ONE HOUR OF LIFE

Sir Walter Scott

One hour of life, crowded to the full with glorious action, and filled with noble risks, is worth whole years of those mean observances of paltry decorum, in which men steal through existence, like sluggish waters through a marsh, without either honour or observation.

PRAYER FOR SERENITY

Reinhold Niebuhr

O God, grant us the serenity to accept
What cannot be changed;
The courage to change what can be changed,
And the wisdom to know the one from the other.

A BIRD IN A GILDED CAGE

Arthur J. Lamb

The ball-room was filled with fashion's throng,
It shone with a thousand lights,
And there was a woman who passed along,
The fairest of all the sights.
A girl to her lover then softly sighed
"There's riches at her command";
"But she married for wealth, not for love," he cried,
"Though she lives in a mansion grand."

(513)

Chorus
She's only a bird in a gilded cage,
A beautiful sight to see,
You may think she's happy and free from care;
She's not, though she seems to be.
'Tis said when you think of her wasted life,
For youth cannot mate with age,
And her beauty was sold for an old man's gold,
She's a bird in a gilded cage.

I stood in a church-yard just at eve,
When sunset adorned the west,
And looked at the people who'd come to grieve,
For loved ones now laid at rest.
A tall marble monument marked the grave
Of one who'd been fashion's queen,
And I thought, "She is happier here at rest,
Than to have people say when seen":

(*Chorus.*)

LOUIS PASTEUR PROCLAIMS THE EXISTENCE OF THE INFINITE

He who proclaims the existence of the Infinite—and none can
avoid it—accumulates in that affirmation more of the supernatural
than is to be found in all the miracles of all the religions; for the
notion of the Infinite presents that double character that forces
itself upon us and yet is incomprehensible. When this notion seizes
upon our understanding we can but kneel. . . . I see everywhere the
inevitable expression of the Infinite in our world: through it the
supernatural is at the bottom of every heart. The idea of God is
a form of the idea of the Infinite. As long as the mystery of the
Infinite weighs on human thought, temples will be erected for the
worship of the Infinite, whether God is called Brahma, Allah, Jehovah
or Jesus, and on the pavement of those temples men will be seen
kneeling, prostrated, annihilated in the thought of the Infinite.
Blessed is he who carries within himself a God, an ideal, and who
obeys it: ideal of art, ideal of science, ideal of the gospel virtues,
therein lie the springs of great thoughts and great actions; they all
reflect light from the Infinite.

(514)

BACK

Wilfrid Gibson

They ask me where I've been,
And what I've done and seen.
But what can I reply
Who knows it wasn't I,
But someone just like me,
Who went across the sea
And with my head and hands
Killed men in foreign lands . . .
Though I must bear the blame
Because he bore my name.

FOR DEFENSE AND PEACE

Book of Common Prayer

O God, who art the author of peace and lover of concord, in knowledge of whom standeth our eternal life, whose service is perfect freedom: defend us thy humble servants in all assaults of our enemies; that we, surely trusting in thy defense, may not fear the power of any adversaries.

O God, from whom all holy desires, all good counsels, and all just works do proceed: Give unto thy servants that peace which the world cannot give; that both our hearts may be set to obey thy commandments, and also by thee we being defended from the fear of our enemies may pass our time in rest and quietness.

SALUTATION OF THE DAWN

Listen to the Exhortation of the Dawn!
Look to this Day!
For it is Life, the very Life of Life.
In its brief course lie all the
Verities and Realities of your Existence:

The Bliss of Growth,
The Glory of Action,
The Splendor of Beauty,
For Yesterday is but a Dream,
And To-morrow is only a Vision:
But Today well-lived makes
Every Yesterday a Dream of Happiness,
And every To-morrow a Vision of Hope.
Look well therefore to this Day!
Such is the Salutation of the Dawn!

(From the Sanskrit,
sometimes attributed to Kalidasa)

MIKE O'DAY

Anonymous

This is the grave of Mike O'Day
Who died maintaining his right of way.
His right was clear, his will was strong,
But he's just as dead as if he'd been wrong.

LITTLE BROWN CHURCH IN THE VALE

William S. Pitts

There's a church in the valley by the wildwood,
No lovelier place in the dale;
No spot is so dear to my childhood
As the little brown church in the vale.

Chorus
Oh, come to the church in the wildwood,
Oh, come to the church in the dale,
No spot is so dear to my childhood
As the little brown church in the vale.

How sweet on a bright Sabbath morning,
To list to the clear ringing bell;
Its tones so sweet are calling
Oh, come to the church in the vale.

FROM THE U. S. SUPREME COURT DECISION
OUTLAWING SEGREGATION IN THE PUBLIC SCHOOLS

We conclude that in the field of public education the doctrine of "separate but equal" has no place. Separate educational facilities are inherently unequal. Therefore, we hold that the plaintiffs and others similarly situated for whom the actions have been brought are, by reason of the segregation complained of, deprived of the equal protection of the laws guaranteed by the Fourteenth Amendment. This disposition makes unnecessary any discussion whether such segregation also violates the Due Process Clause of the Fourteenth Amendment.

Because these are class actions, because of the wide applicability of this decision, and because of the great variety of local conditions, the formulation of decrees in these cases presents problems of considerable complexity. On reargument, the consideration of appropriate relief was necessarily subordinate to the primary question—the constitutionality of segregation in public education.

We have now announced that such segregation is a denial of the equal protection of the laws.

(*Brown vs. Board of Education of Topeka*, May 17, 1954)

IN DISTRUST OF MERITS

Marianne Moore

Strengthened to live, strengthened to die for
    medals and position victories?
They're fighting, fighting, fighting the blind
    man who thinks he sees,—
who cannot see that the enslaver is
enslaved; the hater, harmed. O shining O

firm star, O tumultous
ocean lashed till small things go
as they will, the mountainous
wave makes us who look, know

depth. Lost at sea before they fought! O
star of David, star of Bethlehem,
O black imperial lion
of the Lord—emblem
of a risen world—be joined at last, be
joined. There is hate's crown beneath which all is
death; there's love without which none
is king; the blessed deeds bless
the halo. As contagion
of sickness makes sickness,

contagion of trust can make trust. They're
fighting in deserts and caves, one by
one, in battalions and squadrons;
they're fighting that I
may yet recover from the disease, My
Self; some have it lightly, some will die. "Man's
wolf to man" and we devour
ourselves. The enemy could not
have made a greater breach in our
defenses. One pilot-

ing a blind man can escape him, but
Job disheartened by false comfort knew
that nothing can be so defeating
as a blind man who
can see. O alive who are dead, who are
proud not to see, O small dust of the earth
that walks so arrogantly,
trust begets power and faith is
an affectionate thing. We
vow, we make this promise

to the fighting—it's a promise— "We'll
never hate black, white, red, yellow, Jew,
Gentile, Untouchable." We are
not competent to
make our vows. With set jaw they are fighting,

fighting, fighting,—some we love whom we know.
     some we love but know not—that
         hearts may feel and not be numb.
    It cures me; or am I what
      I can't believe in? Some

in snow, some on crags, some in quicksands,
    little by little, much by much, they
are fighting fighting fighting that where
    there was death there may
be life. "When a man is prey to anger,
he is moved by outside things; when he holds
    his ground in patience
      patience, that is action or
    beauty," the soldier's defense
    and hardest armor for

the fight. The world's an orphan's home. Shall
    we never have peace without sorrow?
without pleas of the dying for
    help that won't come? O
quiet form upon the dust, I cannot
look and yet I must. If these great patient
    dyings—all these agonies
      and woundbearings and blood shed—
    can teach us how to live, these
     dyings were not wasted.

Hate-hardened heart, O heart of iron,
    iron is iron till it is rust.
There never was a war that was
    not inward; I must
fight till I have conquered in myself what
causes war, but I would not believe it.
    I inwardly did nothing.
      O Iscariotlike crime!
    Beauty is everlasting
      and dust is for a time.

ENJOY THE GOOD

Holy Bible, Ecclesiastes 5:18–20

Behold that which I have seen: it is good and comely for one to eat and to drink, and to enjoy the good of all his labor that he taketh under the sun all the days of his life, which God giveth him; for it is his portion.

Every man also to whom God hath given riches and wealth, and hath given him power to eat thereof, and to take his portion, and to rejoice in his labor: this is the gift of God.

For he shall not much remember the days of his life; because God answereth him in the joy of his heart.

LOVE TRIUMPHANT

Frederic Lawrence Knowles

Helen's lips are drifting dust;
Ilion is consumed with rust;
All the galleons of Greece
Drink the ocean's dreamless peace;
Lost was Solomon's purple show
Restless centuries ago;
Stately empires wax and wane—
Babylon, Barbary, and Spain:—
Only one thing, undefaced,
Lasts, though all the worlds lie waste,
And the heavens are overturned.
Dear, how long ago we learned!

There's a sight that blinds the sun,
Sound that lives when sounds are done,
Music that rebukes the birds,
Language lovelier than words,
Hue and scent that shame the rose,
Wine no earthly vineyard knows,
Silence stiller than the shore
Swept by Charon's stealthy oar,

Ocean more divinely free
Than Pacific's boundless sea,—
Ye who love have learned it true.
Dear, how long ago we knew!

THE INNER GLEAM

Ralph Waldo Emerson

A man should learn to detect and watch that gleam of light which flashes across his mind from within, more than the lustre of the firmament of bards and sages. Yet he dismisses without notice his thought, because it is his. In every work of genius we recognize our own rejected thoughts: they come back to us with a certain alienated majesty.

ROBINSON CRUSOE

Charles Edward Carryl

The night was thick and hazy
When the Piccadilly Daisy
Carried down the crew and captain in the sea;
And I think the water drowned 'em,
For they never, never found 'em,
And I know they didn't come ashore with me.

Oh! 'twas very sad and lonely
When I found myself the only
Population on this cultivated shore;
But I've made a little tavern
In a rocky little cavern,
And I sit and watch for people at the door.

I spent no time in looking
For a girl to do my cooking,
As I'm quite a clever hand at making stews;
But I had that fellow Friday
Just to keep the tavern tidy,
And to put a Sunday polish on my shoes.

I have a little garden
That I'm cultivating lard in,
As the things I eat are rather tough and dry;
For I live on toasted lizards,
Prickly pears, and parrot gizzards,
And I'm really very fond of beatle-pie.

The clothes I had were furry,
And it made me fret and worry
When I found the moths were eating off the hair:
And I had to scrape and sand 'em,
And I boiled 'em and I tanned 'em,
Till I got the fine morocco suit I wear.

I sometimes seek diversion
In a family excursion
With the few domestic animals you see;
And we take along a carrot
As refreshment for the parrot,
And a little can of jungleberry tea.

Then we gather as we travel
Bits of moss and dirty gravel,
And we chip off little specimens of stone;
And we carry home as prizes
Funny bugs of handy sizes,
Just to give the day a scientific tone.

If the roads are wet and muddy,
We remain at home and study,—
For the Goat is very clever at a sum,—
And the Dog, instead of fighting,
Studies ornamental writing,
While the Cat is taking lessons on the drum.

We retire at eleven,
And we rise again at seven;
And I wish to call attention, as I close,
To the fact that all the scholars
Are correct about their collars,
And particular in turning out their toes.

GOD

Dante

And in his will is our tranquillity:
It is the mighty ocean, whither tends
Whatever it creates and nature makes.

THE GREAT CREATOR FROM HIS WORK RETURNED

John Milton

"Open, ye everlasting gates!" they sung;
"Open, ye Heavens, your living doors! let in
The great Creator, from his work returned
Magnificent, his six days' work, a World!
Open, and henceforth oft; for God will deign
To visit oft the dwellings of just men
Delighted, and with frequent intercourse
Thither will send his winged messengers
On errands of supernal grace." So sung
The glorious train ascending; he through Heaven,
That opened wide her blazing portals, led
To God's eternal house direct the way—
A broad and ample road, whose dust is gold
And pavement stars, as stars to thee appear
Seen in the Galaxy, that milky way
Which nightly as a circling zone thou seest
Powdered with stars. And now on Earth the seventh
Evening arose in Eden—for the sun
Was set, and twilight from the east came on,
Forerunning night—when at the holy mount
Of Heaven's high-seated top, the imperial throne
Of Godhead, fixed for ever firm and sure,
The Filial Power arrived, and sat him down
With his great Father; for he also went
Invisible, yet stayed (such privilege
Hath Omnipresence) and the work ordained,
Author and end of all things, and from work
Now resting, blessed and hallowed the seventh Day,

As resting on that day from all his work;
But not in silence holy kept; the harp
Had work, and rested not; the solemn pipe
And dulcimer, all organs of sweet stop,
All sounds on fret by string or golden wire,
Tempered soft tunings, intermixed with voice
Choral or unison; of incense clouds,
Fuming from golden censers, hid the mount.
Creation and the Six Days' act they sung.

(From *Paradise Lost*)

THE OLD WOMAN

Joseph Campbell

As a white candle
In a holy place,
So is the beauty
Of an aged face.

As the spent radiance
Of the winter sun,
So is a woman
With her travail done.

Her brood gone from her
And her thoughts as still
As the waters
Under a ruined mill.

ON TOP OF OLD SMOKY

Anonymous

On top of Old Smoky, all covered with snow,
I lost my true lover by a-courting too slow.
Now courting is pleasure, parting is grief;
But a false-hearted lover is worse than a thief.

A thief he will rob you and take what you have,
But a false-hearted lover will take you to your grave.
The grave will decay you and turn you to dust,
But where is the young man a poor girl can trust?

They'll hug you and kiss you and tell you more lies
Than the cross ties on railroads or the stars in the skies;
They'll tell you they love you to give your heart ease;
But the minute your back's turned, they'll court who they please.

On top of Old Smoky, all covered with snow,
I lost my true lover by courting too slow;
Bury me on Old Smoky, Old Smoky so high,
Where the wild birds in heaven can hear my sad cry.

A DENTIST

Anonymous

Stranger! Approach this spot with gravity!
John Brown is filling his last cavity.

WE ARE COMING

Booker T. Washington

Tell them that by way of the shop, the field, the skilled hand, habits of economy and thrift, by way of industrial school and college, we are coming. We are crawling up, working up, yea, bursting up. Often through oppression, unjust discrimination, and prejudice, but through them we are coming up, and with proper habits, intelligence, and property, there is no power on earth that can permanently stay our progress. . . .

Wherever your life touches ours, you make us stronger or weaker. No member of your race in any part of our country can harm the meanest member of mine, without the proudest and bluest blood in Massachusetts being degraded. There is no escape—man drags man down, or man lifts man up.

From SONG OF THE OPEN ROAD

Walt Whitman

Afoot and light-hearted, I take to the open road,
Healthy, free, the world before me,
The long brown path before me, leading wherever I choose.

Henceforth I ask not good fortune—I myself am good-fortune;
Henceforth I whimper no more, postpone no more, need nothing,
Strong and content, I travel the open road. . . .

From this hour, freedom!
From this hour I ordain myself loos'd of limits and imaginary lines,
Going where I list, my own master, total and absolute,
Listening to others, and considering well what they say,
Pausing, searching, receiving, contemplating,
Gently, but with undeniable will, divesting myself, of the holds that
    would hold me.

I inhale great draughts of space;
The east and the west are mine, and the north and the south are
    mine.

I am larger, better than I thought;
I did not know I held so much goodness.
All seems beautiful to me;
I can repeat over to men and women, You have done such good to
    me, I would do the same to you.

I will recruit for myself and you as I go;
I will scatter myself among men and women as I go;
I will toss the new gladness and roughness among them;
Whoever denies me, it shall not trouble me;
Whoever accepts me, he or she shall be blessed, and shall bless me. . . .

Allons! the road is before us!
It is safe—I have tried it—my own feet have tried it well.

Allons! be not detain'd!
Let the papers remain on the desk unwritten, and the book on the
    shelf unopen'd!

Let the tools remain in the workshop! let the money remain unearn'd!
Let the school stand! mind not the cry of the teacher!
Let the preacher preach in the pulpit! let the lawyer plead in the court, and the judge expound the law.

Mon enfant! I give you my hand!
I give you my love, more precious than money,
I give you myself, before preaching or law:
Will you give me yourself? will you come travel with me?
Shall we stick by each other as long as we live?

UNITE AS ONE PEOPLE

Abraham Lincoln

Let us discard all this quibbling about this man and the other man, this race and that race and the other race being inferior, and therefore they must be placed in an inferior position. Let us discard all these things, and unite as one people throughout this land, until we shall once more stand up declaring that all men are created equal.

(1858)

UNIVERSAL PRAYER

Alexander Pope

Father of all; In every age,
 In every clime adored,
By saint, by savage, and by sage,
 Jehovah, Jove, or Lord!

Thou Great First Cause, least understood,
 Who all my sense confined
To know but this, that Thou art good,
 And that myself am blind!

(527)

Yet gave me, in this dark estate,
　To see the good from ill;
And, binding nature fast in fate,
　Let free the human will.

What conscience dictates to be done,
　Or warns me not to do,
This teach me more than hell to shun,
　That, more than heaven pursue.

*　　*　　*　　*

Let not this weak, unknowing hand
　Presume Thy bolts to throw,
And deal damnation round the land
　On each I judge Thy foe.

If I am right, Thy grace impart,
　Still in the right to stay;
If I am wrong, oh, teach my heart
　To find the better way!

Save me alike from foolish pride,
　And impious discontent,
At aught Thy wisdom has denied,
　Or aught Thy goodness lent.

Teach me to feel another's woe,
　To hide the fault I see;
That mercy I to others show,
　That mercy show to me. . . .

This day be bread and peace my lot:
　All else beneath the sun,
Thou know'st if best bestowed or not;
　And let Thy will be done.

To Thee, whose temple is all space,—
　Whose altar, earth, sea, skies,—
One chorus let all beings raise,
　All Nature's incense rise!

TROUBLE

Don Marquis

there is bound to be a certain amount of
trouble running any country
if you are president the trouble happens to you
but if you are a tyrant the trouble happens to other people.

THE TRAVELLERS AND THE BEAR

Aesop

Two men being to travel together through the forest, mutually
promised to stand by each other in any danger they should meet upon
the way. They had not gone far before a Bear came rushing towards
them out of a thicket; upon which one, being a light, nimble fellow,
got up a tree; the other falling flat upon his face, and holding his
breath, lay while the Bear came up and smelled at him; but that
creature, supposing him to be a dead carcass, went back again into
the woods, without doing him the least harm. When all was over,
the Spark who had climbed the tree came down to his companion,
and, with a pleasant smile, asked him what the Bear said to him—
"For," says he, "I took notice that he clapt his mouth very close to
your ear."—"Why," replies the other, "he charged me to take care
for the future not to put any confidence in such cowardly rascals
as you are."

From RABBI BEN EZRA

Robert Browning

Grow old along with me!
The best is yet to be,
The last of life, for which the first was made:
Our times are in his hand
Who saith: "A whole I planned,
Youth shows but half; trust God, see all, nor be afraid."

Ah, but a man's reach should exceed his grasp,
Or what's a heaven for?

THE CANDID FRIEND

George Canning

Give me the avowed, the erect, the manly foe;
Bold I can meet, perhaps return his blow;
But of all plagues, good Heaven, thy wrath can send,
Save, save, oh! save me from the Candid Friend!

THE POWER TO TAX

Chief Justice John Marshall

That the power of taxing [the bank] by the States may be exercised
so as to destroy it, is too obvious to be denied . . . That the power to
tax involves the power to destroy [is] not to be denied.

TWO CAREFREE DAYS

Robert J. Burdette

There are two days in the week about which and upon which I never
worry. Two carefree days, kept sacredly free from fear and apprehension. One of these days is Yesterday. Yesterday with all its cares and
frets, with all its pains and aches, all its faults, and its mistakes and
blunders, has passed forever beyond the reach of my recall. I cannot
undo an act that I wrought. I cannot unsay a word that I said, on
Yesterday. All that it holds of my life, of wrong, regret and sorrow,
is in the hands of the Mighty Love that can bring honey out of the
rock and sweet waters out of the bitterest desert. And the other day
I do not worry about is Tomorrow. Tomorrow with all its possible
adversities, its burdens, its perils, its large promise and poor performance, its failures and mistakes is as far beyond the reach of my
mastery as its dead sister, Yesterday.

THANKSGIVING, 1963

Molly Kazan
(Written shortly after President Kennedy was assassinated)

I think that what he gave us most was pride.
It felt good to have a President like that:
bright, brave and funny and goodlooking.

I saw him once drive down East Seventy-
       second Street
in an open car, in the autumn sun
(as he drove yesterday in Dallas).
His thatch of brown hair looked as though
       it had grown extra thick
the way our wood animals in Connecticut
grow extra fur for winter.
And he looked as though it was fun to be alive,
to be a politician,
to be President,
to be a Kennedy,
to be a man.

He revived our pride.
It felt good to have a President
who read his mail,
who read the papers,
who read books and played touch football.
It was a pleasure and a cause for pride
to watch him take the quizzing of the press
with cameras grinding—
take it in his stride,
with zest.
He'd parry, thrust, answer or duck
and fire a verbal shot on target,
hitting with the same answer, the segregation-
       ists in a Louisiana hamlet and a govern-
       ment in South East Asia.
He made you feel that he knew what was
       going on
in both places.

He would come out of the quiz with an "A"
in Economics, Military Science, Constitutional
        Law, Farm Problems and the moonshot
        program
and still take time to appreciate Miss May
        Craig.

We were privileged to see him on the worst day
(till yesterday),
the Bay of Pigs day,
and we marveled at his coolth and style
and were amazed at an air (that plainly was
        habitual)
of modesty
and even diffidence.
It felt good to have a President
who said, It was my fault.
And went on from there.

It felt good to have a President
who looked well in Vienna, Paris, Rome, Berlin
and at the podium of the United Nations
—and who would go to Dublin,
put a wreath where it did the most good
and leave unspoken
the satisfaction of an Irishman
en route to 10 Downing Street
as head of the U. S. government.

What was spoken
was spoken well.
What was unspoken
needed to be unspoken.
It was none of our business if his back hurt.

He revived our pride.
He gave grist to our pride.
He was respectful of intellect;
he was respectful of excellence;
he was respectful of accomplishment and skill;
he was respectful of the clear and subtle uses of
        our language;
he was respectful of courage.
And all these things he cultivated in himself.

He was respectful of our heritage.
He is now part of it.

He affirmed our future.
Our future is more hopeful
because of his work
but our future is not safe nor sure.
He kept telling us that.
This is a very dangerous and uncertain world.
I quote. He said that yesterday.

He respected facts.
And we must now live with the fact of his
      murder.

Our children cried when the news came. They
      phoned and we phoned
and we cried and we were not ashamed of
      crying but we were ashamed of what
      had happened.
The youngest could not remember any other
      President, not clearly.
She felt as if the world had stopped.

We said, It is a shame, a very deep shame.
But this country will go on
more proudly
and with a clearer sense of who we are
and what we have in us to become
because we had a President like that.
He revived our pride.
We are lucky that we had him for three years.

If a nation expects to be ignorant and free, in a state of
civilization, it expects what never was and never will be.
                                    (Thomas Jefferson, 1816)

UNITY OF MANKIND

Holy Bible, Psalm 133

Behold how good and pleasant it is for brethren to dwell together in unity!

It is like the precious ointment upon the head, that ran down upon the beard, even Aaron's beard: that went down to the skirts of his garment:

As the dew of Hermon, and as the dew that descended upon the mountains of Zion: for there the Lord commanded the blessing, even life for evermore.

GREEN GROW THE LILACS

Anonymous

Oh, green grow the lilacs and so does the rue,
How sad's been the day since I parted from you,
But at our next meeting love we'll renew,
We'll change the green lilacs for the Red, White, and Blue.

I once had a sweetheart but now I have none;
He's gone off and left me to live here alone.
He's gone off and left me contented to be;
He must love another girl better than me.

I passed my love's window both early and late,
The look that he gave me it made my heart ache.
The look that he gave me was painful to see,
For he loves another one better than me.

I wrote my love letters in red rosy lines,
He sent me an answer all twisted in twines,
Saying, "Keep your love letters and I will keep mine,
Just you write to your love and I'll write to mine."

On top of the mountain where green lilacs grow,
And over the valley where the still waters flow,
I met my true love and he proved to be true,
We changed the green lilac for the Red, White, and Blue.

KING LEAR TO THE STORM

William Shakespeare

Blow, winds, and crack your cheeks! rage! blow!
You cataracts and hurricanoes, spout
Till you have drench'd our steeples, drown'd the cocks!
You sulphurous and thought-executing fires,
Vaunt-couriers to oak-cleaving thunderbolts,
Singe my white head! And thou, all-shaking thunder,
Smite flat the thick rotundity o' the world!
Crack nature's moulds, all germens spill at once
That make ingrateful man!

(From *King Lear*)

ADLAI STEVENSON AT CHICAGO, JULY 26, 1952

When the tumult and shouting die, when the bands are gone and the lights are dimmed, there is the stark responsibility in an hour of history haunted with those gaunt, grim specters of strife, dissension, and ruthless, inscrutable, and hostile powers abroad.

The ordeal of the twentieth century—the bloodiest, most turbulent era of the Christian age—is far from over. Sacrifice, patience, understanding, and implacable purpose must be our lot for years to come. . . .

The victory to be won in the twentieth century mocks the pretensions of individual acumen and ingenuity. For it is a citadel guarded by thick walls of ignorance and mistrust which do not fall before the trumpets' blast or the politicians' imprecations or even the generals' baton. They are, my friends, walls that must be directly stormed by the hosts of courage, morality, and of vision, standing shoulder to shoulder, unafraid of ugly truth, contemptuous of lies, half-truths, circuses, and demagoguery.

A GLASS OF BEER

James Stephens

The lanky hank of a she in the inn over there
Nearly killed me for asking the loan of a glass of beer:
May the devil grip the whey-faced slut by the hair,
And beat bad manners out of her skin for a year.

That parboiled ape, with the toughest jaw you will see
On virtue's path, and a voice that would rasp the dead,
Came roaring and raging the minute she looked at me,
And threw me out of the house on the back of my head!

If I asked her master he'd give me a cask a day;
But she, with the beer at hand, not a gill would arrange!
May she marry a ghost and bear him a kitten, and may
The High King of Glory permit her to get the mange.

WAR IS HELL

General William Tecumseh Sherman

I am sick and tired of war. Its glory is all moonshine. It is only those
who have never fired a shot nor heard the shrieks and groans of the
wounded who cry aloud for blood, more vengeance, more desolation.
War is hell.

MY HEART'S IN THE HIGHLANDS

Robert Burns

My heart's in the Highlands, my heart is not here;
My heart's in the Highlands a-chasing the deer;
Chasing the wild deer, and following the roe,
My heart's in the Highlands, wherever I go.

Farewell to the Highlands, farewell to the North,
The birth-place of valor, the country of worth;
Wherever I wander, wherever I rove,
The hills of the Highlands for ever I love.

Farewell to the mountains, high cover'd with snow;
Farewell to the straths and green valleys below;
Farewell to the forests and wild-hanging woods;
Farewell to the torrents and loud-pouring floods.
My heart's in the Highlands, my heart is not here;
My heart's in the Highlands, a-chasing the deer;
Chasing the wild deer, and following the roe,
My heart's in the Highlands, wherever I go.

FROM LINCOLN'S ANNUAL MESSAGE TO CONGRESS

The dogmas of the quiet past are inadequate to the stormy present. The occasion is piled high with difficulty, and we must rise with the occasion. As our case is new, so we must think anew and act anew. We must disenthrall ourselves, and then we shall save our country.

Fellow-citizens, we cannot escape history. We of this Congress and this administration will be remembered in spite of ourselves. No personal significance or insignificance can spare one or another of us. The fiery trial through which we pass will light us down, in honor or dishonor, to the latest generation. We say we are for the Union. The world will not forget that we say this. We know how to save the Union. The world knows that we know how to save it. We—even we here—hold the power and bear the responsibility. In giving freedom to the slave, we assure freedom to the free—honorable alike in what we give and what we preserve. We shall nobly save or meanly lose the last, best hope of earth. Other means may succeed; this could not fail. The way is plain, peaceful, generous, just—a way which, if followed, the world will forever applaud, and God must forever bless.

(1862)

WHEN OUR TWO SOULS STAND UP ERECT AND STRONG

Elizabeth Barrett Browning

When our two souls stand up erect and strong,
Face to face, silent, drawing nigh and nigher,
Until the lengthening wings break into fire
At either curvéd point,—what bitter wrong
Can the earth do to us, that we should not long
Be here contented? Think. In mounting higher,
The angels would press on us and aspire
To drop some golden orb of perfect song
Into our deep, dear silence. Let us stay
Rather on earth, Belovéd,—where the unfit
Contrarious moods of men recoil away
And isolate pure spirits, and permit
A place to stand and love in for a day,
With darkness and the death-hour rounding it.

THE OATH TAKEN BY ATHLETES COMPETING IN THE OLYMPIC GAMES

In the name of all competitors I promise that we will take part in these Olympic Games, respecting and abiding by the rules which govern them, in the true spirit of sportsmanship, for the glory of sport and the honor of our teams.

YE ARE THE TEMPLE OF GOD

Holy Bible, I Corinthians 3:16–17

Know ye not that ye are the temple of God, and that the Spirit of God dwelleth in you?
If any man defile the temple of God, him shall God destroy; for the temple of God is holy, which temple ye are.

YOUNG MEN, AND MEN OF AGE

Francis Bacon

Young men are fitter to invent than to judge, fitter for execution than for counsel, and fitter for new projects than for settled business; for the experience of age, in things that fall within the compass of it, directeth them, but in new things abuseth them. . . . The errors of young men are the ruin of business; but the errors of aged men amount to this—that more might have been done, or sooner. Young men, in the conduct and manage of actions, embrace more than they can hold; stir more than they can quiet; fly to the end, without consideration of the means and degrees; pursue some few principles which they have chanced upon absurdly; care not to innovate, which draws unknown inconveniences; use extreme remedies at first; and that which doubleth all errors, will not acknowledge or retract them; like an unready horse that will neither stop nor turn. . . . Men of age object too much, consult too long, adventure too little, repent too soon, and seldom drive business home to the full period, but content themselves with a mediocrity of success. . . . Certainly it is good to compound employments of both; for that will be good for the present, because the virtues of either age may correct the defects of both; and good for succession, that young men may be learners, while men in age are actors; and, lastly, food for externe accidents, because authority followeth old men, and favor and popularity youth.

NEVER SEEK TO TELL THY LOVE

William Blake

Never seek to tell thy love,
Love that never told can be;
For the gentle wind does move
Silently, invisibly.

I told my love, I told my love,
I told her all my heart,
Trembling, cold, in ghastly fears,
Ah! she doth depart.

(539)

Soon as she was gone from me,
A traveller came by,
Silently, invisibly:
He took her with a sigh.

MACAULAY'S ONE LINE BOOK REVIEW OF ATTERBURY'S "A DEFENSE OF THE LETTERS OF PHALARIS"

The best book ever written by a man on the wrong side of a question of which the author was profoundly ignorant.

THE LOVE SONG OF J. ALFRED PRUFROCK

T. S. Eliot

> *S'o credesse che mia risposta fosse*
> *A persona che mai tornasse al mondo,*
> *Questa fiamma staria senza piu scosse.*
> *Ma perciocche giammai di questo fondo*
> *Non torno vivo alcun, s'i'odo il vero,*
> *Senza tema d'infamia ti rispondo.*

Let us go then, you and I,
When the evening is spread out against the sky
Like a patient etherised upon a table;
Let us go, through certain half-deserted streets,
The muttering retreats
Of restless nights in one-night cheap hotels
And sawdust restaurants with oyster shells:
Streets that follow like a tedious argument
Of insidious intent
To lead you to an overwhelming question . . .
Oh, do not ask, "What is it?"
Let us go and make our visit.

In the room the women come and go
Talking of Michelangelo.

The yellow fog that rubs its back upon the window-panes,
The yellow smoke that rubs its muzzle on the window-panes
Licked its tongue into the corners of the evening,
Lingered upon the pools that stand in drains,
Let fall upon its back the soot that falls from chimneys,
Slipped by the terrace, made a sudden leap,
And seeing that it was a soft October night,
Curled once about the house, and fell asleep.

And indeed there will be time
For the yellow smoke that slides along the street,
Rubbing its back upon the window-panes;
There will be time, there will be time
To prepare a face to meet the faces that you meet;
There will be time to murder and create,
And time for all the works and days of hand
That lift and drop a question on your plate;
Time for you and time for me,
And time yet for a hundred indecisions,
And for a hundred visions and revisions,
Before the taking of a toast and tea.

In the room the women come and go
Talking of Michelangelo.

And indeed there will be time
To wonder, "Do I dare?" and, "Do I dare?"
Time to turn back and descend the stair,
With a bald spot in the middle of my hair—
[They will say: "How his hair is growing thin!"]
My morning coat, my collar mounting firmly to the chin,
My necktie rich and modest, but asserted by a simple pin—
[They will say: "But how his arms and legs are thin!"]
Do I dare
Disturb the universe?
In a minute there is time
For decisions and revisions which a minute will reverse.

For I have known them all already, known them all:—
Have known the evenings, mornings, afternoons,
I have measured out my life with coffee spoons;
I know the voices dying with a dying fall
Beneath the music from a farther room.
So how should I presume?

(541)

And I have known the eyes already, known them all—
The eyes that fix you in a formulated phrase,
And when I am formulated, sprawling on a pin,
When I am pinned and wriggling on the wall,
Then how should I begin
To spit out all the butt-ends of my days and ways?
And how should I presume?

And I have known the arms already, known them all—
Arms that are braceleted and white and bare
[But in the lamplight, downed with light brown hair!]
Is it perfume from a dress
That makes me so digress?
Arms that lie along a table, or wrap about a shawl.
   And should I then presume?
   And how should I begin?

Shall I say, I have gone at dusk through narrow streets
And watched the smoke that rises from the pipes
Of lonely men in shirt-sleeves, leaning out of windows? . . .

I should have been a pair of ragged claws
Scuttling across the floors of silent seas.

And the afternoon, the evening, sleeps so peacefully!
Smoothed by long fingers,
Asleep . . . tired . . . or it malingers,
Stretched on the floor, here beside you and me.
Should I, after tea and cakes and ices,
Have the strength to force the moment to its crisis?
But though I have wept and fasted, wept and prayed,
Though I have seen my head (grown slightly bald) brought in
      upon a platter,
I am no prophet—and here's no greater matter;
I have seen the moment of my greatness flicker,
And I have seen the eternal Footman hold my coat, and snicker,
And in short, I was afraid.

And would it have been worth it, after all,
After the cups, the marmalade, the tea,
Among the porcelain, among some talk of you and me,
Would it have been worth while,
To have bitten off the matter with a smile,

To have squeezed the universe into a ball
To roll it toward some overwhelming question,
To say: "I am Lazarus, come from the dead,
Come back to tell you all, I shall tell you all"—
If one, settling a pillow by her head,
   Should say: "That is not what I meant at all.
   That is not it, at all."

And would it have been worth it, after all,
Would it have been worth while,
After the sunsets and the dooryards and the sprinkled streets,
After the novels, after the teacups, after the skirts that trail along
          the floor—
And this, and so much more?—
It is impossible to say just what I mean!
But as if a magic lantern threw the nerves in patterns on a
          screen:
Would it have been worth while
If one, settling a pillow or throwing off a shawl,
And turning toward the window, should say:
   "That is not it at all,
   That is not what I meant, at all."

No! I am not Prince Hamlet, nor was meant to be;
Am an attendant lord, one that will do
To swell a progress, start a scene or two,
Advise the prince; no doubt, an easy tool,
Deferential, glad to be of use,
Politic, cautious, and meticulous;
Full of high sentence, but a bit obtuse;
At times, indeed, almost ridiculous—
Almost, at times, the Fool.

I grow old . . . I grow old—
I shall wear the bottom of my trousers rolled.

Shall I part my hair behind? Do I dare to eat a peach?
I shall wear white flannel trousers, and walk upon the beach.
I have heard the mermaids singing, each to each.

I do not think they will sing to me.

I have seen them riding seaward on the waves
Combing the white hair of the waves blown back
When the wind blows the water white and black.

We have lingered in the chambers of the sea
By sea-girls wreathed with seaweed red and brown
Till human voices wake us, and we drown.

THE YELLOW ROSE OF TEXAS

Anonymous

There's a yellow rose of Texas
I'm going there to see;
No other fellow knows her,
Nobody, only me,
We never more shall part.

Chorus
She's the sweetest rose of color,
This fellow ever knew,
Her eyes are bright as diamonds,
They sparkle like the dew.
You may talk about your dearest maids
And sing of Rosy Lee,
But the Yellow Rose of Texas
Beats the belles of Tennessee.

Cried so hard when I left her,
It almost broke her heart,
And if we ever meet again,
We never more shall part. (*Chorus.*)

If we could read the secret history of our enemies we
should find in each man's life sorrow and suffering enough
to disarm all hostility.
                                        —Henry Wadsworth Longfellow

SPRING

John Milton

In those vernal seasons of the year, when the air is calm and pleasant, it were an injury and sullenness against nature not to go out and see her riches, and partake in her rejoicing with heaven and earth.

THE FOX AND THE ROOSTER

Aesop

A Fox came toward a Rooster and said to him: "I would fain know if thou canst as well sing as thy father did." And then the Rooster shut his eyes and began to cry and sing. And the Fox took and bare him away. And the people of the town cried: "The Fox beareth away the Rooster!" And then the Rooster said thus to the Fox: "My lord, understandest thou not what the people saith, that thou bearest away their rooster? Tell to them that is thine and not theirs." And as the Fox said, "It is not yours, but it is mine," the Rooster escaped from the Fox's mouth and flew upon a tree.

And then the Rooster said to the Fox: "Thou liest; for I am theirs and not thine." And the Fox began to hit the earth with his mouth and head, saying: "Mouth, thou hast spoken too much! Thou shouldest have eaten the Rooster had not thy words been over many."

And therefore over much talking harmeth, and too much crowing smarteth. Therefore keep thyself from over many words, to the end that thou repentest not.

THE DYING FISHERMAN'S SONG

Anonymous

'Twas midnight on the ocean,
Not a street car was in sight,
The sun was shining brightly
For it had rained all that night.

'Twas a summer's day in winter,
The rain was snowing fast,
As a barefoot girl with shoes on,
Stood sitting on the grass.

'Twas evening and the rising sun
Was setting in the west;
And all the fishes in the trees
Were cuddled in their nests.

The rain was pouring down,
The sun was shining bright,
And everything that you could see
Was hidden out of sight.

The organ peeled potatoes,
Lard was rendered by the choir;
When the sexton rang the dishrag
Someone set the church on fire.

"Holy smokes!" the teacher shouted,
As he madly tore his hair.
Now his head resembles heaven,
For there is no parting there.

OBSTACLES

Boethius

(TRANSLATOR: W. V. Cooper)

When the stars are hidden by black clouds, no light can they afford. When the boisterous south wind rolls along the sea and stirs the surge, the water, now as clear as glass, bright as the fair sun's light is dark, impenetrable to sight, with stirred and scattered sand. The stream, that wanders down the mountain's side, must often find a stumbling-block, a stone within its path torn from the hill's own rock. So too shalt thou: if thou wouldst see the truth in undimmed light, choose the straight road, the beaten path; away with passing joys! away with fear! put vain hopes to flight! and grant no place to grief! Where these distractions reign, the mind is clouded o'er, the soul is bound in chains.

RULES FOR THE ROAD

Edwin Markham

Stand straight;
Step firmly, throw your weight;
The heaven is high above your head
And the good road is faithful to your tread.

Be strong:
Sing to your heart a battle song:
Though hidden foemen lie in wait,
Something is in you that can smile at Fate.

Press through:
Nothing can harm if you are true.
And when the night comes rest:
The earth is friendly as a mother's breast.

ON HIS BOOKS

Hilaire Belloc

When I am dead, I hope it may be said:
'His sins were scarlet, but his books were read.'

AE FOND KISS

Robert Burns

Ae fond kiss, and then we sever;
Ae fareweel, alas, for ever!
Deep in heart-wrung tears I'll pledge thee,
Warring sighs and groans I'll wage thee!

Who shall say that Fortune grieves him
While the star of hope she leaves him?
Me, nae cheerfu' twinkle lights me,
Dark despair around benights me.

(547)

I'll ne'er blame my partial fancy;
Naething could resist my Nancy;
But to see her was to love her,
Love but her, and love for ever.

Had we never loved sae kindly,
Had we never loved sae blindly,
Never met—or never parted,
We had ne'er been broken-hearted.

Fare thee weel, thou first and fairest!
Fare thee weel, thou best and dearest!
Thine be ilka joy and treasure,
Peace, enjoyment, love, and pleasure!

Ae fond kiss, and then we sever!
Ae fareweel, alas, for ever!
Deep in heart-wrung tears I'll pledge thee,
Warring sighs and groans I'll wage thee!

This spot is the sweetest I've seen inmy life,
For it raises my flowers and covers my wife.
—Anonymous

ROMEO AND JULIET IN THE ORCHARD

William Shakespeare

Juliet: Wilt thou be gone? it is not yet near day:
It was the nightingale, and not the lark,
That pierced the fearful hollow of thine ear;
Nightly she sings on yond pomegranate-tree:
Believe me, love, it was the nightingale.

Romeo: It was the lark, the herald of the morn,
No nightingale: look, love, what envious streaks
Do lace the severing clouds in yonder east:

Night's candles are burnt out, and jocund day
Stands tiptoe on the misty mountain tops:
I must be gone and live, or stay and die.

Juliet: Your light is not day-light, I know it, I:
It is some meteor that the sun exhales,
To be to thee this night a torchbearer,
And light thee on the way to Mantua:
Therefore stay yet; thou need'st not be gone.

Romeo: Let me be ta'en, let me be put to death;
I am content, so thou wilt have it so.
I'll say yon grey is not the morning's eye,
'Tis but the pale reflex of Cynthia's brow;
Nor that is not the lark, whose notes do beat
The vaulty heaven so high above our heads:
I have more care to stay than will to go:
Come, death, and welcome! Juliet wills it so.
How is 't, my soul? let's walk: it is not day.

Juliet: It is, it is: hie hence, be gone, away!
It is the lark that sings so out of tune,
Straining harsh discords and unpleasing sharps.
Some say the lark makes sweet division;
This doth not so, for she divideth us:
Some say the lark and loathed toad change eyes;
O, now I would they had changed voices too!
Since arm from arm that voice doth us affray,
Hunting thee hence with hunts-up to the day.
O now be gone; more light and light it grows.

Romeo: More light and light: more dark and dark our woes!
(From *Romeo and Juliet*)

If it wasn't for faith, there would be no living in this
world; we couldn't even eat hash with any safety.
—Josh Billings

JOHN F. KENNEDY

Mary McGrory

He brought gaiety, glamor and grace to the American political scene in a measure never known before. That lightsome tread, that debonair touch, that shock of chestnut hair, that beguiling grin, that shattering understatement—these are what we shall remember.

He walked like a prince and he talked like a scholar. His humor brightened the life of the Republic. While striving for his great office, he had often concealed his amusement with the incongruities of life, lest he be thought not only youthful but frivolous as well. When safely ensconced, he saw no reason to hide his wit. It glinted at every press conference. It informed his private utterance. Shown his latest nephew in August, he commented, "He looks like a fine baby—we'll know more later."

One day he strolled onto the porch outside his office and found an old friend admiring the garden. The lawn was a source of unreasoning pride and constant concern to him; the flowers, while he was uncertain of their names, pleased him. He indicated the tangle of petunias and ageratum and said dryly, "This may go down as the real achievement of this administration."

His public statements were always temperate, always measured. He derided his enemies—he teased his friends. He could be grave, but not for long.

When the ugliness of yesterday is forgotten, we shall remember him, smiling.

(*Washington Star*, November 23, 1963)

WHEN THE ROLL IS CALLED UP YONDER

James M. Black

When the trumpet of the Lord shall sound and time shall be no
    more,
And the morning breaks, eternal, bright and fair;
When the saved of earth shall gather over on the other shore,
And the roll is called up yonder, I'll be there.

On that bright and cloudless morning when the dead in Christ shall
    rise,

And the glory of His resurrection share;
When His chosen ones shall gather to their home beyond the skies,
And the roll is called up yonder, I'll be there.

Let us labor for the Master from the dawn till setting sun,
Let us talk of all His wondrous love and care;
Then when all of life is over and our work on earth is done,
And the roll is called up yonder, I'll be there.

THE UNITED STATES ... THE GREATEST POEM

Walt Whitman

The Americans of all nations at any time upon the earth have probably the fullest poetical nature. The United States themselves are essentially the greatest poem. In the history of the earth hitherto the largest and most stirring appear tame and orderly to their ampler largeness and stir. Here at last is something in the doings of man that corresponds with the broadcast doings of the day and night. Here is not merely a nation but a teeming nation of nations. Here is action untied from strings necessarily blind to particulars and details magnificently moving in vast masses. Here is the hospitality which forever indicates heroes. . . . Here are the roughs and beards and space and ruggedness and nonchalance that the soul loves. Here the performance disdaining the trivial unapproached in the tremendous audacity of its crowds and groupings and the push of its perspective spreads with crampless and flowing breadth and showers its prolific and splendid extravagance. One sees it must indeed own the riches of the summer and winter, and need never be bankrupt while corn grows from the ground or the orchards drop apples or the bays contain fish or men beget children upon woman.

Other states indicate themselves in their deputies . . . but the genius of the United States is not best or most in its executives or legislatures, nor in its ambassadors or authors or colleges or churches or parlors, nor even in its newspapers or inventors . . . but always most in the common people. Their manners speech dress friendships —the freshness and candor of their physiognomy—the picturesque looseness of their carriage . . . their deathless attachment to freedom —their aversion to anything indecorous or soft or mean—the practical acknowledgment of the citizens of one state by the citizens of all

(551)

other states—the fierceness of their roused resentment—their curiosity and welcome of novelty—their self-esteem and wonderful sympathy—their susceptibility to a slight—the air they have of persons
who never knew how it felt to stand in the presence of superiors—
the fluency of their speech—their delight in music, the sure symptom
of manly tenderness and native elegance of soul . . . their good
temper and open-handedness—the terrible significance of their
elections—the President's taking off his hat to them not they to
him—these too are unrhymed poetry. It awaits the gigantic and
generous treatment worthy of it.

(From the Preface of the 1855 edition of *Leaves of Grass*)

HOW THE MONEY ROLLS IN

Anonymous

My sister she works in a laundry,
My father he fiddles for gin,
My mother she takes in washing,
My God, how the money rolls in.

SAMUEL JOHNSON'S COMMENT ON POVERTY

When I was running about this town a very poor fellow, I was a
great arguer for the advantages of poverty; but I was, at the same
time, very sorry to be poor. Sir, all the arguments which are brought
to represent poverty as no evil, show it to be evidently a great evil.
You never find people laboring to convince you that you may live
very happily upon a plentiful fortune.

SATAN

John Milton

. . . His pride
Had cast him out from Heaven, with all his host
Of rebel Angels, by whose aid, aspiring
To set himself in glory above his peers,
He trusted to have equalled the Most High,

If he opposed; and, with ambitious aim
Against the throne and monarchy of God,
Raised impious war in Heaven and battle proud
With vain attempt. Him the Almighty Power
Hurled headlong flaming from the ethereal sky,
With hideous ruin and combustion, down
To bottomless perdition, there to dwell
In adamantine chains and penal fire,
Who durst defy the Omnipotent to arms.
    Nine times the space that measures day and night
To mortal men, he, with his horrid crew,
Lay vanquished, rolling in the fiery gulf,
Confounded, though immortal. But his doom
Reserved him to more wrath; for now the thought
Both of lost happiness and lasting pain
Torments him: round he throws his baleful eyes,
That witnessed huge affliction and dismay,
Mixed with obdurate pride and steadfast hate.
At once, as far as Angels ken, he views
The dismal situation waste and wild.
A dungeon horrible, on all sides round,
As one great furnace flamed; yet from those flames
No light; but rather darkness visible
Served only to discover sights of woe,
Regions of sorrow, doleful shades, where peace
And rest can never dwell, hope never comes
That comes to all; but torture without end
Still urges, and a fiery deluge, fed
With ever-burning sulphur unconsumed.
Such place Eternal Justice had prepared
For those rebellious; here their prison ordained
In utter darkness, and their portion set,
As far removed from God and light of Heaven
As from the centre thrice to the utmost pole.
Oh, how unlike the place from whence they fell!

JAMES BOSWELL'S CONCLUSION ABOUT
DR. SAMUEL JOHNSON

I trust, I shall not be accused of affectation, when I declare, that I find myself unable to express all that I felt upon the loss of such a "Guide, Philosopher, and Friend." I shall, therefore, not say one word of my own, but adopt those of an eminent friend, which he uttered with an abrupt felicity, superior to all studied compositions: —"has made a chasm, which not only nothing can fill up, but which nothing has a tendency to fill up.—Johnson is dead. Let us go to the next best:—there is nobody;—no man can be said to put you in mind of Johnson."

"THOU WILT REVIVE ME"

Holy Bible, Psalm 138:6–8

Though the Lord be high, yet hath he respect unto the lowly: but the proud he knoweth afar off.

Though I walk in the midst of trouble, thou wilt revive me: thou shalt stretch forth thine hand against the wrath of mine enemies, and thy right hand shall save me.

The Lord will perfect that which concerneth me: thy mercy, O Lord, endureth for ever: forsake not the works of thine own hands.

TAKE BACK THE HEART

Claribel

Take back the heart thou gavest,
What is my anguish to thee?
Take back the freedom thou cravest,
Leaving the fetters to me.
Take back the words thou hast spoken.
Fling them aside and be free,
Smile o'er each pitiful token,
Leaving the sorrow to me,

(554)

Drink deep of life's fond illusion,
Gaze on the storm cloud and flee,
Swiftly through strife and confusion,
Leaving the burden to me.

Then when at last overtaken,
Time flings its fetters o'er thee,
Come with a trust still unshaken,
Come back a captive to me,
Come back in sadness or sorrow,
Once more my darling to be,
Come as of old, love, to borrow
Glimpses of sunlight from me.
Love shall resume her dominion,
Striving no more to be free,
When on her world-weary pinion,
Flies back my lost love to me.

ON LADY POLTAGRUE, A PUBLIC PERIL

Hilaire Belloc

The Devil, having nothing else to do,
Went off to tempt My Lady Poltagrue.
My Lady, tempted by a private whim,
To his extreme annoyance, tempted him.

THE QUEEN INTRODUCES ALICE TO A FACT OF MODERN LIFE

Lewis Carroll

Alice never could quite make out, in thinking it over afterwards, how it was that they began; all she remembers is that they were running hand in hand, and the Queen went so fast that it was all she could do to keep up with her; and still the Queen kept crying "Faster! Faster!" but Alice felt she *could not* go faster, though she had no breath left to say so.

(555)

The most curious part of the thing was, that the trees and other things round them never changed their places at all; however fast they went, they never seemed to pass anything. "I wonder if all the things move along with us?" thought poor, puzzled Alice. And the Queen seemed to guess her thoughts, for she cried, "Faster! Don't try to talk!"

Not that Alice nad any idea of doing *that*. She felt as if she would never be able to talk again, she was getting so much out of breath; and still the Queen cried "Faster! Faster!" and dragged her along. "Are we nearly there?" Alice managed to pant out at last.

"Nearly there?" the Queen repeated. "Why, we passed it ten minutes ago! Faster!" And they ran on for a time in silence, with the wind whistling in Alice's ears, and almost blowing her hair off her head, she fancied.

"Now! Now!" cried the Queen. "Faster! Faster!" And they went so fast that at last they seemed to skim through the air, hardly touching the ground with their feet, till suddenly, just as Alice was getting quite exhausted, they stopped, and she found herself sitting on the ground, breathless and giddy.

The Queen propped her up against a tree, and said kindly, "You may rest a little now."

Alice looked around her in great surprise. "Why, I do believe we've been under this tree the whole time! Everything's just as it was!"

"Of course it is," said the Queen; "What would you have it?"

"Well, in *our* country," said Alice, still panting a little, "you'd generally get to somewhere else—if you ran very fast for a long time, as we've been doing."

"A slow sort of country!" said the Queen. "Now, *here*, you see, it takes all the running *you* can do, to keep in the same place. If you want to get somewhere else you must run at least twice as fast as that!"

THOUGHTS IN A GARDEN

Andrew Marvell

How vainly men themselves amaze
To win the palm, the oak, or bays,
And their uncessant labours see
Crown'd from some single herb or tree,

Whose short and narrow-vergéd shade
Does prudently their toils upbraid;
While all the flowers and trees do close
To weave the garlands of repose.

Fair Quiet, have I found thee here,
And Innocence thy sister dear!
Mistaken long, I sought you then
In busy companies of men:
Your sacred plants, if here below,
Only among the plants will grow:
Society is all but rude
To this delicious solitude.

No white nor red was ever seen
So amorous as this lovely green.
Fond lovers, cruel as their flame,
Cut in these trees their mistress' name:
Little, alas, they know or heed
How far these beauties hers exceed!
Fair trees! wheres'e'er your barks I wound,
No name shall but your own be found.

When we have run our passions' heat
Love hither makes his best retreat:
The gods, that mortal beauty chase,
Still in a tree did end their race:
Apollo hunted Daphne so,
Only that she might laurel grow:
And Pan did after Syrinx speed
Not as a nymph, but for a reed.

What wondrous life is this I lead!
Ripe apples drop about my head;
The luscious clusters of the vine
Upon my mouth do crush their wine;
The nectarine and curious peach
Into my hands themselves do reach;
Stumbling on melons, as I pass,
Ensnared with flowers, I fall on grass.

Here at the fountain's sliding foot
Or at some fruit-tree's mossy root,

Casting the body's vest aside,
My soul into the boughs does glide;
There, like a bird, it sits and sings
Then whets and combs its silver wings,
And, till prepared for long flight,
Waves in its plumes the various light.

Such was that happy Garden-state
While man there walk'd without a mate:
After a place so pure and sweet,
What other help could yet be meet!
But 'twas beyond a mortal's share
To wander solitary there:
Two paradises 'twere in one,
To live in Paradise alone.

GRACE BEFORE MEALS

Jewish
Lift up your hands toward the sanctury and bless the Lord. Blessed
art Thou, O Lord our God, King of the universe, who bringest forth
bread from the earth. Amen.

Protestant
Bless, O Lord, this food to our use, and us to Thy services, and make
us ever mindful of the needs of others, in Jesus' Name. Amen.

Roman Catholic
Bless us, O Lord, and these Thy gifts which we are about to receive
from Thy bounty. Through Christ our Lord. Amen.

Eastern Orthodox
The Hungry shall eat and shall be satisfied, and those who seek out
the Lord shall praise Him; their hearts shall live forever. Glory to
the Father, and to the Son, and to the Holy Ghost, both now and
ever, and unto ages of ages. Amen.

I AM THE MONARCH OF THE SEA

Sir William S. Gilbert

I am the monarch of the sea,
The ruler of the Queen's Navee,
Whose praise Great Britain loudly chants;
And we are his sisters and his cousins and his aunts,
And we are his sisters and his cousins and his aunts,
His sisters and his cousins and his aunts.
When at anchor or here I ride
My bosom swells with pride,
And I snap my fingers at a foeman's taunts.
And so do his sisters and his cousins and his aunts,
And so do his sisters and his cousins and his aunts,
His sisters and his cousins and his aunts.
But when the breezes blow
I generally go below
And seek the seclusion that a cabin grants,
And so do his sisters and his cousins and his aunts,
And so do his sisters and his cousins and his aunts,
His sisters and his cousins and his aunts
Whom he reckons up by dozens, and his aunts.

EPITAPH

Anonymous

Within this grave do lie
Back to back, my wife and I;
When the last trump the air shall fill,
If she gets up, I'll just lie still.

BELLS FOR JOHN WHITESIDE'S DAUGHTER

John Crowe Ransom

There was such speed in her little body,
And such lightness in her footfall,
It is no wonder that her brown study
Astonishes us all.

Her wars were bruited in our high window.
We looked among orchard trees and beyond,
Where she took arms against her shadow,
Or harried unto the pond

The lazy geese, like a snow cloud
Dripping their snow on the green grass,
Tricking and stopping, sleepy and proud,
Who cried in goose, Alas,

For the tireless heart within the little
Lady with rod that made them rise
From their noon apple-dreams, and scuttle
Goose-fashion under the skies!

But now go the bells, and we are ready;
In one house we are sternly stopped
To say we are vexed at her brown study,
Lying so primly propped.

HISTORY REPEATS

Charles Dickens

It was the best of times, it was the worst of times, it was the age of wisdom, it was the age of foolishness, it was the epoch of belief, it was the epoch of incredulity, it was the season of Light, it was the season of Darkness, it was the spring of hope, it was the winter of despair, we had everything before us, we had nothing before us, we were all going direct to Heaven, we were all going direct the other way—in short, the period was so far like the present period, that some of its noisiest authorities insisted on its being received, for good or for evil, in the superlative degree of comparison only.

(From A Tale of Two Cities)

THE SYCOPHANTIC FOX AND THE GULLIBLE RAVEN

Guy Wetmore Carryl

A raven sat upon a tree,
  And not a word he spoke, for
His beak contained a piece of Brie
  Or maybe, it was Roquefort.
    We'll make it any kind you please—
    At all events it was a cheese.

Beneath the tree's umbrageous limb
  A hungry fox sat smiling;
He saw the raven watching him.
  And spoke in words beguiling:
    "J'admire," said he, "ton beau plumage,"
    (The which was simply persiflage).

Two things there are, no doubt you know,
  To which a fox is used:
A rooster that is bound to crow,
  A crow that's bound to roost;
    And whichsoever he espies
    He tells the most unblushing lies.

"Sweet fowl," he said, "I understand
  You're more than merely natty,
I hear you sing to beat the band
  And Adelina Patti.
    Pray render with your liquid tongue
    A bit from Götterdämmerung."

This subtle speech was aimed to please
  The crow, and it succeeded;
He thought no bird in all the trees
  Could sing as well as he did.
    In flattery completely doused,
    He gave the "Jewel Song" from *Faust*.

But gravitation's law, of course,
  As Isaac Newton showed it,
Exerted on the cheese its force,
  And elsewhere soon bestowed it.
    In fact there is no need to tell
    What happened when to earth it fell.

I blush to add that when the bird
  Took in the situation
He said one brief, emphatic word,
  Unfit for publication.
    The fox was greatly startled, but
    He only sighed and answered "Tut."

The Moral is: A fox is bound
  To be a shameless sinner.
And also: When the cheese comes round
  You know it's after dinner.
    But (what is only known to few)
    The fox is after dinner, too.

MY MOTHER

Andrew Jackson

There never was a woman like her. She was gentle as a dove and
brave as a lioness. . . . The memory of my mother and her teachings
were after all the only capital I had to start life with, and on that
capital I have made my way.

I do not know the method of drawing up an indictment
against an whole people.

(Edmund Burke, 1775)

ARIEL'S SONG

William Shakespeare

Full fathom five thy father lies;
   Of his bones are coral made;
Those are pearls that were his eyes:
   Nothing of him that doth fade,
But doth suffer a sea-change
Into something rich and strange.
Sea-nymphs hourly ring his knell.
               Ding-dong.
Hark! now I hear them,—Ding-dong, bell.
            (From *The Tempest*)

PIGS IS PIGS

Ellis Parker Butler

Mike Flannery, the Westcote agent of the Interurban Express Company, leaned over the counter of the express office and shook his fist. Mr. Morehouse, angry and red, stood on the other side of the counter, trembling with rage. The argument had been long and heated, and at last Mr. Morehouse had talked himself speechless. The cause of the trouble stood on the counter between the two men. It was a soap box across the top of which was nailed a number of strips, forming a rough but serviceable cage. In it two spotted guinea-pigs were greedily eating lettuce leaves.

"Do as you loike, then!" shouted Flannery, "pay for thim an' take thim, or don't pay for thim and leave thim be. Rules is rules, Misther Morehouse, an' Mike Flannery's not goin' to be called down fer breakin' of thim."

"But, you everlastingly stupid idiot!" shouted Mr. Morehouse, madly shaking a flimsy printed book beneath the agent's nose, "can't you read it here—in your own plain printed rates? 'Pets, domestic, Franklin to Westcote, if properly boxed, twenty-five cents each.'" He threw the book on the counter in disgust. "What more do you want? Aren't they pets? Aren't they domestic? Aren't they properly boxed? What?"

He turned and walked back and forth rapidly, frowning ferociously.

Suddenly he turned to Flannery, and forcing his voice to an artificial calmness spoke slowly but with intense sarcasm.

"Pets," he said, "P-e-t-s! Twenty-five cents each. There are two of them. One! Two! Two times twenty-five are fifty! Can you understand that? I offer you fifty cents."

Flannery reached for the book. He ran his hand through the pages and stopped at page sixty-four.

"An' I don't take fifty cints," he whispered in mockery. "Here's the rule for ut. 'Whin the agint be in anny doubt regardin' which of two rates applies to a shipment, he shall charge the larger. The consign-ey may file a claim for the overcharge.' In this case, Misther Morehouse, I be in doubt. Pets thim animals may be, an' domestic they be, but pigs I'm blame sure they do be, an' me rules says plain as the nose on yer face, 'Pigs Franklin to Westcote, thirty cints each.' An', Misther Morehouse, by me arithmetical knowledge two times thirty comes to sixty cints."

Mr. Morehouse shook his head savagely. "Nonsense!" he shouted, "confounded nonsense, I tell you! Why, you poor ignorant foreigner, that rule means common pigs, domestic pigs, not guinea-pigs!"

Flannery was stubborn.

"Pigs is pigs," he declared firmly. "Guinea-pigs or dago pigs or Irish pigs is all the same to the Interurban Express Company an' to Mike Flannery. Th' nationality of the pig creates no differentiality in the rate, Misther Morehouse! 'Twould be the same was they Dutch pigs or Rooshun pigs. Mike Flannery," he added, "is here to tind to the expriss business and not to hould conversation wid dago pigs in sivinteen languages fer to discover be they Chinese or Tipperary by birth an' nativity."

Mr. Morehouse hesitated. He bit his lip and then flung out his arms wildly.

"Very well!" he shouted, "you shall hear of this! Your president shall hear of this! It is an outrage! I have offered you fifty cents. You refuse it! Keep the pigs until you are ready to take the fifty cents, but, by George, sir, if one hair of those pigs' heads is harmed I will have the law on you!"

He turned and stalked out, slamming the door. Flannery carefully lifted the soap box from the counter and placed it in a corner. He was not worried. He felt the peace that comes to a faithful servant who has done his duty and done it well.

Mr. Morehouse went home raging. His boy, who had been awaiting the guinea-pigs, knew better than to ask him for them. He was a normal boy and therefore always had a guilty conscience when his father was angry. So the boy slipped quietly around the house. There is nothing so soothing to a guilty conscience as to be out of the path of the avenger.

Mr. Morehouse stormed into the house. "Where's the ink?" he shouted at his wife as soon as his foot was across the doorsill.

Mrs. Morehouse jumped guiltily. She never used ink. She had not seen the ink, nor moved the ink, nor thought of the ink, but her husband's tone convicted her of the guilt of having borne and reared a boy, and she knew that whenever her husband wanted anything in a loud voice the boy had been at it.

"I'll find Sammy," she said meekly.

When the ink was found Mr. Morehouse wrote rapidly, and he read the completed letter and smiled a triumphant smile.

"That will settle that crazy Irishman!' he exclaimed. "When they get that letter he will hunt another job, all right!"

A week later Mr. Morehouse received a long official envelope with the card of the Interurban Express Company in the upper left corner. He tore it open eagerly and drew out a sheet of paper. At the top it bore the number A6754. The letter was short. "Subject—Rate on guinea-pigs," it said. "Dear Sir,—We are in receipt of your letter regarding rate on guinea-pigs between Franklin and Westcote, addressed to the president of this company. All claims for overcharge should be addressed to the Claims Department."

Mr. Morehouse wrote to the Claims Department. He wrote six pages of choice sarcasm, vituperation and argument, and then sent them to the Claims Department.

A few weeks later he received a reply from the Claims Department. Attached to it was his last letter.

"Dear Sir," said the reply. "Your letter of the 16th inst., addressed to this Department, subject rate on guinea-pigs from Franklin to Westcote, rec'd. We have taken up the matter with our agent at Westcote, and his reply is attached herewith. He informs us that you refused to receive the consignment or to pay the charges. You have therefore no claim against this company, and your letter regarding the proper rate on the consignment should be addressed to our Tariff Department."

Mr. Morehouse wrote to the Tariff Department. He stated his case clearly, and gave his arguments in full, quoting a page or two from the encyclopedia to prove the guinea-pigs were not common pigs.

With the care that characterizes corporations when they are systematically conducted, Mr. Morehouse's letter was numbered, O.K.'d, and started through the regular channels. Duplicate copies of the bill of lading, manifest, Flannery's receipt for the package and several other pertinent papers were pinned to the letter, and they were passed to the head of the Tariff Department.

The head of the Tariff Department put his feet on his desk and yawned. He looked through the papers carelessly.

"Miss Kane," he said to his stenographer, "take this letter. 'Agent, Westcote, N. J. Please advise why consignment referred to in attached papers was refused domestic pet rates.'"

Miss Kane made a series of curves and angles on her notebook and waited with pencil poised. The head of the department looked at the papers again.

"Huh! guinea-pigs!" he said. "Probably starved to death by this time! Add this to that letter: 'Give condition of consignment at present.'"

He tossed the papers on to the stenographer's desk, took his feet from his own desk and went out to lunch.

When Mike Flannery received the letter he scratched his head.

"Give prisint condition," he repeated thoughtfully. "Now what do thim clerks be wantin' to know, I wonder! 'Prisint condition,' is ut? Thim pigs, praise St. Patrick, do be in good health, so far as I know, but I niver was no veternairy surgeon to dago pigs. Mebby thim clerks wants me to call in the pig docther an' have their pulses took. Wan thing I do know, howiver, which is, they've glorious appytites for pigs of their soize. Ate? They'd ate the brass padlocks off of a barn door! If the paddy pig, by the same token, ate as hearty as these dago pigs do, there'd be a famine in Ireland."

To assure himself that his report would be up to date, Flannery went to the rear of the office and looked into the cage. The pigs had been transferred to a larger box—a dry goods box.

"Wan,— two,— t'ree,— four,— foive,— six,— sivin,— eight!" he counted. "Sivin spotted an' wan all black. All well an' hearty an' all eatin' loike ragin' hippypottymusses." He went back to his desk and wrote.

"Mr. Morgan, Head of Tariff Department," he wrote, "why do I say dago pigs is pigs because they is pigs and will be til you say they ain't which is what the rule books says stop your jollying me you know it as well as I do. As to the health they are all well and hoping you are the same. P. S. There are eight now the family increased all good eaters. P. S. I paid out so far two dollars for cabbage which they like shall I put in bill for same what?"

Morgan, head of the Tariff Department, when he received this letter, laughed. He read it again and became serious.

"By George!" he said, "Flannery is right, 'pigs is pigs.' I'll have to get authority on this thing. Meanwhile, Miss Kane, take this letter: 'Agent, Westcote, N.J. Regarding shipment guinea-pigs, File No. A6754. Rule 83, General Instructions to Agents, clearly states that agents shall collect from consignee all costs of provender, etc., etc., required for livestock while in transit or storage. You will proceed to collect same from consignee.' "

Flannery received this letter next morning, and when he read it he grinned.

"Proceed to collect!" he said softly. "How thim clerks do loike to be talkin'! *Me* proceed to collect two dollars and twinty-foive cints off Misther Morehouse? I wonder do thim clerks *know* Mr. Morehouse? I'll git it! Oh, yes! 'Misther Morehouse, two an' a quarter, plaze.' 'Cert'nly, me dear frind Flannery. Delighted!' *Not!*"

Flannery drove the express wagon to Mr. Morehouse's door. Mr. Morehouse answered the bell.

"Ah, ha!" he cried as soon as he saw it was Flannery. "So you've come to your senses at last, have you? I thought you would! Bring the box in."

"I hev no box," said Flannery coldly. "I hev a bill agin Misther John C. Morehouse for two dollars and twinty-foive cints for kebbages aten by his dago pigs. Wud you wish to pay ut?"

"Pay—Cabbages—!" gasped Mr. Morehouse. "Do you mean to say that two little guinea-pigs—"

"Eight!" said Flannery. "Papa an' mamma an' the six childer. Eight!"

For answer Mr. Morehouse slammed the door in Flannery's face. Flannery looked at the door reproachfully.

"I take ut the con-*sign*-y don't want to pay for thim kebbages," he said. "If I know signs of refusal, the con-*sign*-y refuses to pay for wan dang kebbage leaf an' be hanged to me!"

Mr. Morgan, the head of the Tariff Department, consulted the president of the Interurban Express Company regarding guinea-pigs, as to whether they were pigs or not pigs. The president was inclined to treat the matter lightly.

"What is the rate on pigs and on pets?" he asked.

"Pigs thirty cents, pets twenty-five," said Morgan.

"Then of course guinea-pigs are pigs," said the president.

"Yes," agreed Morgan, "I look at it that way, too. A thing that can come under two rates is naturally due to be classed as the higher. But are guinea-pigs, pigs? Aren't they rabbits?"

"Come to think of it," said the president, "I believe they are more like rabbits. Sort of half-way station between pig and rabbit. I think the question is this—are guinea-pigs of the domestic pig family? I'll ask Professor Gordon. He is an authority on such things. Leave the papers with me."

The president put the papers on his desk and wrote a letter to Professor Gordon. Unfortunately the Professor was in South America collecting zoological specimens, and the letter was forwarded to him by his wife. As the Professor was in the highest Andes, where no white man had ever penetrated, the letter was many months in reaching him. The president forgot the guinea-pigs, Morgan forgot them, Mr. Morehouse forgot them. But Flannery did not. One half of his time he gave to the duties of his agency; the other half was devoted to the guinea-pigs. Long before Professor Gordon received the president's letter, Morgan received one from Flannery.

"About them dago pigs," it said, "what shall I do they are great in family life, no race suicide for them, there are thirty-two now shall I sell them do you take this express office for a menagerie, answer quick."

Morgan reached for a telegraph blank and wrote:

"Agent, Westcote. Don't sell pigs."

He then wrote Flannery a letter calling his attention to the fact that the pigs were not the property of the company but were merely being held during a settlement of a dispute regarding rates. He advised Flannery to take the best possible care of them.

Flannery, letter in hand, looked at the pigs and sighed. The dry goods box had become too small. He boarded up twenty feet of the rear of the express office to make a large and airy home for them, and went about his business. He worked with feverish intensity when out on his rounds, for the pigs required attention and took most of his time. Some months later, in desperation, he seized a sheet of paper and wrote "160" across it and mailed it to Morgan. Morgan returned it asking for an explanation. Flannery replied:

"There be now one hundred sixty of them dago pigs, for heaven's sake let me sell off some, do you want me to go crazy, what?"

"Sell no pigs," Morgan wired.

Not long after this the president of the express company received a letter from Professor Gordon. It was a long and scholarly letter, but the point was the guinea-pig was the *Cavia aparoea*, while the common pig was the genus *Sus* of the family *Suidae*. He remarked that they were prolific and multiplied rapidly.

"They are not pigs," said the president, decidedly, to Morgan. "The twenty-five cent rate applies."

Morgan made the proper notation on the papers that had accumulate in File A6754, and turned them over to the Audit Department.

(568)

The Audit Department took some time to look the matter up, and after the usual delay wrote Flannery that as he had on hand one hundred and sixty guinea-pigs, the property of consignee, he should deliver them and collect charges at the rate of twenty-five cents each.

Flannery spent a day herding his charges through a narrow opening in their cage so that he might count them.

"Audit Dept.," he wrote, when he had finished the count, "you are way off there may be was one hundred and sixty dago pigs once, but wake up don't be a back number. I've got even eight hundred now shall I collect for eight hundred or what, how about sixty-four dollars I paid out for cabbages."

It required a great many letters back and forth before the Audit Department was able to understand why the error had been made of billing one hundred and sixty instead of eight hundred, and still more time for it to get the meaning of the "cabbages."

Flannery was crowded into a few feet at the extreme front of the office. The pigs had all the rest of the room and two boys were employed constantly attending to them. The day after Flannery had counted the guinea-pigs there were eight more added to his drove, and by the time the Audit Department gave him authority to collect for eight hundred Flannery had given up all attempts to attend to the receipts or the delivery of goods. He was hastily building galleries around the express office, tier above tier. He had four thousand and sixty-four guinea-pigs to care for. More were arriving daily.

Immediately following its authorization the Audit Department sent another letter, but Flannery was too busy to open it. They wrote another and then they telegraphed:

"Error in guinea-pig bill. Collect for two guinea-pigs, fifty cents. Deliver all to consignee."

Flannery read the telegram and cheered up. He wrote out a bill as rapidly as his pencil could travel over paper and ran all the way to the Morehouse home. At the gate he stopped suddenly. The house stared at him with vacant eyes. The windows were bare of curtains and he could see into the empty rooms. A sign on the porch said, "To let." Mr. Morehouse had moved! Flannery ran all the way back to the express office. Sixty-nine guinea-pigs had been born during his absence. He ran out again and made feverish inquiries in the village. Mr. Morehouse had not only moved, but he had left Westcote. Flannery returned to the express office and found that two hundred and six guinea-pigs had entered the world since he left it. He wrote a telegram to the Audit Department.

(569)

"Can't collect fifty cents for two dago pigs consignee has left town address unknown what shall I do? Flannery."

The telegram was handed to one of the clerks in the Audit Department, and as he read it he laughed.

"Flannery must be crazy. He ought to know that the thing to do is to return the consignment here," said the clerk. He telegraphed Flannery to send the pigs to the main office of the company at Franklin.

When Flannery received the telegram he set to work. The six boys he had engaged to help him also set to work. They worked with the haste of desperate men, making cages out of soap boxes, cracker boxes, and all kinds of boxes, and as fast as the cages were completed they filled them with guinea-pigs and expressed them to Franklin. Day after day the cages of guinea-pigs flowed in a steady stream from Westcote to Franklin, and still Flannery and his six helpers ripped and nailed and packed—relentlessly and feverishly. At the end of the week they had shipped two hundred and eighty cases of guinea-pigs, and there were in the express office seven hundred and four more pigs than when they began packing them.

"Stop sending pigs. Warehouse full," came a telegram to Flannery. He stopped packing only long enough to wire back, "Can't stop," and kept on sending them. On the next train up from Franklin came one of the company's inspectors. He had instructions to stop the stream of guinea-pigs at all hazards. As his train drew up at Westcote station he saw a cattle-car standing on the express company's siding. When he reached the express office he saw the express wagon backed up to the door. Six boys were carrying bushel baskets full of guinea-pigs from the office and dumping them into the wagon. Inside the room Flannery, with his coat and vest off, was shoveling guinea-pigs into bushel baskets with a coal scoop. He was winding up the guinea-pig episode.

He looked up at the inspector with a snort of anger.

"Wan wagonload more an' I'll quit of thim, an' niver will ye catch Flannery wid no more foreign pigs on his hands. No, sur! They near was the death o' me. Nixt toime I'll know that pigs of whativer nationality is domestic pets—an' go at the lowest rate."

He began shoveling again rapidly, speaking quickly between breaths.

"Rules may be rules, but you can't fool Mike Flannery twice wid the same thrick—whin ut comes to livestock, dang the rules. So long as Flannery runs this expriss office—pigs is pets—an' cows is pets— an' horses is pets—an' lions an' tigers an' Rocky Mountain goats is pets—an' the rate on thim is twenty-foive cints."

He paused long enough to let one of the boys put an empty basket in the place of the one he had just filled. There were only a few guinea-pigs left. As he noted their limited numbers his natural habit of looking on the bright-side returned.

"Well, annyhow," he said cheerfully, "'tis not so bad as ut might be. What if thim dago pigs had been elephants!"

HOW SWEET I ROAM'D

William Blake

How sweet I roam'd from field to field
And tasted all the summer's pride,
Till I the Prince of Love beheld,
Who in the sunny beams did glide!

He shew'd me lilies for my hair,
And blushing roses for my brow;
He led me through his gardens fair,
Where all his golden pleasures grow.

With sweet May dews my wings were wet,
And Phoebus fired my vocal rage;
He caught me in his silken net,
And shut me in his golden cage.

He loves to sit and hear me sing;
Then, laughing, sports and plays with me;
Then stretches out my golden wing,
And mocks my loss of liberty.

Politician: A man who identifies the sound of his own voice with the infallible voice of the people.

—Anonymous

THINK STEADILY AS A ROMAN AND AS A MAN

Marcus Aurelius

(TRANSLATOR: Charles Long)

Every moment think steadily as a Roman and as a man, to do what thou hast in and with perfect and simple dignity, and feeling of affection, and freedom, and justice; and give thyself relief from all other thoughts. And thou wilt give thyself relief, if thou doest every act of thy life as if it were the last, laying aside all carelessness and passionate aversion from the commands of reason, and all hypocrisy and self-love, and discontent with the portion which has been given to thee. Thou seest how few the things are, the which if a man lays hold of, he is able to live a life which flows in quiet, and is like the existence of the gods; for the gods on their part will require nothing more from him who observes these things.

MARK TWAIN RELATES WHAT HAPPENED WHEN THE PREACHER PREACHED TOO LONG

Some years ago in Hartford, I went to church with a group of friends to hear the address of the Reverend Samuel Hawley, a city missionary who was doing a wonderful work in the slums of New York City. He gave us many instances of the heroism and devotion of the poor. I remember he said, "When a man with millions gives, we make a great deal of noise: but it's noise in the wrong place, for it is the widow's mite that counts."

Well, Hawley worked me up to a great pitch. I could hardly wait for him to get through. I had four hundred dollars in my pocket. I wanted to give that and borrow more to give. I looked around at my friends and I could see greenbacks in every eye.

But instead of passing the plate then, Hawley kept on talking and talking, and as he talked it got hotter and hotter, and I got sleepier and sleepier. My enthusiasm went down, down, down—a hundred dollars at a clip—until finally when the plate did come around, I stole ten cents out of it. It all goes to show how a little thing like that can lead to crime!

NIKITA KHRUSHCHEV'S BOAST

About the capitalist states, it doesn't depend on you whether or not we exist. If you don't like us, don't accept our invitations, and don't invite us to come and see you. Whether you like it or not, history is on our side. We will bury you.

(November, 1956)

OUTWITTED

Edwin Markham

He drew a circle that shut me out—
Heretic, rebel, a thing to flout.
But Love and I had the wit to win;
We drew a circle that took him in!

DEMOCRACY

Abraham Lincoln

As I would not be a slave, so I would not be a master. This expresses my idea of democracy. Whatever differs from this, to the extent of the difference is no democracy.

BEAUTIFUL ISLE OF SOMEWHERE

Jessie B. Pounds

Somewhere the sun is shining,
Somewhere the song-birds dwell;
Hush, then thy sad repining,
God lives and all is well.

Chorus
Somewhere, somewhere,
Beautiful isle of somewhere;
Land of the true, where we live anew,
Beautiful isle of somewhere.

(573)

Somewhere the day is longer,
Somewhere the task is done;
Somewhere the heart is stronger,
Somewhere the guerdon won.

Somewhere the load is lifted,
Close by an open gate;
Somewhere the clouds are rifted,
Somewhere the angels wait.

LIMERICK

Anonymous

There was a young monk of Siberia
Who of fasting grew wearier and wearier,
    Till at length with a yell
    He burst from his cell
And devoured the Father Superior.

OTHELLO'S FAREWELL TO HIS CAREER

William Shakespeare

            O, now for ever
Farewell the tranquil mind! farewell content!
Farewell the plumed troop and the big wars
That make ambition virtue! O farewell,
Farewell the neighing steed and the shrill trump,
The spirit-stirring drum, the ear-piercing fife,
The royal banner and all quality,
Pride, pomp and circumstance of glorious war!
And, O you mortal engines, whose rude throats
The immortal Jove's dread clamors counterfeit,
Farewell! Othello's occupation's gone!
                          (From *Othello*)

SANCHO PANZA PRAISES SLEEP

Miguel De Cervantes

(TRANSLATOR: P. A. Matteux)

Now blessings light on him that first invented this same sleep! It covers a man all over, thoughts and all, like a cloak; 'tis meat for the hungry, drink for the thirsty, heat for the cold, and cold for the hot. 'Tis the current coin that purchases all the pleasures of the world cheap; and the balance that sets the king and the shepherd, the fool and the wise man even. There is only one thing, which somebody once put into my head, that I dislike in sleep: it is, that it resembles death; there is very little difference between a man in his first sleep and a man in his last sleep.

WHERE LIES THE LAND?

Arthur Hugh Clough

Where lies the land to which the ship would go?
Far, far ahead, is all her seamen know.
And where the land she travels from? Away,
Far, far behind, is all that they can say.

On sunny noons upon the deck's smooth face,
Linked arm in arm, how pleasant here to pace;
Or, o'er the stern reclining, watch below
The foaming wake far widening as we go.

On stormy nights, when wild north-westers rave,
How proud a thing to fight with wind and wave!
The dripping sailor on the reeling mast
Exults to bear, and scorns to wish it past.

Where lies the land to which the ship would go?
Far, far ahead, is all her seamen know.
And where the land she travels from? Away,
Far, far behind, is all that they can say.

CICERO AGAINST CATILINE

How long, O Catiline, wilt thou abuse our patience! How long shalt thou baffle justice in thy mad career? To what extreme wilt thou carry thy audacity? Art thou nothing daunted by the nightly watch, posted to secure the Palatium? Nothing, by the city guards? Nothing, by the rally of all good citizens? Nothing, by the assembling of the Senate in this fortified place? Nothing, by the averted looks of all here present? Seest thou not that all thy plots are exposed? that thy wretched conspiracy is laid bare to every man's knowledge, here in the Senate? that we are all well aware of thy proceedings of last night; of the night before;—the place of meeting, the company convoked, the measures concerted? Alas, the times! Alas, the public morals? The Senate understands all this. The consul sees it. Yet the traitor lives! Lives? Ay, truly, and confronts us here in Council, takes part in our deliberations, and, with his measuring eye, marks out each man of us for slaughter. And we, all this while, strenuous that we are, think we have amply discharged our duty to the State, if we but shun this madman's sword and fury.

Long since, O Catiline, ought the consul to have ordered thee to execution, and brought upon thine own head the ruin thou hast been meditating against others. There was that virtue once in Rome, that a wicked citizen was held more execrable than the deadliest foe. We have a law still, Catiline, for thee. Think not that we are powerless, because forbearing. We have a decree,—though it rests among our archives like a sword in its scabbard—a decree by which thy life would be made to pay the forfeit of thy crimes. And should I order thee to be instantly seized and put to death, I make just doubt whether all good men would not think it done rather too late than any man too cruelly.

But, for good reasons, I will yet defer the blow long since deserved. Then will I doom thee, when no man is found so lost, so wicked, nay, so like thyself, but shall confess that it was justly dealt. While there is one man that dares defend thee, live! But thou shalt live so beset, so surrounded, so scrutinized, by the vigilant guards that I have placed around thee, that thou shalt not stir a foot against the Republic without my knowledge. Proceed, plot, conspire, as thou wilt; there is nothing you can contrive, nothing you can propose, nothing you can attempt, which I shall not know, hear, and promptly understand. Thou shalt soon be made aware that I am even more active in providing for the preservation of the State, than thou in plotting its destruction.

JOHN WESLEY'S GRACE BEFORE MEALS

Be present at our table, Lord;
Be here and everywhere adored.
Thy creatures bless, and grant that we
May feast in Paradise with Thee.

GOD IS NOW

Henry David Thoreau

Men esteem truth remote, in the outskirts of the system, before Adam and after the last man. In eternity there is indeed something true and sublime. But all these time and places and occasions are now and here. God himself culminates in the present moment, and will never be more divine in the lapse of all the ages. And we are enabled to apprehend at all what is sublime and noble only by the perpetual instilling and drenching of the reality that surrounds us.

ANTHEM FOR DOOMED YOUTH

Wilfred Owen

What passing-bells for these who die as cattle?
Only the monstrous anger of the guns.
Only the stuttering rifles' rapid rattle
Can patter out their hasty orisons.
No mockeries for them from prayers or bells,
Nor any voice of mourning save the choirs,—
The shrill, demented choirs of wailing shells;
And bugles calling for them from sad shires.
What candles may be held to speed them all?
Not in the hands of boys, but in their eyes
Shall shine the holy glimmers of good-byes.
The pallor of girls' brows shall be their pall;
Their flowers the tenderness of silent minds,
And each slow dusk a drawing-down of blinds.

FRET NOT THYSELF BECAUSE OF EVIL DOERS

Holy Bible, Psalm 37:1–4, 7

Fret not thyself because of evil doers, neither be thou envious against the workers of iniquity:

For they shall soon be cut down like the grass, and wither as the green herb.

Trust in the Lord, and do good: so shalt thou dwell in the land, and verily thou shalt be fed.

Delight thyself also in the Lord; and he shall give thee the desires of thine heart. . . .

Rest in the Lord, and wait patiently for him: fret not thyself because of him who prospereth in his way, because of the man who bringeth wicked devices to pass.

CHRISTMAS BELLS

Henry Wadsworth Longfellow

I heard the bells on Christmas Day
Their old, familiar carols play,
Then from each black, accursèd mouth
The cannon thundered in the South,
    And with the sound
    The carols drowned
Of peace on earth, good-will to men!

It was as if an earthquake rent
The hearth-stones of a continent,
    And made forlorn
    The households born
Of peace on earth, good-will to men!

And in despair I bowed my head;
"There is no peace on earth," I said:
    "For hate is strong,
    And mocks the song
Of peace on earth, good-will to men!"

Then pealed the bells more loud and deep:
"God is not dead; nor doth he sleep!
    The Wrong shall fail,
    The Right prevail,
With peace on earth, good-will to men!"

A MAN'S HOME

William Pitt

The poorest man may in his cottage bid defiance to all the forces of the Crown. It may be frail; its roof may shake; the wind may blow through it; the storms may enter, the rain may enter,—but the King of England cannot enter; all his forces may not dare cross the threshold of the humblest home.

HEART-HURT

Anonymous

He laughed derision when his foes
    Against him cast, each man, a stone;
His friend in anger flung a rose—
    And all the city heard him moan.

WORLD WARS

Anonymous

World War I
The officers get all the steaks
And all we get is the bellyache.
The general got the croix-de-guerre,
And the son of a gun was never there.

World War II
The Wacs and Waves will win the war;
So what the hell are we fighting for?

World War III
I won't print and you won't see
The verses written on World War Three.

QUOTES FROM HARRY TRUMAN

When Eisenhower was about to succeed Truman as President:
He'll sit there and he'll say, "Do this! Do that!" and nothing will
happen. Poor Ike—it won't be a bit like the Army.

When preparing to leave the Presidency, Mr. Truman said: If I
had known there would be so much work leaving this place, I'd have
run again.

Whenever the press quits abusing me, I know I'm in the wrong
pew.

*During a campaign speech, a woman listener called out to him,
"Mr. Truman, you sound as if you have a cold." Mr. Truman replied*: That's because I ride around in the wind with my mouth
open.

If you can't stand the heat, get out of the kitchen.

When President, Mr. Truman kept this motto on his desk:
THE BUCK STOPS HERE.

THERE'S A CERTAIN SLANT OF LIGHT

Emily Dickinson

There's a certain slant of light,
On winter afternoons,
That oppresses, like the weight
Of cathedral tunes.

Heavenly hurt it gives us;
We can find no scar,
But internal difference
Where the meanings are.

None may teach it anything
'Tis the seal, despair,—
An imperial affliction
Sent us of the air.

When it comes, the landscape listens,
Shadows hold their breath;
When it goes, 'tis like the distance
On the look of death.

DEMOSTHENES' FAREWELL

(TRANSLATOR: Rufus Choate)

(When the Macedonians finally conquered Greece after forty years
of struggle, Demosthenes, who strove desperately to save his country,
was forced to flee to the temple of Poseidon. The Thracian soldiers
who pursued him dared not violate the temple, but tried to tempt
Demosthenes to surrender by promising his pardon. This was
Demosthenes' reply. After responding, he took poison and died.)

I dread the clemency you offer more than the torture and death
which I had reason to expect, for I cannot bear that it be reported
that the king had corrupted me by the promise of life to desert the
ranks of Greece and stand in those of Macedon. Glorious and
beautiful I should have thought if it my life could have been guarded
by my country; by the fleet; by the walls which I have built; by the
treasury which I have filled; by her constitution giving liberty to her
people; by her ancestral glory; by her assemblies of freemen; by the
love of my brother Athenians who so often have crowned me; by
Greece which hitherto I have been able to save. But since this may
not be, since this temple, these altars and sanctities cannot keep me
from the court of the king of Macedon; a spectacle—a slave—I,
Demosthenes, whom Nature never formed for disgrace—I who have
drunk in from Xenophon and Plato the hope of immortality—I, for
the honor of Athens, prefer death to bondage and thus wrap myself
in liberty, the finest winding sheet.

LOVE

Samuel Taylor Coleridge

All thoughts, all passions, all delights,
　Whatever stirs this mortal frame,
All are but ministers of Love,
　　　　And feed his sacred flame.

Oft in my waking dreams do I
　Live o'er again that happy hour,
When midway on the mount I lay
　　　　Beside the ruin'd tower.

The moonshine stealing o'er the scene
　Had blended with the lights of eve;
And she was there, my hope, my joy,
　　　　My own dear Genevieve!

She lean'd against the arméd man,
　The statue of the arméd knight;
She stood and listen'd to my lay,
　　　　Amid the lingering light.

She listen'd with a flitting blush,
　With downcast eyes and modest grace;
And she forgave me, that I gazed
　　　　Too fondly on her face.

She wept with pity and delight,
　She blush'd with love and virgin shame;
And like the murmur of a dream,
　　　　I heard her breathe my name.

Her bosom heaved—she stepp'd aside,
　As conscious of my look she stept—
Then suddenly, with timorous eye
　　　　She fled to me and wept.

She half enclosed me with her arms,
　She press'd me with a meek embrace;
And bending back her head, look'd up,
　　　　And gazed upon my face.

'Twas partly love, and partly fear,
  And partly 'twas a bashful art,
That I might rather feel, than see,
    The swelling of her heart.

I calm'd her fears, and she was calm,
  And told her love with virgin pride;
And so I won my Genevieve,
    My bright and beauteous Bride.

THE AMERICANS AND THE RUSSIANS

Alexis de Tocqueville

There are at the present time two great nations in the world which seem to tend toward the same end, although they started from different points. I allude to the Russians and the Americans. . . . All other nations seem to have nearly reached their natural limits; but these are still in the act of growth. All the others are stopped, or continue to advance with extreme difficulty; these are proceeding with ease and celerity along a path to which the human eye can assign no term. . . .

The Anglo-American relies upon personal interest to accomplish his ends, and gives free scope to the unguided exertions and common sense of the citizens. The Russian centers all the authority of society in a single arm. The principal instrument of the former is freedom; of the latter, servitude. Their starting points are different and their courses are not the same; yet each of them seems to be marked out by the will of Heaven to sway the destinies of half the globe.

(1835)

JOHN WESLEY'S RULE

Do all the good you can,
By all the means you can,
In all the ways you can,
In all the places you can,
At all the times you can,
To all the people you can,
As long as ever you can.

COME DOWN, O MAID

Alfred, Lord Tennyson

"Come down, O maid, from yonder mountain height:
What pleasure lives in height (the shepherd sang),
In height and cold, the splendour of the hills?
But cease to move so near the Heavens, and cease
To glide a sunbeam by the blasted Pine,
To sit a star upon the sparkling spire;
And come, for Love is of the valley, come,
For Love is of the valley, come thou down
And find him; by the happy threshold, he,
Or hand in hand with Plenty in the maize,
Or red with spirited purple of the vats,
Or foxlike in the vine; or cares to walk
With Death and Morning on the silver horns,
Nor wilt thou snare him in the white ravine,
Nor find him dropt upon the firths of ice,
That huddling slant in furrow-cloven falls
To roll the torrent out of dusky doors:
But follow; let the torrent dance thee down
To find him in the valley; let the wild
Lean-headed Eagles yelp alone, and leave
The monstrous ledges there to slope, and spill
Their thousand wreaths of dangling watersmoke,
That like a broken purpose waste in air:
So waste not thou; but come; for all the vales
Await thee; azure pillars of the hearth
Arise to thee; the children call, and I
Thy shepherd pipe, and sweet is every sound,
Sweeter thy voice, but every sound is sweet;
Myriads of rivulets hurry thro' the lawn,
The moan of doves in immemorial elms,
And murmuring of innumerable bees.

HE WAS FROM MISSOURI

Willard Duncan Vandiver

I come from a state that raises corn and cotton and cockleburs and Democrats, and frothy eloquence neither convinces nor satisfies me. I am from Missouri. You have got to show me.

DIOGENES TO THE PEOPLE OF SYNOPE, HIS NATIVE CITY

My countrymen:

You have banished me, my countrymen, and I on the contrary desire that you be confined to your homes, for while you inhabit Synope, I live at Athens. You spend your time with none but mercenary traders, while I converse daily with philosophers. You deal in nothing but vile merchandise, while I continually read both men and books. Pity me not then, but rather envy me in that being removed from you, I lead a much happier life than when I was with you. I then wallowed in all kinds of sloth and luxury; I now am obliged to labor for my living; I then lived at large, but now am confined to rules. What then hinders me from pitying you in your condition, men of Synope, in that having so great wealth you want knowledge, and in wanting that, want everything?

Your banishing me, I look upon with favour, and value your threats so little, that I had rather be accused than applauded by you. In a word, I would choose to be a vagabond all over the earth, before I would consent to live a wealthy, but unknown citizen of Synope.

Farewell.

BATTER MY HEART

John Donne

Batter my heart, three person'd God; for, you
As yet but knocke, breathe, shine, and seeke to mend,
That I may rise, and stand, o'erthrow me and bend
Your force, to breake, blowe, burn and make me new.
I, like an usurpt towne, to another due,

Labour to'admit you, but Oh, to no end;
Reason, your viceroy in mee, mee should defend,
But is captiv'd, and proves weake or untrue.
Yet dearely' I love you and would be loved faine,
But am bethroth'd unto your enemie:
Divorce mee, 'untie, or breake that knot againe,
Take mee to you, imprison mee, for I
Except you'enthrall mee, never shall be free,
Nor ever chaste, except you ravish mee.

NOTICE

Persons attempting to find a motive in this narrative will be prosecuted; persons attempting to find a moral in it will be banished; persons attempting to find a plot in it will be shot.

By Order of the Author,
Per G.G., Chief of Ordnance
(From Mark Twain's *Huckleberry Finn*)

ON AN OLD SUN DIAL

Time flies,
Suns rise
And shadows fall.
Let time go by.
Love is forever over all.

THE STARS

Ralph Waldo Emerson

If a man would be alone, let him look at the stars. The rays that come from those heavenly worlds will separate between him and what he touches.

One might think the atmosphere was made transparent with this design, to give man, in the heavenly bodies, the perpetual presence of the sublime. Seen in the streets of cities, how great they are!

(586)

If the stars should appear one night in a thousand years, how would men believe, and adore, and preserve for many generations, the remembrance of the city of God which had been shown? But every night come out these envoys of beauty, and light the universe with their admonishing smile.

LOVE ME, AND THE WORLD IS MINE

David Reed, Jr.

I wander on as in a dream,
My goal a paradise must be,
For there an angel waits 'twould seem,
Yet lo, dear heart, 'tis only thee.
Suns may shine to light my way dear,
Wealth be mine for ever dear,
Queens may pledge their riches too;
Yet the world would still be lonely,
With such virtues only.
Life to me dear, means just you.
I care not for the stars that shine,
I dare not hope to e'er be thine,
I only know I love you.
Love me, and the world is mine.

THE DAYS OF THE MONTH

Anonymous

Thirty days hath September,
April, June and November;
All the rest have thirty-one,
Excepting February alone,
Which hath but twenty-eight, in fine,
Till leap-year gives it twenty-nine.

THE LADIES

Rudyard Kipling

I've taken my fun where I've found it;
  I've rogued an' I've ranged in my time;
I've 'ad my pickin' o' sweet'earts,
  An' four o' the lot was prime.
One was an 'arf-caste widow,
  One was a woman at Prome,
One was the wife of a *jemedar-sais,* *
  And one is a girl at 'ome.

Now I aren't no 'and with the ladies,
  For, takin' 'em all along,
You never can say till you've tried 'em,
  An' then you are like to be wrong.
There's time when you'll think that you mightn't,
  There's times when you'll know that you might;
But the things you will learn from the Yellow an' Brown,
  They'll 'elp you a lot with the White!

I was a young un at 'Oogli,
  Shy as a girl to begin;
Aggie de Castrer she made me,
  An' Aggie was clever as sin;
Older than me, but my first un—
  More like a mother she were—
Showed me the way to promotion and pay,
  An' I learned about women from 'er!

Then I was ordered to Burma,
  Actin' in charge o' Bazar,
An' I got me a tiddy live 'eathen
  Through buyin' supplies off 'er pa.
Funny an' yellow an' faithful—
  Doll in a teacup she were,
But we lived on the square, like a true-married pair,
  An' I learned about women from 'er!

* Head-groom

(588)

Then we was shifted to Neemuch
   (Or I might ha' been keepin' 'er now),
An' I took with a shiny she-devil,
   The wife of a nigger at Mhow;
Taught me the gipsy-folks' *bolee*;*
   Kind of volcano she were,
For she knifed me one night 'cause I wished she was white,
   An' I learned about women from 'er!

Then I come 'ome in a trooper,
   'long of a kid of sixteen—
Girl from a convent at Meerut,
   The straightest I ever 'ave seen.
Love at first sight was 'er trouble,
   She didn't know what it were;
An' I wouldn't do such, 'cause I loved 'er too much,
   But—I learned about women from 'er!

I've taken my fun where I've found it,
   An' now I must pay for my fun,
For the more you 'ave known o' the others
   The less will you settle to one;
An' the end of it's sittin' and thinkin',
   An' dreamin' Hell-fires to see;
So be warned by my lot (which I know you will not),
   An' learn about women from me!

What did the Colonel's Lady think?
   Nobody ever knew.
Somebody asked the Sergeant's wife,
   An' she told 'em true!
When you get to a man in the case,
   They're like as a row of pins—
For the Colonel's Lady an' Judy O'Grady
   Are sisters under their skins!

* Slang

FROM PRESIDENT EISENHOWER'S FAREWELL ADDRESS TO THE NATION

Crises there will continue to be. In meeting them, whether foreign or domestic, great or small, there is a recurring temptation to feel that some spectacular and costly action could become the miraculous solution to all current difficulties. A huge increase in newer elements of our defenses; development of unrealistic programs to cure every ill in agriculture; a dramatic expansion in basic and applied research—these and many other possibilities, each possibly promising in itself, may be suggested as the only way to the road we wish to travel.

But each proposal must be weighed in the light of a broader consideration; the need to maintain balance in and among national programs—balance between the private and the public economy, balance between the cost and hoped for advantages—balance between the clearly necessary and the comfortably desirable; balance between our essential requirements as a nation and the duties imposed by the nation upon the individual; balance between actions of the moment and the national welfare of the future.

But we can no longer risk emergency improvisation of national defense. We have been compelled to create a permanent armaments industry of vast proportions. Added to this, three and a half million men and women are directly engaged in the defense establishment. We annually spend on military security alone more than the net income of all United States corporations.

Now this conjunction of an immense military establishment and a large arms industry is new in the American experience. The total influence—economic, political, even spiritual—is felt in every city, every state house, every office of the Federal Government. We recognize the imperative need for this development. Yet we must not fail to comprehend its grave implications. Our toil, resources and livelihood are all involved; so is the very structure of our society.

In the councils of Government, we must guard against the acquisition of unwarranted influence, whether sought or unsought, by the military-industrial complex. The potential for the disastrous rise of misplaced power exists and will persist.

We must never let the weight of this combination endanger our liberties or democratic processes. We should take nothing for granted. Only an alert and knowledgeable citizenry can compel the proper meshing of the huge industrial and military machinery of defense with our peaceful methods and goals, so that security and liberty may prosper together.

The prospect of domination of the nation's scholars by Federal employment, project allocations and the power of money is ever present, and is gravely to be regarded.

Yet, in holding scientific research and discovery in respect, as we should, we must also be alert to the equal and opposite danger that public policy could itself become the captive of a scientific-technological elite.

It is the task of statesmanship to mold, to balance, and to integrate these and other forces, new and old, within the principles of our democratic system—ever aiming toward the supreme goals of our free society.

Another factor in maintaining our balance involves the element of time. As we peer into society's future, we—you and I, and our Government—must avoid the impulse to live only for today, plundering, for our own ease and convenience, the precious resources of tomorrow.

We cannot mortage the material assets of our grandchildren without risking the loss also of their political and spiritual heritage.

(January 17, 1961)

THE BLADES OF GRASS

Stephen Crane

In Heaven,
Some little blades of grass
Stood before God.
"What did you do?"
Then all save one of the little blades
Began eagerly to relate
The merits of their lives.
This one stayed a small way behind,
Ashamed.
Presently, God said,
"And what did you do?"
The little blade answered, "Oh, my Lord,
Memory is bitter to me,
For, if I did good deeds,
I know not of them."
Then God, in all His splendor,
Arose from His throne,
"Oh, best little blade of grass!" He said.

(591)

FOLLOW THE GLEAM

Alfred, Lord Tennyson

Not of the sunlight,
Not of the moonlight,
Not of the starlight!
O young Mariner,
Down to the haven,
Call your companions,
Launch your vessel,
And crowd your canvas,
And, ere it vanishes
Over the margin,
After it, follow it,
Follow the Gleam.

THE WITCHING TIME OF NIGHT

William Shakespeare

'Tis now the very witching time of night,
When churchyards yawn, and hell itself breathes out
Contagion to this world: now could I drink hot blood,
And do such bitter business as the day
Would quake to look on. Soft! now to my mother,
O heart, lose not thy nature; let not ever
The soul of Nero enter this firm bosom:
Let me be cruel, not unnatural:
I will speak daggers to her, but use none;
My tongue and soul in this be hypocrites;
How in words soever she be shent,
To give them seals, never, my soul, consent!

(From *Hamlet*)

From the *Charter of the United Nations*

We, the people of the United Nations, determined to save succeeding generations from the scourge of war, which twice in our lifetime has brought untold sorrow to mankind, and to reaffirm faith in fundamental human rights, in the dignity and worth of the human person, in the equal right of men and women and of nations large and small. . . .

And for these ends to practice tolerance and live together in peace with one another as good neighbors . . .

Have resolved to combine these efforts to accomplish our aims.

(June, 1945)

I DON'T WANT TO PLAY IN YOUR YARD

Philip Wingate

Once there lived side by side two little maids,
Used to dress just alike, hair down in braids,
Blue gingham pinafores, stockings of red,
Little sun bonnets tied on each pretty head.
When school was over secrets they'd tell,
Whispering arm in arm, down by the well.
One day a quarrel came, hot tears were shed:
"You can't play in our yard," but the other said:

Chorus
"I don't want to play in your yard, I don't like you anymore,
You'll be sorry when you see me, sliding down our cellar door,
You can't holler down our rain-barrel, you can't climb our apple
     tree,
I don't want to play in your yard if you won't be good to me."

Next day two little maids each other miss.
Quarrels are soon made up, sealed with a kiss,
Then hand in hand again, happy they go,
Friends all through life to be, they love each other so.
Soon school days pass away, sorrows and bliss,
But love remembers yet quarrels and kiss;
In sweet dreams of childhood, we hear this cry:
"You can't play in our yard," but the other said: (*Chorus*)

(593)

BUDDHA COUNSELS A GRIEVING MOTHER

The Gospel of Buddha
(TRANSLATOR: Paul Carus)

And Kisā Gotamī had only one son, and he died. In her grief she
carried the dead child to all her neighbors, asking them for medicine, and the people said: "She has lost her senses. The boy is dead."

At length Kisā Gotamī met a man who replied to her request: "I
cannot give thee medicine for thy child, but I know a physician who
can."

And the girl said: "Pray tell me, sir; who is it?" And the man
replied: "Go to Sayamuni, the Buddha."

Kisā Gotamī repaired to the Buddha and cried: "Lord and
Master, give me the medicine that will cure my boy."

The Buddha answered: "I want a handful of mustard-seed." And
when the girl in her joy promised to procure it, the Buddha added:
"The mustard-seed must be taken from a house where no one has
lost a child, husband, parent, or friend."

Poor Kisā Gotamī now went from house to house, and the people
pitied her and said: "Here is a mustard-seed, take it!" But when she
asked, "Did a son or daughter, a father or mother, die in your
family?" they answered her: "Alas! the living are few, the dead are
many. Do not remind us of our deepest grief." And there was no
house but some beloved had died in it.

Kisā Gotamī became weary and hopeless, and sat down at the wayside, watching the lights of the city, as they flickered up and were
extinguished again. At last the darkness of the night reigned everywhere. And she considered the fate of man, that their lives flicker up
and are extinguished. And she thought to herself: "How selfish am I
in my grief! Death is common to all; yet in this valley of desolation
there is a path that leads him to immortality who has surrendered all
selfishness."

Putting away the selfishness of her affection for her child, Kisā
Gotamī had the dead body buried in the forest. Returning to the
Buddha, she took refuge in him and found comfort in the Dharma,
which is a balm that will soothe all the pain of our troubled hearts.

The Buddha said: "The life of mortals in this world is troubled
and brief and combined with pain. For there is not any means by
which those that have been born can avoid dying; after reaching old
age there is death; of such a nature are living beings. . . .

"Mark! while relatives are looking on and lamenting deeply, one
by one mortals are carried off, like an ox that is led to the slaughter.

"So the world is afflicted with death and decay, therefore the wise do not grieve, knowing the terms of the world. . . .

"Not from weeping nor from grieving will any one obtain peace of mind; on the contrary, his pain will be the greater and his body will suffer. He will make himself sick and pale, yet the dead are not saved by his lamentation. . . .

"He who seeks peace should draw out the arrow of lamentation, and complaint, and grief.

"He who has drawn out the arrow and has become composed will obtain peace of mind; he who has overcome all sorrow will become free from sorrow, and be blessed."

HOLY, HOLY, HOLY!

Reginald Heber

Holy, Holy, Holy! Lord God Almighty!
  Early in the morning our song shall rise to thee:
Holy, Holy, Holy! merciful and mighty!
  God in Three Persons, blessèd Trinity.

Holy, Holy, Holy! all the saints adore thee,
  Casting down their golden crowns around the glassy sea;
Cherubim and Seraphim falling down before thee,
  Which wert, and art, and evermore shalt be.

Holy, Holy, Holy! though the darkness hide thee,
  Though the eye of sinful man thy glory may not see,
Only thou art holy; there is none beside thee,
  Perfect in power, in love, and purity.

Holy, Holy, Holy! Lord God Almighty!
  All thy works shall praise thy Name, in earth, and sky, and sea;
Holy, Holy, Holy! merciful and mighty!
  God in Three Persons, blessèd Trinity.

THE SEVEN WONDERS OF THE ANCIENT WORLD

Anonymous

The Pyramids first, which in Egypt were laid;
Next Babylon's Garden, for Amytis made;
Then Mausolos' Tomb of affection and guilt;
Fourth, the Temple of Dian in Ephesus built;
The Colossus of Rhodes, cast in brass, to the Sun;
Sixth, Jupiter's Statue, by Phidias done;
The Pharos of Egypt comes last, we are told,
Or the Palace of Cyrus, cemented with gold.

GO TO THE ANT, THOU SLUGGARD

Holy Bible, Proverbs 6:6–11

Go to the ant, thou sluggard: consider her ways and be wise:
Which having no guide, overseer, or ruler,
Provideth her meat in the summer, and gathereth her food in the
    harvest.
How long wilt thou sleep, O sluggard? when wilt thou arise out of
    thy sleep?
Yet a little sleep, a little slumber, a little folding of the hands to
    sleep:
So shall thy poverty come as one that travelleth, and thy want as an
    armed man.

WITH RUE MY HEART IS LADEN

A. E. Housman

With rue my heart is laden
    For golden friends I had,
For many a rose-lipt maiden
    And many a lightfoot lad.

By brooks too broad for leaping
The lightfoot boys are laid;
The rose-lipt girls are sleeping
In fields where roses fade.

BROKEN FRIENDSHIP

Samuel Taylor Coleridge

Alas! they had been friends in youth,
But whispering tongues can poison truth!
And constancy lives in realms above!
And life is thorny, and Youth is vain!
And to be wroth with one we love,
Doth work like madness in the brain!
They parted—ne'er to meet again!
But never either found another
To free the hollow heart from paining!
They stood aloof, the scars remaining;
Like cliffs which had been rent asunder!
A dreary sea now flows between;
But neither heat, nor frost, nor thunder,
Shall wholly do away, I ween,
The marks of that which once had been.

RETIRE UNTO THYSELF

Marcus Aurelius

(TRANSLATOR: Charles Long)

Men seek retreats for themselves, houses in the country, sea-shores
and mountains, and thou too are wont to desire such things very
much. But this is altogether a mark of the most common sort of man,
for it is in thy power whenever thou shalt choose to retire into thyself. For nowhere either with more quiet or more freedom from
trouble does a man return into his own soul, particularly when he

has within him such thoughts that by looking into them he is immediately in perfect tranquillity; and I affirm that tranquillity is nothing else than the good ordering of the mind.

SONG

Thomas Carew

Ask me no more where Jove bestows,
When June is past, the fading rose;
For in your beauty's orient deep
These flowers, as in their causes, sleep.

Ask me no more whither do stray
The golden atoms of the day;
For, in pure love, heaven did prepare
Those powers to enrich your hair.

Ask me no more whither doth haste
The nightingale, when May is past;
For in your sweet dividing throat
She winters, and keeps warm her note.

Ask me no more where those stars light
That downwards fall in dead of night;
For in your eyes they sit, and there
Fixèd become, as in their sphere.

Ask me no more if east or west
The Phoenix builds her spicy nest;
For unto you at last she flies,
And in your fragrant bosom dies.

Marriage resembles a pair of shears, so joined that they can not be separated; often moving in opposite directions, yet always punishing anyone who comes between them.
—Sydney Smith

FRIENDSHIP

Mark Twain

The holy passion of Friendship is of so sweet and steady and loyal and enduring a nature that it will last through a whole lifetime, if not asked to lend money.

AH, FADING JOY

John Dryden

Ah, fading joy, how quickly art thou past!
    Yet we thy ruine haste:
As if the cares of Humane Life were few,
    We seek out new,
And follow Fate that does too fast pursue.

See how on ev'ry Bough the Birds express
    In their sweet notes their happiness.
    They all enjoy and nothing spare;
But on their Mother Nature lay their care:
Why then should Man, the Lord of all below,
    Such troubles chuse to know,
As none of all his Subjects undergo?

IT PAYS TO ADVERTISE

Anonymous

The codfish lays ten thousand eggs,
    The homely hen lays one.
The codfish never cackles
    To tell you what she's done.
And so we scorn the codfish,
    While the humble hen we prize,
Which only goes to show you
    That it pays to advertise.

BRUTUS EXPLAINS WHY HE MURDERED CAESAR

William Shakespeare

Romans, countrymen, and lovers! hear me for my cause, and be silent, that you may hear: believe me for mine honor, and have respect to mine honor, that you may believe: censure me in your wisdom, and awake your senses, that you may the better judge. If there be any in this assembly, any dear friend of Caesar's, to him I say that Brutus' love to Caesar was no less than his. If then that friend demand why Brutus rose against Caesar, this is my answer: not that I loved Caesar less, but that I loved Rome more. Had you rather Caesar were living, and die all slaves, than that Caesar were dead, to live all freemen? As Caesar loved me, I weep for him; as he was fortunate, I rejoice at it; as he was valiant, I honor him; but as he was ambitious, I slew him. There is tears for his love; joy for his fortune; honor for his valor; and death for his ambition. Who is here so base that would be a bondman? If any, speak; for him have I offended. Who is here so rude that would not be a Roman? If any, speak; for him have I offended. Who is here so vile that will not love his country? If any, speak; for him have I offended. I pause for a reply.

(From *Julius Caesar*)

THE CHURCH'S ONE FOUNDATION

Samuel J. Stone

The Church's one foundation
　Is Jesus Christ her Lord;
She is his new creation
　By water and the word:
From heaven he came and sought her
　To be his holy bride;
With his own blood he bought her,
　And for her life he died.

Elect from every nation,
　Yet one o'er all the earth,
Her charter of salvation,
　One Lord, one faith, one birth;

One holy Name she blesses,
  Partakes one holy food,
And to one hope she presses,
  With every grace endued.

Though with a scornful wonder
  Men see her sore opprest,
By schisms rent asunder,
  By heresies distrest;
Yet saints their watch are keeping,
  Their cry goes up, "How long?"
And soon the night of weeping
  Shall be the morn of song.

'Mid toil and tribulation,
  And tumult of her war,
She waits the consummation
  Of peace for evermore;
Till with the vision glorious
  Her longing eyes are blest,
And the great Church victorious
  Shall be the Church at rest.

Yet she on earth hath union
  With God the Three in One,
And mystic sweet communion
  With those whose rest is won.
O happy ones and holy!
  Lord, give us grace that we
Like them, the meek and lowly,
  On high may dwell with thee.

TRUST THYSELF

Ralph Waldo Emerson

Trust thyself: every heart vibrates to that iron string. . . . Who so
would be a man, must be a nonconformist. He who would gather
immortal palms must not be hindered by the name of goodness, but
must explore if it be goodness. . . .

Insist on yourself; never imitate. Your own gift you can present every moment with the cumulative force of a whole life's cultivation; but of the adopted talent of another you have only an extemporaneous half possession. That which each can do best, none but his Maker can teach him. No man yet knows what it is, nor can, till that person has exhibited it. . . .

Nothing can bring you peace but yourself. Nothing can bring you peace but the triumph of principles.

PIAZZA PIECE

John Crowe Ranson

  —I am a gentleman in a dustcoat trying
  To make you hear. Your ears are soft
         and small
  And listen to an old man not at all,
  They want the young men's whispering
         and sighing.
  But see the roses on your trellis dying
  And hear the spectral singing of the moon;
  For I must have my lovely lady soon,
  I am a gentleman in a dustcoat trying.

  —I am a lady young in beauty waiting
  Until my truelove comes, and then we kiss.
  But what grey man among the vines is this
  Whose words are dry and faint as
         in a dream?
  Back from my trellis, Sir, before I scream!
  I am a lady young in beauty waiting.

Orthodoxy is my doxy; heterodoxy is another man's doxy.

        —Bishop William Warburton

A FACE ON WHICH TIME MAKES BUT
LITTLE IMPRESSION

Thomas Hardy

A Saturday afternoon in November was approaching the time of twilight, and the vast tract of unenclosed wild known as Egdon Heath embrowned itself moment by moment. Overhead the hollow stretch of whitish cloud shutting out the sky was as a tent which had the whole heath for its floor.

The heaven being spread with this pallid screen and the earth with the darkest vegetation, their meeting-line at the horizon was clearly marked. In such contrast the heath wore the appearance of an instalment of night which had taken up its place before its astronomical hour was come: darkness had to a great extent arrived hereon, while day stood distinct in the sky. Looking upwards, a furze-cutter would have been inclined to continue work; looking down, he would have decided to finish his faggot and go home. The distant rims of the world and of the firmament seemed to be a division in time no less than a division in matter. The face of the heath by its mere complexion added half an hour to evening: it could in like manner retard the dawn, sadden noon, anticipate the frowning storms scarcely generated, and intensify the opacity of a moonless midnight to a cause of shaking and dread.

In fact, precisely at this transitional point of its nightly roll into darkness the great and particular glory of the Egdon waste began, and nobody could be said to understand the heath who had not been there at such a time. It could best be felt when it could not clearly be seen, its complete effect and explanation lying in this and the succeeding hours before the next dawn: then, and only then, did it tell its true tale. The spot was, indeed, a near relation of night, and when night showed itself an apparent tendency to gravitate together could be perceived in its shades and the scene. The sombre stretch of rounds and hollows seemed to rise and meet the evening gloom in pure sympathy, the heath exhaling darkness as rapidly as the heavens precipitated it. And so the obscurity in the air and the obscurity in the land closed together in a black fraternization toward which each advanced half-way.

The place became full of a watchful intentness now; for when other things sank brooding to sleep the heath appeared slowly to awake and listen. Every night its Titanic form seemed to await something; but it had waited thus, unmoved, during so many centuries, through the crises of so many things, that it could only be imagined to await one last crisis—the final overthrow.

It was a spot which returned upon the memory of those who loved it with an aspect of peculiar and kindly congruity. Smiling champaigns of flowers and fruit hardly do this, for they are permanently harmonious only with an existence of better reputation as to its issues than the present. Twilight combined with the scenery of Egdon Heath to evolve a thing majestic without severity, impressive without showiness, emphatic in its admonitions, grand in its simplicity. . . .

The most thorough-going ascetic could feel that he had a natural right to wander on Egdon: he was keeping within the line of legitimate indulgence when he laid himself open to influences such as these. Colours and beauties so far subdued were, at least, the birthright of all. Only in summer days of highest feather did its mood touch the level of gaiety. Intensity was more usually reached by way of the solemn than by way of the brilliant, and such a sort of intensity was often arrived at during winter darkness, tempests, and mists. Then Egdon was aroused to reciprocity; for the storm was its lover, and the wind its friend. Then it became the home of strange phantoms; and it was found to be the hitherto unrecognized original of those wild regions of obscurity which are vaguely felt to be compassing us about in midnight dreams of flight and disaster, and are never thought of after the dream till revived by scenes like this.

(Opening of *The Return of the Native*)

ASPIRATION

Henry David Thoreau

Did you ever hear of a man who had striven all his life faithfully and singly toward an object and in no measure obtained it? If a man constantly aspires, is he not elevated? Did ever a man try heroism, magnanimity, truth, sincerity, and find that there was no advantage in them,—that it was a vain endeavor?

IT CAME UPON THE MIDNIGHT CLEAR

Edmund Hamilton Sears

It came upon the midnight, clear,
  That glorious song of old,
From angels bending near the earth
  To touch their harps of gold;
"Peace on earth, good will to men
  From heaven's all-gracious King"—
The world in solemn stillness lay
  To hear the angels sing.

For lo! the days are hastening on
  By prophet bards foretold,
When with the ever circling years
  Comes round the age of gold;
When peace shall over all the earth
  In ancient splendors fling,
And the whole world gives back the song
  Which now the angels sing.

LIMERICK

Anonymous

There was once a maiden of Siam
  Who said to her lover, young Kiam,
    If you kiss me, of course,
    You will have to use force,
But God knows you are stronger than I am.

SELF-RELIANCE

Ralph Waldo Emerson

I do not wish to expiate, but to live. My life is not an apology, but a life. It is for itself and not for a spectacle. I much prefer that it should be a lower strain, so it be genuine and equal, than that it should be glittering and unsteady. . . .

(605)

What I must do is all that concerns me, not what the people think. This rule, equally arduous in actual, and in intellectual life, may serve for the whole distinction between greatness and meanness. It is the harder because you will always find those who think they know what is your duty better than you know it. It is easy in the world to live after the world's opinion; it is easy in solitude to live after our own; but the great man is he who in the midst of the crowd keeps with perfect sweetness the independence of solitude.

A PARTING GUEST

James Whitcomb Riley

What delightful hosts are they—
    Life and Love!
Lingeringly I turn away,
    This late hour, yet glad enough
They have not withheld from me
    Their high hospitality.
So, with face lit with delight
    And all gratitude, I stay
    Yet to press their hands and say,
"Thanks.—So fine a time! Good night."

ON BEING CAESAR'S FRIEND

Epictetus

(TRANSLATOR: Elizabeth Carter)

What then, is this evil thus hurtful, and to be avoided? "Not to be the friend of Caesar," saith one. He is gone, he fails in the adapting, he is embarrassed, he seeks what is nothing to the purpose. For, if he gets to be Caesar's friend, he is nevertheless distant from what he sought. For what is it that every man seeks? To be secure, to be happy, to do what he pleases without restraint and without compulsion. When he becomes the friend of Caesar, then, doth he cease

(606)

to be restrained? To be compelled? Is he secure? Is he happy? Whom shall we ask? Whom can we better credit than this very man, who hath been his friend? Come forth and tell us whether you sleep more quietly now, or before you were the friend of Caesar? You presently hear him cry, "Leave off, for heaven's sake, and do not insult me. You know not the miseries I suffer; there is no sleep for me; but one comes, and saith that Caesar is already awake; another, that he is just going out. Then follow perturbations, then cares." Well, and when did you use to sup more pleasantly, formerly, or now? Hear what he says about this, too. When he is not invited, he is distracted; and if he is, he sups like a slave with his master, solicitous all the while not to say or do anything foolish. And what think you? Is he afraid of being whipped like a slave? How can he hope to escape so well? No; but as becomes a great man, Caesar's friend, of losing his head.—And when did you bathe more quietly; when did you perform your exercises more at your leisure; in short, which life would you rather wish to live, your present, or the former? I could swear, there is no one so stupid and insensible as not to deplore his miseries, in proportion as he is more the friend of Caesar.

No one fears Caesar himself, but death, banishment, loss of goods, prison, disgrace. Nor doth any one love Caesar, unless he be a person of great worth; but we love riches, the tribunate, the praetorship, the consulship. When we love and hate and fear these things, they who have the disposal of them must necessarily be our masters.

AMERICAN NAMES

Stephen Vincet Benét

I have fallen in love with American names,
The sharp names that never get fat,
The snakeskin-titles of mining-claims,
The plumed war-bonnet of Medicine Hat,
Tucson and Deadwood and Lost Mule Flat.

Seine and Piave are silver spoons,
But the spoonbowl-metal is thin and worn,
There are English counties like hunting-tunes
Played on the keys of a postboy's horn,
But I will remember where I was born.

I will remember Carquinez Straits,
Little French Lick and Lundy's Lane,
The Yankee ships and the Yankee dates
And the bullet-towns of Calamity Jane.
I will remember Skunktown Plain.

I will fall in love with a Salem tree
And a rawhide quirt from Santa Cruz,
I will get me a bottle of Boston sea
And a blue-gum nigger to sing me blues,
I am tired of loving a foreign muse.

Rue des Martyrs and Bleeding-Heart-Yard,
Senlis, Pisa, and Blindman's Oast,
It is a magic ghost you guard
But I am sick for a newer ghost,
Harrisburg, Spartanburg, Painted Post.

Henry and John were never so
And Henry and John were always right?
Granted, but when it was time to go
And the tea and the laurels had stood all night,
Did they never watch for Nantucket Light?

I shall not rest quiet in Montparnasse.
I shall not lie easy at Winchelsea.
You may bury my body in Sussex grass,
You may bury my tongue at Champmédy.
I shall not be there. I shall rise and pass.
Bury my heart at Wounded Knee.

THE SULTAN'S HAREM

Anonymous

The sultan got sore on his harem,
And invented a scheme to scare 'em;
He caught him a mouse
Which he loosed in the house;
(The confusion is called harem scarem.)

From THE BALLAD OF EAST AND WEST

Rudyard Kipling

O East is East, and West is West, and never the twain shall meet,
Till Earth and Sky stand presently at God's great Judgment Seat;
But there is neither East nor West, Border, nor Breed, nor Birth,
When two strong men stand face to face, though they come from the
    ends of earth!

THE LAST WORD

Matthew Arnold

Creep into thy narrow bed,
Creep, and let no more be said!
Vain thy onset! all stands fast.
Thou thyself must break at last.

Let the long contention cease!
Geese are swans, and swans are geese.
Let them have it how they will!
Thou art tired; best be still.

They out-talk'd thee, hiss'd thee, tore thee?
Better men fared thus before thee;
Fired their ringing shot and pass'd,
Hotly charged—and sank at last.

Charge once more, then, and be dumb!
Let the victors, when they come,
When the forts of folly fall,
Find thy body by the wall!

ACCEPTANCE

Marcus Aurelius

(TRANSLATOR: Charles Long)

If the gods have determined about me and about the things which must happen to me, they have determined well, for it is not easy even to imagine a deity without forethought; and as to doing me harm, why should they have any desire toward that? for what advantage would result to them from this or to the whole, which is the special object of their providence? But if they have not determined about me individually, and they have certainly determined about the whole at least, and the things which happen by way of sequence in this general arrangement I ought to accept with pleasure and be content with them.

JOHN HENRY

Anonymous

John Henry said to his captain,
"A man ain't nothing but a man.
And before I'll let your steam drill beat me down,
Die with the hammer in my hand, Lawd, Lawd!
Die with the hammer in my hand."

John Henry got a thirty pound hammer,
Beside the steam drill he did stand.
He beat that steam drill three inches down,
An' died with his hammer in his hand, Lawd, Lawd!
Died with the hammer in his hand.

John Henry had a little woman
And she was always dressed in blue,
She went down track never looking back,
Says, "John Henry, I am always true to you, Lawd, Lawd!
John Henry, I am always true to you."

"Who gonna shoe your pretty feet,
Who gonna comb your bangs?
Who gonna kiss your rose-red lips,
Who gonna be your man, Lawd, Lawd!
Who gonna be your man?"

"Sweet Papa gonna shoe your pretty feet,
Sister gonna comb your bangs,
Mamma gonna kiss your rose-red lips,
John Henry gonna be your man, Lawd, Lawd!
John Henry gonna be your man."

John Henry had a pretty little boy,
Sittin' in the palm of his hand.
He hugged and kissed him an' bid him farewell,
"O son, do the best you can, Lawd, Lawd!
Son, do the best you can."

They took John Henry to the graveyard
An' they buried him in the sand,
An' ev'ry locomotive come roarin' by
Says, "Dere lays a steel-drivin' man, Lawd, Lawd!
Dere lays a steel-drivin' man."

SOLOMON JUDGES BETWEEN TWO WOMEN DISPUTING OVER A CHILD

Holy Bible, I Kings 3:16–27

Then came there two women, that were harlots, unto the king, and stood before him.

And the one woman said, O my lord, I and this woman dwell in one house; and I was delivered of a child with her in the house.

And it came to pass, the third day after that I was delivered, that this woman was delivered also: and we were together; there was no stranger with us in the house, save we two in the house.

And this woman's child died in the night; because she overlaid it.

And she arose at midnight, and took my son from beside me, while thine handmaid slept, and laid it in her bosom, and laid her dead child in my bosom.

(611)

And when I arose in the morning to give my child suck, behold, it was dead; but when I had considered it in the morning, behold, it was not my son which I did bear.

And the other woman said, Nay; but the living is my son, and the dead is thy son. And this said, No; but the dead is thy son, and the living is my son. Thus they spake before the king.

Then said the king, The one saith, This is my son that liveth, and thy son is the dead; and the other saith, Nay; but thy son is the dead, and my son is the living.

And the king said, Bring me a sword. And they brought a sword before the king.

And the king said, Divide the living child in two, and give half to one, and half to the other.

Then spake the woman whose the living child was unto the king, for her bowels yearned upon her son, and she said, O my lord, give her the living child, and in no wise slay it. But the other said, Let it be neither mine nor thine, but divide it.

Then the king answered and said, Give her the living child, and in no wise slay it: she is the mother thereof.

I LOVE TO TELL THE STORY

Katherine Hankey

> I love to tell the story
>   Of unseen things above,
> Of Jesus and his glory,
>   Of Jesus and his love.
> I love to tell the story,
>   Because I know 'tis true;
> It satisfies my longings
>   As nothing else could do.
>
> *Refrain*:
>   I love to tell the story,
>   'Twill be my theme in glory,
>   To tell the old, old story
>   Of Jesus and his love.

I love to tell the story;
  More wonderful it seems
Than all the golden fancies
  Of all our golden dreams.
I love to tell the story,
  It did so much for me;
And that is just the reason
  I tell it now to thee.

I love to tell the story;
  'Tis pleasant to repeat
What seems, each time I tell it,
  More wonderfully sweet.
I love to tell the story,
  For some have never heard
The message of salvation
  From God's own holy word.

I love to tell the story;
  For those who know it best
Seem hungering and thirsting
  To hear it, like the rest.
And when, in scenes of glory,
  I sing the new, new song,
'Twill be the old, old story
  That I have loved so long.

DETERMINATION

Anonymous

Sir Andrew Barton said, I'm hurt,
  I'm hurt, but I'm not slain.
I will lay me down and bleed awhile,
  Then rise and fight again.

SUMER IS ICUMEN IN

Anonymous

Sumer is icumen in,
  Lhude sing cuccu;
Groweth sed and bloweth med
  And springth the wudè nu.
    Sing cuccu!
Awe bleteth after lomb,
  Lhouth after calvè cu;
Bulluc sterteth, buckè verteth;
  Murie sing cuccu.
    Cuccu, cuccu,
  Wel singès thu, cuccu,
  Ne swik thu naver nu.
Sing cuccu nu! Sing cuccu!
Sing cuccu! Sing cuccu nu!

WISE SAYINGS OF BENJAMIN FRANKLIN

Love your neighbors, but don't pull down your hedges.

Don't think to hunt two hares with one dog.

He that is rich need not live sparingly, and he than can live sparingly need not be rich.

None preaches better than the ant, and she says nothing.

A long life may not be good enough, but a good life is long enough.

God heals, and the doctor takes the fee.

If you'd have a good servant that you like, serve yourself.

A good example is the best sermon.

Search others for their virtues, thyself for thy vices.

Proclaim not all thou knowest, all thou owest, all thou hast, nor all thou canst.

If you would keep your secret from an enemy, tell it not to a friend.

THE SPACIOUS FIRMAMENT

Joseph Addison

The spacious firmament on high,
With all the blue ethereal sky,
And spangled heavens, a shining frame,
Their great Original proclaim.
The unwearied sun from day to day
Does his Creator's power display,
And publishes to every land
The work of an Almighty hand.

Soon as the evening shades prevail,
The moon takes up the wondrous tale,
And nightly to the listening earth
Repeats the story of her birth;
Whilst all the stars that round her burn,
And all the planets in their turn,
Confirm the tidings as they roll,
And spread the truth from pole to pole.

What though in solemn silence, all
Move round this dark terrestrial ball?
What though nor real voice nor sound
Amidst their radiant orbs be found?
In Reason's ear they all rejoice,
And utter forth a glorious voice,
Forever singing as they shine:
"The hand that made us is divine!"

LOVE

Anonymous

I love you,
Not only for what you are,
But for what I am
When I am with you.

I love you,
Not only for what
You have made of yourself,
But for what
You are making of me.

I love you
For the part of me
That you bring out;
I love you
For putting your hand
Into my heaped-up heart
And passing over
All the foolish, weak things
That you can't help
Dimly seeing there,
And for drawing out
Into the light
All the beautiful belongings
That no one else had looked
Quite far enough to find.

I love you because you
Are helping me to make
Of the lumber of my life
Not a tavern
But a temple;
Out of the works
Of my every day
Not a reproach
But a song.

I love you
Because you have done
More than any creed
Could have done
To make me good,
And more than any fate
Could have done
To make me happy.

You have done it
Without a touch,
Without a word,
Without a sign.
You have done it
By being yourself,
Perhaps that is what
Being a friend means,
After all.

THE WORDS OF POPE JOHN XXIII

(TRANSLATOR: Salvator Attanasio)

What did I feel upon learning that I had been elected Pope? Much emotion, to be sure, and a host of anxieties. But also the same sensation as a baby in swaddling clothes, because the cassock which they had slipped over me was very tight and I felt as though I were wrapped like a mummy.

Formerly the public had been forbidden access to the cupola of St. Peter's so that people would not see the Pope as he took his stroll through the Vatican Gardens. John XXIII had this restriction lifted, declaring: But why can't the faithful watch me? I don't do anything that would give cause for scandal.

Walking through the streets of Rome one day, Pope John heard a woman, taken back by the Pope's obesity, remark to her companion: God, but he's fat!

Pope John turned around and benignly observed: But Madame, you must know that the conclave is not exactly a beauty contest!

A few minutes before receiving President and Mrs. Kennedy, Pope John, evincing an air of vague concern, inquired for the proper mode of addressing the wife of the President of the United States. The monsignor in charge of protocol replied: Your Holiness can choose either Madame President or simply Madame.

Ah!: *said the Pope with a thoughtful air.*

But on entering the audience chamber, he spontaneously opened his arms, smiled broadly and exclaimed: Ah, Jacqueline!

A diplomat newly accredited to the Holy See was received by the Pope. He asked the Pontiff how many persons worked at the Vatican. Winking an eye John XXIII replied: Oh, no more than half of them!

John XXIII recounted that in the first months of his pontificate he often awoke during the night, thinking himself still a cardinal and worried over a difficult decision to be made. At these times, he said, he would say to himself: I'll talk it over with the Pope!

Then he would remember where he was. He would say to himself: But *I'm* the Pope! *After which he would conclude:* Well, I'll talk it over with Our Lord!

Let us look at each other without mistrust, meet each other without fear, talk with each other without surrendering principle.

Unity in necessary things, freedom in doubtful things, charity in all things.

To Maione Roméo: This morning I must receive cardinals, princes and important representatives of the Government. But in the afternoon I want to spend a few minutes with some ordinary people who have no other title save their dignity as human beings and children of God.

In the first days of his pontificate John XXIII received a letter from a twelve-year old boy named Bruno. It read:
My dear Pope: I am undecided. I want to be a policeman or a Pope. What do you think?
The Pope replied:
My little Bruno, if you want my opinion, learn how to be a policeman, because that cannot be improvised. As regards being pope, you will see later. Anybody can be a pope; the proof of this is that I have become one. If you ever should be in Rome, come to see me. I would be glad to talk all this over with you.

Pope John asked a child: What's your name? *When the child answered* Arcangelo, *the Pope said:* Oh, poor me! I'm just plain Angelo!

ST. TERESA'S BOOK-MARK

(TRANSLATOR: Henry Wadsworth Longfellow)

Let nothing disturb thee,
Nothing affright thee;
All things are passing;
God never changeth;
Patient endurance
Attaineth to all things;
Who God possesseth
In nothing is wanting;
Alone God sufficeth.

MY GAL SAL

Paul Dresser

Everything is over and I'm feeling bad,
I lost the best pal that I ever had;
'Tis but a fortnight, since she was here,
Seems like she's gone though for twenty year.
Oh how I miss her, my old pal,
O how I'd kiss her, my Gal Sal.
Face not so handsome, but eyes don't you know,
That shone just as bright as they did years ago.

Chorus:
They called her frivolous Sal,
A peculiar sort of gal,
With a heart that was mellow,
An all 'round good fellow,
Was my old pal.
Your troubles, sorrows and care,
She was always willing to share.
A wild sort of devil,
But dead on the level,
Was my Gal Sal.

(619)

Brought her little dainties just afore she died,
Promised she would meet me, on the other side;
Told her how I loved her, she said: "I know Jim,
Just do your best, leave the rest to Him;"
Gently I pressed her to my breast,
Soon she would take her last long rest.
She looked at me and murmured "pal"
And softly I whispered "Good-bye Sal."

THE PLEASURE OF PAINTING

William Hazlitt

"There is a pleasure in painting which none but painters know. In writing, you have to contend with the world; in painting, you have only to carry on a friendly strife with Nature. You sit down to your task, and are happy. From the moment that you take up the pencil, and look Nature in the face, you are at peace with your own heart. No angry passions rise to disturb the silent progress of the work, to shake the hand, or dim the brow: no irritable humours are set afloat: you have no absurd opinions to combat, no point to strain, no adversary to crush, no fool to annoy—you are actuated by fear or favour to no man. There is "no juggling here," no sophistry, no intrigue, no tampering with the evidence, no attempt to make black white, or white black: but you resign yourself into the hands of a greater power, that of Nature, with the simplicity of a child, and the devotion of an enthusiast—"study with joy her manner, and with rapture taste her style." The mind is calm, and full at the same time. . . .

The painter thus learns to look at nature with different eyes. He before saw her "as in a glass darkly, but now face to face." He understands the texture and meaning of the visible universe, and "sees into the life of things," not by the help of mechanical instruments, but of the improved exercise of his faculties, and an intimate sympathy with nature. . . . He perceives form, he distinguishes character. He reads men and books with an intuitive eye. He is a critic as well as a connoisseur. The conclusions he draws are clear and convincing, because they are taken from the things themselves. He is not a fanatic, a dupe, or a slave; for the habit of seeing for himself also disposes him to judge for himself.

THE THINGS I PRIZE

Henry van Dyke

These are the things I prize
And hold of dearest worth:
Light of the sapphire skies,
Peace of the silent hills,
Shelter of the forests, comfort of the grass,
Music of birds, murmurs of little rills,
Shadows of cloud that swiftly pass,
    And, after showers,
    The smell of flowers
    And of the good brown earth,—
And best of all, along the way, friendship and mirth.

DAY IS DYING IN THE WEST

William F. Sherwin

Day is dying in the west,
Heaven is touching earth with rest;
Wait and worship while the night
Sets her evening lamps alight
    Thro' all the sky.

Refrain:
Holy, holy, holy,
Lord God of Hosts!
Heaven and earth are full of thee,
Heaven and earth are praising thee,
    O Lord most high.

Lord of life, beneath the dome
Of the universe, thy home,
Gather us, who seek thy face,
To the fold of thy embrace,
    For thou art nigh.

(621)

While the deep'ning shadows fall,
Heart of Love, enfolding all,
Thro' the glory and the grace
Of the stars that veil thy face,
    Our hearts ascend.

When for ever from our sight
Pass the stars, the day, the night.
Lord of angels, on our eyes
Let eternal morning rise,
    And shadows end.

PRESIDENT ANDREW JACKSON'S MOTHER WRITES HIM A FINAL LETTER

Andrew, if I should not see you again I wish you to remember and treasure up some things I have already said to you: In this world you will have to make your own way. To do that you must have friends. You can make friends by being honest, and you can keep them by being steadfast. You must keep in mind that friends worth having will in the long run expect as much from you as they give to you. To forget an obligation or be ungrateful for a kindness is a base crime—not merely a fault or a sin but an actual crime. Men guilty of it sooner or later must suffer the penalty. In personal conduct be always polite, but never obsequious. No one will respect you more than you esteem yourself. Avoid quarrels as long as you can without yielding to imposition. But sustain your manhood always. Never bring a suit of law for assault and battery or for defamation. The law affords no remedy for such outrages that can satisfy the feelings of a true man. Never wound the feelings of others. Never brook wanton outrage upon your own feelings. If ever you defend your honor do it calmly. If angry at first, wait till your wrath cools before you proceed.

LOVE NOT ME FOR COMELY GRACE

Anonymous

Love not me for comely grace,
For my pleasing eye or face,
Nor for any outward part:
No, nor for a constant heart!
For these may fail or turn to ill:
   So thou and I shall sever.
Keep therefore a true woman's eye,
And love me still, but you know not why!
So hast thou the same reason still
   To dote upon me ever.

WHERE GO THE BOATS?

Robert Louis Stevenson

Dark brown is the river,
   Golden is the sand.
It flows along for ever,
   With trees on either hand.

Green leaves a-floating,
   Castles of the foam,
Boats of mine a-boating—
   Where will all come home?

On goes the river
   And out past the mill,
Away down the valley,
   Away down the hill.

Away down the river,
   A hundred miles or more,
Other little children
   Shall bring my boats ashore.

(623)

LOVE

Robert G. Ingersoll

Love is the only bow on life's dark cloud. It is the Morning and the Evening Star. It shines upon the cradle of the babe, and sheds its radiance upon the quiet tomb. It is the mother of Art, inspirer of poet, patriot and philosopher. It is the air and light of every heart, builder of every home, kindler of every fire on every hearth. It was the first to dream of immortality. It fills the world with melody, for Music is the voice of Love. Love is the magician, the enchanter, that changes worthless things to joy, and makes right royal kings and queens of common clay. It is the perfume of the wondrous flower— the heart—and without that sacred passion, that divine swoon, we are less than beasts; but with it, earth is heaven and we are gods.

MADONNA OF THE EVENING FLOWER

Amy Lowell

All day long I have been working,
Now I am tired.
I call: "Where are you?"
But there is only the oak tree rustling in the wind.
The house is very quiet,
The sun shines in on your books,
On your scissors and thimble just put down,
But you are not there.
Suddenly I am lonely:
Where are you?
I go about searching.

Then I see you.
Standing under a spire of pale blue larkspur,
With a basket of roses on your arm.
You are cool, like Silver,
And you smile.

I think the Canterbury bells are playing little tunes,
You tell me that the peonies need spraying,
That the columbines have overrun all bounds,
That the pyrus japonica should be cut back and rounded.

(624)

You tell me these things.
But I look at you, heart of silver,
White heart-flame of polished silver,
Burning beneath the blue steeples of the larkspur,
And I long to kneel instantly at your feet,
While all about us peal the loud, sweet *Te Deums* of the
Canterbury bells.

THE EDUCATED MAN

Socrates

Whom do I call educated? First, those who manage well the circumstances which they encounter day by day and those who possess a judgment which is accurate in meeting occasions as they arise and rarely miss the expedient course of action. Next, those who are decent and honorable in their intercourse with all men, bearing easily and good-naturedly what is unpleasant and offensive in others, and being as agreeable and reasonable to their associates as it is humanly possible to be. Furthermore, those who hold their pleasures always under control and are not ultimately overcome by their misfortunes, bearing up under them bravely and in a manner worthy of our common nature. Finally, and most important of all, those who are not spoiled by their successes, who do not desert their true selves, but hold their ground steadfastly as wise and sober-minded men, rejoicing no more in the good things that have come to them through chance than in those which, through their own nature and intelligence, are theirs since birth. Those who have a character which is in accord, not with one of these things, but with all of them—these I maintain are educated and whole men possessed of all the virtues of a man.

FOR EVENING

Sabine Baring-Gould

Now the day is over,
    Night is drawing nigh;
Shadows of the evening
    Steal across the sky;

Jesus, give the weary
  Calm and sweet repose;
With Thy tenderest blessing
  May our eyelids close.

Grant to little children
  Visions bright of thee;
Guard the sailors tossing
  On the deep, blue sea.

Comfort every sufferer
  Watching late in pain;
Those who plan some evil
  From their sins restrain.

Through the long night watches,
  May thine angels spread
Their white wings above me,
  Watching round my bed.

When the morning wakens,
  Then may I arise
Pure, and fresh, and sinless
  In Thy holy eyes. Amen.

COMMUTER

E. B. White

Commuter—one who spends his life
In riding to and from his wife;
A man who shaves and takes a train
And then rides back to shave again.

HOLY GOD, WE PRAISE THY NAME

Clarence Walworth

Holy God, we praise Thy name;
Lord of all, we bow before Thee;
All on earth Thy sceptre claim,
All in heaven above adore Thee.

Infinite Thy vast domain,
Everlasting is Thy reign.

Hark, the loud celestial hymn
Angel choirs above are raising;
Cherubim and Seraphim,
In unceasing chorus praise Thee;
Fill the heaven with sweet accord;
Holy, holy, holy Lord.

THE "KITTY"

Anonymous

There was a young man from the city,
Who met what he thought was a kitty;
He gave it a pat,
And said, "Nice little cat!"
And they buried his clothes out of pity.

O, WHAT A ROGUE AND PEASANT SLAVE AM I!

William Shakespeare

O, what a rogue and peasant slave am I!
Is it not monstrous that this player here,
But in a fiction, in a dream of passion,
Could force his soul so to his own conceit
That from her working all his visage wann'd;
Tears in his eyes, distraction in 's aspect,
A broken voice, and his whole function suiting
With forms to his conceit? and all for nothing!
For Hecuba!
What's Hecuba to him, or he to Hecuba,
That he should weep for her? What would he do,
Had he the motive and the cue for passion
That I have? He would drown the stage with tears
And cleave the general ear with horrid speech,
Make mad the guilty and appal the free,
Confound the ignorant, and amaze indeed
The very faculties of eyes and ears.

Yet I,
A dull and muddy-mettled rascal, peak,
Like John-a-dreams, unpregnant of my cause,
And can say nothing; no, not for a king,
Upon whose property and most dear life
A damn'd defeat was made. Am I a coward?
Who calls me villain? breaks my pate across?
Plucks off my beard, and blows it in my face?
Tweaks me by the nose? gives me the lie i' the throat,
As deep as to the lungs? who does me this?
Ha!
Swounds, I should take it: for it cannot be
But I am pigeon-liver'd and lack gall
To make oppression bitter, or ere this
I should have fatted all the region kites
With this slave's offal: bloody, bawdy villain!
Remorseless, treacherous, lecherous, kindless villain!
O, vengeance!
Why, what an ass am I! This is most brave,
That I, the son of a dear father murder'd,
Prompted to my revenge by heaven and hell,
Must, like a whore, unpack my heart with words,
And fall a-cursing, like a very drab,
A scullion!

(From *Hamlet*)

WRITTEN ON THE EVE OF EXECUTION

Chidiock Tichbourne

My prime of youth is but a frost of cares,
  My feast of joy is but a dish of pain,
My crop of corn is but a field of tares,
  And all my good is but vain hope of gain;
My life is fled, and yet I saw no sun;
And now I live, and now my life is done.

My tale was heard, and yet it was not told;
  My fruit is fallen, and yet my leaves are green;
My youth is spent, and yet I am not old;
  I saw the world, and yet I was not seen;

(628)

My thread is cut, and yet it is not spun;
And now I live, and now my life is done.

I sought my death and found it in the womb,
   I lookt for life and saw it was a shade,
I trod the earth and knew it was my tomb,
   And now I die, and now I was but made;
My glass is full, and now my glass is run,
And now I live, and now my life is done.

HELL

T. S. Eliot

What is hell? Hell is oneself,
Hell is alone, the other figures in it
Merely projections.
      (From *The Cocktail Party*)

I AM THE CAPTAIN OF THE PINAFORE

Sir William S. Gilbert

Captain:
I am the Captain of the Pinafore!

Chorus:
And a right good captain, too!

Captain:
You're very, very good,
And be it understood,
I command a right good crew.

Chorus:
We're very, very good,
And, be it understood,
He commands a right good crew.

Captain:
Though related to a peer,
I can hand, reef and steer,
Or ship a selvagee;
I am never known to quail
At the fury of a gale,
And I'm never, never sick at sea!

Chorus:
What, never?

Captain:
No, never!

Chorus:
What, *never?*

Captain:
Hardly ever!

Chorus:
He's hardly ever sick at sea!
Then give three cheers, and one cheer more,
For the hardy Captain of the Pinafore!

Captain:
I do my best to satisfy you all!

Chorus:
And with you we're quite content.

Captain:
You're exceedingly polite,
And I think it only right
To return the compliment.

Chorus:
We're exceedingly polite,
And he thinks it only right
To return the compliment.

Captain:
Bad language or abuse,
I never, never use,
Whatever the emergency;

Though "bother it" I may
Occasionally say,
I never use a big, big D!

Chorus:
What, *never?*

Captain:
No, never!

Chorus:
What, *never?*

Captain:
Hardly ever!

Chorus:
Hardly ever swears a big, big D!
Then give three cheers, and one cheer more,
For the well-bred Captain of the Pinafore!

SCIENCE'S LESSON

Thomas Huxley

Science seems to me to teach in the highest and strongest manner the great truth which is embodied in the Christian conception of entire surrender to the will of God. Sit down before a fact as a little child, be prepared to give up every preconceived notion, follow humbly wherever and to whatever abyss nature leads, or you shall learn nothing. I have only begun to learn content and peace of mind since I have resolved at all risks to do this.

IN NO STRANGE LAND

Francis Thompson

O world invisible, we view thee,
O world intangible, we touch thee,
O world unknowable, we know thee,
Inapprehensible, we clutch thee!

(631)

Does the fish soar to find the ocean,
The eagle plunge to find the air—
That we ask of the stars in motion
If they have rumour of thee there?

Not where the wheeling systems darken,
And our benumbed conceiving soars!—
The drift of pinions, would we hearken,
Beats at our own clay-shuttered doors.

The angels keep their ancient places;—
Turn but a stone, and start a wing!
'Tis ye, 'tis your estrangèd faces,
That miss the many-splendoured thing.

But, when so sad thou canst not sadder,
Cry—and upon thy so sore loss
Shall shine the traffic of Jacob's ladder
Pitched betwixt Heaven and Charing Cross.

Yea, in the night, my Soul, my daughter,
Cry—clinging Heaven by the hems;
And lo, Christ walking on the water
Not of Gennesareth, but Thames!

WHERE SHALL WISDOM BE FOUND?

Holy Bible, Job 28:12–20, 28

But where shall wisdom be found? and where is the place of under-standing?

Man knoweth not the price thereof: neither is it found in the land of the living.

The depth saith, It is not in me: and the sea saith, It is not with me.

It cannot be gotten for gold, neither shall silver be weighed for the price thereof.

It cannot be valued with the gold of Ophir, with the precious onyx, or the sapphire.

The gold and the crystal cannot equal it: and the exchange of it shall not be for jewels of fine gold.

No mention shall be made of coral, or of pearls: for the price of wisdom is above rubies.

The topaz of Ethiopia shall not equal it, neither shall it be valued with pure gold.

Whence then cometh wisdom? and where is the place of understanding? . . .

And unto man he said, Behold, the fear of the Lord, that is wisdom; and to depart from evil is understanding.

SHANGRI-LA

James Hilton

[The High Lama is speaking:]

"Now let me begin by sketching for you a very agreeable picture. You are still, I should say, a youngish man by the world's standards; your life, as people say, lies ahead of you; in the normal course you might expect twenty or thirty years of only slightly and gradually diminishing activity. By no means a cheerless prospect, and I can hardly expect you to see it as I do—as a slender, breathless, and far too frantic interlude. The first quarter-century of your life was doubtless lived under the cloud of being too young for things, while the last quarter-century would normally be shadowed by the still darker cloud of being too old for them; and between those two clouds, what small and narrow sunlight illumines a human lifetime! But you, it may be, are destined to be more fortunate, since by the standards of Shangri-La your sunlit years have scarcely yet begun. It will happen, perhaps, that decades hence you will feel no older than you are today—you may preserve, as Henschell did, a long and wondrous youth. But that, believe me, is only an early and superficial phase. There will come a time when you will age like others, though far more slowly, and into a condition infinitely nobler; at eighty you may still climb to the pass with a young man's gait, but at twice that age you must not expect the whole marvel to have persisted. We are not workers of miracles; we have made no conquest of death or even of decay. All we have done and can sometimes do is to slacken the *tempo* of this brief interval that is called life. We do this by methods which are as simple here as they are impossible elsewhere; but make no mistake; the end awaits us all.

"Yet it is, nevertheless, a prospect of much charm that I unfold for you—long tranquilities during which you will observe a sunset as man in the outer world hear the striking of a clock, and with far less care. The years will come and go, and you will pass from fleshly enjoyments into austerer but no less satisfying realms; you may lose the keenness of muscle and appetite, but there will be gain to match your loss; you will achieve calmness and profundity, ripeness and wisdom, and the clear enchantment of memory. And, most precious of all, you will have Time—that rare and lovely gift that your Western countries have lost the more they have pursued it. Think for a moment. You will have time to read—never again will you skim pages to save minutes, or avoid some study lest it prove too engrossing. You have also a taste for music—here, then, are your scores and instruments, with Time, unruffled and unmeasured, to give you their richest savor. And you are also, we will say, a man of good fellowship—does it not charm you to think of wise and serene friendships, a long and kindly traffic of the mind from which death may not call you away with his customary hurry? Or, if it is solitude that you prefer, could you not employ our pavilions to enrich the gentleness of lonely thoughts?"

The voice made a pause which Conway did not seek to fill.

"You make no comment, my dear Conway. Forgive my eloquence— I belong to an age and a nation that never considered it bad form to be articulate. . . . But perhaps you are thinking of wife, parents, children, left behind in the world? Or maybe ambitions to do this or that? Believe me, though the pang may be keen at first, in a decade from now even its ghost will not haunt you. Though in point of fact, if I read your mind correctly, you have no such griefs."

Conway was startled by the accuracy of the judgment. "That's so," he replied. "I'm unmarried; I have few close friends and no ambitions."

"No ambitions? And how have you contrived to escape those widespread maladies?"

For the first time Conway felt that he was actually taking part in a conversation. He said: "It always seemed to me in my profession that a good deal of what passed for success would be rather disagreeable, apart from needing more effort than I felt called upon to make. I was in the Consular Service—quite a subordinate post, but it suited me well enough."

"Yet your soul was not in it?"

"Neither my soul nor my heart nor more than half my energies. I'm naturally rather lazy."

The wrinkles deepened and twisted till Conway realized that the High Lama was very probably smiling. "Laziness in doing stupid things can be a great virtue," resumed the whisper. "In any case, you will scarcely find us exacting in such a matter. Chang, I believe, explained to you our principle of moderation, and one of the things in which we are always moderate is activity. I myself, for instance, have been able to learn ten languages; the ten might have been twenty had I worked immoderately. But I did not. And it is the same in other directions; you will find us neither profligate nor ascetic. Until we reach an age when care is advisable, we gladly accept the pleasures of the table, while—for the benefit of our younger colleagues—the women of the valley have happily applied the principle of moderation to their own chastity. All things considered, I feel sure you will get used to our ways without much effort. Chang, indeed, was very optimistic—and so, after this meeting, am I. But there is, I admit, an odd quality in you that I have never met in any of our visitors hitherto. It is not quite cynicism, still less bitterness; perhaps it is partly disillusionment, but it is also a clarity of mind that I should not have expected in any one younger than—say, a century or so. It is, if I had to put a single word to it, passionlessness."

Conway answered: "As good a word as most, no doubt. I don't know whether you classify the people who come here, but if so, you can lable me '1914-1918.' I used up most of my passions and energies during the years I've mentioned, and though I don't talk much about it, the chief thing I've asked from the world since then is to leave me alone. I find in this place a certain charm and quietness that appeals to me, and no doubt, as you remark, I shall get used to things."

"Is that all, my son?"

"I hope I am keeping well to your own rule of moderation."

"You are clever—as Chang told me, you are very clever. But is there nothing in the prospect I have outlined that tempts you to any stronger feeling?"

Conway was silent for an interval and then replied: "I was deeply impressed by your story of the past, but to be candid, your sketch of the future interests me only in an abstract sense. I can't look so far ahead. I should certainly be sorry if I had to leave Shangri-La to-morrow or next week, or perhaps even next year; but how I shall feel about it if I live to be a hundred isn't a matter to prophesy. I can face it, like any other future, but in order to make me keen it must have a point. I've sometimes doubted whether life itself has any; and if not, long life must be even more pointless."

"My friend, the traditions of this building, both Buddhist and Christian, are very reassuring."

"Maybe. But I'm afraid I still hanker after some more definite reason for envying the centenarian."

"There *is* a reason, and a very definite one indeed. It is the whole reason for this colony of chance-sought strangers living beyond their years. We do not follow an idle experiment, a mere whimsy. We have a dream and a vision. It is a vision that first appeared to old Perrault when he lay dying in this room in the year 1789. He looked back then on his long life, as I have already told you, and it seemed to him that all the loveliest things were transient and perishable, and that war, lust, and brutality might some day crush them until there were no more left in the world. He remembered sights he had seen with his own eyes, and with his mind he pictured others; he saw the nations strengthening, not in wisdom, but in vulgar passions and the will to destroy; he saw their machine power multiplying until a single-weaponed man might have matched a whole army of the Grand Monarque. And he perceived that when they had filled the land and sea with ruin, they would take to the air. . . . Can you say that his vision was untrue?"

"True indeed."

"But that was not all. He foresaw a time when men, exultant in the technique of homicide, would rage so hotly over the world that every precious thing would be in danger, every book and picture and harmony, every treasure garnered through two millenniums, the small, the delicate, the defenseless—all would be lost like the lost books of Livy, or wrecked as the English wrecked the Summer Palace in Peking."

"I share your opinion of that."

"Of course. But what are the opinions of reasonable men against iron and steel? Believe me, that vision of old Perrault will come true. And that, my son, is why *I* am here, and why *you* are here, and why we may pray to outlive the doom that gathers around on every side."

"To outlive it?"

"There is a chance. It will all come to pass before you are as old as I am."

"And you think that Shangri-La will escape?"

"Perhaps. We may expect no mercy, but we may faintly hope for neglect. Here we shall stay with our books and our music and our meditations, conserving the frail elegancies of a dying age, and seeking such wisdom as men will need when their passions are all spent. We have a heritage to cherish and bequeath. Let us take what pleasure we may until that time comes."

"And then?"

"Then, my son, when the strong have devoured each other, the Christian ethic may at last be fulfilled, and the meek shall inherit the earth."

A shadow of emphasis had touched the whisper, and Conway surrendered to the beauty of it; again he felt the surge of darkness around, but now symbolically, as if the world outside were already brewing for the storm. And then he saw that the High Lama of Shangri-La was actually astir, rising from his chair, standing upright like the half-embodiment of a ghost. In mere politeness Conway made to assist; but suddenly a deeper impulse seized him, and he did what he had never done to any man before; he knelt, and hardly knew why he did.

"I understand you, Father," he said.

He was not perfectly aware of how at last he took his leave; he was in a dream from which he did not emerge till long afterwards. He remembered the night air icy after the heat of those upper rooms, and Chang's presence, a silent serenity, as they crossed the starlit courtyards together. Never had Shangri-La offered more concentrated loveliness to his eyes; the valley lay imaged over the edge of the cliff, and the image was of a deep unrippled pool that matched the peace of his own thoughts. For Conway had passed beyond astonishments. The long talk, with its varying phases, had left him empty of all save a satisfaction that was as much of the mind as of the emotions, and as much of the spirit as of either.

(From *Lost Horizon*, 1933)

BEDOUIN SONG

Bayard Taylor

From the Desert I come to thee
  On a stallion shod with fire;
And the winds are left behind
  In the speed of my desire.
Under thy window I stand,
  And the midnight hears my cry:
I love thee, I love but thee,
  With a love that shall not die
    Till the sun grows cold,
    And the stars are old,
    And the leaves of the Judgment
        Book unfold!

Look from thy window and see
  My passion and my pain;
I lie on the sands below,
  And I faint in thy disdain.

Let the night-winds touch thy brow
  With the heat of my burning sigh,
And melt thee to hear the vow
  Of a love that shall not die
      Till the sun grows cold,
      And the stars are old,
      And the leaves of the Judgment
          Book unfold!

My steps are nightly driven,
  By the fever in my breast,
To hear from thy lattice breathed
  The word that shall give me rest.
Open the door of thy heart,
  And open thy chamber door,
And my kisses shall teach thy lips
  The love that shall fade no more
      Till the sun grows cold,
      And the stars are old,
      And the leaves of the Judgment
          Book unfold!

GOD'S GRANDEUR

Gerard Manley Hopkins

The world is charged with the grandeur of God
It will flame out, like shining from shook foil;
It gathers to a greatness, like the ooze of oil
Crushed. Why do men then now not reck his rod?
Generations have trod, have trod, have trod;
And all is seared with trade; bleared, smeared with toil;
And wears man's smudge and shares man's smell: the soil
Is bare now, nor can foot feel, being shod.
And for all this, nature is never spent;
There lives the dearest freshness deep down things;
And though the last lights off the black West went
Oh, morning, at the brown brink eastward, springs—
Because the Holy Ghost over the bent
World broods with warm breast and with ah! bright wings.

GOD GOVERNS IN THE AFFAIRS OF MEN

Benjamin Franklin

I have lived, sir, a long time. And the longer I live, the more convincing proofs I see of this truth—that God governs in the affairs of men. And if a sparrow cannot fall on the ground without his notice, is it probable that an empire can rise without his aid? We have been assured, sir, in the sacred writings that except the Lord build the house, they labor in vain that build it. I firmly believe this; and I also believe that without his concurring aid we shall succeed in this political building no better than the builders of Babel; our projects will be confounded and we ourselves shall become a reproach and a byword down to future ages.

OH THERE IS BLESSING IN THIS GENTLE BREEZE

William Wordsworth

Oh there is blessing in this gentle breeze,
A visitant that while it fans my cheek
Doth seem half-conscious of the joy it brings
From the green fields, and from yon azure sky.
Whate'er its mission, the soft breeze can come
To none more grateful than to me; escaped
From the vast city, where I long had pined
A discontented sojourner: now free,
Free as a bird to settle where I will.
What dwelling shall receive me? in what vale
Shall be my harbour? underneath what grove
Shall I take up my home? and what clear stream
Shall with its murmur lull me into rest?
The earth is all before me. With a heart
Joyous, nor scared at its own liberty.
I look about; and should the chosen guide
Be nothing better than a wandering cloud,
I cannot miss my way. I breathe again!
Trances of thought and mountings of the mind
Come fast upon me: it is shaken off,
That burthen of my own unnatural self,

The heavy weight of many a weary day
Not mine, and such as were not made for me.
Long months of peace (if such bold word accord
With any promises of human life),
Long months of ease and undisturbed delight
Are mine in prospect; whither shall I turn,
By road or pathway, or through trackless field,
Up hill or down, or shall some floating thing
Upon the river point me out my course?

DEATH OF THE AGED

Robert G. Ingersoll

After all, there is something tenderly appropriate in the serene death of the old. Nothing is more touching than the death of the young, the strong. But when the duties of life have all been nobly done; when the sun touches the horizon; when the purple twilight falls upon the past, the present, and the future; when memory, with dim eyes, can scarcely spell the blurred and faded records of the vanished days—then, surrounded by kindred and friends, death comes like a strain of music. The day has been long, the road weary, and the traveler gladly stops at the welcome inn.

Nearly forty-eight years ago, under the snow, in the little town of Cazenovia, my poor mother was buried. I was but two years old. I remember her as she looked in death. That sweet, cold face has kept my heart warm through all the changing years.

SONG

James Thomson

Let my voice ring out and over the earth,
   Through all the grief and strife,
With a golden joy in a silver mirth:
   Thank God for life!

Let my voice swell out through the great abyss
   To the azure dome above,
With a chord of faith in the harp of bliss:
   Thank God for Love!

Let my voice ring out beneath and above,
   The whole world through,
O my Love and Life, O my Life and Love,
   Thank God for you!

MISFORTUNES NEVER COME SINGLY

Harry Graham

Making toast at the fireside,
Nurse fell in the grate and died;
And what makes it ten times worse,
All the toast was burnt with nurse.

GOD OUR REFUGE

Richard Chenevix Trench

If there had anywhere appeared in space
   Another place of refuge where to flee,
Our hearts had taken refuge in that place,
   And not with Thee.

For we against creation's bars had beat
   Like prisoned eagles, through great worlds had sought
Though but a foot of ground to plant our feet,
   Where Thou were not.

And only when we found in earth and air,
   In heaven or hell, that such might nowhere be—
That we could not flee from Thee anywhere,
   We fled to Thee.

(641)

BECAUSE

Edward Teschemacher

Because you come to me with naught save love,
And hold my hand and lift mine eyes above,
A wider world of hope and joy I see,
Because you come to me.

Because you speak to me in accents sweet,
I find the roses waking round my feet,
And I am led through tears of joy to see,
Because you speak to me.

Because God made thee mine I'll cherish thee
Through light and darkness, through all time to be,
And pray His love may make our lives divine.
Because God made thee mine.

EPITAPH

Remember man, that passeth by,
As thou is now so once was I;
And as I am now so must thou be:
Prepare thyself to follow me.
   Under this someone wrote:
To follow you I'm not content,
Until I learn which way you went.
         (Churchyard;
    Linton, England, 1825)

The God who gave us life, gave us liberty at the same time.

—Thomas Jefferson

(642)

YOUTH'S IMMORTALITY

William Hazlitt

No young man believes he shall ever die. It was a saying of my brother's, and a fine one. There is a feeling of Eternity in youth which makes us amends for everything. To be young is to be as one of the Immortals. One half of time indeed is spent—the other half remains in store for us with all its countless treasures, for there is no line drawn, and we see no limit to our hopes and wishes. . . . We look round in a new world, full of life and motion, and ceaseless progress, and feel in ourselves all the vigour and spirit to keep pace with it, and do not foresee from any present signs how we shall be left behind in the race, decline into old age, and drop into a grave. . . . Like a rustic at a fair, we are full of amazement and rapture, and have no thought of going home, or that it will soon be night. We know our existence only by ourselves, and confound our knowledge with the objects of it. We and Nature are therefore one.

ASK ME NO MORE

Alfred, Lord Tennyson

Ask me no more: the moon may draw the sea;
    The cloud may stoop from heaven and take shape,
    With fold to fold, of mountain or of cape;
But O too fond, when have I answer'd thee?
        Ask me no more.

Ask me no more: What answer should I give?
    I love not hollow cheek or faded eye:
    Yet O my friend, I will not have thee die!
Ask me no more, lest I should bid thee live;
        Ask me no more.

Ask me no more: thy fate and mine are seal'd:
    I strove against the stream and all in vain:
    Let the great river take me to the main:
No more, dear love, for at a touch I yield;
        Ask me no more.

(643)

AN IRISH WISH

Anonymous

May the road rise to meet you.
May the wind be ever at your back
May the Good Lord keep you
    in the hollow of His hand.
May your heart be as warm
    as your hearthstone.
And when you come to die
    may the wail of the poor
    be the only sorrow
    you'll leave behind.
May God bless you always.

ENVOY

Robert Louis Stevenson

Go, little book, and wish to all
Flowers in the garden, meat in the hall,
A bin of wine, a spice of wit,
A house with lawns enclosing it,
A living river by the door,
A nightingale in the sycamore!

If I have seen further (than you and Descartes) it is by
standing upon the shoulders of Giants.
    (Sir Isaac Newton, in a letter to Robert Hooke, 1675)

INDEX OF TITLES

(647)

INDEX OF FAMILIAR LINES

NOTE: Many of the selections in this book contain more than one familiar line. But this index contains only one familiar line from each selection. Consequently, the choosing of lines has often been arbitrary, representing only the editor's opinion of what is most familiar.

(656)

(661)

(665)

(668)

INDEX OF AUTHORS

(673)

(680)